The Cambridge Companion to Emily Dickinson

Emily Dickinson, one of the most important American poets of the nineteenth century, remains an intriguing and fascinating writer. *The Cambridge Companion to Emily Dickinson* includes eleven new essays by accomplished Dickinson scholars. They cover Dickinson's biography, publication history, poetic themes and strategies, and her historical and cultural contexts. As a woman poet, Dickinson's literary persona has become incredibly resonant in the popular imagination. She has been portrayed as singular, enigmatic, and even eccentric. At the same time, Dickinson is widely acknowledged as one of the founders of American poetry, an innovative pre-modernist poet as well as a rebellious and courageous woman. This volume introduces new and practiced readers to a variety of critical responses to Dickinson's poetry and life, and provides several valuable tools for students, including a chronology and suggestions for further reading.

CAMBRIDGE COMPANIONS TO LITERATURE

CAMBRIDGE COMPANIONS TO CULTURE

THE CAMBRIDGE
COMPANION TO
EMILY DICKINSON

EDITED BY
WENDY MARTIN

Professor of American Literature and American Studies
Claremont Graduate University

CAMBRIDGE
UNIVERSITY PRESS

CAMBRIDGE UNIVERSITY PRESS
Cambridge, New York, Melbourne, Madrid, Cape Town, Singapore, São Paulo, Delhi

Cambridge University Press
The Edinburgh Building, Cambridge CB2 8RU, UK

Published in the United States of America by Cambridge University Press, New York

www.cambridge.org
Information on this title: www.cambridge.org/9780521001182

First published 2002
Sixth printing 2008

Printed in the United Kingdom at the University Press, Cambridge

A catalogue record for this publication is available from the British Library

Library of Congress Cataloguing in Publication data
The Cambridge companion to Emily Dickinson / edited by Wendy Martin.
p.   cm. – (Cambridge companions to literature)
Includes bibliographical references and index.
ISBN 0 521 80644 5 – ISBN 0 521 00118 8 (pbk)
1. Dickinson, Emily, 1830–1886 – Criticism and interpretation –
Handbooks, manuals, etc.   2. Women and literature – United States – History –
19th century – Handbooks, manuals, etc.   I. Title: Emily Dickinson.
II. Martin, Wendy, 1940–   III. Series.
PS1541.Z5 C28   2002
811'.4 – dc21   2002067682

ISBN 978-0-521-80644-2 hardback
ISBN 978-0-521-00118-2 paperback

CONTENTS

NOTES ON CONTRIBUTORS

WENDY BARKER has authored three book collections of poetry and a chapbook, as well as a study of Dickinson, *Lunacy Of Light: Emily Dickinson and the Experience of Metaphor* (1987). With Sandra M. Gilbert, she has also edited a collection of essays on the poet Ruth Stone. Two new books are forthcoming: a selection of translations from the Bengali of Rabindranath Tagore (with Saranindranath Tagore), and an edition of her poems with accompanying essays. Recipient of NEA and Rockefeller Fellowships, the Violet Crown Book Award and the Mary Elinore Smith Poetry Prize, she served as Fulbright Senior Lecturer at St. Kliment Ohridski University of Sofia in Bulgaria. She is professor of English at the University of Texas at San Antonio.

CHRISTOPHER BENFEY is Professor of English at Mount Holyoke College. He has written widely on Emily Dickinson, including his first book, *Emily Dickinson and the Problem Of Others* (1984). He is also the author of *The Double Life of Stephen Crane* (1992) and *Degas in New Orleans: Encounters in the Creole World of Kate Chopin and George Washington Cable* (1997). Benfey has held fellowships from the Guggenheim Foundation, the National Endowment for the Humanities, and the American Council of Learned Societies. He lives with his wife and two sons in Amherst, less than a mile from the Dickinson Homestead.

PAULA BERNAT BENNETT is a Bunting and an AAS-NEH fellow. She is the author of *My Life a Loaded Gun: Female Creativity and Feminist Poetics* (1986) and *Emily Dickinson: Woman Poet* (1990) and the editor of *Nineteenth-Century American Women Poets: An Anthology* (1998) and *Palace-Burner: The Selected Poetry of Sarah Piatt* (2001) in the American Poetry Recovery Series, University of Illinois Press. Her articles have appeared in *Signs*, *ALH* and *PMLA*. She has just completed a manuscript, *Ironizing Sentimentality: The Emergence of Modern Subjectivities in*

United States Women's Poetry: 1825–1900, under advance contract with Princeton University Press.

BETSY ERKKILA is Chair of English and Henry Sanborn Noyes Professor of English at Northwestern University. Her publications include *Walt Whitman Among the French: Poet and Myth* (1980), *Whitman the Political Poet* (1989), *The Wicked Sisters: Women Poets, Literary History, and Discord* (1992), *Visiting Emily: Poems Inspired by the Life and Work of Emily Dickinson* (2000), and *Mixed Bloods and Other American Crosses* (forthcoming). She is co-editor of *Breaking Bounds: Whitman and American Cultural Studies* (1996), *Ezra Pound: The Contemporary Reviews* (forthcoming), and a new Riverside edition of Edgar Allan Poe.

SUZANNE JUHASZ is Professor of English at the University of Colorado at Boulder. Her books on Emily Dickinson include *The Undiscovered Continent: Emily Dickinson and the Space of the Mind* (1983), *Feminist Critics Read Emily Dickinson* (1983), and with Cristanne Miller and Martha Nell Smith, *Comic Power in Emily Dickinson* (1993). Her other books include *Reading from the Heart: Women Writers, Women Readers, and the Story of True Love* (1994) and the forthcoming *A Desire for Women: Relational Psychoanalysis, Writing, and Relationships between Women*. She is the Founding Editor of *The Emily Dickinson Journal*.

WENDY MARTIN is Professor of American Literature and American Studies at the Claremont Graduate University. Her publications include the following books: *An American Sisterhood: Feminist Writing from the Colonial Times to the Present* (1972); *An American Triptych: The Lives and Work of Anne Bradstreet, Emily Dickinson and Adrienne Rich* (1984); *Critical Essays on Kate Chopin* (1988); *We Are The Stories We Tell: Best Short Stories by North American Women Writers* (1990); *Colonial American Travel Narratives* (1994); and *The Beacon Book of Essays By Contemporary American Women* (1996). Professor Martin is on the editorial board of *The Heath Anthology of American Literature*; in addition, she founded *Women's Studies: An Interdisciplinary Journal* in 1972 and continues to be the editor of the journal.

CRISTANNE MILLER is the W. M. Keck Distinguished Service Professor of English at Pomona College. She has served as president of the Emily Dickinson International Society and written several books and articles on Emily Dickinson, including *Comic Power in Emily Dickinson* (1993), with Suzanne Juhasz and Martha Nell Smith, and *Emily Dickinson: A Poet's Grammar* (1987). Professor Miller has co-edited *The Emily Dickinson*

Handbook (1998), with Gundrun Grabher and Roland Hagenbuchle, and *Emily Dickinson: A Celebration for Readers* (1989), with Suzanne Juhasz. She is also the author of *Marianne Moore: Questions of Authority* (1995) and has co-edited *The Selected Letters of Marianne Moore* (1997) with Bonnie Costello and Celeste Goodridge.

DOMHNALL MITCHELL is Professor of Nineteenth-Century American Literature at the Norwegian University of Science and Technology, Trondheim. He has written articles on Dickinson for *American Literature*, *Nineteenth-Century Literature* and *The Emily Dickinson Journal*. His book, *Emily Dickinson: Monarch of Perception*, was published by the University of Massachusetts Press in 2000.

DAVID S. REYNOLDS is Distinguished Professor of English and American Studies at Baruch College and the Graduate Center of the City University of New York. He is the author of *Walt Whitman's America: A Cultural Biography* (1995), winner of the Bancroft Prize and the Ambassador Book Award and finalist for the National Book Critics Circle Award. His other books include *Beneath the American Renaissance: The Subversive Imagination in the Age of Emerson and Melville* (1988), winner of the Christian Gauss Award and Honorable Mention for the John Hope Franklin Prize, *George Lippard* (1982), and *Faith in Fiction: The Emergence of Religious Literature in America* (1981). He is the editor of *George Lippard, Prophet of Protest: Writings of an American Radical* (1986) and the coeditor of *The Serpent in the Cup: Temperance in American Literature* (1997) and of a new edition of three works by the popular nineteenth-century novelist George Thompson.

MARTHA NELL SMITH is Professor of English and Director of the Maryland Institute for Technology in the Humanities (MITH) at the University of Maryland. Her numerous publications include three award-winning books – *Open Me Carefully: Emily Dickinson's Intimate Letters to Susan Dickinson* (1998), coauthored with Ellen Louise Hart, *Comic Power in Emily Dickinson* (1993), coauthored with Cristanne Miller and Suzanne Juhasz, *Rowing in Eden: Rereading Emily Dickinson* (1992) – and more than thirty articles in such journals as *Studies in the Literary Imagination*, *South Atlantic Quarterly*, *Women's Studies Quarterly*, *Profils Americains*, *San Jose Studies*, and *The Emily Dickinson Journal*. The recipient of numerous awards from NEH and ACLS for her work on Dickinson and in new media, Smith is also coordinator and general editor of the *Dickinson Electronic Archives* project at the Institute for Advanced Technology in the

Humanities (IATH) at the University of Virginia (http://jefferson.village. virginia.edu/dickinson).

DANEEN WARDROP is Associate Professor of English at Western Michigan University. She has written *Emily Dickinson's Gothic: Goblin With a Gauge* (1996), as well as essays in journals such as *ATQ, BSQ, Texas Studies in Literature and Language*, and *African-American Review*.

FRED D. WHITE is Associate Professor of English at Santa Clara University, where he teaches courses in composition, poetry, and a seminar on Emily Dickinson. His articles have appeared in *Arizona Quarterly, College Literature, North Dakota Quarterly, San Jose Studies, South Dakota Review, Walt Whitman Review*, and elsewhere.

SHIRA WOLOSKY received her Ph.D. in Comparative Literature from Princeton University. She was an Associate Professor of English at Yale University before moving to the Hebrew University of Jerusalem, where she is now Full Professor of English and American Literature. She has written *Emily Dickinson: A Voice of War* (1984); *Language Mysticism* (1995); "Poetry and Public Discourse" for the *Cambridge History of American Literature* (forthcoming) and *The Art of Poetry* (2001), as well as articles on poetry and literary theory.

ACKNOWLEDGMENTS

A very special acknowledgment of appreciation to Danielle Hinrichs, a doctoral candidate in American Literature at the Claremont Graduate University who was involved in every phase of this project from its initial conceptualization to its organization throughout. Danielle Hinrichs has participated in the solicitation of papers, correspondence with contributors, crafting the Introduction, and compiling the bibliography. Without her disciplined commitment at the highest levels of professional engagement, this project would not have been done.

I would also like to express my sincere gratitude to Margaret Barry, who completed her M. A. in English at the Claremont Graduate University in 1998, for her invaluable and insightful assistance in the early stages of this volume. Finally, my thanks to Cambridge University Press, and particularly Ray Ryan and Nikki Burton, for their support.

CHRONOLOGY

1828   Dickinson's parents, Edward Dickinson, a lawyer, and Emily
        Norcross, marry on 6 May.
1829   Dickinson's brother, William Austin is born on 16 April.
1830   Dickinson is born on 10 December in Amherst, Massachussetts.
1833   Dickinson's sister, Lavinia, is born on 28 February.
1835   Edward Dickinson is appointed Treasurer at Amherst College.
1840   Dickinson enters Amherst Academy.
1847   Dickinson graduates from Amherst Academy and enters Mount
        Holyoke Female Seminary.
1848   Dickinson returns home from Mount Holyoke.
1852   Edward Dickinson is elected Representative to Congress.
1855   Emily Norcross Dickinson becomes ill. In the same year, Dickinson
        meets the Reverend Charles Wadsworth in Philadelphia.
1856   William Austin Dickinson marries Susan Gilbert.
1857   Ralph Waldo Emerson speaks in Amherst and visits members of the
        Dickinson family.
1858   Dickinson begins recording her poems in fascicles.
1860   Wadsworth visits Dickinson in Amherst.
1861   "I taste a liquor never brewed" published in the *Springfield
        Republican* under the title, "The May-Wine." In the same year,
        Austin and Susan Dickinson's first child, Edward, is born.
1862   "Safe in their Alabaster Chambers" published by the *Republican*.
        Dickinson begins corresponding with Thomas Wentworth
        Higginson.
1864   "Some keep the Sabbath Going to Church" published by the
        Roundtable, and "Blazing in Gold, and Quenching in Purple"
        published by the *Republican*. Austin Dickinson is drafted to fight
        in the Civil War; he pays $500 for a substitute.

1866 "A narrow fellow in the grass" published by the *Republican*. Susan and Austin Dickinson's second child, Martha, is born.

1870 Higginson spends time with Dickinson in Amherst.

1872 Edward Dickinson resigns as Treasurer of Amherst College.

1873 Higginson visits Dickinson for a second time.

1874 Edward Dickinson dies.

1875 Emily Norcross Dickinson is paralyzed. Susan and Austin Dickinson's third child, Thomas Gilbert, is born.

1878 "Success is counted sweetest" published in *A Masque of Poets*.

1882 Wadsworth dies is April. Emily Norcross Dickinson dies in November after a long and debilitating illness.

1883 Dickinson's nephew, Thomas Gilbert, dies at age eight.

1886 Dickinson dies on 15 May. Her funeral takes place on 19 May.

1890 Higginson and Mabel Loomis Todd publish the first posthumous volume of Dickinson's *Poems*.

1891 Todd and Higginson publish the second series of Dickinson's *Poems*.

1894 Todd publishes the *Letters of Emily Dickinson*.

1895 William Austin Dickinson dies.

1896 Todd publishes the third series of Dickinson's *Poems*. In the same year, Lavinia Dickinson files a suit against Todd and wins.

1899 Lavinia Dickinson dies.

1913 Dickinson's close friend and sister-in-law, Susan Dickinson, dies.

DEA   Martha Nell Smith, Ellen Louise Hart, and Marta Werner, eds. *Dickinson Electronic Archives*. Online since 1995. Institute for Advanced Technology in the Humanities (IATH), University of Virginia. Available: http://jefferson.village.virginia.edu/dickinson/

Fas   Franklin, R. W., ed. *The Manuscript Books of Emily Dickinson*. Cambridge, MA and London: The Belknap Press of Harvard University Press, 1981. References to manuscript books or groups in this edition will use the abbreviation "Fas" and cite the number assigned by Franklin.

Fr   Franklin, R. W., ed. *The Poems of Emily Dickinson: Variorum Edition*. 3 vols. Cambridge, MA and London: The Belknap Press of Harvard University Press, 1998. References will use these initials and the number assigned by Franklin.

J   Johnson, Thomas H, eds. *The Poems of Emily Dickinson: Variorum Edition*. 3 vols. Cambridge, MA and London: The Belknap Press of Harvard University Press, 1955. References will use this initial and the number assigned by Johnson.

L   Johnson, Thomas H. and Theodora Ward, eds. *The Letters of Emily Dickinson*. 3 vols. Cambridge, MA and London: The Belknap Press of Harvard University Press, 1958. References will use this initial and the number assigned by Johnson and Ward.

LED   Sewall, Richard Benson. *The Life of Emily Dickinson*. 2 vols. New York: Farrar, Straus, and Giroux, 1974.

NAWP   Bennett, Paula Bernat, ed. *Nineteenth-Century American Women Poets: An Anthology*. Oxford: Blackwell Publishers, 1998.

OMC   Hart, Ellen Louise and Martha Nell Smith, eds. *Open Me Carefully: Emily Dickinson's Intimate Letters to Susan Huntington Dickinson*. Ashfield, MA: Paris Press, 1998. References will use these initials and will cite the number assigned in the volume.

WSD   Martha Nell Smith, Laura Elyn Lauth, Lara Vetter, eds. *Writings by Susan Dickinson*. Online since 1998. Institute for Advanced Technology in the Humanities (IATH), University of Virginia. Available: http://jefferson.village.virginia.edu/dickinson/susan/. A critical edition of Susan's work housed at the Houghton Library, Harvard University, and at the John Hay Library, Brown University.

YH   Leyda, Jay. *The Years and Hours of Emily Dickinson.* 2 vols. New Haven and London: Yale University Press, 1960.

Note: The publisher has used its best endeavors to ensure that the URLs for external websites referred to in this book are correct and active at the time of going to press. However, the publisher has no responsibility for the websites and can make no guarantee that a site will remain live or that the content is or will remain appropriate.

WENDY MARTIN

Introduction

Born in 1830 in Amherst, Massachusetts, Emily Dickinson led a privileged life with a financially comfortable and well-respected family in a deeply Calvinist New England community. Her father was elected a representative to Congress and served as Treasurer of Amherst College for thirty-seven years, a post later occupied by Dickinson's brother, Austin. The Dickinson family hosted many important visitors, including the famed essayist and poet Ralph Waldo Emerson. Emily Dickinson had numerous correspondents and attended both Amherst Academy and Mount Holyoke Female Seminary. For most of her life, however, the poet spent much of her time secluded within her family's home, writing poetry and helping to run the household. She sent numerous letters and poems to her intimate friend and sister-in-law Susan Gilbert Dickinson, and she, with her sister, Lavinia, nursed her ailing mother throughout her lengthy illness and until her death, just four years before the poet's own. Dickinson's poetry expresses her struggles with her faith, with her father, with mortality, and with the challenges of being a woman and a poet.

Emily Dickinson has emerged as a powerful and persistent figure in American culture. As a woman poet, Dickinson has been portrayed as singular and enigmatic and even eccentric. Often, Dickinson is painted as a young woman in white, closeted in the upper rooms of her home, isolated not only from her neighbors and friends, but also from the historical and cultural events taking place outside her door. Her poems speak most noticeably of "the Heaven of God," "the starkest Madness," or the "Infinite" rather than of worldly events. She has been perceived as agoraphobic, deeply afraid of her surroundings, and as an eccentric spinster. At the same time, Dickinson is widely acknowledged as one of the founders of American poetry, an innovative pre-modernist poet as well as a rebellious and courageous woman.

Since her poems were first published posthumously in 1890, critical responses to Emily Dickinson's work have been both abundant and unceasing, steadily gathering force with every new version of her collected poems and each poem newly discovered in her letters and manuscripts. Continuous publication of Dickinson's poems and manuscripts has been spurred by vigorous scholarly inquiry and by public interest in her poetry and her life. Emily Dickinson's vast appeal lies not only in her writings but also in her literary persona, one that has become extraordinarily resonant in the popular imagination. An exhibition at the Mead Art Museum in Amherst, 1997, demonstrates the poet's palpable presence in today's culture in images of the white dress she famously wore, in various versions of the solitary woman and her "letter to the world," and in the incorporation of words from her poems in contemporary art. One of the most persistent images of the poet in both public perception and literary scholarship has been that of Dickinson as a private woman who remained isolated within her New England home, and who included her poems in private letters rather than public books and journals. Dickinson's position in both the public and private sphere, however, is being re-evaluated by critics today, revealing her to be both more fully connected to her cultural surroundings and more strategic in her withdrawals: "The Soul selects her own Society – / Then – shuts the Door –" (J 303).

One of the most often quoted facts of Emily Dickinson's life is that she published only a few poems during her lifetime. Although she wrote to the writer and editor, Thomas Wentworth Higginson, to ask his opinion of her poetry, she did not openly seek publication, and most of the poems published during her lifetime were submitted by Dickinson's friends, not by the poet herself. In 1858, she began to record poems in folded pages hand-bound with string, often called fascicles. In this way, she collected and organized, and some say self-published, her poetry. Although Dickinson asked her sister, Lavinia, to destroy the poems upon her death, Lavinia sought instead to organize, or reorganize, them for publication, igniting a tumultuous battle for control over Dickinson's poems and their appearance in print. The publication history that followed her death has been marked by considerable controversy, resulting most recently in the increasing use and availability of Dickinson's poems in their original manuscript form.

This movement toward the examination of Dickinson's original manuscripts has lead to a more detailed exploration of the peculiarly visual aspects of Dickinson's poetry – her dashes of varying lengths, unusual capitalization, the placement of poems on the page, and her insertion of variant word choices in many poems. Her unusual poetic form was both lauded and denounced by early critics, and often "cleaned up" by editors, but its fragmented, multiple, and imagistic qualities have more recently been compared to modernist poetic strategies. An examination of the letters in which Dickinson included many of her poems even calls into question the boundaries that divide poetic and epistolary genres, leading readers to fascinating questions about the perimeters and possibilities of poetry.

Dickinson's stark style, her ambiguous punctuation and capitalization, her variant word choices and multiple versions of poems, and her practice of expunging clearly historical references from her poetry, all contribute to creating poems that are extraordinarily open to varying, sometimes even contradictory, interpretations that perplex, startle, and amaze readers. At times, her poems seem to embody multiple voices that perform various personae. Many of the contributors to this volume suggest that such contradiction lies at the very center of Dickinson's poems and her conception of herself as poet. Although we can identify many cohesive trends and persistent topics in Dickinson studies, Dickinson scholarship can be characterized by similar dialogue and movement, by its fervently debated interpretations and its groundbreaking and startling new readings, all of which demonstrate the brilliant possibilities of Dickinson's poetry and the importance of her work and her life in American culture.

This companion begins with Dickinson's manuscripts and her biography. Focusing in part on the editorial battle that began between Dickinson's sister-in-law, Susan Dickinson, and her husband's mistress, Mabel Loomis Todd, Betsy Erkkila's essay, "The Emily Dickinson wars," provides a thorough and nuanced overview of the publication history of Dickinson's poems. Erkkila argues that controversy over what we read when we read a Dickinson poem constitutes a "scene of struggle in which significant social and cultural values have been both produced and contested." In particular, Erkkila asserts that debate about Dickinson's poetry has continued to circulate around questions of authorial intention, the individual author, and traditional aesthetic categories "despite the efforts of feminists, new historicists, multiculturalists, and cultural studies critics to move the study of literature toward a more historically contingent, interdisciplinary, and worldly focus." Scholarly outrage over editorial changes to Dickinson's poems, including altered punctuation, capitalization and line breaks, choices of variant words, and the alteration and removal of poems from Dickinson's letters, has led to increased focus on Dickinson's original manuscripts. This movement, which attempts to maintain intentionality in Dickinson's work and respect for Dickinson as a "great poet," further isolates the poet from her social world and her poems from their cultural contexts. Erkkila seeks a transformation in Dickinson studies that will accompany our move into the twenty-first century: "Whereas in the past, contests over Dickinson have tended to focus on her poetic genius, her intentions, her singularity, and the private and essentially gendered dimensions of her art, in the new millennium one can imagine enlarged definitions of 'context' and other possible 'wars' – social as well as literary, cultural as well as individual, international as well as national and familial – that might enrich our understanding of the historical locations and occasions for writing through renewed acts of critical attention to Emily Dickinson and the world she lived in."

In "Emily Dickinson and the American South," Christopher Benfey turns to the critical reception of Dickinson's work; like Erkkila, he emphasizes the cultural and ideological forces that shape readings of Dickinson's poetry. Benfey argues that many early critics of Dickinson's poems perceived Dickinson as avant-garde, a modern rebel rejecting all social norms. Nevertheless, a significant group of critics, Benfey suggests, viewed Dickinson as a conservative New England traditionalist. Southern agrarianists like Allen Tate adopted Dickinson as an "honorary southerner" and believed that Dickinson's seclusion constituted a rejection of the increasing industrialism and urbanism of her age. These critics, Benfey posits, have had a significant impact on Dickinson literary criticism of recent decades, including feminist criticism. Feminist critics like Sandra Gilbert and Susan Gubar drew heavily on Tate's writings and similarly argued that Dickinson's seclusion constituted a rejection of her society, but with a difference. Feminists argued that Dickinson voluntarily shut out society as a rejection of its patriarchal values. These seemingly different critical traditions are joined, Benfey argues, in their similar assumption that Dickinson's "poems are best read in their relation to some version of 'Old New England,' defined as patriarchal, religious, marked by quiet habits and intense piety." In the end, Benfey asserts the need for a recognition of rebellion that "goes beyond American national boundaries."

Martha Nell Smith's "Susan and Emily Dickinson: their lives, in letters" focuses on the relationship between Emily Dickinson and her close friend and sister-in-law Susan Dickinson. Perhaps above all, their relationship was an epistolary one; Emily wrote nearly 500 letters and sent numerous poems to Susan. In response, Susan offered insights, observations and suggestions. Contrary to the narrative of the isolated poetess, this correspondence reveals the poet's connection and interaction with her sister-in-law on intensely personal and deeply artistic levels. It also places Dickinson squarely in the manuscript culture of the nineteenth century, one in which binding poems into fascicles and enclosing poems in letters was not at all unusual. Indeed, the letters between the two women intermingle reflections on daily life and poetry. Smith suggests that the "facts of this correspondence challenge not only widely held notions about the individual author Emily Dickinson, but also literary traditions that have drawn sharp distinctions between 'poetic' and 'domestic' subjects." Relating evidence of Susan's immense contribution to Emily Dickinson's poetic practices and strategies, Smith describes

Susan's place at the center of the editorial battles that began after Emily Dickinson's death and continue today. According to Smith, "the editing of Emily Dickinson was, from the very beginning, driven, inflected by, and/or entangled with biography."

The next group of essays in this companion looks more closely at Dickinson's poems, her themes, and her strategies. Wendy Barker begins this discussion in "Emily Dickinson and poetic strategy" by examining Dickinson's own references to prose and poetry in her poems and letters. Throughout Dickinson's poetry, the term prose is associated with oppressive sunlight, sermons, religious practices, patriarchy, and constraint. Poetry, on the other hand, is allied with liberating darkness and inner freedom. Dickinson used her poetry as a force of liberation that allowed her to move outside of the prose boundaries constructed by her father, the church, and her culture, all of which hemmed her into a confined space. For Dickinson, Barker argues, "To be...wide open to the moment, oblivious to prosaic social demands and stultifying theological ones, is poetry, possibility, and perhaps even paradise."

For Fred White, in "Emily Dickinson's existential dramas," Dickinson's poetry dwells less in paradise than in the limited nature of humanity. White demonstrates Dickinson's dramatic portrayal of existentialism. He argues that "Instead of directly conveying the poet's own thoughts and feelings about the subject, Dickinson prefers the aesthetically richer indirection of a dramatic rendering, whereby characters – personae – speak in their own disparate voices, thereby creating a richer and more complex work of art." The voices of her characters demonstrate major existential themes, "choos[ing] existence over essence" and "champion[ing] the existential over the transcendent." In many ways, White asserts, Dickinson's poetry is written against Emersonian transcendentalism, showing that "word and world – mind and nature – are separated by an unbridgeable gulf." We see in Dickinson's poetry that "*existence* is bound by temporality, individual limitation and isolation," yet these very barriers to transcendence make her "most of all a poet of the deliberately lived moment, of physical presence, of life's unstoppable movement."

Cristanne Miller and Suzanne Juhasz's "Performances of gender in Dickinson's poetry" similarly attends to the dramatic voices of Dickinson's poetry, viewing the "space of the poem...as a stage, whereon the poet may play a multitude of self-positionings." In this essay, Dickinson's performativity allows her to take on various subject positions and to enact gender. For Miller and Juhasz, the performance unfolds not just in the voice of Emily Dickinson but in the dramatic interplay between reader and text. They argue that "the poem demands of readers that they perform its 'script' along with the poem's speaker or 'voice.'" In Dickinson's lyric poetry, the speaker's self, and its gendered identity, is "a self that is done – enacted, performed by the reader." Thus, despite the traditional view of Dickinson as isolated from the world, her "poems are particularly open to – indeed, demanding of – readerly participation."

Shira Wolosky's "Emily Dickinson: being in the body," begins with the poem, "I am afraid to own a body," taking up the question of embodiment in relation to identity. Dickinson's emphasis on body and soul seems radically different from Whitman's inclusive and expansive "I am the poet of the Body and I am the poet of the Soul," but, Wolosky argues, both poets respond to American cultural forces that promise correlation, "implicit claims that the various levels of experience and of identity are mutually confirming and culturally coherent." For Whitman, this correlation is approximated but with some tension, but for Dickinson, just as various levels of meaning seem to be reaching correlation, they are stymied and the reader experiences a shift in meaning and a contest of contradictory ideas. Dickinson's greater agonistic tendencies, Wolosky argues, have in large part to do with her often contradictory positions as woman, poet, and American. "These analogical slips," Wolosky states, "textually enact a kind of cultural slippage in which a female gender complicates or contradicts assertions of American or Romantic selfhood; material progress in the world subverts or opposes, rather than realizes spiritual longings; self-fulfillment contests self-denial; and body remains in tension with soul, including poetic embodiment as against some pure artistic essence." Such representational collisions are more than the poet's personal contests; they reflect broad cultural controversy.

In "Emily Dickinson and the Gothic in Fascicle 16," Daneen Wardrop examines Dickinson's use of Gothic images to explore identity in the particular context of her self-bound fascicles. She looks specifically at the way in which the visual elements of the manuscripts, dashes, line- and page-breaks, and handwriting, as well as the arrangement of the poems, influence the Gothic elements of the eleven poems included in Fascicle 16. Wardrop presents Dickinson as a forerunner of modernist and postmodernist ideas of identity, demonstrating in her poetry the "splitting, conflicted, shattering subject" so present throughout twentieth- and twenty-first-century literary works. Like Wolosky, Wardrop finds interdependence, contradiction, and collision at the center of Dickinson's poems. Using strategies of disorientation to heighten suspense and to unsettle the reader, Dickinson conveys identities that are unstable, "always in process," that move between singular and plural and male and female subject positions in disconcerting, shifting pronouns. Words crossed out or written above lines, blank pages, and multiple versions of the poems all contribute to the multiplicity of meaning in Dickinson's poems; the fascicle manuscripts reveal the poems as "elastic, in process, a workshopping entity, alive."

The final three essays in this companion pay particular attention to the cultural contexts of Dickinson's poems. In "Emily Dickinson and popular culture" David Reynolds again departs from Dickinson scholarship's traditional emphasis on the poet's isolation and discusses the many ways in which Dickinson's poetry engages with and was influenced by the popular culture of nineteenth-century America. "[H]aunted themes," some very similar to those Wardrop discusses, appear here as evidence of Dickinson's tremendous interest in the popular newspapers and pamphlets of her day, which increasingly reported the sometimes gruesome details of crimes and mysteries. In addition, Dickinson's poems register the mid-nineteenth-century's controversy over sermon styles, reflecting an interest in "imaginative preaching," which emphasized anecdote and adventure over doctrinal formality. She also takes up the topic of temperance, manipulating and playing off of popular images of this movement. Her successful poetic use of such popular images occurs, according to Reynolds, through "radically personalizing [them] by redirecting [them] toward quotidian experience and private emotion," and through "direct[ing] such images inward, using them as metaphors for the recesses of the psyche." Reynolds's essay concludes with a discussion of the influence of the expansion of women's literature between 1858 and 1866, Dickinson's most productive years. Reynolds argues that this literature, sometimes referred to as the "literature of misery" because it focused on the inner grief and anger of women, had a great influence on Dickinson's own imagery, particularly her "repeated use of volcano imagery." Dickinson's poetry stands out, Reynolds argues, "for its playful fusion of opposing views."

Other scholars, however, like Domhnall Mitchell, choose to emphasize Dickinson's seeming disregard of egalitarianism. In "Emily Dickinson and class," Mitchell argues that Dickinson's comments on class and race situate "her in an American tradition of thought and writing that responds with alarm to the dangers perceived as latent in a democratic system." Mitchell analyzes several of Dickinson's most well-known poems in light of their class implications, arguing that they demonstrate a regard for observation over action and reveal Dickinson's paradoxical positions of exclusivity and exclusion. Mitchell explains that "Dickinson's position as a female member of the provincial gentry in Amherst almost certainly contributed to the formation of a consciousness that felt special and even superior, but also excluded from the public spheres of action and power. The result is the frequent promotion in her writing of non-involvement, strategic withdrawal, deferral, anonymity, and witness."

Whereas Reynolds and Mitchell tend in the end to distinguish Dickinson and her poetry from the lives and literature of other nineteenth-century women writers, Paula Bennett seeks to reintegrate Dickinson with her female peers. Bennett asserts that discussions of other nineteenth-century women poets have been pursued in Dickinson studies mainly as a way to elevate Dickinson above other writers, to demonstrate "Dickinson's genius and her ability to transcend the limits of her time, place, and gender." Bennett's essay, "Emily Dickinson and her American women poet peers," argues against this exceptionality. Dickinson struggles, Bennett suggests, with two competing positions: an immersion in domestic life and a quest for literary immortality. The complications of this contest are most evident in Dickinson's image of the spider, a figure that combines the images of sewing and weaving so common in women's writing with a masculine representation of a solitary spider "spinning delicate webs out of a secret self, a self known, finally, only to God." Bennett looks closely at two of Dickinson's spider poems, "The Spider holds a Silver Ball" and "A Spider sewed at Night," in the context of other nineteenth-century women's poetry about weaving in order to demonstrate Dickinson's struggle to mediate issues of transcendence and materiality.

Dickinson prevails as a powerful poetic voice and literary figure. Part of her genius lies in the fact that she was deeply a part of her own culture; at the same time, she anticipated the psychological preoccupations and poetic themes and practices that we grapple with today and will continue to engage throughout the twenty-first century.

BIOGRAPHY AND
PUBLICATION HISTORY

I

BETSY ERKKILA

The Emily Dickinson wars

We see – Comparatively –
The Thing so towering high
– Emily Dickinson

"There was a 'war between the houses,'" wrote Mary Lee Hall of the disputes between Lavinia Dickinson (Emily Dickinson's sister), Susan Gilbert Dickinson (Dickinson's intimate friend and the wife of her brother, Austin Dickinson), and Mabel Loomis Todd (Austin's lover for thirteen years) over the first volumes of Emily Dickinson's *Poems* and *Letters* edited and published by Todd and Thomas Higginson in the 1890s.[1] This early and primarily female "war," which "had as its site and center the volcanic and transgressive love relationship between Dickinson and Sue,"[2] has continued into the present with disputes between male editors such as R. W. Franklin and feminist critics such as Susan Howe over the proper editing of Dickinson; the 1993 publication of *New Poems of Emily Dickinson*, edited by William H. Shurr, proposes to add 498 "new" poems to the Dickinson canon; and the 1998 publication of Franklin's long-awaited and already much-debated variorum edition of *The Poems of Emily Dickinson* adds seventeen poems to the Dickinson canon and promises to replace the standard edition of *The Poems of Emily Dickinson* edited by Thomas H. Johnson in 1955. As Christopher Benfey observes, "For a century now...the editing of Emily Dickinson's poetry has been entangled with human passions, sex, and blindered partiality, as though the editors were (and sometimes they were)...despairing lovers tossing on their beds."[3] This is the stuff of American soap opera. And yet these ongoing Dickinson wars have produced a heady mix of sex and text that has left its mark not only on past and recent editions of Dickinson's work but also on the making of American literary history.

My own interests in entering the Dickinson "wars" are more social and cultural than editorial. Rather than tracing the editorial history of Dickinson's work as stages in an ongoing telos of bringing Dickinson into proper representation and circulation, I want to use the occasion of the new millennium, which might be said to mark the centennial of the first publication of Dickinson's poetry and the rise of her critical reputation in the 1890s, to reflect on Dickinson's publication history as a scene of struggle in which significant social and cultural values have been both produced and contested. That is, rather than seeking to wrest Dickinson's writing from the hands of seemingly adulterous, mutilating, or otherwise inadequate editors, I am more interested in the precise kinds of cultural, political, and ideological work that the figure of Emily Dickinson and her writing have been called upon to do. In other words, what is finally at stake in the Emily Dickinson wars?

1 Poetic genius

Although the volumes of Dickinson's *Poems* and *Letters* edited by Todd and Higginson in the 1890s have been widely criticized for producing a conventionalized version of Dickinson that would appeal to the popular literary taste of the time, these early editions are in fact quite interesting in suggesting the ways certain founding assumptions continue to frame Dickinson studies and literary studies more generally at the beginning of the twenty-first century. Like Susan and Lavinia Dickinson, who emphasized Dickinson's "seclusion and intellectual brilliancy," her "peculiar and wonderful genius," and the separation of her poems from any specifically "personal experiences," or "love disaster,"[4] Higginson and Todd represent Dickinson as an isolated and individual artist-genius whose poems exist against and beyond time and history. "The verses of Emily Dickinson belong emphatically to what Emerson long since called 'the Poetry of the Portfolio,'" Higginson wrote in his "Preface" to *Poems by Emily Dickinson* (1890); they were "something produced absolutely without the thought of publication, and solely by way of expression of the writer's own mind" (p. iii). Dickinson was, Higginson asserted in an article in the *Atlantic Monthly* written to promote the second edition of *Poems* (1891), "a wholly new and original poetic genius."[5]

Although Higginson's representation of Dickinson as a solitary and original "poetic genius" might appear to be natural and self-evident, the notions of the individual "author," "poetic genius," "mind," "art," and "imagination" that he and Todd invoke in their prefaces to Dickinson's work are actually quite recent and heavily contested concepts. The notion of author as individual genius whose imagination and art are forms of intellectual property arose simultaneously with free enterprise and the literary marketplace in the late eighteenth and early nineteenth century as "genius" and "culture" were redefined not as something public and *outside*, as in Alexander Pope's *An Essay on Criticism* (1711) – "True Wit is Nature to Advantage drest / What oft was Thought, but ne'er so well Exprest" – but as something *inside* and private, as in Emerson's words in "The Poet" (1844): "Thou shalt leave the world, and know the muse only. Thou shalt not know any longer the times, customs, graces, politics, or opinions of men, but shalt take all from the muse."[6]

At a time of massive social transformation, when a new industrial elite of money and business was eroding the traditional power, rank, and privilege of the old landed gentry, and labor was engaging in increasingly violent confrontations with capital, the figure of Emily Dickinson and her work were presented as a reaffirmation of the cultural power of mind and genius against the debased imperatives of both the capital marketplace and the democratic masses. In the words of one of Dickinson's earliest reviewers, William Dean Howells, writing as editor of *Harper's Magazine* in 1891, "If nothing else had come out of our life but this strange poetry we should feel that in the work of Emily Dickinson America, or New England rather, had made a distinctive addition to the literature of the world, and could not be left out of any record of it; and the interesting and important thing is that this poetry is as characteristic of our life as our business enterprise, our political turmoil, our demagogism, our millionarism."[7] Against the apparent crassness of both the new money and the new masses, "the work of Emily Dickinson" is invoked as a figure of what Perry Miller would later call *The Mind of New England* assuming its rightful and culturally dominant position as a representative not only of United States mind but of all mind on the stage of world literature.

As one of the founding assumptions of Dickinson studies, the notion of Dickinson as "a wholly new and original poetic genius" representative at once of New England genius and US genius, has in its turn come to shape later responses to the Todd-Higginson volumes as a site of adulteration (and literal adultery between Austin and Mabel) where the uniqueness and radicalism of Dickinson's work has been mutilated and defiled. And yet, as Lavinia wrote to Higginson after the publication of the first edition of *Poems* in 1890, "But for Mrs Todd & your self, 'the poems' would die in the box where they were found."[8] Ironically, if it had not been for the editorial labors of Todd and Higginson, we might not have Dickinson's writing – or at least significant parts of it – at all: in fact, Todd's carefully made transcriptions of the Dickinson holographs are, in some cases, the only copies we have. What the editing of Dickinson makes visible is the ways in which the editor, like the author, is engaged in acts of cultural production and interpretation that are collective and social rather than private and individual.

In their effort to produce a Dickinson that would appeal to popular audiences, Todd and Higginson were enormously successful. The first edition of *Poems* sold some 10,000 copies and, in the words of Higginson, enjoyed a "suddenness of success almost without parallel in American literature" ("Dickinson's Letters," p. 444). While it is not my purpose to present a detailed analysis of these 1890s volumes, I want to suggest that if we were not so singly focused on the process of bringing Dickinson into proper – meaning scholarly rather than popular – representation, we might examine the material dimensions of these early volumes of Dickinson's work and their subsequent reception for what they reveal not only about the ways Dickinson was socialized, marketed, and consumed by her first editors and readers, but also about the history of the author, the book, editorial practice, and literary taste at a crucial moment in the simultaneous emergence of aestheticism and mass culture, literary modernism and the culture of consumption.

Despite the efforts of Todd and Higginson to conventionalize Dickinson's work, her poems still seemed formally aberrant enough to cause some reserve, especially among genteel critics. It was Dickinson's form rather than her content that unnerved Thomas Aldrich in his influential review of Dickinson's *Poems* for the *Atlantic* in 1892. Dickinson's "versicles" were, he wrote, both aesthetically "fatal" and "queer," terms that inadvertently mark the relation between the danger of Dickinson's formal deviance and other forms of "queerness" or deviancy in her work.⁹ These early volumes of poems, which were later included in *The Complete Poems of Emily Dickinson* (1924) and *The Poems of Emily Dickinson* (1930), edited by Dickinson's niece, Martha Dickinson Bianchi, were also radical enough to make Dickinson a cultural icon among several modernists, including most notably Amy Lowell, Conrad Aiken, Hart Crane, Yvor Winters, John Crowe Ransome, and Allen Tate, whose 1932 article "New England Culture and Emily Dickinson," begins by setting Dickinson as a New Critical embodiment of mind and culture against the "intellectual chaos" of Marxian criticism and the kinds of political writing associated with the depression: Dickinson's poetry is "a poetry of ideas," he says, "and it demands of the reader a point of view – not an opinion of the New Deal or the League of Nations, but an ingrained philosophy that is fundamental, a settled attitude that is almost extinct in this eclectic age."¹⁰

2 Property

The historically contingent relation between marketplace notions of individualism and private property and the emergence of modern notions of poetic genius, the author, and the work as forms of intellectual property is particularly legible in Dickinson studies because as a field of cultural and academic study it cannot finally be separated from its origins in a property dispute between Lavinia Dickinson and Mabel Loomis Todd. Todd was the lover of Austin Dickinson to whom Lavinia deeded a piece of Dickinson's land (at Austin's request) in partial repayment for her work on Dickinson's manuscripts. As a result of this highly publicized legal battle, the Dickinson manuscripts were divided between the house of Dickinson and the house of Todd, whose descendants, Martha Dickinson Bianchi (Susan Dickinson's daughter and Dickinson's niece) and Millicent Todd Bingham (Todd's daughter) parsed out a bewildering series of publications – including *The Single Hound: Poems of a Lifetime* (1914), *Complete Poems* (1924), *Further Poems* (1929), *Poems* (1930), *Unpublished Poems* (1935), *Poems* (1937), and *Bolts of Melody* (1945) – in response to the growing public appetite for Dickinson's work.

"The world will not rest satisfied till every scrap of her writings, letters as well as literature, has been published," wrote one reviewer in 1892 in response to the first and second volumes of Dickinson's *Poems* (Buckingham, *Reception*, p. 294). Whatever else one might say about these first editions and the earliest public response to her work, Emily Dickinson, the "Recluse Woman of Genius" (Buckingham, *Reception*, p. 182), had emerged as an author, and as such her "mind" would continue to be bought, sold, marketed, exchanged, litigated, and owned as a form of private property. Just as in the late nineteenth and early twentieth century, the division and dissemination of Dickinson's writings were marked by the simultaneous sexual and legal terms of a property dispute between the house of Dickinson and the house of Todd, so in 1950, a further legal battle over the ownership of Dickinson's work ensued when Alfred Leete Hampson, Bianchi's companion and heir, sold Dickinson's manuscripts to Harvard University, which peremptorily claimed ownership and possession of all Dickinson's work. When Todd Bingham successfully challenged Harvard's claim, the Dickinson manuscripts were once again divided, this time between the Houghton Library at Harvard, which owns the manuscripts of Susan and Lavinia, and the Amherst College Library, which owns Todd's share of the Dickinson manuscripts.

"Publication – is the Auction / Of the Mind of Man – ," Dickinson wrote in one of her most frequently cited poems (Fr 788). The irony, of course, is that the "Mind" of Emily Dickinson, who refused to go to market and resisted commodification by what she called "Disgrace of Price," is now owned collectively by Harvard University and Amherst College, where access to and circulation of her writing is vigorously policed and controlled.[11] If you want to quote from or publish the work of Dickinson you must ask for the privilege and pay the price; if, on the other hand, Dickinson had gone to market, her work, like the work of many of her contemporaries, would now be in the public domain.

3 Cultural contests

During the thirties, Emily Dickinson became a key figure in the formulation of a New Critical methodology grounded in close reading, formal analysis, and the individual poem as self-enclosed aesthetic object. "The greatness of Emily Dickinson" is not going to be found in anything outside the poem, R. P. Blackmur averred. "It is going to be found in the words she used and in the way she put them together," he argued, in an essay that carefully discriminates between Dickinson's "mob of verses" and a very few poems in which she attains the ideal of "poetry" as "a rational and objective art" especially "when the theme is self-expression."[12] Deployed as a weapon against the political, ideological, and popular approaches to literature associated with the Left, the masses, and the thirties, in the criticism of Tate, Blackmur, Yvor Winters, and others, Dickinson's poems became both the exempla and the occasion for modernist and New Critical definitions of the literary – grounded in distinctions between poetry and history, aesthetics and politics, high art and mass culture, form and feeling – that came to dominate academic criticism and literary studies in the United States during the Cold War period.

"[T]he fact is that [Dickinson] did not live in history and held no view of it, past or current," wrote Thomas Johnson, whose three-volume edition of *The Poems of Emily Dickinson*, published by Harvard University Press in 1955, reaffirmed both the formalist and New Critical protocols of the American academy and an ongoing tendency among editors and critics to banish or repress the social location and formation of Dickinson's work.[13] But here the "Mind" of the poet is given a patriarchal and particularly fifties twist. Completely eliding the historical fact of Susan Dickinson's erotic, muse-like presence at the sources of Dickinson's poetic art (Erkkila, *Wicked*, pp. 27–8), Johnson's edition of the poems locates Dickinson's genius not in herself or in her lifelong love relationship with Susan (to whom Dickinson sent some 250 poems between 1853 and 1884), but in the spectral and safely heteronormative figure of the "Master," Charles Wadsworth. "Whereas [Benjamin] Newton as muse had awakened her to a sense of her talent," Johnson writes in his introduction to the *Poems*, "Wadsworth as muse made her a poet" (p. xxii).

As the first edition since the 1890s to have access to Dickinson materials in both the Todd and the Dickinson collections, the first collection of Dickinson's *Poems* edited by a literary scholar, and the first to seek to preserve Dickinson's unconventional spelling, capitalization, and punctuation, Johnson's edition of Dickinson's *Poems* represented a landmark literary event that had a major impact on the direction and practice of American poetry, writing, editing, and criticism – especially Dickinson criticism – over the next half-century. But Johnson's work on Dickinson also bears the editorial battle scars of the ongoing "war between the houses" over the ownership of Dickinson's work. Allowed access to the Dickinson manuscripts in the Todd collection on only two occasions (because Bingham's ownership was still being disputed by Harvard), Johnson was forced to work from photostats, which led to errors in transcription, interpretation, and judgment.

Although Johnson's edition of Dickinson's *Poems* along with his three-volume edition of *The Letters of Emily Dickinson* (1958) have served several generations of students, teachers, writers, and scholars as the standard editions of Dickinson's work, these editions have also been an ongoing site of contest in the Dickinson wars. In *The Editing of Emily Dickinson* (1967), Franklin criticized Johnson for errors, inconsistencies, and misrepresentations; and in 1981, Franklin himself published a two-volume facsimile edition of *The Manuscript Books of Emily Dickinson*, which seeks to make "the manuscript books of the poet available for the first time, restored as closely as possible to their original order and, through facsimile reproduction, presented much as she left them for Lavinia and the world."[14] Intended as a kind of manuscript counterpart and corrective to Johnson's print edition of the poems, Franklin's edition of Dickinson's hand-sewn manuscript books, or "fascicles" (as Todd called them), and unbound "sets" of poems has spurred a whole new series of contests about Dickinson's irregularities of grammar, punctuation, and capitalization, her line and stanza divisions, her use of alternative words and phrases, and finally, what one reads when one reads a Dickinson "poem." Critical of the editorial work of both Johnson and Franklin, who published his own corrected, expanded, and probably now "standard" edition of Dickinson's *Poems* in 1998, poet-scholars such as Susan Howe and textual critics and editors, such as Jerome McGann, Ellen Louise Hart, and Martha Nell Smith, have urged us to return to Dickinson's original manuscripts as the site of what Howe calls Dickinson's "visual intentionality" and her most radical literary experiments.[15]

William Shurr's 1993 edition of *New Poems of Emily Dickinson* is another story. Marketed as "a stunning new literary discovery – nearly five hundred new Dickinson poems... expanding the canon of Dickinson's known poems by almost one-third and making a major addition to the study of American literature,"[16] *New Poems* and William Shurr have provoked widespread controversy among Dickinson scholars and in the larger literary community, with charges ranging from hoax and sham, to claims that Shurr neglected the work of other scholars who had already "discovered" some of the poems he presents, to more general charges that he has ridden ignorantly and roughshod over the complexities and ambiguities of Dickinson's sexual and textual practice and the corresponding difficulties of editorial reproduction and translation. Whereas Howe, McGann, and Smith would return us to the origin of Dickinson's art in her manuscript productions, Shurr bypasses the manuscripts altogether, preferring to "excavate" and "elevate" 498 new poems into the Dickinson canon, not through a careful reading of Dickinson's manuscripts but through a close reading of the already edited and interpreted volumes of Dickinson's *Letters* by Johnson and Ward. Where Howe, McGann, and Smith re-enact Dickinson's own resistance to the market and print by leading us back to the holograph page, Shurr openly plays the market, feeding the public "appetite" for Dickinson and staging his putative "discovery" of new poems as a media event. "[W]e continue to hope that there are stores of Dickinson material still to be discovered, works to feed the appetite of those who would like to have more of her poems," Shurr writes in his Introduction (*New Poems*, p. 2).

There are many things wrong with Shurr's edition. Shaped by notions of the author, poetry, and the aesthetic, which were set in place by the first editorial and critical constructions of Dickinson and reaffirmed by the formalist and New Critical frames of academic criticism in the forties and fifties, Shurr's editorial practice is grounded in the assumption that poems are "freestanding, contextless productions" that must be extricated from "their original contexts" – personal, social, cultural, historical – and relocated in a canonical and ultimately transcendent realm called "art": "It is only when they are isolated and presented as freestanding poems that we can focus on them as the works of art they are," Shurr writes. All signs of history and the social context must be banished: "In order further to isolate them for study," he says, "I have organized them by genre rather than by chronology" (Shurr, *New Poems*, p. 10).

Although Shurr acknowledges that "Dickinson's tendency to use the same rhythm and meter for her prose indicates that the line between her poetry and prose is not entirely fixed" (p. 102), his entire project is driven by a desire to "fix it" – to redraw the boundaries and reassert the fundamental distinctions between poetry and prose, art and history, text and context, work and life. Thus, whereas Hart in her essay, "The Encoding of Homoerotic Desire," recovers a hitherto unnoticed poem in one of Dickinson's letters to Susan, but refuses to separate this poem, which she calls "Morning," from its context either in the letters or in the erotic and lifelong love relationship between Emily and Susan Dickinson, Shurr includes the same poem among his "discoveries," refusing to acknowledge either the homoerotic contexts of the poem or the fact that it was Hart who originally called attention to this and other "letter-poems" that do not appear in Johnson's edition of the *Poems*. But Shurr contradicts himself: while he erases the homoerotic contexts of Dickinson's "letter-poems" addressed to Susan, he keeps the "Master" plot and the heteronormative frames of Dickinson studies in play by consistently locating the heterosexual "contexts" of these "new poems" in Dickinson's relationship with Charles Wadsworth, Samuel Bowles, and Otis Lord.

In "What Is an Author?" Foucault asks, "What if, within a workbook filled with aphorisms, one finds a reference, the notation of a meeting or of an address, or a laundry list: Is it a work, or not? Why not?"[17] Foucault's questions suggest that once the author function is in place, there can be no end to what counts as a "work," or, in Shurr's terms, a "poem" by Emily Dickinson. Although Dickinson's letters are not laundry lists, Shurr's editorial strategy of scouting out any prose passage that smacks of a "fourteener" (a tetrameter followed by a trimeter line) and reformatting it as a poem suggests the "author function" has run amuck. In fact, Shurr himself appears to recognize that the potentially absurd logic of his editorial project would be to reformat all of Dickinson's letters as poems: "The recording of such brilliant scraps could be almost endless and would cite virtually every page of the three volume *Letters*" (Shurr, *New Poems*, p. 84).

To compare Shurr's *New Poems* to recent textual studies of Dickinson's work is, writes Margaret Dickie, "to descend rapidly to another area of scholarship entirely, where the refined sensibility of Howe, the wide-ranging energies of McGann, the scrupulous attention of Smith, and the elaborate designs of Cameron have no place."[18] But while reviews of Shurr have put him in his place as an instance of what one reviewer called "the critical grotesque," I want to suggest that as a site of cultural contest, the controversy stirred by Shurr's edition is also instructive in revealing the ways notions of the poet, the poem, the individual author, language, and the aesthetic as relatively distinct categories of analysis and inquiry continue to frame Dickinson studies, despite the efforts of feminists, new historicists, multiculturalists, and cultural studies critics to move the study of literature toward a more historically contingent, interdisciplinary, and worldly focus.

Like reponses to the Todd-Higginson, Johnson, and Franklin editions of Dickinson as sites of editorial defilement and mutilation, reviews of Shurr present Dickinson as a "major poet" whose language, texts, intentions, and integrity as an author must not be violated. "This is sad business," writes a reviewer for the *Chicago Tribune*. "It should be enough that Dickinson is one of the world's greatest poets." "Dickinson is a truly major poet, and her writing should not be cavalierly handled," asserts a reviewer for the *Christian Science Monitor*. "Unfortunately, the 'new poems' are not new, nor are they true poems," observes another reviewer in the *Boston Globe*. "Where we might ask, are the poet's clear intentions taken into account?" she asks, noting that Shurr should have "respected the 'prose-formatted poems' and discussed them as they were written."[19]

The fact that some of the poems that Shurr presents might be said to be better than ones already in the Dickinson canon suggests that the issue is not so much poetry – or even what counts as a poem – but the necessity of maintaining the integrity and purity of Dickinson's intentions as individual author and origin of the poetry. The reaction to Shurr suggests the potential conflict between an editorial practice framed by intentionalism and a critical practice that has come to discount not only authorial intentions, in accord with W. K. Wimsatt and Monroe C. Bearsley's "The Intentional Fallacy" (1946), but also, under the pressure of poststructuralist theory, traditional constructions of the subject, the author, language, and representation. Critical of Shurr for his failure to indicate "that the letters are literary works with their own integrity" and his failure to make use of Dickinson's manuscripts, where he might have noticed that "line breaks in Dickinson's poems and letters are intentional visual strategies," Hart asserts, "Dickinson, a poet unpublished during her lifetime, left her work in hand-written manuscripts, and it is essential for an editor to return to them."[20] While I agree that Shurr should have made use of Dickinson's manuscripts, even if he had, this would not have given him any unmediated access to Dickinson's intentions. Are the line breaks in Dickinson's letters and poems "intentional visual strategies" as Howe has argued or merely matters of "arbitrary convenience" as R. W. Franklin has argued? Are Dickinson's letters "literary" letters as Todd suggested, "letter-poems" as Hart and Smith have argued, "prose-formatted poems" as Shurr claims, or, as some might argue, simply letters. These and other questions about Dickinson's intentions in her manuscripts are radically undecideable.

As McGann observes in *The Textual Condition*, the concept of "author's intentions" is "ambiguous and unstable" and "misrepresents the interactive procedures by which texts are constituted."[21] What the various alterations, excisions, and editorial translations of Dickinson's "work" suggests is the socially constituted, interactive, and collaborative nature of authors and texts. Rather than leading us to recognize the social location of the writer and writing, however, recent contests over the editing of Dickinson appear to be leading us – or at least some of us – in just the opposite direction: backward toward the room, and the box, and the manuscripts where Dickinson locked the purity of her authorial intentions.

4 Pure intentionality

The nostalgia for some pure intentionality originating in the author as a figure of mind and genius writing for eternity is particularly evident in Susan Howe's work on Emily Dickinson. With its verbal and visual gaps, markings, variants, erasures, stutters, spaces, and indeterminacies, Dickinson's poetry, as Howe presents it, reflects – or one might say inflects – Howe's interests as a L-A-N-G-U-A-G-E poet. Howe herself acknowledges this: "[Dickinson's] poems and her middle and later letters encompass whatever I want to bring to them. Need to bring to them. I often worry that I may be imposing my particular obsessions on her" (*Birth-Mark*, p. 155). Unlike past and recent editors whose appeal to Dickinson's intentions often masks their historical mediation, Howe accentuates her own poetic intervention by entitling her book on Dickinson, *My Emily Dickinson* (1985).

Howe's *The Birth-Mark: Unsettling the Wilderness in American Literary History*, which includes her influential essay, "These Flames and Generosities of the Heart: Emily Dickinson and the Illogic of Sumptuary Value," has been hailed as "[a]n astonishing work re-presenting the American past, its history, literature, texts and critics" (Rachel Blau Du Plessis, book jacket). But Howe's subtitle, "Unsettling the Wilderness," does not mean restoring the land to its original inhabitants or even relocating Native American cultures at the center rather than the margins of the story of American literary emergence. Rather, it means displacing the land as the actual site of historical struggle between indigenous cultures and their European conquerors with the symbolic wilderness of white mind and white writing. Like *My Emily Dickinson*, *Birth-Mark* is in fact wholly Eurocentric in its mytho-poetic reading of both Emily Dickinson and American literary history.

Drawing on the work of Perry Miller, Howe's attempt to locate what she calls "a distinctive American voice" (*Birth-Mark*, p. 156) reinstates the mythic narrative of America's errand into the wilderness with all its perdurable racial, sexual, and imperial coordinates: the origins of American culture in New England; American exceptionalism as it is represented by what Howe calls the "singularly North American ... literary expression of Emerson, Thoreau, Melville, Dickinson, and to a lesser degree Hawthorne" (*Birth-Mark*, p. xi); the savage/civilized binary; and the notion of writing as a sacred practice, "a physical event of immediate revelation" (*Birth-Mark*, p. 1), which exists against and beyond history, or "actuality."

In Howe's reading, the "wilderness" and its inhabitants, which she signifies metonymically as "tomahawks, powwows, quickhatch and wampumpeag" are continually represented as "other" in relation to the European mind working out its sacred national "errand" and destiny in America (*Birth-Mark*,

Foundationalists

antifoundationalist

p. 90). "The antinomian controversy was," she asserts, "the primordial struggle of North American literary expression" (*Birth-Mark*, pp. 3–4). Read within the context of current work in the field of comparative American cultural studies, however, what Howe calls "the primordial struggle" might be better understood in Walter Benjamin's terms as repeated acts of "barbarism" committed in the name of American "civilization" – against Native Americans, women, blacks, Mexicans, and other sexual and social outsiders – as the Anglo-American voice of New England seeks to naturalize its voice as *the* distinctive "North American literary expression."[22]

The cornerstone of Howe's vision of history is the mind and art of Emily Dickinson, whose "wild" poetic creation ultimately displaces and comes to stand in for the multiple indigenous cultures that actually inhabited what Howe calls the American "wilderness." "Really alone at a real frontier," which is in fact intellectual and symbolic, Dickinson is celebrated as a poetic "genius" – "Outside authority, eccentric, unique" – who "sings the sound of the imagination as learner and founder, sings of liberation into an order beyond gender" and "indifferent to worldly chronology" (*My Emily*, pp. 76, 28, 13).

Re-enacting Dickinson's refusal to go to market, Howe advocates a return to Dickinson's original markings on her manuscripts as a means of fully appreciating her "visual intentionality," "her naked Expression," and the "physical immediacy" of her "spiritual improvisations" (*Birth-Mark*, pp. 146, 148). It is here, at the originary scene of writing, that we "see what *she, Emily Dickinson*, reveals of her most profound self in the multiple multilayered scripts, sets, notes, and scraps she left us" (*Birth-Mark*, p. 20). Drawing attention to "Dickinson's word variants, directional dashes, and crosses" as "another kind of writing" (*Birth-Mark*, p. 9), Howe calls for a "facsimile edition" – a "presentation of the author's, Emily Dickinson's texts" – that would "show the layerings and fragile immediacies of her multifacted [sic] visual and verbal productions" (*Birth-Mark*, pp. 19–20).

Howe's visionary and revisionary reading of Dickinson raises important questions about the ways we read, edit, translate, and interpret Dickinson's writing – or any writing. But her critical focus on Dickinson's "scrawls," "strokes," "cuts," and marks on the page as signs of poetic genius and sites of aesthetic significance also suggests the extent to which the mind of the individual author and a primarily aesthetic focus on questions of language and craft continue to circumscribe even the most adventurous new work on Dickinson. There are other questions we might ask. Is it only to gain access to the poet's "most profound self" or her intentions, visual or otherwise, that we read Dickinson? Are there other cultural, social, psychological, philosophical, or affective reasons for reading Dickinson beyond the intrinsic value of the literary text? Why should a primarily aesthetic focus on the author's language and craft, her originality, her poetic genius, or in Howe's words, her status as "one of the greatest poets who ever wrote in English" (*Birth-Mark*, p. 19) continue to mark the horizon and limit of Dickinson studies or any literary study in the new millennium?

What gets written out of Howe's focus on Dickinson's holographs as the site of some originary purity of language, intention, and meaning is once again the social location not only of the writer and writing but also language itself as part of a complex process of social, historical, and cultural production and articulation. "When she created herself author, editor, publisher," Howe asserts, "she situated her production in a field of free transgressive prediscovery" (*Birth-Mark*, p. 147). But even in her holographs Dickinson's language does not exist in some pre-discursive realm outside history: language is itself a social and multi-accentual medium. "Language is not a neutral medium that passes freely and easily into the private property of the speaker's inentions," writes Mikhail Bakhtin; it is populated – overpopulated – with the intentions of others.[23]

Historically, Dickinson worked and wrote toward the end of a period of transition between the patronage of an older aristocratic system and the more democratic forms of patronage and participation opened by the market and what Jurgen Habermas calls the "public sphere" of print.[24] As I argue in "Emily Dickinson and Class," Dickinson's mode of manuscript production did not represent some distinctive manifestation of pure artistic creation "untainted" by the social: her hand-sewn manuscripts (her "fascicles") and her circulation of poems in letters and poems as letters represented a residual mode of aristocratic production and circulation that set itself against the twin processes of industrialization and democratization that radically transformed material, social, and cultural relations in nineteenth-century America. If Dickinson's refusal to print was a sign of her resistance to the commodification of art and "Mind" in the capitalist and patriarchal marketplace, it was also a sign of her aristocratic refusal of the democratic possibilities of public and mass circulation.[25] And yet, even in those poems that had no other audience but herself, Dickinson's poems represented what she called "my letter to the World" (Fr 519) – acts of communication, of social expression, that existed in an intermediate sphere of "letters," between private and public, silence and speech.

"No manufactured print. No outside editor/'robber,'" Howe writes prose-poetically in *My Emily Dickinson* (p. 23). "The idea of a printed book appears as a trap," she asserts in *Birth-Mark* (p. 170). But against Howe's demonization of print as the site of art's defilement and vulgarization, one might set Benjamin's argument, in "The Work of Art in the Age of Mechanical Reproduction," that the technology of reproduction opened the possibility of a politicized art of the masses that "constituted a revolutionary criticism of traditional concepts of art."[26] These "traditional concepts" include what Benjamin calls the "outmoded concepts" of "Creativity and genius, eternal value and mystery" (p. 218) – the very concepts that Howe and others seek to reaffirm in returning us to Dickinson's holograph, or "scriptures," as the absolute ground of her "work."

More so than other writers, Dickinson appears to elicit a desire for greater and greater intimacy and a corresponding belief that proximity to the scene of writing – of hand to paper transcription – will bring some immediate access not available in the print medium. But while a return to Dickinson's manuscripts may give us a fuller appreciation of her literary and aesthetic radicalism – and even this has been vigorously contested – it will also return us to the more privileged, class-based modes of aristocratic cultural production in which she was engaged. Rather than repeating Dickinson's own acts of reclusion and withdrawal, we might want to ask: Aside from a select group of academics and L-A-N-G-U-A-G-E poets who have the cultural and educational capital to read "Cancelations, variants, insertions, erasures, marginal notes, stray marks and blanks" (*Birth-Mark*, p. 9) as signs of aesthetic significance, who would be the audience for the facsimile edition of all of Dickinson's poems, letters, and fragments that Howe proposes? The edition of Dickinson proposed by Howe would not only not reach that vague but much invoked figure the "common reader"; it would also reinstate some of the more ethnocentric, ahistorical, and exclusionary terms of canonical American literary studies.

5 Horizons

In *Textual Condition* McGann observes that "Dickinson's texts...despite her enormous popularity as a poet, have yet to be even minimally socialized" (p. 86). He calls for a "critical reimagination of critical editing" that would recognize the social nature of texts (p. 67). Challenging not only "authorial intention" as the ground of textual editing, but also the notion of a single text as the "correct" one, McGann emphasizes the "indeterminacy" of an archive that includes "not just original manuscripts, proofs, and editions but all the subsequent textual constitutions which the work undergoes in its historical passages" (p. 62). "The transmission history of a poetical work," he argues, "is as much a part of the poetry as is the 'original' work of the author" (p. 147).

And yet, as important as McGann's work has been to the formulation of a social theory of texts, in his discussion of the "visual aspect" of Dickinson's manuscripts in *Black Riders*, he, too, invokes Dickinson's holographs and her "visual" intentions as the "final horizon" of any editorial translation. For him, as for Howe, Dickinson's hand-sewn manuscripts are the site of some ultimate transparency where her intentions may be clearly read. Franklin's facsimile edition of the manuscripts "makes it clear," McGann writes, "that Dickinson's texts are what would later be called (by Charles Olson) 'composition by field'" (*Black Riders*, p. 27). Dismissing the notion that Dickinson's "odd lineations are unintentional," he argues that "certain textual moments reveal such a dramatic use of page space as to put the questions of intentionality beyond consideration" (*Black Riders*, p. 28). But Franklin's facsimile edition of the manuscripts does *not* put Dickinson's intentions *beyond* question – least of all to Franklin himself, who has consistently argued that Dickinson's unusual marks of punctuation, her lineation, her multiple variants, and her organization of her poems into fascicles have no particular significance, aesthetic or otherwise. What McGann's modernist interpretation of Dickinson's manuscripts in fact suggests is that in the context of his *own* reading of the "objectivist" poetics of Pound, Stein, Olson, and Zukovsky, McGann's experience of Dickinson's writing as "composition by field" is so "dramatic" that he has projected it back onto her manuscripts as "authorial intention."

Critical of Johnson's edition for going "astray," for misrepresenting Dickinson's writing by approaching "her work as if it aspired to a typographical existence," McGann argues that "Dickinson's scripts cannot be read as if they were 'printer's copy' manuscripts, or as if they were composed with an eye toward some state beyond their handcrafted textual condition." Dickinson's hand-sewn manuscripts are, McGann insists, her "work's initial horizon of finality," a horizon that is further circumscribed by McGann's exclusive focus on "*the aesthetic or expressive*" significance of her "scriptural forms." McGann concludes, "When we come to edit her work for bookish presentation . . . we must accommodate our typographical conventions to her work, not the other way around" (*Black Riders*, p. 38).

But if Dickinson's hand-sewn manuscripts are, as McGann argues, the "horizon of finality," then they were possibly not meant to be read or edited at all. So who exactly is the ideal reader that McGann and others invoke in describing how "we" must read and edit Dickinson? Moreover, what exactly constitutes the "work" whose "aspirations" and "horizon" McGann reads so clearly? We do not know the intentions of Dickinson's hand-sewn manuscripts; nor do we know if "her work" "aspired to a typographical existence." What we do know is that Lavinia discovered hundreds of Dickinson's hand-written poems in a box shortly after her death in May 1886. If we are going to follow Dickinson's "intentions" exactly, wouldn't a further logic be that we not "edit" Dickinson's work for publication at all, in fact, that we put her manuscripts back into the box where she left them and not read them at all. Or perhaps we should just destroy Dickinson's manuscripts altogether since silence and death may have been part of what McGann calls "the work's initial horizon of finality."[27]

I am, of course, being facetious. But what I am trying to suggest is that there is no "horizon of finality." We do not know Dickinson's intentions, nor, short of the miraculous discovery of some real rather than Shurr-like "trove" of Dickinson papers, will we ever know her intentions or what constitutes "her work" in any traditional sense of the term. Lavinia chose to save Dickinson's poetic manuscripts, and we must choose and take responsibility for the precise forms in which Dickinson's work is edited and circulated, the kinds of cultural work it is asked to do, and the particular kinds of cultural and political interventions it might be asked to make.

As we move into the new millennium, we might want to reflect back upon and reconsider the histories and intellectual categories through which we have come to know and interpret Dickinson's work. Why, we might ask, has the "Mind" of the poet and the categories of the author, the aesthetic, literature, and Dickinson's status as the "greatest" American or woman poet of all time so persistently framed the kinds of questions we ask? What are the categories that organize and divide Dickinson studies? Why is gender so often separated from history and culture, and language and editing separated from both? Why does the category of the private consistently trump political and ideological analysis? Why does a focus on gender take precedence over questions of race and class? Are there other ways of organizing Dickinson studies that might bring these seemingly distinct modes of inquiry and analysis into a more fluid and fully interactive relation with each other?

Rather than reinstating the hierarchized sets of binaries – private/public, poetry/sexuality, literature/history, aesthetics/politics, high art/mass culture, holograph/print, individual authorship/cultural production – that continue to structure not only Dickinson studies but the institutional spaces we inhabit, we might want to consider other ways of approaching the relations among literature, culture, society, and world. Art is never only private and individual; it is also and always collective and social. Whereas in the past critics have measured the blank space on Dickinson's manuscript pages as a means of gauging her poetic intentions, in the future critics might want to examine her manuscript production in relation to the cultural production, poetics, and writing practices of her place and time. Was Dickinson's manuscript production unique, or was it part of what Emerson called a broader cultural "revolution" in the production of the poetry of "the portfolio over the book?" (Emerson, p. 1169). If Dickinson resisted what Smith calls the "fixity" and "finality" of print, how do we account for Whitman's radical experiments with the fluidity and indeterminacy of print in the 1855 and later editions of *Leaves of Grass*? Whereas in the past, contests over Dickinson have tended to focus on her poetic genius, her intentions, her singularity, and the private and essentially gendered dimensions of her art, in the new millennium one can imagine enlarged definitions of "context" and other possible "wars" – social as well as literary, cultural as well as individual, international as well as national and familial – that might enrich our understanding of the historical locations and occasions for writing through renewed acts of critical attention to Emily Dickinson and the world she lived in.

NOTES

1 Letter of Mary Lee Hall to Millicent Todd Bingham, 5 August 1933, reprinted in *LED*, p. 258. Mabel Loomis Todd and Thomas Wentworth Higginson (eds.), *Poems of Emily Dickinson* (Boston: Roberts Brothers, 1890); Todd and Higginson (eds.) *Poems by Dickinson* (Boston: Roberts Brothers, 1891); Todd (ed.) *Letters of Emily Dickinson*, 2 vols. (Boston: Roberts Brothers, 1894); Todd and Higginson (eds.) *Poems by Emily Dickinson* (Boston: Roberts Brothers, 1896).

2 Betsy Erkkila, *The Wicked Sisters: Women Poets, Literary History, and Discord* (New York: Oxford University Press, 1992), p. 29.

3 Christopher Benfey, "The Mystery of Emily Dickinson," *New York Times Book Review*, 8 April 1999, p. 39.

4 Susan Gilbert Dickinson, "Miss Emily Dickinson of Amherst," *Springfield Republican*, 18 May 1886, in Willis J. Buckingham (ed.), *Emily Dickinson's Reception in the 1890s: A Documentary History* (University of Pittsburgh Press, 1989), p. 551. Lavinia Dickinson, cited in *LED*, p. 153.

5 Higginson, "Emily Dickinson's Letters," *Atlantic Monthly*, 68 (October 1891), p. 445.

6 John Butt *et al.* (eds.), *The Poems of Alexander Pope*, 6 vols. (New Haven: Yale University Press, 1953), vol. 1, pp. 272–3; Ralph Waldo Emerson, *Essays and Lectures*, ed. Joel Porte (New York: Library of America, 1983), p. 467.

7 Howells, "Editor's Study" *Harper's New Monthly Magazine*, 82 (January 1891), p. 320.

8 Millicent Todd Bingham, *Ancestor's Brocades: The Literary Debut of Emily Dickinson* (New York and London: Harper & Brothers, 1945), p. 87.

9 Aldrich, "*In Re* Emily Dickinson," *Atlantic Monthly*, 69 (January 1892), p. 144.

10 Tate, "New England Culture and Emily Dickinson," *Symposium: A Quarterly Journal in Modern Foreign Literature*, 3 (April 1932), p. 206.

11 The only scholar to have total access to Dickinson's original manuscripts at Harvard University is Franklin. When Johnson prepared his edition, he was

allowed to see the Todd collection on only two occasions (Franklin, *Poems*, vol. I, p. 6).

12 R. P. Blackmur, "Emily Dickinson: Notes on Prejudice and Fact," *The Southern Review* 3 (Autumn 1937), pp. 332, 324, 347. John Crowe Ransom later cited Blackmur's essay on Dickinson as a model of the new critical method in *The New Criticism* (Norfolk, CT: New Directions, 1941), pp. vii–x. *Understanding Poetry: An Anthology for College Students* (New York: Henry Holt and Company, 1938), edited by Cleanth Brooks and Robert Penn Warren, includes an extended New Critical analysis of language, image, form, and tone in "After great pain, a formal feeling comes – " (pp. 468–71). See also Tate, "New England Culture"; and Yvor Winters, "Emily Dickinson and the Limits of Judgment," in *Maule's Curse: Seven Studies in the History of American Obscurantism* (Norfolk, CT: New Directions, 1938), pp. 149–68.

13 Johnson's comment on Dickinson appeared in the Introduction to *The Letters of Emily Dickinson* (Cambridge, MA.: The Belknap Press of Harvard University Press, 1958), p. xx.

14 Franklin (ed.), *The Manuscript Books of Emily Dickinson*, 2 vols. (Cambridge, MA.: Harvard University Press, 1981), p. ix.

15 Susan Howe, *My Emily Dickinson* (Berkeley: North Atlantic Books, 1985); Howe, *The Birth-Mark: Unsettling the Wilderness in American Literary History* (Hanover: Wesleyan University Press of New England, 1993); Jerome J. McGann, *Black Riders: The Visible Language of Modernism* (Princeton University Press, 1993); McGann, "Emily Dickinson's Visible Language," *Emily Dickinson Journal*, 2 (1993), pp. 40–51; Ellen Louise Hart, "The Encoding of Homoerotic Desire: Emily Dickinson's Letters and Poems to Susan Dickinson, 1850–1886," *Tulsa Studies in Women's Literature*, 9 (1990), pp. 251–72; Martha Nell Smith, *Rowing in Eden: Rereading Emily Dickinson* (Austin: University of Texas Press, 1992); Hart and Smith (eds.), *Open Me Carefully: Emily Dickinson's Intimate Letters to Susan Huntington Dickinson* (Ashfield, MA: Paris Press, 1998). See also Sharon Cameron, *Choosing Not Choosing: Dickinson's Fascicles* (University of Chicago Press, 1992).

16 Comment appears on the book jacket of William H. Shurr (ed.), with Anna Dunlap and Emily Grey Shurr, *New Poems of Emily Dickinson* (Chapel Hill: University of North Carolina Press, 1993).

17 Michel Foucault, "What is an Author?" trans. Josué V. Harari, in *The Foucault Reader*, ed. Paul Rabinow (New York: Pantheon Books, 1984), pp. 103–104.

18 Margaret Dickie, "Dickinson in Context," *American Literary History* 7 (1995), p. 330.

19 Fredric Koeppel, *Chicago Tribune*, 14 October 1993, sec. 5, p. 3; Paul O. Williams, *Christian Science Monitor*, 29 October 1993, p. 15; Marcy L. Tanter, *Boston Globe*, 25 October 1993, p. 39.

20 Hart, "Poetic License," *Women's Review of Books*, 9 (January 1994), p. 24.

21 Jerome J. McGann, *The Textual Condition* (Princeton University Press, 1991), p. 67.

22 "There is no document of civilization which is not at the same time a document of barbarism," Walter Benjamin writes in "Theses on the Philosophy of History," in Hannah Arendt (ed.), *Illuminations: Essays and Reflections*, trans. Harry Zohn (New York: Schocken Books, 1969), p. 256.

23 Mikhail Bakhtin, in Michael Holquist (ed.), *The Dialogic Imagination: Four Essays*, trans. Caryl Emerson and Michael Holquist (Austin: University of Texas Press, 1981), p. 294.

24 Jurgen Habermas, *The Structural Transformation of the Public Sphere: An Inquiry into a Category of Bourgeois Society*, trans. Thomas Burger (Cambridge, MA: MIT Press, 1991).

25 Erkkila, "Emily Dickinson and Class," *American Literary History* 4 (1992), pp. 1–27.

26 Benjamin, "The Work of Art in the Age of Mechanical Reproduction" (*Illuminations*, p. 231).

27 In her will, which is dated 19 October 1875, Dickinson leaves her entire estate to Lavinia: "I give devise and bequeath to my only sister Lavinia N. Dickinson all my estate, real and personal, to have and to hold the same to her and her heirs, and assigns forever"; in *The Years and Hours of Emily Dickinson*. Ed. Jay Leyda (New Haven: Yale University Press, 1960), vol. 2, p. 236. Although Sewall writes that "All of Emily's correspondence was destroyed by Lavinia after Emily's death, by Emily's direction" (*Life*, p. 96), the precise nature of Dickinson's "direction" to Lavinia remains unclear. According to Mabel Loomis Todd, Lavinia was uncertain about Dickinson's exact "wishes": "Soon after her death her sister Lavinia came to me, as usual in late evening, actually trembling with excitement. She told me she had discovered a veritable treasure – quantities of Emily's poems which she had had no instructions to destroy. She had already burned without examination hundreds of manuscripts, and letters to Emily, many of them from nationally known persons, *thus, she believed, carrying out her sister's partly expressed wishes, but without intelligent discrimination*. Later she bitterly regretted such inordinate haste. But these poems, she told me, must be printed at once" (Todd, "Emily Dickinson's Literary Début," *Harper's Monthly Magazine* [March 1930], pp. 463–464, *emphasis added*).

GUIDE TO FURTHER READING

Cameron, Sharon. *Choosing Not Choosing: Dickinson's Fascicles*. University of Chicago Press, 1992.

Erkkila, Betsy. *The Wicked Sister: Women Poets, Literary History, and Discord*. New York: Oxford University Press, 1992.

Howe, Susan. *The Birth-Mark: Unsettling the Wilderness in American Literary History*. Hanover: Wesleyan University Press of New England, 1993.

My Emily Dickinson. Berkeley: North Atlantic Books, 1985.

McGann, Jerome. *Black Riders: The Visible Language of Modernism*. Princeton University Press, 1993.

The Textual Condition. Princeton University Press, 1991.

Smith, Martha Nell. *Rowing in Eden. Rereading Emily Dickinson*. Austin: University of Texas Press, 1992.

2

CHRISTOPHER BENFEY

Emily Dickinson and the American South

> I taste a liquor never brewed –
> From Tankards scooped in Pearl –
> Not all the Vats upon the Rhine
> Yield such an Alcohol!
> (*Poems*, 1890)

When Emily Dickinson's poems began appearing in slim volumes during the 1890s, many readers viewed her as an avant-garde writer. Her innovations and transgressions in subject and style were the occasion for either censure or celebration. "'Alcohol' does not rhyme to 'pearl,'" sniffed one English reviewer, scowling at the first stanza of "I taste a liquor never brewed" – while implying that the intoxicating experiment did not go well with aesthetic, "pearly" permanence. "She reminds us," he added, "of no sane or educated writer."[1] Alice James, the brilliant sister of William and Henry James, noted with patriotic delight that British critics were deaf to Dickinson's peculiar, and peculiarly American, excellence. "It is reassuring to hear the English pronouncement that Emily Dickinson is fifth-rate," she reflected in January 1892, "they have such a capacity for missing quality; the robust evades them equally with the subtle."[2]

The influential American novelist and critic William Dean Howells, by contrast, had singled out "I taste a liquor never brewed" – "something that seems compact of both Emerson and Blake, with a touch of Heine too" – as exemplifying Dickinson's up-to-date-ness.[3] In this, he was following the lead of Mabel Loomis Todd's apt defense of Dickinson's "daring" in her preface to the second series of *Poems*:

> Like Impressionist pictures, or Wagner's rugged music, the very absence of conventional forms challenges attention. In Emily Dickinson's exacting hands, the special, intrinsic fitness of a particular order of words might not be sacrificed to anything virtually extrinsic; and her verses all show a strange cadence of inner rhythmical music. Lines are always daringly constructed, and the

"thought-rhyme" appears frequently, – appealing, indeed, to an unrecognized sense more elusive than hearing.[4]

The off-rhyme of "alcohol" and "pearl" was presumably just such a "thought-rhyme," appealing to what T. S. Eliot called the "auditory imagination." Dickinson's use of "slant" or approximate rhymes, of slang, of rhythms that pushed the limits of her metrical schemes – all these led some American reviewers to greet her posthumously published work as the very latest thing.

And when anomalous or experimental poems by other poets were published during the 1890s, it was often to Emily Dickinson that they were compared. The ironic, free-verse parables in Stephen Crane's *Black Riders*, perhaps the most original poetic production of the decade, displayed for one critic an "audacity of . . . conception, suggesting a mind not without kinship to Emily Dickinson's."[5] Meanwhile, Dickinson's aging mentor and editor Thomas Wentworth Higginson, reviewing Crane's book anonymously in *The Nation*, discerned "an amplified Emily Dickinson," and remarked that Crane "grasps his thought as nakedly and simply" as she did.[6] One reviewer even claimed a direct "influence," reporting (with no independent confirmation) that William Dean Howells himself had read aloud from Dickinson's poems in Crane's presence.[7]

Emily Dickinson's poetry seemed resolutely "modern" to many sophisticated, turn-of-the-century readers. She was "unconventional" and "daring," heedless of traditional forms and rules, a distinctively American poet. During the twentieth century, this view of her achievement has recurred from time to time, especially during the years just after the 1955 publication of the complete poems. At that historical moment after World War II, American critics were eager to consolidate a century (since the 1855 publication of Whitman's *Leaves of Grass*) of American modernist writing. David Porter's magisterial and forcefully argued *Dickinson: The Modern Idiom* makes the strongest possible case for Emily Dickinson's modernity.[8]

But this view of Dickinson as "modern" has by no means been the dominant interpretation of her achievement during the past one hundred years. From the beginning, Dickinson's poetry strongly appealed to traditionalists as well, especially to those who felt that she captured perfectly a certain lost New England world, an austere landscape of the spirit all but eliminated by Gilded Age excesses. It is this version of Dickinson, in many ways a "conservative" Dickinson, that this essay will explore most fully. In my view, this interpretation of Dickinson has prevailed since the first publication of her poems. Several other interpretations, differing sharply in certain details, have nonetheless taken their terms from this traditionalist account. It is this division in Dickinson's legacy – and its regional coordinates – to which my title points, rather than the more familiar "war of the houses" often invoked in accounts of Dickinson's fate at the hands of her editors.

In his handsome tribute in *Harper's*, Howells claimed that in Dickinson's work "America, or New England rather, had made a distinctive addition to the literature of the world," adding that "this poetry is as characteristic of our life as our business enterprise, our political turmoil, our demagogism, our millionairism."[9] Howells saw in Dickinson a sort of spiritual counterweight to the capitalist economy of the northeast. That qualifying specification, "or New England rather," claims for that region its traditional role (since the generation of Emerson, Channing, and Thoreau) of reminding the United States of its true purpose. In this regard, Howells might have quoted Dickinson herself, who once described "a quality of loss" on the spring landscape, as though "Trade had suddenly encroached/Upon a Sacrament" (Fr 962).

The most eloquent tribute to Emily Dickinson as a custodian of old New England values came from Samuel Ward, Margaret Fuller's close friend and an early writer for the *Dial*. Ward wrote to his friend Higginson shortly after the publication of the first edition of Dickinson's *Poems*:

> I am, with all the world, intensely interested in Emily Dickinson. No wonder six editions have been sold, every copy, I should think to a New Englander. She may become world famous, or she may never get out of New England. She is the quintessence of that element we all have who are of the Puritan descent *pur sang*. We came to this country to think our own thoughts with nobody to hinder . . . We conversed with our own souls till we lost the art of communicating with other people. The typical family grew up strangers to each other, as in this case. It was *awfully* high, but awfully lonesome.   (*LED*, p. 26)

Higginson promptly forwarded Ward's letter to Mabel Todd, calling it "the most remarkable criticism yet made on E. D." (*LED*, p. 26). It is also fair to say that Ward's letter, quoted prominently in his second chapter, "The New England Dickinson and the Puritan Heritage," dominates Richard Sewall's influential view of Dickinson in his two-volume biography. Sewall acknowledged that "the following chapters [of his biography] will both confirm and qualify [though not overturn] Ward's analysis" (*LED*, p. 26). He specifically endorsed Ward's identification of Dickinson as a New Englander of "pure blood": "for the Dickinsons were pure stock, without even a wife in seven generations from outside New England" (*LED*, p. 26).

Paradoxically, however, the strongest argument for Dickinson as the quintessential, "pure-blooded" upholder of New England traditions came not from New Englanders like Higginson and Ward, but from writers of the American South, who found in Dickinson's poetry a voice strangely kindred to their own. After the initial flurry of response that greeted the publication of the three volumes of the 1890s, Dickinson received little attention from poets or critics during the first two decades of the twentieth century. Dickinson remained a subterranean taste from about 1897 to 1924. Barely mentioned in literary histories of the time and rarely included in anthologies, she had a brief success in 1914 with the publication of *The Single Hound* (mostly poems that Dickinson had sent to Susan Gilbert, edited by her daughter, Martha Dickinson Bianchi).

Then, in 1924, the Savannah-born poet Conrad Aiken edited a selection of Dickinson's poems for British readers, with a preface that is the first major essay on Dickinson's work. Calling her "the most perfect flower of New England Transcendentalism," Aiken – the first in a long line of poet-critics to write about Dickinson – noticed in her work the "singular mixture of Puritan and free thinker."

Nothing in Aiken's own fluent and mellifluous poetry reminds us of Dickinson's (in his words) "bare, bleak, and fragmentary" work. He is Southern opulence and ease; she is New England granite. He complained that "her poetry seldom became 'lyrical,' seldom departed from the colorless sobriety of its bare iambics and toneless assonance." (Aiken's own poetry was, if anything, *too* "lyrical," too in love with its tuneful vowels.) But he relished her "freedom of utterance," the way "anything went by the board if it stood in the way of thought." Freedom was paramount in Aiken's assessment of Dickinson's biography as well. "It is apparent," Aiken wrote, "that Miss Dickinson became a hermit by deliberate and conscious choice."[10]

Aiken's essay makes a strong case for Dickinson's centrality in American literature. His Dickinson, part Puritan and part free thinker, is herself divided. It was the Puritan part, however, that remained a barrier for sophisticated American readers during the 1920s. One might have expected Dickinson's originality, waywardness, and embrace of freedom to have triumphed in the heroic 1920s of American writing, when, as Alfred Kazin remarked in a famous passage from *On Native Grounds*, "all the birds began to sing . . . [and] the emergence of our modern American literature after a period of dark ignorance and repressive Victorian gentility was regarded as the world's eighth wonder, a proof that America had at last 'come of age.'"[11] But Dickinson was not included in this "emergence" of "modern American literature." It was Walt Whitman, instead, who seemed, to the poets and novelists of the 1920s, the lyrical liberator who, with his expansive lines and explosive social philosophy, had heroically slipped the yoke of European convention.

Even those poets who leaned towards a more cryptic phrasing and a smaller canvas looked less often to Dickinson than one might suppose. You will not find Dickinson's name in the manifestos of T. S. Eliot or Ezra Pound. You might expect to find her work exerting an influence on that loosely convened school of British and American poets – including Pound, H. D., and Amy Lowell – who wished to make a break with the traditions of "genteel" poetry in English. These self-styled "Imagists" aimed for a new precision in their use of language, uncluttered with what was conventionally considered "poetic." But Dickinson seems to have been a negligible presence for them as well.

Among the Imagists, who coalesced as a group during the years after 1913, only Amy Lowell regarded Dickinson as a significant precursor. After completing her two-volume life of Keats in 1923, Lowell toyed with the idea of writing a biography of Dickinson. Mabel Todd, seeking an ally against the biography planned by Dickinson's niece Martha Bianchi, strongly encouraged Lowell to do so, sending her Dickinson manuscripts and letters from her own hoard. Lowell died of a stroke before she could seriously begin work on the project, however. That Lowell thought of writing a biography and not a critical work is itself significant, as though something about the prevailing line on Dickinson's life was preventing a generation of readers from having full access to her work.

Part of the problem, perhaps, was a sense that Dickinson's life – or at least what little was known of it – did not sufficiently express that escape from "repressive Victorian gentility" that Kazin had invoked. Aiken, in a hooded aside, mentioned the "spinsterly angularity" of her writing, as though marriage would have somehow "rounded" it. And William Carlos Williams, whose lean, imagistic lines in *Spring and All* (1921) have some of the miniaturist clarity of Dickinson's verse, took aim at American women poets generally, and Dickinson in particular, in a difficult and disturbing passage in his own attack on Victorian gentility, *In the American Grain* (1925):

> It is the women above all – there never have been women, save pioneer Katies; not one in flower save some moonflower Poe may have seen, or an unripe child. Poets? Where? They are the test. But a true woman in flower, never. Emily Dickinson, starving of passion in her father's garden, is the very nearest we have ever been – starving.
>
> Never a woman: never a poet. That's an axiom. Never a poet saw sun here.[12]

Williams's phrase "woman in flower," and his nasty epigram "Never a woman [i.e., a heterosexually "fulfilled" woman]: never a poet," hearkens back to Aiken's hint that virginity was somehow a hindrance to full poetic expression.

Clearly, an unusually perceptive temperament was needed to find in Dickinson's work, during the 1920s, a heroism comparable to Whitman's noisier, self-celebrating "barbaric yawp." Hart Crane, who himself knew something about "starving of passion" in his father's garden, had such a temperament. Mulling over his own outsider status, as a homosexual amid masculinist poets like Williams and Ezra Pound, Crane had already, in his great poem "The Bridge," revealed a more vulnerable side of Whitman than the bluff caricature of many 1920s evocations. In 1927, a few years before his suicide, Crane began his sonnet "To Emily Dickinson" with that hunger Williams had sensed in Dickinson: "You who desired so much – in vain to ask – / You fed your hunger like an endless task." Crane saw Dickinson as a reconciler of opposites – "Some reconcilement of remotest mind"; and he answered the bloomless flower claim of Williams and Aiken with the line, " – Truly no flower yet withers in your hand,/ The harvest you descried and understand/ Needs more than wit to gather, love to bind." Crane also paid tribute, in the very un-Dickinsonian form of the sonnet, to Dickinson's genius in the use of abstractions and exotic diction ("Leaves Ormus rubyless, and Ophir chill").[13]

Interestingly, the image of Dickinson "starving of passion in her father's garden" has not gone away. Indeed, it has dominated a good deal of biographically based feminist criticism of Dickinson during recent decades. As the feminist poet-critic Sandra Gilbert recently remarked, Williams correctly understood that imaginatively "Dickinson *was* starving in Victorian Massachusetts . . . and that she couldn't be – in the 'ordinary' sense – either a woman or a poet."[14] One reason why Amy Lowell was drawn to the life of Dickinson is, presumably, the many ways in which her own life resembled Dickinson's. "Starving of passion in her father's garden" is a pretty good description of what we know of Amy Lowell's life – until her imposing father's death and his generous bequest made it possible for her to move in with her female lover and become the poet she had always wished to become.

The real trumpet blast that heralded Dickinson's arrival on the American literary map (or, to change metaphors, in the canon) came from Crane's friend Allen Tate, the reactionary Southern poet and brilliant critic, in an essay of 1932 – when Tate could still complain that "Miss Dickinson's poetry has not been widely read." By then, enough of Dickinson's poems had appeared, especially after the *Complete Poems* of 1924, to make critics feel – erroneously, since the manuscripts in Mabel Todd's hands remained unpublished for another two decades – reasonably confident that they had her entire oeuvre in hand.

Tate was a leading figure in the Southern literary movement of the 1920s generally referred to as the Agrarians (for their attachment to allegedly rural and agricultural values and their rejection of northern industrialism) or the Fugitives (for the literary magazine that they founded at Vanderbilt in Nashville). The Fugitives attacked what they perceived as the money-grubbing tendencies of the United States (what Howells had called "our millionairism"), and looked to what they considered the best traditions of the Old South – especially religious and family traditions – for alternative modes of living. Though they regretted the presence of slavery in the antebellum South, they were inclined to interpret the Civil War as a conflict between northern industrialism and southern agrarianism, and not as a battle over freedom.

The line of descent from this group of Southern critics and writers to the school of criticism that came to be known, after World War II, as the New Criticism is direct. Tate and his associates among the Fugitives – John Crowe Ransom, Robert Penn Warren, Cleanth Brooks – were leaders in turn among the New Critics, who argued that the "poem itself" as an "organic" whole was the proper subject of literary study. While the New Critics avoided explicit political statements in their analysis of literary texts, implicit in their practice was a preference for the sort of society – hierarchical, ritualized, and traditional – that could produce sophisticated and complex writing of the kind they most admired.

In an essay published in 1935 called "The Profession of Letters in the South," Tate praised the "feudal" past of the South, when "the artist was a member of an organic society."[15] This organic society – a *Gemeinschaft* of common cultural values rather than a *Gesellschaft* of shared economic interests, to borrow two influential German sociological terms – was destroyed, according to Tate, by "finance-capitalism and its creature, machine-production." By the Civil War, according to Tate, the transformation was almost complete, and those traditions he valued most – reverence for God, land, and family – were on the verge of extinction.

In Tate's view, only two regions of the country had been sufficiently imbued with theological convictions and rural traditions to resist to some degree the "rising plutocracy" – namely, the South and New England. And even they were in danger of surrendering to "the machine."

> By 1825 its [i.e., industrialism's] growth in the East was rank enough to begin choking out the ideas and habits of living that New England along with Virginia had kept in unconscious allegiance to Europe . . . Theocracy was on the decline, and industrialism was rising – as Emerson, in an unusually lucid moment, put it, "Things are in the saddle." The energy that had built the meeting-house ran the factory.
> (*Man of Letters*, p. 212)

By 1850, according to Tate, "the Gilded Age had already begun. But culture, in the true sense, was disappearing." "Puritan theocracy" had given a "final, definite meaning to life," and "an heroic proportion and a tragic mode to the experience of the individual," while the "new order" of capitalism "tended to flatten it out in a common experience" (*Man of Letters*, p. 213).

For Allen Tate, Emily Dickinson was a heroic voice raised against industrialism and all it stood for. While lamenting, in the "Profession of Letters" essay, that the South "had no... Emily Dickinson," Tate managed to turn Dickinson into a sort of honorary Southerner, "a deep mind writing from a deep culture," untouched by "the rising plutocracy of the East" (*Man of Letters*, p. 224). He argues that Dickinson was a poet of *transition*. "Born into the equilibrium of an old and a new order," she came of age at the ideal time for a poet – hers was "the perfect literary situation" (p. 223). She had the advantage of an orthodox and highly structured set of theological beliefs and intellectual traditions, namely those of Puritan New England, but this world was on the wane – "The spiritual community" was "breaking up" – and she could dwell in it without being imprisoned within it. Instead, this whole rich theological world was available to her imagination: religious ideas and abstractions were "momently toppling from the rational plane to the level of perception" (p. 221).

Tate had an equally bold interpretation of Dickinson's "withdrawal" from the world. Endorsing Conrad Aiken's view that Dickinson became a hermit by "deliberate and conscious choice," Tate pushed her motivations beyond the merely psychological and into the realm of the cultural and political. For Tate, Dickinson's withdrawal was her way of deliberately turning her back on the ravages of industrialism. "It must have been her sole way of acting out her part in the history of her culture, which made, with the variations of circumstance, a single demand upon its representatives" – i.e., to make money (*Man of Letters*, p. 216). Tate cavalierly brushed away the "modern prejudice... that no virgin can know enough to write poetry." "All pity for Miss Dickinson's 'starved life' is misdirected," Tate eloquently concluded. "Her life was one of the richest and deepest ever lived on this continent" (p. 216).

Emily Dickinson was a rebel, in Tate's view, but she was a rebel of reaction, staunchly upholding values that her elders were giving up. In this regard, she closely resembles Henry James's fictional Catherine Sloper, the dutiful daughter in *Washington Square* who refuses to adapt to Gilded Age values and fashions. The daughters end up (as James and Tate portray them) more patriarchal than the patriarchs. As New York City and Amherst grow and prosper, Catherine and Emily dig in their heels, refusing to budge from their ancestral addresses. Their fathers die; rejected suitors line their solitary paths. Their loneliness, deliberate and chosen, takes on a heroic dimension.

Allen Tate managed to give a "Southern" turn to his reading of specific poems by Emily Dickinson. The poem that Tate singled out as "one of the greatest in the English language" (p. 219), one that "illustrates better than anything else she wrote the special quality of her mind" (p. 218), has become one of her most familiar poems. Shorn of its fourth stanza by Higginson and Todd, the poem was already an anthology piece by the 1930s, under the title "The Chariot" that its first editors had provided. Here is the version Tate had to work with, included in the first volume of Dickinson's *Poems* of 1890:

> THE CHARIOT
> Because I could not stop for death,
> He kindly stopped for me;
> The carriage held but just ourselves
> And immortality.
>
> We slowly drove, he knew no haste,
> And I had put away
> My labor, and my leisure too,
> For his civility.
>
> We passed the school where children played,
> Their lessons scarcely done;
> We passed the fields of gazing grain,
> We passed the setting sun.
>
> We paused before a house that seemed
> A swelling of the ground;
> The roof was scarcely visible,
> The cornice but a mound.
>
> Since then 'tis centuries; but each
> Feels shorter than the day
> I first surmised the horses' heads
> Were toward eternity.

There are, of course, many possible ways to interpret this poem. Richard Sewall, for example, suggested that the poem "commemorates the birth of the poet in her, the time of poetic awakening," as well as "her recognition of her all-encompassing theme . . . the meaning of eternity in the light of which all things, from childhood to the grave, must now be seen" (*LED*, p. 572).

What is most striking in Tate's reading of the poem, in an intense page of analysis, is how strangely "Southern" it is in image and theme. The poem becomes, in Tate's hands, an evocation of genteel life as it might have been lived on a Southern plantation before the Civil War:

> The content of death in the poem eludes explicit definition. He is a gentleman taking a lady out for a drive. But note the restraint that keeps the poet from

carrying this so far that it becomes ludicrous and incredible; and note the subtly interfused erotic motive, which the idea of death has presented to most romantic poets, love being a symbol interchangeable with death. The terror of death is objectified through this figure of the genteel driver, who is made ironically to serve the end of Immortality.   (*Man of Letters*, pp. 219–20)

The poem, for Tate, records one of those stately rituals of a conservative society: "a gentleman taking a lady out for a drive." Tate's "genteel driver" embodies the Southern ideal of chivalry. It is essential to his view of the poem that it has a rural, and specifically agricultural, setting: "The sharp *gazing* before *grain* instills into nature a cold vitality of which the qualitative richness has infinite depth" (*Man of Letters*, p. 219). The images at the heart of "Because I could not stop for death" arise from one of those "organic" and "deep" agrarian societies that Tate most admired.

Of course, Dickinson meets Tate halfway. Her poem *does* portray a stately social encounter between a lady of "leisure" and a man of "civility." The adverbs in the first two stanzas – "He *kindly* stopped for me"; "We *slowly* drove, he knew no haste" – confirm the genteel world of ritual and gallantry evoked in Tate's reading. Even the title that Higginson and Todd provided, "The Chariot," suggests an antique world – perhaps the lost world of the Negro spiritual "Swing low, sweet chariot." (There may even be a specific allusion here. Before the Civil War, Higginson had made a tour of the South, and was one of the first to collect spirituals – what he called "slave songs." Higginson may have preceded Tate in sensing an affinity between the stately arrival of death's chariot in Dickinson's poem and the angelic chariot in "Swing low.")

What Tate ignores, or glosses over in his line about "the genteel driver ... made ironically to serve the end of Immortality," is that there are three characters in the poem, not two. As the poet-critic Randall Jarrell, another Southerner, who had studied with Tate and Ransom in his youth, pointed out, the poem was like someone saying, "We have a nice hotel room. The girl, myself, and the Sphinx."[16] Tate's erasure of the third figure is significant, and indicates just how committed he is to a certain scene – genteel, agrarian, ritualized – evoked in his mind by the poem. This mysterious third figure, whom Dickinson names "Eternity," complicates the picture of a gentleman and lady taking a drive. A chaperon, perhaps?

There is, to be sure, a certain unintended irony in Tate's view of Emily Dickinson as the voice of a pre-industrial society, a poet who "had nothing to do with ... the rising plutocracy of the East." For if Dickinson's father and brother did not excel in the "rising plutocracy," it was not for lack of effort; in any case, the two treasurers of Amherst College did well enough in the world. Edward Dickinson invested in all sorts of financial schemes.

"I must make some money in some way," he wrote his wife in 1835, "and if I don't speculate in the lands, at the 'East,' I must at the 'West.'"[17] One wouldn't know from Dickinson's deliberately naïve poem "I like to see it lap the miles" that her Whig father lobbied and labored hard to bring the railroad – that symbol of the Gilded Age, dear to all Whig politicians – to water-power-poor Amherst, in order to improve prospects of commerce and trade. (A locomotive was named in his honor.) Emily Dickinson attended the opening ceremonies for the Amherst railroad station, a stone's throw from the Homestead on Main Street. But Tate will take the carriage poem, thank you, and not the railroad poem.

Tate's Southern reading of "Because I could not stop for death" raises an interesting question. Could Emily Dickinson's poetry owe something to her own direct experience of Southern ways of life? Emily Dickinson made one trip to the South, in February and March 1855, during her father's tenure in Congress. It was certainly the furthest she ever traveled, and, except for her sojourn in Boston because of eye trouble nine years later, it was her longest period away from Amherst. The trip has inspired a great deal of speculation, centered upon the two weeks Dickinson spent in Philadelphia on the return trip, when she is rumored to have had her crucial encounter with the Reverend Charles Wadsworth, minister of the Arch Street Presbyterian Church. (For many years, Wadsworth has headed the list of Dickinson's possible lovers.)

The Southern segment of the trip – three weeks in Washington DC with at least one foray into Virginia – has received far less attention. But two letters from the trip, one to the Gilbert sisters and one to Mrs. Holland, make clear that Dickinson was drawn to the genteel manners, the polished elegance, and the soft weather of the South. In a letter to Susan and Martha Gilbert, sent from Washington on 28 February, Dickinson reveled in the Southern spring:

> Sweet and soft as summer, Darlings, maple trees in bloom and grass green in the sunny places – hardly seems it possible this is winter still; and it makes the grass spring in this heart of mine and each linnet sing, to think that you have come [back to Amherst]. (L 178)

In a letter to Mrs. Holland dated 18 March, she recounted a visit she had made with her sister, Lavinia, to Mount Vernon:

> I will not tell you what I saw – the elegance, the grandeur; you will not care to know the value of the diamonds my Lord and Lady wore, but if you haven't been to the sweet Mount Vernon, then I *will* tell you how on one soft spring day we glided down the Potomac in a painted boat, and jumped upon the shore – how hand in hand we stole along up a tangled pathway till we reached the tomb of General George Washington, how we paused beside it, and no one

spoke a word, then hand in hand, walked on again, not less wise or sad for that marble story; how we went within the door – raised the latch he lifted when he last went home – thank the Ones in Light that he's since passed in through a brighter wicket! Oh, I could spend a long day, if it did not weary you, telling of Mount Vernon – and I will sometime if we live and meet again, and God grant we shall! (L 179)

These letters reveal a pleasure in the "soft" spring of the South, and in the "elegance" and "grandeur" of the great plantation of Mount Vernon. "We have had many pleasant times," Dickinson told Mrs. Holland, "and seen much that is fair, and heard much that is wonderful – many sweet ladies and noble gentlemen have taken us by the hand and smiled upon us pleasantly – and the sun shines brighter for our way thus far." The sisters befriended a Mrs. James Brown of Alabama who later sent them a novel by Elizabeth Stuart Phelps as a gift. It is easy to imagine those sweet Southern ladies and noble gentlemen making their way into poems like "Because I could not stop for death."

I want to close this discussion of the "conservative" Dickinson with a final chapter in the twentieth-century reception of Emily Dickinson, namely, the extraordinary body of feminist criticism during the last third of the century. I think it is fair to say that this has been the dominant wing of Dickinson criticism for the past twenty-five years or so. I believe, though, that the true roots of this criticism, at least as it regards Emily Dickinson, go back to the Agrarian idea of Dickinson as cultural custodian and reactionary rebel. A further impetus, also stemming in part from the Agrarians, was the so-called "confessional" poetry of the late 1950s and 1960s, which made Dickinson's voice "audible" in new and compelling ways.

When Emily Dickinson's complete poems were published more or less in the form in which she wrote them, in 1955, the Southern interpretation once again prevailed. John Crowe Ransom, a leading figure in the old Agrarian circles and a key "New Critic," argued, in an essay called "Emily Dickinson: A Poet Restored," that "the principal literary event of these last twenty years or so [i.e., from 1935 to 1955] has ... been the restoration just now of an old poet" who "in most ways ... was surely not one of our 'moderns.'"[18] Ransom's analysis of Dickinson's biographical situation turned out to have an unexpectedly powerful influence among feminist critics of her poetry.

Ransom's essay recapitulates Tate's cultural analysis of Dickinson's Amherst – "where in her time the life and the metaphysics were still in the old Puritan tradition, being almost boastfully remote from what went on across the state in Boston." He quotes "Because I could not stop for death," with its restored fourth stanza, but his interpretation is essentially Tate's genteel one: "Death's victim now is the shy spinster, so he presents himself as a decent civil functionary making a call upon a lady to take her for a drive" (Ransom, "Poet Restored," p. 90).

Ransom's essay is of particular interest, however, for the way in which it recasts certain questions about Dickinson's relation to the vocation of poetry. What Ransom notices is the singular split between Dickinson's daily life as "a little home-keeping person" (p. 89), extraordinarily ill at ease with other people, and the explosive and confident persona we encounter in so many of her poems. It is a disjunction he finds to be typical of poets. She has adopted what William Butler Yeats called the "poet's mask: the personality which was antithetical to her natural character and identical with her desire" (p. 97). Ransom draws a parallel between Dickinson and Whitman in this regard:

> By nature gentle but indecisive, plain in looks, almost anonymous in her want of any memorable history, she chose as an artist to claim a heroic history which exhibited first a great passion, then renunciation and honor, and a passage into the high experiences of a purified Soul. That is the way it would seem to figure out. And we have an interesting literary parallel if we think in these terms about the poetry of her contemporary, Walt Whitman. A good deal of notice has been paid lately to Whitman by way of pointing out that he was an impostor, because the aggressive masculinity which he asserted so blatantly in the poems was only assumed. But that would be Walt Whitman's mask. (pp. 97–8)

Ransom's view of the shy spinster adopting the bold mask would seem, on the face of it, to have little to do with the feminist interpretation of Dickinson that began to emerge a couple of decades later. And yet, the line from his essay to the influential treatment of Dickinson in the classic feminist work *The Madwoman in the Attic* is direct, as the authors, Sandra Gilbert and Susan Gubar, implicitly acknowledge. Ransom is the single most invoked figure in their discussion of Dickinson. How did this come about? We will have to make a bit of a detour to explain it.

During the 1950s, it was as a poet of religious structures that Dickinson appeared in some of the most influential literary criticism. Tate's emphasis on Dickinson's religious vocabulary and traditional culture found persuasive expression in Richard Wilbur's elegant poem "Altitudes" (1956), with its comparison (or rather equation) of two perspectives, the dome of St. Peter's in Rome and Emily Dickinson's cupola in Amherst. In an important essay published the same year, which recapitulates much of Tate's argument, Wilbur chose Dickinson's oxymoronic phrase "Sumptuous Destitution" to name what he took to be the central strategy in her work – a sort of less-is-more attitude. This "paradox that privation is more plentiful than plenty" could – in Wilbur's view – make a Rome of Amherst.[19] Of course, this was another turn in the old argument about Dickinson's deliberate "withdrawal." Wilbur,

Tate, and the rest believed that Dickinson had gained something important – some spiritual boon – by turning her back on "plenty."

But something else was happening as well during the late 1950s. American poetry, long in thrall to modernist notions of "impersonality," took an autobiographical or "confessional" turn. Poets such as Randall Jarrell, Robert Lowell, and John Berryman (soon followed by Sylvia Plath and Anne Sexton) began to quarry their own lives for material, and the first-person singular returned to poetry with a vengeance. It was at just this moment that Emily Dickinson was "restored," and this group of poets was particularly attuned to her own version of "confessional" poetry. The autobiographical turn that dominated American poetry in the late 1950s and early 1960s made Dickinson's poetry, with its forceful, "I"-dominated voice, particularly audible. Several members of the group of American poets who came of age during the 1950s – the "middle generation" that included Randall Jarrell, Elizabeth Bishop, and Robert Lowell – were intensely interested in Dickinson. The Southerner Jarrell was taking notes for an extended essay on Dickinson at the time of his apparent suicide in 1965. His tentative title for the essay was "The Empress of Calvary," clearly another version of the idea of "Sumptuous Destitution." In some of his own most effective later poems, Jarrell had been experimenting with women's voices, not so much in the older mode of the dramatic monologue – the creation of "believable" women characters – as in an uncanny attempt to probe his own androgynous self. As he read through Dickinson's complete poems, Jarrell was thrilled to find what he perceived to be confirmation (and provocation) for his experiments in Dickinson's practice. He reminded himself to "Notice change in versions" of poem Fr 346 (from "I showed her Heights she never saw" to "He showed me Hights I never saw – "), and in the contrasting versions of "Going to Him! Happy letter!" and "Going – to – Her! Happy – Letter."[20] Current readers may be more inclined to see, especially in the second instance, experimentation with sexual orientation rather than gender. Nonetheless, the importance for "confessional" writing is obvious.

Berryman too was proud of his skill in what he called "the administration of pronouns." Without playing with "ambiguous pronouns," he claimed, he could never have written his first major poem, *Homage to Mistress Bradstreet*. Berryman didn't much like the poetry of his "muse," the seventeenth-century American poet Anne Bradstreet; she concerned him, he admitted, "almost from the beginning, as a woman, not much as a poetess." His "impersonation" of her was an attempt to inhabit her body, and to experience imaginatively such female experiences as childbirth.[21]

But late in his life, Berryman (like Jarrell) became obsessed with Dickinson. Having modeled the sprawling form of his *Dream Songs* on Whitman's

Song of Myself, he tried in his last few books to learn all he could from Dickinson's leaner poetry. Judging from his late tribute to her, "Your Birthday in Wisconsin You Are 140," it was a certain wildness in the language and behavior of "Squire Dickinson's cracked daughter" that appealed to him most, as his own life unraveled in alcoholism and eventual suicide. Some biographical details are garbled in his poem – Dickinson deflected Judge Otis Lord's romantic attentions, not the reverse – but it remains a handsome rebuttal to Higginson's early qualms about Dickinson's poetry.[22]

Higginson's response to Dickinson's "cracked" poetry (more alcohol than pearl, in his view) is also the starting point for Adrienne Rich's very different (and far more effective) poem of 1964. "'I Am in Danger – Sir'" is, among other things, a meditation on the peculiar fate of Dickinson's posthumous reception, which Rich sees as a sort of embattled museum of relics, scraps, and objects that fail to cohere. Rich shares Berryman's sympathy for Dickinson's subversive "wildness" (in marked contrast to Wilbur's decorous version of her). And Rich, like Jarrell, is interested in Dickinson's subverting of gender: "you, woman, masculine/ in single-mindedness." Rich's poem makes a fine pendant for her classic essay on Dickinson, "Vesuvius at Home" (1975), which develops some of the same ideas of the explosive imagination lurking behind the "feminine" decorum of Dickinson's daily life.[23] Rich's excavation of Dickinson's life and work, and her focus on such theretofore neglected poems as "My Life had stood – a Loaded Gun," set the agenda for feminist criticism of Dickinson's life and work.

In *The Madwoman in the Attic*, Sandra Gilbert and Susan Gubar are at pains to define what they call "the 'problem' of lyric poetry by women" (p. 582). While women writers have excelled in prose fiction, and especially in Gothic narrative, in both verse and prose, lyric poetry has remained largely the province of male writers. The problem, as they see it, turns on the kind of self-assertion demanded of poets but denied women. They invoke the Dickinson critic Suzanne Juhasz's concept of the "double-bind" of the woman poet: "on the one hand, the impossibility of self-assertion for a woman, on the other hand, the necessity of self-assertion for a poet" (p. 584). Dickinson's "solution" to the problem was that of the literary persona. "In the context of a dramatic fiction, Dickinson could metamorphose from a real person (for whom aggressive speech is forbidden) into a series of characters of supposed persons (for whom assertive speeches must be supplied)" (p. 584).

Gilbert and Gubar identify as their antagonists such "masculinist" critics as Ransom, and yet their argument, as they are forced to acknowledge, closely resembles his idea of the poet's mask (p. 557). But Gilbert and Gubar make one further move. They argue that Dickinson was not content (as Ransom suggested) to have explosive poetry compensate for the confined daily life of a shy spinster. They argue, instead, that Dickinson turned her own daily life into a Gothic tale, a "yarn of pearl." Gender relations were at the center of this story: "Dickinson's attitude toward the powerful male Other who ruled women's days and lives is at the heart of the gothic 'Novel' into which she transformed her own life" (p. 594). Dickinson's life, they argue, "became a kind of novel or narrative poem in which, through an extraordinarily complex series of maneuvers, aided by costumes that came inevitably to hand, this inventive poet enacted and eventually resolved both her anxieties about her art and her anger at female subordination..." (p. 583).

Where is that "fictional shape Dickinson gave her life" to be found if not in the poetry? Well, in her adoption of white dresses – one of those "costumes that came inevitably to hand." "By literally and figuratively impersonating 'a woman – white,' Dickinson wove her life into a gothic 'Yarn of Pearl' that gave her exactly the 'Amplitude' and 'Awe' she knew she needed in order to write great poetry" (p. 586). In that imaginative space Dickinson is, they argue, the "inebriate of air" who settles for "Sumptuous Destitution," though she is also, in their approving view, "greedy, angry, secretly or openly self-assertive" (p. 564). For Gilbert and Gubar, the questions surrounding Dickinson's "withdrawal" are again key. They endorse the Aiken-Tate conviction that the withdrawal was deliberate and not imposed by some psychological disorder or trauma. And they repeat Tate's powerful interpretive move from biographic to cultural motivations. All these critics share a view of Dickinson's society as "patriarchal." Where they differ is in the value they place on that society.

Tate's view is that Dickinson's withdrawal represented a rejection of the new, money-based values of the Gilded Age, and a return to the religious values of "Old New England." For Tate, Dickinson embraces patriarchy. It is why a poem like "Because I could not stop for death" means so much to him.

Quite differently, Gilbert and Gubar's view is that Dickinson's withdrawal represented a rejection of patriarchy new and old – for what "Old New England" and Gilded Age New England had in common was a social order ("Puritan-Victorian society," they call it [p. 588]) in which women had few options beyond overworked motherhood or isolated spinsterhood. This is why a poem like "My life had stood – a Loaded Gun" is so significant in feminist criticism. Instead of death arriving in a carriage to take the speaker for a ride, the speaker herself deals in death. "This woman poet," as Adrienne Rich wrote, "perceives herself as a lethal weapon."[24] Gilbert and Gubar add that "This Gun clearly is a poet, and a Satanically ambitious poet at that" (Madwoman, p. 609). They conclude that "this enigmatically powerful poem is an astounding assertion of 'masculine' artistic freedom" (p. 610).

Gilbert and Gubar return biographical considerations to the center of their analysis. That Dickinson's own father was "temperamentally as well as culturally a remote, powerful, and grim patriarch" (p. 597) is key to their interpretation of the rebellious daughter. For Gilbert and Gubar, Dickinson's rebellion does not represent a return to earlier values but an emphatic rejection of them. "In poem after poem, as we have seen, this 'gentle spinster' [an allusion to Ransom] enacts the part of a defiant childwoman who resents her tyrannical husband/father and longs to be delivered from his fierce Requirements" (p. 595). In their account, Dickinson more closely resembles Emily Bronte's Catherine Earnshaw than Henry James's Catherine Sloper.

A century of Emily Dickinson criticism and biography has been dominated by one idea: that her poems are best read in relation to some version of "Old New England," defined as patriarchal, religious, marked by quiet habits and intense piety. This conviction is as central to the Southern or "Agrarian" reading of her poetry as it is to feminist readings of it. Both Agrarians and feminists agree in viewing Dickinson as, in some sense, a rebel against this patriarchy. Both see in her use of personae and slippery pronouns a key to her rebelliousness. They differ in the direction they see this rebellion taking. For Agrarian critics like Tate and Ransom, Dickinson's rebellion is directed towards the "Gilded Age" and its money-grubbing tendencies in favor of an earlier set of religious and cultural values. For Adrienne Rich and her followers, Dickinson's rebellion is directed towards the patriarchs themselves, in favor of greater freedom for women in their actual and imaginative lives.

It is in her language that Dickinson's "withdrawal" is most evident. She assiduously guarded her privacy and spoke, to Higginson and others, in a deliberately riddling way, shrugging off his questions ("You ask of my Companions Hills – Sir – and the Sundown"). "All men say 'What' to me," she told him, "but I thought it a fashion." As a consequence of her reticence, it has been easy for her many and diverse admirers to invent their own private Emily: Emily the fierce feminist; Emily the pliant lover; Emily the "voice of war"; Emily the prophet of modernism; Emily the guardian of old New England; and so on. But it is the reticence itself that tells us most about Emily Dickinson. Dickinson was out to purge her own language of deadness. This is what she meant when she asked Higginson whether her verse was "alive." This is what she was trying to explain when she told him that she shunned men and women "because they talk of hallowed things, aloud, and embarrass my dog." This is why people constantly disappointed her, including Higginson, who remarked after an intense visit with Dickinson in 1870 that "She often thought me *tired*." With Higginson, with Susan, and others, infatuation yielded to a friendly formality, as Dickinson increasingly preferred the company of children, animals, and people of her father's more restrained generation.

The overwhelming impression conveyed in Dickinson's letters and poems is of someone who couldn't stand – who had a visceral shudder in the presence of – the flatulent rhetoric of church and state around her. Already, in her teenage years at Mount Holyoke, Dickinson had shown her intellectual honesty in her refusal to count herself among the "saved." Hollow religious language disgusted her: "He preached upon 'Breadth' till it argued him narrow ... The Truth never flaunted a Sign – / Simplicity fled from his counterfeit presence / As Gold the Pyrites would shun" (Fr 1266).

Dickinson was immune to the war fever around her as well. Scholars have combed her verse and prose for mention of the Civil War, which coincided with her greatest outpouring of verse. But her inspiration during those years seems to have been more resistance to high rhetoric than acceptance of it. A reference to bells tolling here and to bullets there have been adduced to show her awareness of the war. (As though she could have been oblivious to it!) Many critics may be right in claiming that she never specifically referred to the Civil War in her poetry. While Julia Ward Howe was writing her saber-rattling "Battle Hymn of the Republic," and Whitman his *Drum-Taps*, Dickinson was quietly demolishing myths of heroic pomposity, as in her two-stanza unraveling of the Jason myth, which begins with the act of finding and counts down to the devastating finale:

> Fourth, no Discovery –
> Fifth, no Crew –
> Finally, no Golden Fleece –
> Jason, sham, too –
>
> (Fr 910)

Her father's commitment to the Whig values of compromise – he had campaigned before the Civil War for the Southern Whig presidential candidates Zachary Taylor and Henry Clay – may well have tempered Dickinson's own response to the war. Once the war had begun, and the casualties, in Amherst and elsewhere, rose, her family joined in the patriotic fervor. But she did not move in radical circles. Such friends as Samuel Bowles, Nathaniel Banks, and Dr. Holland were unlikely to fan any flames, before the war or after. Banks spent a weekend at the Dickinson Homestead in 1860, when he was governor of Massachusetts, and attended the Amherst College commencement tea there – the last before the Civil War. Two years later, Banks found himself in charge of the occupation of New Orleans, and systematically dismantled the arrangements that his predecessor, the radical Benjamin Butler, had made to empower blacks and their supporters in the city. After the war, Holland commissioned a book called *The Great South*, by a former *Springfield Republican* reporter, Edward King. The book, sharply critical of Reconstruction policies, was meant to encourage northern investment in the South.[25] Higginson was a radical, of course, a secret supporter of John Brown's raid and commander of a Negro regiment. But Dickinson and Higginson seem not to have discussed politics in their correspondence or in their personal encounters.

More importantly, I think, Dickinson's response to the Civil War was elegiac rather than accusatory. She is sorry for the deaths of northern boys, but does not hunger for Southern deaths to avenge them. Those poems that have been tied to the war lament rather than indict; she does not take sides, and is never *engagé*. Her letters, such as the famous one commemorating the death of Frazar Stearns, son of the president of Amherst College, also avoid indictment. In this regard, Dickinson did not poison her writing for Southern readers, as Emerson, Thoreau and Stowe did. She joins Melville and Hawthorne – writers dear to the South – in assuming an attitude of tragic resignation.

Dickinson's brittle language, oblique and sharply objective, can be seen as a passionate response to the degraded verbiage of the Civil War era, and the Gilded Age pieties that followed. The Agrarian critics and the feminist critics are right to detect rebellion in her voice – as Allen Tate wrote, only partly in jest, "Cotton Mather would have burnt her for a witch" (*Man of Letters*, p. 226). But Dickinson's reach in this regard goes beyond American national boundaries. She speaks for all those who feel hemmed in by official rhetoric and ideology. This is one explanation for the special appeal of her work for such poets and translators of Dickinson as Paul Celan and Eugenio Montale. These poets carved out a kindred prosody of obliquity and harsh specificity in the face of the degradation of the Italian language under Mussolini and the German language under the Nazis. That the leading German-language poet of the post-Nazi era and the leading Italian poet of this century looked to Emily Dickinson should invite us to read her in this way, as a voice raised against the pompous posturing of both sides.[26]

She once mentioned to Higginson her adamant resolution to "never try to lift the words which I cannot hold." She never did.

NOTES

1 Andrew Lang, writing anonymously, "The Newest Poet," *Daily News* (London), 2 January 1891, reprinted in Willis J. Buckingham (ed.), *Emily Dickinson's Reception in the 1890s: A Documentary History* (University of Pittsburgh Press, 1989), p. 81.

2 Quoted in Jean Strouse, *Alice James: A Biography* (New York: Bantam, 1982), p. 320.

3 William Dean Howells, "Editor's Study," *Harper's New Monthly Magazine* (January 1891). Quoted in Buckingham, *Reception*, p. 78.

4 Mabel Loomis Todd, "Preface" to Emily Dickinson, *Poems* (1891).

5 See Christopher Benfey, *The Double Life of Stephen Crane* (New York: Knopf, 1992), p. 131.

6 *Ibid.*

7 *Ibid.*

8 Porter, *Dickinson: The Modern Idiom* (Cambridge, MA: Harvard University Press, 1981).

9 Howells, "Editor's Study," *Harper's New Monthly*, 82 (January 1891): 320.

10 Conrad Aiken, "Emily Dickinson," from *A Reviewer's ABC* (1935), reprinted in Richard B. Sewall (ed.), *Emily Dickinson: A Collection of Critical Essays* (Englewood Cliffs, NJ: Prentice-Hall, 1963), pp. 12, 13, 15.

11 Alfred Kazin, *On Native Grounds: An Interpretation of Modern American Prose Literature* (San Diego: Harcourt Brace, 1982), p. xiii.

12 William Carlos Williams, *In the American Grain* (New York: New Directions, 1925), p. 179.

13 Hart Crane, "To Emily Dickinson," *The Poems of Hart Crane*, ed. Marc Simon (New York: Liveright Publishing Company, 1986).

14 Sandra M. Gilbert, " 'If a lion could talk...': Dickinson Translated," *Emily Dickinson Journal* 2, 2 (1993): 5.

15 Allen Tate, *The Man of Letters in the Modern World: Selected Essays: 1928–1955* (Cleveland: Meridian, 1955), p. 306.

16 William H. Pritchard, *Randall Jarrell: A Literary Life* (New York: Farrar, Straus, and Giroux, 1990), p. 278.

17 Quoted in Sandra M. Gilbert and Susan Gubar, *The Madwoman in the Attic: The Woman Writer and the Nineteenth-Century Literary Imagination* (New Haven: Yale University Press, 1979), p. 597.

18 Ransom, "Emily Dickinson: A Poet Restored," in Sewall (ed.), *Critical Essays.*

19 Wilbur, " 'Sumptuous Destitution,' " in *Responses: Prose Pieces, 1953–1976* (New York: Harcourt Brace, 1976), pp. 3–15.

20 On Jarrell and Emily Dickinson, see Benfey, " 'The Wife of Eli Whitney': Jarrell and Dickinson," in David Sofield and Herbert F. Tucker (eds.), *Under Criticism: Essays for William H. Pritchard* (Athens, OH: Ohio University Press, 1998).

21 See Benfey, "The Woman in the Mirror: John Berryman and Randall Jarrell," in Richard J. Kelly and Alan K. Lathrop (eds.), *Recovering Berryman: Essays on a Poet* (Ann Arbor: University of Michigan Press, 1993), p. 158.

22 See Benfey, "Woman in the Mirror."

23 Rich, "Vesuvius at Home: The Power of Emily Dickinson," in *On Lies, Secrets, and Silences: Selected Prose, 1966–1978* (New York: Norton, 1979), pp. 157–83.

24 *Ibid.*

25 On Butler and King, see Benfey, *Degas in New Orleans: Encounters in the Creole World of Kate Chopin and George Washington Cable* (New York: Knopf, 1997), pp. 50–2, 105–12.

26 Montale's versions of Dickinson are included in Marisa Bulgheroni (ed.), *Emily Dickinson: tutte le Poesie* (Milan: Mondadori, 1997). Celan's eight translations date from 1961.

GUIDE TO FURTHER READING

Gilbert, Sandra M. and Gubar, Susan. *The Madwoman in the Attic: The Woman Writer and the Nineteenth-Century Literary Imagination*. New Haven: Yale University Press, 1979.

Rich, Adrienne. "Vesuvius at Home: The Power of Emily Dickinson," in *On Lies, Secrets, and Silence: Selected Prose 1966–1978*. New York: W.W. Norton, 1979.

Sewall, Richard B. (ed.). *Emily Dickinson: A Collection of Critical Essays*. Englewood Cliffs, NJ: Prentice-Hall, 1963.

Tate, Allen. *The Man of Letters in the Modern World: Selected Essays, 1928–1955*. Cleveland: Meridian Books, 1955.

Twelve Southerners (John Crowe Ransom, Donald Davidson, *et al.*). *I'll Take My Stand: The South and the Agrarian Tradition*. First published 1930. Baton Rouge: Louisiana State University Press, 1977.

3

MARTHA NELL SMITH

Susan and Emily Dickinson:
their lives, in letters

She [Lavinia Dickinson] feels a little baffled by my possession of so many mss. of Emily's.
 – Susan Dickinson to William Hayes Ward, editor of *The Independent*,
 14 March 1891

The first poem "To Sue" is beautiful. I could have wept over it. Some are rather obscure – I must read them many times.
 Such genius and mysticism as Emily possessed often transcends mortal comprehension.
 – Kate Anthon, long-time friend of Susan and Emily, to Martha Dickinson
 Bianchi upon publication of *The Single Hound*, "a volume offered as a
 memorial to the love of these 'Dear, dead Women,'" in 1914

> *...Do you remem-*
> *ber what whis-*
> *pered to*
> *"Horatio"?*

 – Emily to Susan Dickinson, spring 1886, within weeks of Emily's death. As
 Hamlet lay dying, he whispered "Report me and my cause aright" and
 "tell my story" to Horatio. (*OMC* 253)

During the first century of public distribution of her literary work, many facts about Emily Dickinson's writing practices and about her decades-long alliance with her sister-in-law, Susan Huntington Gilbert Dickinson, have become clearer. As her poems moved from manuscript and hand circulation to printed volumes and various editions, tools such as Thomas H. Johnson's variorum *The Poems of Emily Dickinson* (1955), his three-volume *The Letters of Emily Dickinson* (1958) with Theodora Ward, Jay Leyda's two-volume *Years and Hours of Emily Dickinson* (1960), R. W. Franklin's two-volume *The Manuscript Books of Emily Dickinson* (1981), and his three-volume variorum *The Poems of Emily Dickinson* (1998) have proved indispensable for Dickinson scholars. Yet the facts about Susan and Emily Dickinson's relationship lack what Susan and Emily called "phosphorescence" and Percy Bysshe Shelley called the "uncommunicated lightning" of mind in his introduction to *Prometheus Unbound*. Echoing Shelley, Emily remarked to Susan that some had "the Facts but not the Phosphorescence," or understanding, "of Knowledge" (*WSD*, "Notes Toward a Volume of ED's Writing"). All of the above lack understanding of Susan and Emily Dickinson's relationship because the facts they convey about it have neither been adequately interrogated nor read in a framework making clear their profound significance for understanding Dickinson's poetic project. These perplexities in interpretation are perhaps inevitable in a culture with a limited (and heterosexualized) range of storylines for scripting poetic influence and erotic devotions. This essay will review those facts, analyze the history of their "lives" in Dickinson study, and will conclude by discussing the importance of recovering the biography of this relationship for understanding Emily Dickinson's writing practices.

Born nine days after Emily Dickinson on 19 December 1830, about ten miles away from Amherst in Old Deerfield, Massachusetts, and dying 12 May 1913, almost twenty-seven years to the day after Emily, Susan and Emily have been called "nearly twins" by some,[1] and indeed they enjoyed many mutual passions – for literature, especially poetry, gardening, recipes, music, and nature. Here are a few facts about Emily Dickinson, her writing practices, and her relationship with Susan: Emily sent Susan substantially more writings than were addressed to any other person (more than twice the number sent to her next most frequently addressed correspondent, Thomas Wentworth Higginson), and these nearly 500 writings constitute one of two major corpora that Dickinson bequeathed to the world at her death (the other being the more than 800 poems in the fascicles). The number of texts alone testify that Susan was Emily's most trusted reader and critic, and the record shows that the two engaged in a literary dialogue that lasted for decades, and the better part of Dickinson's life. Correspondents for nearly forty years and next door neighbors for three decades, their relationship was constant, from the time they were girls together until Emily's death in 1886. Emily and Susan began writing to one another when they were in their late teens, perhaps earlier. Their mutual passions, especially for literature, were well-known to their contemporaries, and at least one – their common friend, editor Samuel Bowles, in an 1862 letter to Susan – acknowledged their writing together. As Emily writes more and more to Susan, poetry emerges within and from the epistolary scriptures, and her lyrics become significantly bolder in theme, imagery, and form. Material evidence in Susan's papers shows that Emily was sending Susan pencilled, or what appear to be draft versions of poems that she would record in her manuscript books, or "fascicles," in ink.

This is especially significant since critics, editors, and biographers have long believed that Emily did not share drafts of her poems with any other contemporary. Other material evidence in Susan's papers and in the writings to her husband, Emily's brother Austin, shows that someone had sought to expunge affectionate expressions by Emily to and about Susan. As readers will see, Mabel Loomis Todd, one of the first two editors producing volumes of Dickinson's poems, wanted to obfuscate the centrality of Susan's roles in Emily's writing processes, and went to great lengths to suppress any trace of Susan as literary collaborator and confidante.

However, though mentioned in biographies and tabulated in editions, these facts have remained dispersed and scattered, and thus generally uninterpreted. In other words, the story these facts tell has not been uttered, until recently. Simply and succinctly put, these facts show that as most beloved friend, influence, muse, and adviser whose editorial suggestions Dickinson sometimes followed, Susan played a primary role in Emily's creative processes.

Facts about the relationship's constancy and longevity were well known to their contemporaries, but they have been passed along to posterity through a variety of testimonies, two of which are the central players in determining the relationship's reception. Closest to the source of any and all is Martha Dickinson Bianchi, Susan's daughter and Emily's niece, who has generally (and unfairly) been received as nearly always unreliable. The other key source is one who knew the relationship only from a distance. Though received by many as objective, this was hardly possible for the source was Mabel Loomis Todd, Susan's husband's mistress. In the course of her affair with Emily's brother Austin, Loomis Todd served as editor of the first three volumes of Emily's poems. So while editing Susan's best friend's poems, she played the role of satisfying mistress to Susan's disappointing wife. Not surprisingly, then, the story about Susan's role in Emily Dickinson's writing life has never been uttered in a full, coherent narrative, but has only been relayed in partial and competing versions, with many key facts hidden or trivialized.

Other key facts about the writings of this relationship have been available but have either gone unnoticed or have not been analyzed for their significance, even by those who have access to them. In effect, these facts have been privatized, reserved for editors and scholars engaged in manuscript study. Indeed, what is signaled by the fact that Emily wrote to Susan in pencil while she almost always wrote to all others in the more formal medium of ink? And what is signaled by the fact that Emily wrote to Susan on diverse types of paper (graph, scrap, and formal embossed paper of all sizes) while with other correspondents she almost always used more formal, often gilt-trimmed stationery, in effect dressing her texts like a gift edition of poetry or a deluxe edition of biblical scripture? Like "scattered pieces of a puzzle" this knowledge has lain in scholarly books and articles and in manuscript collections but has remained "unknown because 'its logically related parts . . . have never become known to any one person'" who could then transmit that knowledge to the public.[2] Even as attention to Dickinson's manuscripts has increased exponentially, witnessed by the fact that so many books of Dickinson criticism published in the 1990s feature some facsimile image of her scripture on their covers,[3] the prevailing assumption has been that any knowledge discovered through analyses of the original documents is of primary interest to specialists. The meanings of facts regarding the materiality of Dickinson's manuscripts for literary history and for understanding the poet Emily Dickinson's writing projects have thus been inaccessible to the general reader.

The textual body of Dickinson's manuscripts is a powerful witness to Susan's entanglements in Emily's compositional and distribution practices. Sending another writings in one's casual script, in handwriting similar to one's private notes, is an act that speaks trust, familiarity, and routine. Sometimes placing those writings on less formal stationery, scraps of paper lacking gilt edges or elegant embossments to impress, likewise signals the intimacy of comfortable quotidian exchange, a correspondence not bound by and to special occasions, but an everyday writing habit taking as its subject any element of life's course, from the monumental death of a beloved to the presumably negligible nuisance of indigestion. These expressions to and about Susan uttered in pencil and ink, on elegant stationery and on the backs of envelopes were powerful enough to drive Susan herself to destroy those "too personal and adulatory ever to be printed" (WSD, "Correspondence with William Hayes Ward," 14 March 1891) and to provoke someone else to scissor half of a sheet out of one of Emily's early, four-page letters to Austin, to erase several lines out of another and words out of others, and to ink over every line of "One Sister have I in our house" (Fas 2, J 14, Fr 5; see also OMC 30).

Public and private forces have thus worked in concert to leave untold stories about the fact that so many poems were sent to a single contemporary and about what might motivate readers (including the addressee herself) to feel justified in suppressing writings to Dickinson's primary audience. Following the conventions of typographical bookmaking, editors first working with the Dickinson documents were more focused on relaying the linguistic elements of her writings and the stories embedded therein and ignored the stories conveyed by the material elements of her writings altogether. As the first century of reading Dickinson progressed and editors such as Johnson and Franklin began to grapple more and more with the material elements, the amount of information to be gleaned, sorted, and evaluated proved to be astounding. Conventional principles of selection discouraged recognition of the salience of material facts like paper type and size that are so telling in the Susan corpus. At the same time, a particular reception of Susan's relevance to Emily's writing had been set, one that held that Susan was important but was more interested in her own daughter's career. Consequently, this extraordinary body – "so many mss. of Emily's" in Susan's possession – and their many characteristics, especially physical aspects that relay information about the nature of this relationship (such as the pictorial elements, drawings, and cutouts, to which Susan herself called attention), tended to confound late twentieth-century readers and editors.

The lives of the facts in Dickinson study

Emily Dickinson died in 1886, and her poems were introduced to the reading public in 1890 as *Poems by Emily Dickinson*, edited by Mabel Loomis Todd and Thomas Wentworth Higginson. During her lifetime, Dickinson circulated her writings primarily through her correspondences, but posthumous editors have circulated her writings in printed books. Thus her writings moved from the realm of gift exchange to that of commodities bought and sold, from a world where Emily's "Mine" was Susan's "your own" (*OMC* 243) and "Copyright" mutual (*OMC* 244) to a province where "Publication – is the Auction" (Fas 37, J 704, Fr 788), law prevails, and copyright is mandated by courts. In commodification's geography of being poetry is not so much "my sermon – my hope – my solace – my life" (*WSD*, "Letter to Curtis Hidden Page") as it was to Susan, but is "my property." Authors in the realm of literary trade are celebrities, and audience desires and expectations begin to shape publishers' notions of authors, even of what authors look like, and popular images begin to function as stereotypes. Just as the composite biography of a rock star – an image of especially long, spikey, flourescent, or otherwise unusual hair, provocative dress, and easy access to lots of sex and drugs – still lurks around the performance of any rock & roller today, so the composite (stereotypical) biography of the poetess lurked in the minds of all her nineteenth-century readers (including herself). In 1890, audiences were prepared to receive a reclusive figure who robed herself in white and harbored some "secret sorrow" quietly as she wrote poems at home, and publishers knew that a solitary literary figure was marketable.[4] So when Loomis Todd and Higginson edited their volume, the conventional image of the poetess was in their minds, in the mind of their publisher, and in the minds of their audience. But theirs was not the first plan for a posthumous volume of Emily Dickinson's poems.

Knowing that Susan had been Emily's most trusted literary audience, Emily's sister Lavinia first turned to Susan to accomplish the task of editing the poems for print. Between Dickinson's death and the first printed volume of her work four years later, Susan began to work on what one might call her "Book of Emily's Writings." As Dickinson's primary audience, Susan determined that including writings that were "rather more full, and varied" (December 1890 letter to Higginson)[5] than the conventional presentation made in *Poems by Emily Dickinson* was in order. Loomis Todd and Higginson had separated the poems from their original contexts in letters and in manuscript books and divided them into the predictable subjects anticipated by audiences – books of poetry tended to organize lyrics into categories such as "Life, Love, Time & Eternity, Nature," the sections used for all three books of *Poems by Emily Dickinson* in which Loomis Todd had a hand. In telling contrast, Susan wanted to showcase Emily's "early letters quite surpassing the correspondence of Gunderodi[e] with Bettine [von Arnim]" (a romantic friendship celebrated by Goethe), use "quaint bits to [her] children," with "illustrations of her (Emily's) own, showing her witty humorous side" which was "all . . . left out of" that first printed volume (*WSD*, letter to Higginson; and "Correspondence with William Hayes Ward," 23 March 1891). When Susan broached her idea to Higginson, he evidently told her that such a gathering of literary work, the "more full and varied" volume she had first imagined, was "un-presentable" (December 1890 letter).

In addition to all the writings that Susan had in her possession, forty manuscript books and scores of poems on loose sheets were found after Dickinson's death, and Lavinia (Vinnie) wanted poems from that trove incorporated into the printed volume she asked Susan to compile. Susan struggled with how to make a book from those fascicles, reading through the astonishing production of her dearest friend and marking individual lyrics with the initials D, F, L, N, P, S, W, and X in order to categorize them, not only in deference to Vinnie's wishes but also bowing to Higginson's market judgment. In other words, Susan tried to make *their* "Book of Emily" but could not because it went against her better judgment influenced by decades of her creative collaboration with Emily. As her correspondence with William Hayes Ward shows, Susan thought Higginson's verdict of "un-presentable" underestimated public taste and ability "to recognize the power of so many that were ruled out of the [1890] volume just printed" (*WSD*, "Correspondence with William Hayes Ward," 8 February 1891). Conflicted, distracted, and grieved by the loss of Emily and by her husband's flagrant affair with Mabel, Susan moved slowly, and Vinnie grew impatient and demanded that the fascicle poems be returned so that another editor, one who could get the job done more quickly, could work on the project. As Edward Dickinson's

(Emily's nephew Ned) notebook and Martha Dickinson Bianchi's accounts of making *The Single Hound* show, Susan was to work on designs for a book based on the writings Emily sent her throughout the 1890s and then for the rest of her life (*WSD*, "Notes Toward a Volume of Emily Dickinson's Writings," and *DEA*, "Ned's Notebook"). Nevertheless, she returned the fascicle poems. Not long thereafter, Loomis Todd, her husband's mistress, began copying and reorganizing the poems in the manuscript books to make a printed volume.

At that point, when Emily's poems passed from Susan's hands to Mabel Loomis Todd's, personal and cultural forces converged to suppress Susan's crucial role as audience for Emily's poetry.[6] In addition to the restrictions inherent in making volumes divided into the four categories so familiar to the consumer, editors worked under the shadow of the fact that the most marketable image of a woman poet was the reclusive white-clad figure, noted earlier. This romanticized figure wrote all alone, and an immediate audience for her poetry, especially on the domestic front, would not be viewed as a part of the stereotypical biography for "poetess." Wanting for rather obvious reasons to suppress that Emily Dickinson's primary audience was in fact the "wife forgotten" (*OMC* 9) – who completed the triangle of Mabel and her lover, Emily's brother Austin – Loomis Todd was more than happy to play up the image of the solitary woman writer in her editorial productions. In a letter to her parents, Loomis Todd flatly declared her awareness that Amherst stories of Emily's life were very much "like a book" (*YH* II, p. 357), and for reasons that were not entirely professional, her iterations of the life of the poet conformed to audience expectations that de-emphasized the writer's audience. She refused Higginson's recommendation that Susan's obituary of Emily, which pointed out that she kept her own company but was certainly "not disappointed with the world,"[7] serve as the introduction to the 1890 *Poems*. Instead, she used a three-paragraph introduction by Higginson that proclaimed that Emily was "a recluse by temperament and habit" (iv), an image more aligned with the composite "poetess" than the vibrant figure of Susan's obituary.[8] Not surprisingly, when Loomis Todd produced *The Letters of Emily Dickinson* (1894), Dickinson's primary correspondent of several decades is not even mentioned, nor are any of the hundreds of letters to her reproduced, though Susan's sister Martha, to whom Emily sent a handful of letters, is mentioned.

As is obvious from the story recounted above, the editing of Emily Dickinson was, from the very beginning, driven, inflected by, and/or entangled with biography. What is not so obvious is that biography persists as a key element in the editing of Dickinson. Even our contemporaries whose focus is her textual condition predicate analyses on beliefs about her biographical condition. R. W. Franklin accounts for her "motive[s] . . . in constructing" her handmade books as a desire "to reduce disorder in her manuscripts" (Fr *x*), and Marta Werner, coeditor of the *Dickinson Electronic Archives*, accounts for her seemingly random choice of writing materials – "whatever lies close by" – by characterizing her process as "cometary," demanding to be "written even before one's thoughts have been ordered" (*Open Folios*, p. 21), while maintaining that "agoraphobia" (or imitating agoraphobia) accounts for her modes of existence (p. 27). With the plain goal of fostering serious analysis of Emily and Susan's literary, amorous, and other bonds, Ellen Louise Hart and I published *Open Me Carefully* in 1998. Thus some conception of the author and her relations tends to color all interpretation of Emily Dickinson, no matter how textually centered.

The lack of a clear biographical account of, as well as a lack of a cultural model for, Susan and Emily Dickinson's relationship makes the following set of facts, available in part since 1914 and almost in full since 1955–8 (when Johnson published the *Poems* and *Letters*), difficult to interpret. "I am not suited dear Emily with the second verse," Susan wrote to her beloved friend and sister-in-law in about 1861. In this, Susan responds to a revised version of "Safe in their Alabaster Chambers," one that featured an entirely new second stanza. Among the ten lyrics known to be printed during the poet's lifetime, "Safe in their Alabaster Chambers" offers the only example of Emily Dickinson responding directly to a reader's advice. At the behest of Susan, Dickinson revised this poem several times. She labored over its composition, searching for an appropriate second stanza, and in the process wrote four different verses for possible coupling with the striking first (*OMC* 58–63). These facts are especially important since Dickinson is perhaps best known for her isolation, for purportedly writing in complete solitude. Until the 1990s, critics and biographers had been virtually silent on what this exchange between the two women meant. Both of them were writers, yet neither was what one would call a professional writer. Both were readers, yet neither was what one would call a professional reader, a critic, or an "expert." If this exchange were between Wordsworth and Coleridge, or Hawthorne and Melville, or Elizabeth Barrett and Robert Browning, interpreters would declare literary liaison with certainty. Yet most have balked, hesitated, and some have shrugged, saying this is the exception (of Emily reaching out to another concerning the writing of a poem) that proves the rule (that reaching out was not her habit). However, the ease with which Emily approaches Susan and with which Susan delivers her response suggests that this exchange was a habit of their relationship, that this kind of give and take between them was the rule.

Turning to an example frequently (and accurately) remarked upon to document Dickinson's resistance to advice helps clarify interpretation of the exchange with Sue. Suppose readers insert Higginson – a professional man of letters and widely published essayist, well-known agitator for women's rights, abolitionist, and correspondent of Dickinson's for almost twenty-five years – into the position of first person singular saying "I am not suited – dear Emily." When one imagines Higginson as speaker, the relationship connoted by the exchange is easily read as one of poet consulting a trusted audience, a mentor of notable *public* standing. The many drafts of poems forwarded to Susan over the entire course of Emily's decades-long writing career make visible Susan's role as consultant, collaborator, and liaison. The most extensive single example of her contributions to Emily Dickinson's writing of a poem is Susan Dickinson's responses to different versions of "Safe in their Alabaster Chambers," which indicate that she critiqued the text while Dickinson was in the process of writing, and that the effects of Susan's responses to reading the poem are evident in its various incarnations. Susan wrote to Emily when she saw the poem published in the *Springfield Daily Republican* and is likely to be responsible for its printing in the newspaper read by the Dickinson households. In other words, from their writing back and forth about the poem, it is clear that Susan was a vital participant in its composition and transmission (*OMC* 58–62; "Emily Dickinson Writing a Poem," *DEA*). Had the same exchange occurred between Dickinson and Higginson, readers would have approached these facts with anything but the critical indifference with which they have in fact usually been handled. Had Higginson been the player instead of Susan, this exchange would have been at the center of Dickinson studies.

Important for reading and understanding Susan and Emily's exchange and the critical responses (or lack thereof) to the situation are the structure of "public" and "private" prime audiences that receive Higginson as authoritative, legitimate critic and Susan as amateur. The picture is additionally complicated by the fact that their passionate relationship throughout adulthood until Emily's death resists paradigms for standardizing emotional alliances. Although their relationship has strong elements of romantic friendship and also might be called prototypically lesbian, as well as mutually mentoring, their dynamic devotion does not fit comfortably into any standard category – lover, sister, mentor, best friend, neighbor, or companion – though it has elements of each. In *Open Me Carefully*, Hart and I present their mutual preoccupations with textuality, well aware of the fact that for Susan and Emily poetry and love "coeval come" (*OMC* 140). The conflation of poetry with biography, or life, began long before the print productions of the 1890s.

Even from the present record, which is surely incomplete, there is an astonishing range of writings sent from Emily to Susan over a lifetime – from a note joking about flatulence (*OMC* 24) to poems interrogating the role of romantic love in women's lives and women's circumstance in nineteenth-century America, to letter-poems posing questions of faith and doubt, to poems spoofing on Charles Dickens's sentimental characterization of "Little Nell" and others on her father's strict rules, to emotionally wrenching letter-poems on the death of Susan and Austin's youngest child Gib at the tender age of eight. Dickinson's poetry flourished in her writings to Susan, and her hybrid genre, "letter-poems" (*WSD*, "Correspondence with William Hayes Ward"), seems to have originated in their exchanges; the writings showcase changes in style and experimentations with punctuation, lineation, drawings, mixing media via layouts (e.g., attaching illustrations from novels and standard textbooks like the *New England Primer* to her poems to make "cartoons"), and even calligraphic orthography. These letters repeatedly display Dickinson's vivacious sense of humor and her highly self-conscious textual play as well as her devoted affections.

Throughout their correspondence, there are frequent allusions that attest to their voraciousness as readers, a fact that is likewise corroborated by the vast holdings of both household libraries, especially the Evergreens. There are also linguistic and material allusions to their mutual writing endeavors: from one of the earliest letters (*OMC* 7, April 1852), readers learn that Emily wants to get Susan's journal bound; a letter of but a couple of months later (*OMC* 10, 11 June 1852) has two holes on each third of the folds similar to some of those made in the fascicles, as if the missive was at some point prepared for binding; Emily at one point christens herself and Sue "Combined Girl" for their artistic affinities (*OMC* 85); a mid-1860s letter to Sue from Samuel Bowles, publisher of the *Republican* and dear family friend, remarks, "Speaking of writing, do you & Emily give us some gems for the" *Springfield Musket*, "& then come to the Fair" (*YH* II, p. 93).[9]

The writing and reading workshop did not end with Dickinson's death. Susan made transcripts of numerous poems, sometimes more than one (e.g., of "On this wondrous sea"; H B73, H ST 23e, H ST 24, J 4, Fr 3),[10] evidently to send to friends or editors, and she submitted a few poems to magazines such as the *Independent*, *Scribner's*, and *The Century*. Susan's initials on fascicle poems and on other writings addressed to her appear to note topical categorization of Emily's poems – "D," for "Death," "L" for "Love," "N" for "Nature," "S" for "Sun" or for "Susan" herself, "W" for "Wind," a meteorological element in which both women had deep investments as a metaphor for unseen but nevertheless effective power – and "X's" and numbers on the documents appear to have a similar taxonomizing function. Sometimes Susan turned the topical indicators into titles, as did Emily when she called "A narrow Fellow/in the Grass" (H B 193; J 986, Fr 1096) her

"Snake" (L 316). On 31 December 1886, the last day of the year in which Emily died, Susan writes to the editor of *The Century*, "I enclose a poem of Miss Emily Dickinson's on the 'Wind' thinking you might like to print it" (quoted in Bingham, *Ancestors' Brocades*, p. 86), and forwarded "The Wind – tapped like/a tired Man – " (Fas 29, J 436, Fr 621).

Her pencilled lines across paragraphs in the early documents, publication of a few poems in the 1890s, and extensive work with son Ned and daughter Martha transcribing Aunt Emily's poems indicate that she was indeed preparing a volume for publication and continued to work on developing the project even when her husband Austin forbade her to do so in order to promote the editorial efforts of his mistress Loomis Todd. Most of their transcriptions can be viewed in "Notes Toward a Volume of Emily Dickinson's Writings" in *Writings by Susan Dickinson* and "Ned's Notebook" (*DEA*). Mentioning Emily's love of flowers, her improvisational piano playing, her attitude toward women, and quoting the "facts but not the phosphorescence of knowledge," Bianchi's introduction to *The Single Hound* follows Susan's outline of memories of Emily.[11] Significantly, of the first volume he edited with Todd, Susan writes to Higginson with editorial and emotional authority, correcting a mistranscription, and thanking him "for her as well as for myself" for its publication (December 1890 and January 1891). For his part, Higginson followed Susan's advice, correcting the 1890 edition according to her critical commentary. A 13 February 1914 letter of Martha's to her friend Charles Brownell, an editor at *Scribner's*, likewise testifies to Susan's decisive authority as stylist and wordsmith on the inside of Emily's creative process: "my reasons [in matters of publication] are mamma's, and if I publish at all it must be as she wished. . . . I have no advisor now, and Dolly [Susan, who had died in May 1913] was always so *sure* of everything, I miss her wise decision unspeakably."[12] Though the Higginson-Todd endeavor was by no means ideal as far as she was concerned, Susan applauded his launching more of "Our Fleet," as she had called ushering the poems into print when writing to Emily about publication of "Safe in their Alabaster Chambers" in the *Republican* in March 1862 (*OMC* 58).

The facts of this correspondence challenge not only widely held notions about the individual author Emily Dickinson, but also literary traditions that have drawn sharp distinctions between "poetic" and "domestic" subjects. Comments about routine household and family matters in Dickinson's writings have been received as household detritus, interesting for biography but separate from her writing poetry. Clearly integrating the spiritual, complexly cerebral, and exceptional with the quotidian and mundane, these women shared recipes and household news, as well as critiques of literature and speculations about God and eternity, often within a few lines of writing. The record shows that Emily and Susan Dickinson integrated the "high" poetic and the "low" domestic and thus agreed with Ralph Waldo Emerson's declaration in "The Poet": the Poet is one who shall "not be able to find a condition inopportune or ignoble" as a poetic subject. For Susan and Emily, possessing and being possessed by poetry was not a matter of royalties and copyrights but was an ennobling endowment of spirit, grace, humor, passion, and comfort. Fettering poetry with dollars per line and fee per use was "so foul a thing," subjecting the chariot of the "Human soul" (J 1263, Fr 1286) to printer's proofs fouled by corrections. Poetry leavened and enlivened all experience, routine or sublime, and attaching any "Price" to it was a "Disgrace" (Fas 37, J 709, Fr 788), as was divorcing it from the everyday.

In their writings regarding Dickinson's poetic project, both Emily and Susan emphasized the distinction between the often synonymously used terms *publish* and *print*. When she wrote to Higginson about the appearance of "The Snake" in the *Republican*, Dickinson did not say, "I had told you I did not *publish*"; she said, "I had told you I did not *print*" [emphasis added] (BPL Higg 59, L 316).[13] Also, when she smiles at Higginson's conjecture that she delays "to publish," quotation marks make it plain that she uses his words when she utters the more commonplace term for works produced in the literary marketplace instead of her more precise "to print" (BPL Higg 52, L 265). Writing on 18 February 1891, to William Hayes Ward, superintending editor of the *Independent*, Susan corrected herself: "I recognize fully all Miss Emily's lack of rhyme and rhythm, but have learned to accept it for the bold thought, and everything else so unusual about it . . . I think if you do not feel that your own literary taste is compromised by it, I would rather the three verses of the 'Martyrs' ['Through the Straight Pass / of Suffering' (Fas 36; J 792, Fr 187)] should be published if any. I shall not be annoyed if you decide not to publish at all. I should have said *printed*" (*WSD*, "Correspondence with William Hayes Ward"). Surrounded by lawyers (Dickinson's father and brother), these women are somewhat legalistic in their differentiations, using *publish* in the special sense "to tell or noise abroad" (*OED*).[14] That mutually careful specificity to distinguish between works printed and works published is not a negligible fact. Yet until the past decade, it had hardly been remarked in Dickinson criticism and/or biography.

The lives in Dickinson study

It goes without saying that there are many lives of Emily Dickinson. By the end of the twentieth century, *The Belle of Amherst* has become *EMILY*

Unplugged; Simon and Garfunkel sing about her in "The Dangling Conversation" while the Lemonheads croon "My Life had stood a Loaded Gun" (J 754, Fr 764), and the familiar gingerbread-bearing figure in the white dress occasionally makes cameo appearances in prime time shows such as "Cheers" and "thirtysomething." Jamie Fuller imagines *The Diary of Emily Dickinson* while Judith Farr envisions her life at South Hadley Female Seminary (now Mt. Holyoke College) in *I Never Came to You in White*. Richard Sewall's *The Life of Emily Dickinson* has been reprinted by Harvard University Press, which has also reissued Johnson and Ward's *The Letters of Emily Dickinson* in one volume. It is significant that the "little home-keeping person" haunts all of these Emily Dickinsons.[15] Equally significant is the fact that, with the exception of the unabashedly feminist *EMILY Unplugged*, all of these Dickinson lives either leave out Emily's primary audience Susan altogether or depict her as highly problematic, even distasteful and despicable. These omissions and seemingly hostile iterations of Susan perpetuate the portrayals of the most frequently consulted biographical sources, Sewall's book and Johnson's biographical blurbs.

Simply in the course of doing business, Johnson sentences women to linguistic mortality. In the words of Sandra Gilbert and Susan Gubar, "instead of [graphing women] by distinguished inscriptions," his identifying descriptions render women so that they "leave indistinguishable traces."[16] In his blurbs and indices, the first names of thirteen women have disappeared and they are known only as "the wife of." Often, though the wife was the primary correspondent, his blurb is focused on the husband. That overarching bias may in part account for Johnson's handling (or rather mishandling) of Susan in her son Gib's biography: "His sudden and unexpected death from typhoid fever, 5 October 1883, was a blow from which neither his father nor his Aunt Emily fully recovered" (L, p. 938). Conscious or unconscious, his omission signals some bias against Susan, for he writes as if a 52-year-old mother would be unscathed by the death of her youngest child when he was but a boy of eight. In fact, Gib's death devastated Susan and she withdrew from society for more than a year. Sewall likewise underplays Susan's role in Emily's literary life. His valuable story is understandably a partial one because he wrote his biography at the behest of Millicent Todd Bingham, Loomis Todd's daughter, who "wanted, she said, 'the whole story' of her mother's involvement told – but told in the setting of the larger story of Emily Dickinson" (*LED*, p. xiv).

Sewall's attentions are directed by those of a woman (Loomis Todd) who received fewer than a score of poems and letters from Emily, but who printed hundreds of Emily's poems and became so attached to them that she refused to return the fascicles and other writings in her possession when Lavinia demanded them back in 1896–8. In the late 1920s her daughter Millicent complained bitterly to Josephine Pollitt that some of the poems Bianchi published in *Further Poems of Emily Dickinson* (1929) "are *my mother's poems!*"[17] Susan, however, received more than twenty score writings from Emily, but printed fewer than a score of her poems even though she was most likely the agent for almost all of the ten printings Dickinson witnessed during her lifetime (Smith, *Rowing*, p. 155–6). Though the commonplace biography set in motion by Loomis Todd holds that Emily and Susan did not see one another for fifteen years or more, Emily's letters and notes to Susan document uninterrupted contact from the late 1840s until 15 May 1886 (Smith, *Rowing*, pp. 156–7). According to the Todd-Bingham-Sewall account of things, Emily only came out to see Susan upon Gib's death. Otherwise, the story usually goes, for the last fifteen years or so, she did not have face-to-face contact. But Emily's niece Bianchi marks Gib's death as a time of great family pain: "Mother . . . would not even be driven through the village for more than a year"; "Father, manlike, hardened his will after the first outburst of despair"; and Aunt Emily became "remote, inaccessible."[18] As Jean McClure Mudge points out, "Emily's notes document regular happy rendezvous with Sue in the Mansion [Homestead] until 1883 . . . After 1883, it appears, Sue did not come to the Mansion anymore. She had two good reasons. That year, her eight-year-old son Gilbert died and she withdrew from society for months [actually for more than a year]. At the same time, Austin began his affair with Mabel Loomis Todd" ("Dickinson and 'Sister Sue,'" p. 105). Emily's notes and poems to Susan during this period are "solace" (OMC 234, 235, 236, 237, 238, 240), and though Emily became "remote" at this time, Bianchi tells that, within days of her death, "Aunt Emily still came down to chat with us by the fire, looking just the same, dramatic in her expression of all she said as ever – she somehow seemed like a winter sun moving further from us, nearer those final answers she had always been trying to find" (*Life Before Last*, pp. 148–9). According to Sewall, Emily refused to see "doctors or dressmakers" (*LED*, p. 154), but Bianchi tells delightful stories about "Aunt Emily" allowing the dressmaker Mrs. Shaw to "try on the pinafore white aprons she made for wear in cooking hours, and gave her goodies to take home to a sick daughter. Mrs. Shaw 'thought a sight of Miss Emily' and when Aunt Emily said some funny thing to make her laugh, she would exclaim, 'Why, the very *idea*! Who'd a thought of such a thing! How you make me laugh!' – which made Aunt Emily talk more and funnier" (*Life Before Last*, p. 80).

Besides competing with Sewall's assertion that Dickinson refused to see anyone, based on the knowledge of Mabel Loomis Todd, who never met

Emily face-to-face, this account of Bianchi's also contradicts those who depict Susan as snobbish and aloof. In the paragraph immediately preceding this one, Bianchi writes that her mother valued Mrs. Shaw "highly and made a pet of her, always having some favorite dish of hers when she was here 'by the day'" (*Life Before Last*, p. 79). Such a depiction of Susan corroborates that of John Erskine, who met Mabel, Millicent, Susan and Martha, and describes Susan as "cultured, intelligent, and kind" and characterizes the "attacks on Susan's character" (by Todd, Bingham, and their sympathizers) as "little short of a disgrace to American biography."[19] Erskine also calls Susan a "scholar" who "had a mind much above the ordinary" (pp. 135, 132).

A powerfully intellectual (she was a mathematician and math teacher in Baltimore in 1851–2), vivacious, charismatic, sometimes arrogant, often generous, acutely and astutely well-read woman and devoted mother, Susan, her life stories, and their meanings for Emily Dickinson were bound to become sites of contestation in a culture with limited storylines for women, their accomplishments, and their contributions to the literary and artistic welfare of society. Dickinson herself characterized their relationship in literary terms – comparing her love for Susan to Dante's love for Beatrice, Swift's for Stella, and Mirabeau's for Sophie de Ruffey (*OMC* 165), and comparing her tutelage with Susan to one with Shakespeare (*OMC* 229). Clearly, she valued Susan's opinions about writing and reading, and both women shared an affective theory of poetry. Of "Safe in their Alabaster Chambers," Susan wrote that the first verse is so compelling that "I always go to the fire and get warm after thinking of it, but I never *can* again" (*OMC* 61); a few years later, Thomas Higginson paraphrased Emily's critical commentary, echoing Susan's – "If I read a book [and] it makes my whole body so cold no fire ever can warm me I know *that* is poetry" (L 342a).

When Susan compares her relationship with Emily and the lifetime of writing exchanged between them to a relationship that was written up in *Goethe's Correspondence with a Child* in a letter to Higginson, she underscores their relationship's literary, intellectual nature, as well as the intensity of their emotional engagement. Susan proceeds to speak with quiet but unassailable authority about his and Loomis Todd's editing of Emily's poems. Making clear that she is thoroughly acquainted with Emily's poetic corpus, Susan approves of most of the titles used in the 1890 *Poems* and, in a 4 January 1891 letter corrects "a blunder (of the printer I suppose)," "afar" to "ajar" in "I know some lonely Houses / off the Road" (Fas 13, J 289, Fr 311). As we have seen, Higginson took Susan's suggestion and in subsequent editions the word was changed.

Though a century of scholarship has approached this relationship with the assumption that Emily was the writer and Susan the reader, always,

Writings by Susan Dickinson shows that Susan wrote essays, reviews, journals, poems, letters, and memorials constantly throughout her life, and produced commonplace books and scrapbooks of her own publications in the *Springfield Republican*, as well as of clippings about admired figures such as Queen Victoria, and of favorite poems, essays, and stories of other writers, including Emily.[20] Very early in their relationship Dickinson enthuses over "Susie" keeping a journal, exclaiming that she wants "to get it bound – at my expense" (*OMC* 7), and among the papers found in the Evergreens is a journal Susan kept of a trip to Europe in 1905, when she was seventy-five years old. As an elderly traveler and inveterate writer, Susan visited Paris, Nice, Cologne, Zurich, Verona, Venice, Florence, Rome, the Hague, and London, reveling in the architectural majesty of church buildings and in the sublime beauty of the "Alpine peaks snow tipped...all so wholesome after Paris" and taking care to record her observations and encounters with acquaintances new and old, usually in a literary or poetical vein. On the ship returning home, her journal entries compare "layers of clouds" to the "White Alps pointing upward" (*WSD*).

Besides apparently keeping journals throughout her life, Susan published several stories in the *Springfield Republican* – "A Hole in Haute Society" (2 August 1908), "The Passing of Zoroaster" (March 1910), "The Circus Eighty Years Ago" (early 1900s), and possibly "The Case of the Brannigans" (though this may be by her daughter, Martha). In January 1903, writing from Rome, Susan published a lengthy review of "Harriet Prescott's [Spofford] Early Work" as a letter to the editor of the *Republican*. Arguing for republication of Spofford's early work, she quotes "my sister-in-law, Emily Dickinson" as an authority, reiterating the latter's delighted reader's response – "That is the only thing I ever saw in my life I did not think I could have written myself. You stand nearer the world than I do. Send me everything she writes" – and quoting Dickinson's declaration, "for love is stronger than death," in her own critique of Prescott's "Circumstance." In "Annals of the Evergreens," a typescript that was not published until the 1980s, Susan praises Prescott's "Pomegranate Flowers" at the outset, then proceeds to describe an Evergreen's life rich in cultural exchange, one in which she was reading the Brownings, Thomas de Quincey, Julia Ward Howe, Thomas Carlyle, and Shakespeare, and entertaining many distinguished visitors – Ralph Waldo Emerson, Harriet Beecher Stowe, abolitionist Wendell Phillips, and landscape designer Frederick Olmsted. Personalities more intimately associated with the Dickinson circle also grace these pages as Susan relates luscious accounts of lunches with "fresh asparagus" and "salad from our own garden" and dinners of "very nice lamb and strawberries" with editor Samuel Bowles, his wife Mary, friend Maria Whitney, Josiah and Elizabeth Holland, and Judge Otis P. Lord, and recounts fondly his recital of a hymn complemented by "a most remarkable artistic performance" by Vinnie (*WSD*, "Annals of the Evergreens" 18).

Among Susan's surviving papers are scores of letters that show her to be a most attentive mother and friend, numerous essays on subjects as diverse as the valiant work of nurses and the art of architecture, reviews of "Autumn's Divine Beauty Begins" (an anonymous essay celebrating the season printed in the *Republican*) and *Wind of Destiny*, a popular novel by Arthur Sherburne Hardy, which she finds most "refreshing" because "it does not presuppose idiocy in the reader but makes a little demand upon a moderate equipment of mind and imagination" (a remark that just as well characterizes her appreciation as Emily's most staunch contemporary audience). Besides collecting paeans to Queen Victoria, Susan's own writings honor strong pioneering women. Her memoir of Elizabeth Blackwell (the first female doctor in the United States, known not only for her medical practice but also for working to open the profession to women), relates how "of course women deplored" this intellectual female working out of her sphere but speaks of her with great admiration and within the context of Susan's own quest for knowledge, a lifelong journey to which her thousands of books attest (*WSD*, "A Memory of Dr. Elizabeth Blackwell").

Her surviving writings witness her care and passion for the word – drafts of essays and poems show careful searching for the most effective vocabulary and syntax. Among several poems in Susan's papers are typescript and ink drafts, with pencil revisions, of "What offering have I, dear Lord," the poem reiterated in typescript and included in "Annals" (*WSD*). That Susan did not regard the printed word as final is obvious from the fact that several clippings of her own work placed in a scrapbook show her revising after their appearance in the *Republican*. That she was confident of her intellectual abilities and critical acumen is apparent from the fact that Susan corresponded about such matters not only with Higginson and Bowles, but also with other leading editors of the day. Among her letters are several to William Hayes Ward, editor of the *Independent*, about publishing Emily's poems, and her scrapbooks show that in March 1902 she sent W. C. Brownell a favorable review of his *Victorian Prose Masters* and received a most warm reply. Significantly, "Annals of the Evergreens" parallels the trajectories of Susan's correspondences, revealing that her role was more than that of a social leader who entertained prominent guests, for she was clearly a most capable conversationalist who held her own with Emerson and was known by many for her intellectual acumen. Just as Emily's writing was commonly known, so was Susan's "hard reading" (*YH* II, p. 78). By the time of Amherst College's 1877 commencement, Bowles wanted to honor Susan's intellect and social dexterity with an honorary degree.

Besides publishing critical pieces and stories, Susan published at least one poem, "Love's Reckoning," in the *Republican*, and wrote quite a few others including "To me through every season dearest," "Did I but purpose to embark with thee," and "Irony" or "Crushed before the Moth" (*WSD*). Though more conventional in form and to our twenty-first century tastes not nearly as "good" as Emily's, Susan's poems attend to many of the same subjects – "There are three months of the Spring" distinctly echoes both "These are the days when Birds come back" (*OMC* 25) and "The Crickets / sang / And set the / Sun" (*OMC* 122), and Susan's focus on nature recalls Emily's own extended attentions to narrow fellows in the grass and the sun "Blazing in Gold – and / Quenching – in Purple!" (*OMC* 68) and "stooping – stooping – low" (*OMC* 52). Her lyric tribute in memoriam to Emily remarks that "Summer always kept her for it's own" but assures that "in the Autum . . . I know she'll come with outstretched hands!" ("I'm waiting but she comes not back," *WSD*). Their correspondence was a creative wellspring for Susan as well as for Emily – on Susan's copy of "The Crickets / sang / And Set the / Sun" are several lines of Susan's response to Emily's work, recounting a few lines from Milton's *Comus*:

> I was all ear
> And took in strains that
> might create a seal
> Under the ribs of death

And, upside down, Susan added a few lines from Sir Walter Scott's *Redgauntlet*:

> Despair is treason
> toward man
> And blasphemy
> to Heaven.

By folks who knew her as intimately as Lavinia, her sister-in-law a little more than two years younger, Susan has been roundly criticized for not seeing Emily's poems into print with good speed. Indeed, this is an important part of her story as it bears on the study of Dickinson. By her own account in the aforementioned letters to Higginson and to Ward, the volume Susan describes highlighting Emily's wit as well as the eroticized correspondence of Emily and Susan is a much more holistic volume than the epitome of the late nineteenth-century poetry book produced by Higginson and Todd. Hers would have been filled with drawings and jokes as well as profound lyrics, and her outline for production shows that rather than divide the poems into conventional categories Susan would have emphasized poetry's integration with quotidian experience, Emily's intellectual prowess, and her philosophical interrogations of the spiritual, corporeal, emotional, and mental realms (*WSD*, "Notes Toward a Volume of Emily Dickinson's Writings"). Her critiques of the printed volumes and descriptions of how she would have managed preparing a production performance of Emily's writings for auction to the world are, for twenty-first century readers, immured in mechanical and high-tech images of print and screen, avenues into the nineteenth-century manuscript culture of literary exchange in which Susan and Emily were constant participants.

Among Susan's papers are fascicles of favorite poems that both she and her sister Martha copied out sometime in the 1850s. Rooted in a culture where modes of literary exchange frequently included sending consolation poems and making fascicles of favorite poems as well as commonplace books and scrapbooks of treasured literary pieces, Dickinson's fascicle assembly of her own poems and distribution of her poems in epistolary contexts are anything but eccentric (*WSD*, "Commonplace Book"). The distinction these two women writers draw between the terms "publish" and "print" is, as is Susan's description of what her volume of Emily's writings would have featured, a sign of the literary culture in which their works were so deeply embedded, a literary culture of vital manuscript exchange in which even printed works were recirculated in holograph form. This manuscript culture that Emily and Susan knew so well and in which each practiced as writers is one about which late twentieth-century literary history tends to have amnesia. Had Susan produced a volume modeled on the practices of this culture for the world at large, Dickinson's readers would have had a much broader sense of the range of Emily's writings from the beginning, and would have had a much stronger sense of the manuscript culture in which Emily Dickinson's poetic project was far from an aberration. Instead of remaking Emily's writings to fit the contours, categories, and poetic forms driven by the machine of the printed book, Susan's volume would have been oriented and shaped by those hand-fashioned modes of literary exchange and opened up a sense of that nineteenth-century literary world practically lost to twentieth-century readers.

As is evident from many of Susan's titles for Dickinson's poems, from her journal entries, and from the subjects of her reviews, a profound love and deep appreciation for nature pervades her sensibilities, and she clearly favors art focused on the natural world's splendors, on the "Eden, always eligible" (L 391). Her regard for nature is intense enough to be characterized as religious or spiritual, and Susan was indeed devoutly religious from her late teens and throughout her adulthood. Late in her life, Susan turned more and more to the rituals of High Church and even pondered becoming a Roman Catholic, but was dissuaded by Bishop F. Dan Huntington "who himself had abandoned Harvard Unitarianism to don the sacerdotal robes of American Anglicanism" (*WSD*, "Letters from Bishop Huntington"). Yet her religious devotions were far more than ceremonial, for Susan spent almost every Sabbath for six years in the 1880s establishing a Sunday school in Logtown, a poor village not far from Amherst later known as Belchertown, and she often prepared baskets of food for those far less fortunate than the upper-middle-class Dickinsons.

Susan's enactment of simple ritual for profound utterance is perhaps best displayed in the plain flannel robe she designed and in which she dressed Emily for death, laying her out in a white casket, cypripedium and violets (symbolizing faithfulness) at her neck, two heliotropes (symbolizing devotion) in her hand.[21] This final act over Emily's body underscores "their shared life, their deep and complex intimacy" and that they both anticipated a "postmortem resurrection" of that intimacy.[22] Besides swaddling her beloved friend's body for burial, Susan penned Emily's obituary, a loving portrayal of a strong, brilliant woman, devoted to her family and to her neighbors, and to her writing, for which she had the most serious objectives and highest ambitions. Though "weary and sick" at the loss of her dearest friend (*WSD*, "Obituary for Emily Dickinson" 12), Susan produced a piece so powerful that Higginson wanted to use it as the introduction to the 1890 *Poems*. Beginning to tell her friend's story, Susan concludes the obituary by pointing readers' attentions to Emily as writer, and to the fact that her words would live on. Among her daughter Martha's papers is evidence that these same four lines were used again in a Dickinson ceremony, perhaps to conclude Susan's own (or Ned's or Lavinia's) funeral (Brown 16:35:1):

> Morns like these we parted;
> Noons like these she rose,
> Fluttering first, then firmer,
> To her fair repose.

That these lines are quoted from memory by Susan and other members of her family demonstrates, especially when one takes into account all the other facts of these writing lives, that for Susan and Emily poetry was not property, nor a commodity to be possessed and auctioned, but was spiritual sustenance, and, as Susan was to tell a famous editor at the turn of the nineteenth century, "sermon ... hope ... solace ... life." For these Dickinsons, poetry, practically a member of the family, "breathed" (L 260). That is at least one significant part of the story the records of their relationship tell. The study of Emily and

Susan Dickinson's relationship, indeed of all of Dickinson's relationships with her female correspondents, answers the call not only of scholars such as Wendy Martin, who called for extended analyses of the friendships that "sustained her as an artist,"[23] but also of Emily Dickinson herself, who, in asking Susan to recall "what whispered to Horatio?" (*OMC* 253), asked her to "report me and my cause aright / To the unsatisfied" (*Hamlet* V, ii, 338–9).

NOTES

1 See Jean McClure Mudge, "Emily Dickinson and 'Sister Sue,'" *Prairie Schooner*, 52 (1978): 90–108, here 93.

2 Harold Love, *Scribal Publication in Seventeenth-Century England* (Oxford: Clarendon Press, 1993), p. 9.

3 All of the following feature photographic reproductions of a manuscript: Sharon Cameron, *Choosing Not Choosing: Dickinson's Fascicles* (University of Chicago Press, 1992); Susan Howe, *The Birth-Mark: Unsettling the Wilderness in American Literary History* (Hanover: University of New England Press, 1993); Judy Jo Small, *Positive as Sound: Emily Dickinson's Rhyme* (Athens: University of Georgia Press, 1990); Smith, *Rowing in Eden: Rereading Emily Dickinson* (Austin: University of Texas Press, 1992); Marta Werner, *Emily Dickinson's Open Folios: Scenes of Reading, Surfaces of Writing* (Ann Arbor: University of Michigan Press, 1995).

4 Cheryl Walker, *The Nightingale's Burden: Women Poets and American Culture Before 1900* (Bloomington: Indiana University Press, 1982), pp. 82–9. The degree to which this literary figure imbued Dickinson's literary culture is poignantly exemplified by her friend J. G. Holland, using the nom de plume Timothy Titcomb, in "No. 15 of his 'Letter to the Joneses,' To Miss Felicia Hemans Jones, Concerning her Strong Desire to Become an Authoress": "It is not unfrequently true that those whose affections have been unsatisfied at home – whose plans of domestic life have miscarried... – turn to the public life for that which has been denied them at home." (*YH* ii, p. 81).

5 Also see Millicent Todd Bingham, *Ancestors' Brocades: The Literary Debut of Emily Dickinson* (New York and London: Harpers Brothers Publishers), pp. 86–7.

6 Martha Nell Smith, "Suppressing the Books of Susan in Emily Dickinson," in Amanda Gilroy and W. M. Verhoeven (eds.), *Epistolary Histories: Letters, Fiction, Culture* (Charlottesville and London: University Press of Virginia, 2000), pp. 101–25.

7 *Republican*, 18 May 1886.

8 Though Loomis Todd refused to use the obituary as introduction to the 1890 *Poems*, she mined it but a year later for her introduction to the 1891 *Poems* (see Smith, *Rowing*, pp. 207–8).

9 Leyda misquotes slightly the name of the local newspaper to which Bowles refers, the *Springfield Musket*, a Civil War publication; in his account, Leyda misreads "Musket" as "Market." I would like to thank Karen Dandurand for bringing Leyda's error to my attention and for apprising me of the *Musket's* existence.

10 Manuscripts at the Houghton Library, Harvard University, are cited with the initial H and the library catalog numbers.
11 Emily Dickinson, *The Single Hound: Poems of a Lifetime* (Boston: Little Brown, 1914), pp. vii, x, xi.
12 Quoted in Elizabeth Horan, "To Market: The Dickinson Copyright Wars," *The Emily Dickinson Journal* 5.1 (1996): 88–120.
13 The Thomas Wentworth Higginson Papers, Galatea Collection at the Boston Public Library, are cited with the initials BPL Higg and the library catalog numbers.
14 Both Emily and Sue Dickinson consistently apply this distinction. In three other letters to Ward, Susan uses "print" for mass reproduction and distribution of poetry (*WSD*, "Correspondence with William Hayes Ward," 8 February 1891, 14 March 1891, 23 March 1891). In the 1890s when Sue or her daughter Martha marked one of Dickinson's manuscripts to indicate that the poem has already appeared in print, she wrote "printed" (not published) on the document. In a letter to her brother, Emily writes, "I should be pleased with a line when you've published your work to Father" (L 108, 18 March 1853). In "It would never be Common – / more – I said – " (Fas 19, J 430, Fr 388), the poem's speaker writes that her joy was such that she "felt it publish – in my Eye." As late as 1876, book publishers at the US Centennial in Philadelphia were debating the meaning of the term "publish."
15 John Crowe Ransom, "Emily Dickinson: A Poet Restored," in Richard B. Sewall (ed.) *Emily Dickinson: A Collection of Critical Essays* (Englewood Cliffs, NJ: Prentice-Hall, Inc., 1963), pp. 88–100, here p. 89.
16 In their critique of Ruth Stone's *Second-Hand Coat: Poems New and Selected* (Boston: David R. Godine, 1987), Gilbert and Gubar emphasize what Johnson's apparatus "manifests – that such systematic erasure is not a trivial matter, but distorts our history as it translates all characters and relationships into terms making males Primary." See Sandra Gilbert and Susan Gubar, "Ceremonies of the Alphabet: Female Grandmatologies and the Female Authorgraph," in Domna C. Stanton (ed.), *Female Autograph: Theory and Practice of Autobiography from the Tenth to the Twentieth Century* (Chicago and London: University of Chicago Press, 1987), pp. 21–48, here p. 26.
17 Citation from manuscripts at the John Carter Brown Library at Brown University, A94–67 1:1.
18 Bianchi, *Life Before Last: Reminiscences of a Country Girl*, ed. Barton Levi St. Armand and Martha Nell Smith (forthcoming).
19 Erskine, "The Dickinson Feud," in *The Memory of Certain Persons* (Philadelphia & New York: J. B. Lippincott Co., 1947), p. 136.
20 These materials are all in the Martha Dickinson Bianchi Collection which was donated by Mary Landis Hampson to the John Hay Library, Brown University, Providence, RI. See esp. Susan's "Commonplace Book" (Brown 16:35:1; *WSD*, http://jefferson.village.virginia.edu/dickinson/susan/shdcpbdex.html), and her Notebook, 1895– (Brown MO5.0). All quotations from this collection are courtesy of the John Carter Brown Library at Brown University.
21 Barton Levi St. Armand, *Emily Dickinson and Her Culture: The Soul's Society* (Cambridge University Press, 1984), pp. 74–5.

22 See Ellen Louise Hart, "The Encoding of Homoerotic Desire: Emily Dickinson's Letters and Poems to Susan Dickinson, 1850–1886," *Tulsa Studies in Women's Literature* 9.2 (1990): 251–72, here 255; and Vivian Pollak, *Dickinson: The Anxiety of Gender* (Ithaca and London: Cornell University Press, 1984), p. 137.

23 Martin, *An American Triptych: Anne Bradstreet, Emily Dickinson, Adrienne Rich* (Chapel Hill & London: University of North Carolina Press, 1984), p. 82.

GUIDE TO FURTHER READING

Bianchi, Martha Dickinson. *Life Before Last: Reminiscences of a Country Girl*, ed. Barton Levi St. Armand and Martha Nell Smith (forthcoming).

Erskine, John. "The Dickinson Feud," *The Memory of Certain Persons*. Philadelphia and New York: J. B. Lippincott Co., 1947.

Gilbert, Sandra Mortola and Susan Dreyfuss David Gubar. "Ceremonies of the Alphabet: Female Grandmatologies and the Female Authorgraph." In Domna C. Stanton, ed. *Female Autograph: Theory and Practice of Autobiography from the Tenth to the Twentieth Century*. Chicago and London: University of Chicago Press, 1987, pp. 21–48.

Love, Harold. *Scribal Publication in Seventeenth-Century England*. Oxford Clarendon Press, 1993.

Martin, Wendy. *An American Triptych: Anne Bradstreet, Emily Dickinson, Adrienne Rich*. Chapel Hill and London: University of North Carolina Press, 1984.

Pollak, Vivian. *Dickinson: The Anxiety of Gender*. Ithaca and London: Cornell University Press, 1984.

Ransom, John Crowe. "Emily Dickinson: A Poet Restored." In Richard B. Sewall, ed. *Emily Dickinson: A Collection of Critical Essays*, Englewood Cliffs, NJ: Prentice-Hall Inc., 1963, pp. 88–100.

St. Armand, Barton Levi. *Emily Dickinson and Her Culture: The Soul's Society*. Cambridge University Press, 1984.

Smith, Martha Nell. *Rowing in Eden: Rereading Emily Dickinson*. Austin: University of Texas Press, 1992.

"Suppressing the Books of Susan in Emily Dickinson." In Amanda Gilroy and W. M. Verhoeven, eds. *Epistolary Histories: Letters, Fiction, Culture*. Charlottesville and London: University Press of Virginia, 2000, pp. 101–125.

Stone, Ruth. *Second-Hand Coat: Poems New and Selected*. Boston: David R. Godine, 1987.

Walker, Cheryl. *The Nightingale's Burden: Women Poets and American Culture Before 1900*. Bloomington: Indiana University Press, 1982.

POETIC STRATEGIES
AND THEMES

4

WENDY BARKER

Emily Dickinson and poetic strategy

"I dwell in Possibility – / A fairer House than Prose – ," Emily Dickinson begins a poem that describes how, simply by "spreading wide" her "narrow hands," she gathers "Paradise" (Fr 466, J 657).[1] However, this "house" of possibility is not a dwelling providing shelter in the usual sense but is instead composed of trees and sky. The house of possibility is "More numerous of windows" and "Superior of doors" than "Prose," which is not only enclosed by humanly constructed dimensions but is also, the poet suggests, more constraining than protecting, more imprisoning than liberating.

Prose: the genre, what is not poetry; prosy: what is matter-of-fact and dry; prosaic: what is lacking in imagination or spirit, what is dull. In "I held a Jewel in my fingers – " the poet explains that, confident her jewel would "keep," she allows herself to fall asleep in the warm day with its "prosy" winds, until, as she laments,

> I woke – and chid my honest fingers,
> The Gem was gone –
> And now, an Amethyst remembrance
> Is all I own –   (Fr 261, J 245)

Whatever possibility the "Jewel" might offer is lost entirely, leaving only a memory. And whatever this "Gem" might suggest, whether a cherished friend, or an idea for a poem, clearly it is a metaphor for something valuable, and it vanishes not because of the poet's "honest fingers," but due to the distracting, detracting forces of the day's "prosy" winds, which are the antithesis of the muses' breezes, of the breeze as inspiration. Soporific, these prosy winds seduce the poet into falling asleep, into losing her wakefulness, her consciousness. If not outright thieves, they are agents, causes of the poet's impotence to protect her "Gem." Barbara Mossberg argues that this is a poem about writing – since these "honest" fingers can hold not only a "Gem" but also a pen, this is a poem about the forces that keep the poet from her own creativity.[2]

In another poem Dickinson insists, "They shut me up in Prose" because "they liked me 'still'" (Fr 445, J 613). But "They shut me up in Prose" is not a bitter, resentful diatribe. The "Prose" within which the "me" has been shut is powerless to stop her mind, her brain, which, she declares, continues to "go round." The "They" of the poem, she boasts, might as well "have lodged a Bird / For Treason – in the Pound." And like a bird, she too "has but to will / And easy as a Star / Look down upon Captivity – / And laugh" (Fr 445).[3] Although it might at first strike a reader as an overly dramatic, perhaps even childish complaint, the poem is a statement of victorious assertion.

* * *

The original meaning for "prose," which comes from the Latin *prosa*, is "straightforward discourse." According to the *Oxford English Dictionary*, it is "The ordinary form of written or spoken language, without metrical structure." It is "Plain, simple, matter-of-fact, (and hence) dull or commonplace expression, quality, spirit." It can refer to "A dull, commonplace, or wearisome discourse or piece of writing." And, in an archaic colloquial meaning, it can refer to "familiar talk, chat, gossip."

Metaphorically, Emily Dickinson was enclosed, all but engulfed by what she thought of as "prose." At home, her mother's unimaginative use of hackneyed language drew the poet's scorn; in reporting her mother's urging her "to turn over a new leaf," the poet drolly commented, "I call that the Foliage Admonition" (L II: 571). On a more weighty level, Dickinson's father's censorious opinions and directives would have been prose of the most ponderous sort and yet, as paterfamilias in this traditional New England family, his word would have been law. The prosy chat of a mother who did not understand her daughter's brilliant wit, the prose admonitions of a stern and demanding father, and the wearisome, lengthy sermons delivered by pastors of Amherst's First Church of Christ would all have been reason enough for Dickinson to do everything she could to "Abolish" her "Captivity," with a brain, that no matter how often "they" tried to shut her up "in Prose," continued to "go round."

And as she does in "I held a Jewel in my fingers," the poet often equates loss of something she values not only with prose, but also with the "Day" itself, and its governing star, the sun. In a letter dated 6 July 1851 she wrote to her much-missed intellectual companion, her brother Austin: "I have just come in from Church very hot, and faded, having witnessed a couple of Baptisms, three admissions to church, a Supper of the Lord, and some other minor transactions time fails me to record" (L I: 46). Not only is Dickinson's wit in high gear in this passage, but, metaphorically, she is associating the language of the Calvinist church, its doctrine and its rituals, with the enervating effects of July's heat. And by saying she is "faded," the youthful Dickinson even suggests to her brother that the "climate" within the church dims her, as if in the "light" of its liturgy she is wiped out, erased – perhaps in danger of losing her "Gem."

In another letter to Austin, also written in 1851 but in October, when presumably the weather would have been cooler, Dickinson confides:

> I am at home from meeting on account of the storm and my slender con-sitution, which I assured the folks, would not permit me accompanying them today.
>
> It is Communion Sunday, and they will stay a good while – what a nice time pussy and I have to enjoy ourselves! Just now the sun peeped out. I tell you I chased it back again behind the tallest cloud, it has not my permission to show its face again till after all the meeting, then it may shine, shine, for all pussy and I care! (L I: 54)

Again we see Dickinson playing "hooky" from church, and metaphorically associating the *lack* of sun with the peace and privacy caused by the absence of "the folks." Rather than being forced to spend her Sunday listening to the pastor's sermon (that would have been sandwiched between chat and gossip before and after the service), she can keep her own company, and, uncensored, articulate her own thoughts to the family member whose companionship she most valued. Dickinson's letter takes the form of "prose"; the texts of the Watts hymns sung by the congregation of the First Church of Christ were written as "poetry"; yet in these letters Dickinson clearly experiences more "possibility" at home alone, privately engaged in an epistolary tête-à-tête, than she does "shut up" in church, publicly lifting her voice in common meter with the congregation.[4]

Church, of course, as the House of God, would have been a structural embodiment of the Word of God, from which Dickinson shrank, as she did from the "eyes of God," which she describes as "triple lenses" that "burn upon" her "Escapade" (Fr 1076, J 894). Rebelling against her culture's dominant definition of Jehovah, the poet in one poem insists that God's "Watch" is quite simply "wrong" (Fr 427, J 415). Whether questioning the accuracy of his pocket watch or the efficacy of his guardianship, she makes it clear how out of sync she feels in a community dominated by nineteenth-century New England Calvinist theology. "I never felt at Home – Below," she explains, "And in the Handsome Skies / I shall not feel at Home – I know – / I dont like Paradise // ... If God could make a visit – / Or ever took a Nap – / So not to see us – but they say / Himself – a Telescope // Perennial beholds us." If it were not for "Judgment Day," she confides, she would "run away / From Him" (Fr 437, J 413). But she knows that, even as an escapee from the bounds of conventional Calvinist thought, she will nevertheless be found out, be seen by those all-powerful telescopic eyes, and will be judged.

In an earlier poem, she writes of wanting to climb a fence to gather strawberries, worrying, "But – if I stained my Apron – / God would certainly scold" (Fr 271, J 251). Associated with cultural voices that told young women not to gather their own fruits, not to hike up their skirts to climb over an obstacle to reach what they desired, God is also associated with those who would see – and criticize – what she has been up to. The speaker of the poem wants the berries – "Berries are nice!" – but if she were to try to reach for them, her apron (as Mossberg has observed, an emblem of femininity itself)[5] would be "stained." She would be seen, found out, publicly known to be sinful. Whether the image of "berries" suggests simply berries, or serves as metaphor for the fruits of sexual experience, or even poetry,[6] "Over the fence" serves as another example of the poet's sense of the eye of God as constraining and judging, as responsible for her being "shut up" in "prose."

As Margaret Homans has argued, Dickinson linked snakes with the power of language, with the power she valued most, but she could only see her own poetic power as "bad," since it needed to assert itself away from the sunny world of culturally condoned, even expected, dress fittings and calling cards.[7] No wonder Dickinson often described herself as "wicked";[8] she not only fears being judged as a sinner, but she doesn't even like "Paradise." Although in another poem she frets, "Why – do they shut me out of Heaven?" she all but answers her own question in asking immediately, "Did I sing – too loud?" adding, with seeming docility but underlying sarcasm, "But – I can say a little 'minor' / Timid as a Bird" (Fr 268, J 248). God's heaven for Dickinson seems a vast grim parlor where young ladies remain still, their hands folded in clean aprons (when they are not dutifully carrying out household duties) and silent, or at least very quiet, speaking only when spoken to, and in timid, low voices, while he, bright as the noonday sun, inspects them all. A heaven dominated by the "prosy" voice of this prying, scolding, constraining, silencing deity is no dwelling place of possibility for this poet.

Inwardly a theological rebel, Dickinson nevertheless outwardly enacted the role of a dutiful daughter for most of her life:[9] she was an almost thirty-nine-year-old adult when she complained to her sister-in-law Susan, "I am so hurried with Parents that I run all Day with my tongue abroad, like a Summer Dog" (L II: 333). Emily Dickinson's life may have been "privileged" because of her father's position in law and politics and her family's social prominence, but that same prominence added to the already burdensome, ongoing housework necessary in any nineteenth-century household. And this was a family who, at least during the poet's youth, entertained visitors often. Simply for Sunday dinner, chickens would have to be slaughtered and plucked, the spices ground for breads and pies, or puddings. The designated family baker, Dickinson (whose father preferred his elder daughter Emily's bread to that made by anyone else) rose before dawn to make the fires and to prepare the family breakfast. Even with one family household servant, chores were endless, and fell to the women of the family. And since Dickinson's mother was frequently ill, much of the burden fell on the shoulders of the two Dickinson daughters, Emily and her sister Vinnie. It was during an illness of the poet's mother that Dickinson complained to her close friend Abiah Root, "Father and Austin still clamor for food, and I, like a martyr am feeding them . . . God keep me from what they call *households*" (L I: 36). About two-and-a-half years later, she wrote to her friends, the Hollands, "if it wasn't for broad daylight, and cooking stoves, and roosters, I'm afraid you would have occasion to smile at my letters often." In this same passage, she describes her letter-writing as a way of attempting "Immortality," complaining that even a crow from a nearby "farm-yard dissipates the illusion" (L I: 133).

The broad daylight of household demands, the heat of the church and its enervating strictures – these for this poet were the stuff of dry prose. Feeling neither at home "below" in the "normal" daily life of this earth, or anticipatory of the life hereafter in a Christian heaven, Dickinson is, metaphorically, herself in conflict with the very light of day, which is of course literally caused by the sun. Dickinson was supremely aware of climate, of degrees of light, of the progression of a twenty-four-hour period we call a "day." The words "sun" and "day" are the most frequently used nouns in the poems (sun is used 170 times, day 232 times, light 82 times, noon 76 times).[10] Over and over in her poems, the sun is the antithesis of nurturing. It is "supercilious" (Fr 1116, J 950), "superfluous" (Fr 1013, J 999), and it can be downright destructive. In "The Butterfly's Numidian Gown," the sun causes a butterfly to pant, out of breath, exhausted (perhaps like "a summer dog"), needing to "lean" on a clover leaf "As if it were undone" (Fr 1395, J 1387). In "To Pack the Bud – oppose the Worm – ," a bud has hard work of it to "Adjust the Heat" so it can "Obtain its right of Dew" (Fr 1038, J 1058). In this poem, no mention is made of the challenge to receive *enough* light – the difficulty for the developing bloom is that there will be too much sun that will evaporate or destroy the "Dew," the moisture the bud needs in order to grow. In all of these poems, the sun itself is enervating rather than energizing. In "Angels, in the early morning," the angels are "smiling" as, early in the day, among the "Dews," they pluck the buds of flowers, but later, "when the sun is hottest," they are "sighing" as they "bear along" the "parched flowers" from the "sands" (J 94, Fr 73). Whether these flowers are simply flowers or are metaphors for larger beings, perhaps young women, this poem clearly suggests a kind of destruction of young life, of waste and pointlessness, that peaks at the zenith of the sun's power.

Perhaps the most extreme example of the poet's fear of the sun's force as inimical to her own energy and integrity appears in a letter to her dearest friend, Susan Gilbert, about to become the bride of the poet's brother (a letter so dramatic that almost every Dickinson critic has commented on its significance),[11] in which the twenty-two-year-old poet meditates on the subject of wifehood:

> You and I have been strangely silent upon this subject, Susie, we have often touched upon it, and as quickly fled away, as children shut their eyes when the sun is too bright for them...you have seen flowers at morning, satisfied with the dew, and those same sweet flowers at noon with their heads bowed in anguish before the mighty sun; think you these thirsty blossoms will now need naught but – *dew*? No, they will cry for sunlight, and pine for the burning noon, tho' it scorches them, scathes them; they have got through with peace – they know that the man of noon, is *mightier* than the morning and their life is henceforth to him. Oh Susie it is dangerous... (L I: 93)

About eleven years later, Dickinson writes what might almost be a "gloss" of this passage:

> Doom is the House without the Door –
> 'Tis entered from the Sun –
> And then the Ladder's thrown away,
> Because Escape – is done –
> (Fr 710, J 475)

If marrying meant becoming dependent upon a husband who, as a "mighty sun," would either "dower and deprive" (Fr 1692, J 1675), or, perhaps worse, "scorch," or "scathe" his bride with his culturally approved, even culturally decreed, dominance; if such "Doom" is entered from the sun; and, if the sun represents "prosy" constraints, societal and religious pressures (such as marrying) that would rob the poet of her "Gem," then no wonder Dickinson looked away from the sun, looked "oppositely," to darkness, even at times to winter and to snow, and to the moon, for her "Kingdom of Heaven" (Fr 1072, J 959).[12]

* * *

Sometime in 1863, Dickinson "reckoned"

> First – Poets – Then the Sun –
> Then Summer – Then the Heaven of God –

adding that poetry "so seems"

> To Comprehend the Whole –
> The Others look a needless Show –
> So I write – Poets – All –
> (Fr 533, J 569)

Such "reckoning" is reminiscent of a passage in a letter of 1851 to Susie: "We are the only poets, and everyone else is *prose*" (L 1: 56). Friendship with Susan, as Martha Nell Smith posits, was probably the most rewarding and intimate relationship of the poet's life.[13] If these two dear friends are the only "real" poets in a world of prose – or two "Nobody"s surrounded by "public" frogs croaking drearily in a bog (Fr 260, J 288) – then poetry is language that affords genuine intimacy between trusting friends, language that allows dialogue as a free exchange of uncensored thoughts. Poetry is the antithesis of prosy language spoken by "Brittle" ladies of "Dimity Convictions" who express "a horror so refined / Of freckled [or imperfect, or actual] human nature" (Fr 675, J 401); of the language of the poet's father's dictatorial "real life" (L 1: 65); the language of sermons and speechifying, language that comes, one-directional, from "on high," laying down rules, confinements, constrictions, and expectations that would keep society's members, including the "Wayward" (Fr 745, J 722) Emily Dickinson "in line." Poetry for Dickinson is the antithesis of bland, tired phrasings, of the status quo.

Instead, the poet values an intensity of experience few would "dare" to share: "Dare you see a Soul *at the White Heat*? / Then crouch within the door" (Fr 401, J 365). Not doom, not reached from – or because of – the sun or its light, this level of intense experience is achieved inside an enclosed, darkened space where fire can melt and mold metal. An entirely different force from the enervating, fading heat of the "normal" external day, this is an internal heat that turns a formerly solid, rigid shape into liquid, a transforming fire that changes "utterly," as Yeats would have put it. Following the poem's metaphoric logic, what is within the forge has become molten, liquid, devoid of rigid boundaries, transformed from its everyday function in "broad daylight" (as a horseshoe, a handle), open to being reshaped into a new form – open to possibility. Whether in the process of being repaired, or of being shaped for the first time, this is an object undergoing transformation. "Dimity Convictions" could not withstand such a blaze.

Raw heat. Heat from within, from an inner core: that is poetry. Light from dark. Language culled from extremities of experience, expressed but undiluted, undimmed by culturally determined categories and definitions: that is poetry. And whereas Dickinson often associated external conflicts over religious, cultural, social, and familial definitions and expectations with "broad daylight" or the sun, she could describe internal conflict in terms of extreme cold, comparing the private, "*gallanter*" fighters "within the bosom" to "Angels," God's messengers, who walk "with even feet / And Uniforms of Snow" (Fr 138, J 126). In associating such private, intense spiritual or emotional experience with that of the angels, she lifts her own difficulties to a heavenly status. And there is no external judgment here: "none observe" this individual intensity. "I think the Hemlock likes to stand / Upon a Marge of Snow" (Fr 400, J 525), Dickinson, wrote; it "satisfies an awe / That men, must slake in wilderness" – "The Hemlock's nature thrives – on cold," she reiterates. She would have agreed with Gaston Bachelard's comment that dreamers like a severe winter because "the winter cosmos is a simplified cosmos."[14] In a northern climate like New England, the cold provides a climate less congenial to social "niceties," and more congenial to privacy and introspection.

"If I read a book [and] it makes my whole body so cold no fire ever can warm me I know *that* is poetry," wrote Dickinson to Higginson. "If I feel physically as if the top of my head were taken off, I know *that* is poetry. These are the only ways I know it," the poet continues in her letter (L II: 342a). No overheating, wilting, fading suns in these images. Rather, the body is intensely alive, alert, quiveringly awake, shivering, almost orgasmic. Immediately after, she asks, "How do most people live without any thoughts?" Emily "had to think," (*LED*, p. 128) said the poet's sister Vinnie, and for Dickinson, poetry is the language of intense thought, of extreme experience, whether internally "*at the White Heat*" or in "uniforms of snow." A private language, a language different from the language of the "majority," poetry is not for everybody. It is perhaps a language of two "Nobody"s, and if only the "pair of us" dare to speak and understand, then fine, let the rest of the world croak away with their faded platitudes, pieties, and preachments in broad daylight from their public ponds (Fr 260, J 288).

Reading, of course, allowed for a private language shared by two, between writer and reader, and Dickinson was an avid reader, of current magazines, and of much "fiction" and "poetry," especially enamored of George Eliot, the Brontës, and Elizabeth Barrett Browning and Robert Browning.[15] In a tribute to Barrett Browning written in 1863, Dickinson describes the "Conversion of the Mind" that enabled her to construct – metaphorically – her house of possibility, and enact her poetics, her "Gem-Tactics":

> I think I was enchanted
> When first a sombre Girl –
> I read that Foreign Lady –
> The Dark – felt beautiful –

And whether it was noon at night –
Or only Heaven – at noon –
For very Lunacy of Light
I had not power to tell –

The poem continues by describing a series of transformations in which bees "became as Butterflies," and "Butterflies – as Swans," the "Days" now stepping to "Mighty Metres" of "Titanic Opera." Through what she calls a "Lunacy of Light," the poet experiences the "Dark" as "beautiful" as she undergoes a "Conversion of the Mind" that leads to "a Divine Insanity" (Fr 627, J 593). "The Danger" is that she would, at some later time, return to a state where she is once more "sane." Whether in the seventh stanza, we read "The Danger to be sane," or, as in an alternative version, "The Sorrow to be sane," the poem makes clear that to experience "sanity" again – to become part of the conventional, or "normal" daylight world – would be an enormous loss. This paradoxical association of "Lunacy" or insanity (and/or the moon) with deity and the delight of possibility, and of "sanity" with danger, sorrow, constriction, and loss echoes another poem also written in 1863: "Much Madness is divinest sense – / To a discerning Eye – / Much Sense – the starkest Madness – / 'Tis the Majority / In this, as all, prevail" (Fr 620, J 4365). But the "Antidote" in case such dangerous sanity (or "Sense" that to the poet is *non*-sense) is experienced remains: these "tomes" of "Solid Witchcraft," Barrett Browning's poems (and possibly the works of other foreign ladies in whose writing Dickinson also revelled, Charlotte Brontë, for example), will "keep," will not be lost like the "Gem" in the "prosy winds" of daylight, but, "Like Deity," will continue to exist as reliable resources. Reading Barrett Browning has allowed Dickinson to find nothing short of "Jubilee," a heaven on earth, which might seem "Lunacy" to the "Majority," to those possessed of "Dimity Convictions," but for the poet, creates unlimited "Possibility."

From a darkness at least as potent for possibility as the forge, this "Lunacy of Light" causes amazing transformations. No scorching of daisies or brides here: butterflies are not only *not* "undone," but are in the process of being transformed from bees to swans, the tiniest creatures expanding beyond their "normally" perceived boundaries. Like metal that is melted, losing its fixed rigidity, its former clearly defined shape, the insects in this poem are no longer the prosy, everyday creatures they had been. After this "Conversion of the Mind," in which "the Dark felt beautiful," there are no bounds, no limits. Even the smallest creatures, even the most ordinary noises of an ordinary day have become part of a "Titanic Opera," an entire community making glorious music. Operas usually consist of full orchestras, choruses, as well as soloists, with arias and recitatives that are often performed double forte to large audiences. In "I think I was enchanted" there are no closets, no keeping "still" – this joyful "Conversion of the Mind" allows the smallest creatures of the field their voices, and not just on an operatic, but on a "Titanic" scale, one commensurate with the gods, in fact, with the forerunners of the gods, the Ur-gods – the primal forces of the universe.

As if the smallest creatures ("I was the slightest in the House – / I took the smallest Room" (Fr 473, J 486), wrote the poet, in one of many instances in which she describes herself as small, or in which she identifies with small creatures or objects), after this "Conversion of the Mind," became gods themselves, equal to, and invulnerable to the judgmental eyes of a Calvinist God. Dickinson's copy of *Aurora Leigh* was not only much read but also marked – Elizabeth Barrett Browning's novel in verse must have served as a model for the Amherst poet, for whom fitting within the boundaries of genteel nineteenth-century American definitions of "true womanhood" was anathema. Barrett Browning's Aurora, a woman poet named for the dawn, achieves absolute victory in that she never loses her "Gem" – she writes her poetry, achieves recognition, refuses the man who wants her for the wrong reasons, and finally unites with him when he (now sightless) sees things her way, and comes to her on her terms. Aurora refuses to submit to conventional definitions for female behavior; ultimately, she is writer, public figure, friend, surrogate mother, and lover. She has it all. And Barrett Browning's narrative has it all: it is both a novel and a poem, crossing and blurring the boundaries of genre: both/and, not either/or.

Dickinson's "Gem-tactics" involve a valorizing of that which is not fixed by social or religious decree; divinity for this poet is a fluid thing. Dickinson might have said along with Gerard Manley Hopkins, "Glory be to God for dappled things." In her delighting in "freckled human nature," and in the wild and spotted "Leopard," which "Civilization spurns" (Fr 276, J 492), she makes clear that she values what is "unrefined," unboxed, uncategorized, what is not "black or white," what is not pinned down by a single definition, seen only according to one "light." "The Dark" can feel "beautiful" according to this "Lunacy of Light," according to what Dickinson described elsewhere as "another way to see" (Fr 696, J 627).

Metaphorically abandoning the "broad daylight" that, in effect, abandoned her, by dictating that she be confined to conventional expectations, this is a poet who writes "Good Morning – midnight – I'm coming Home" (Fr 382, J 485). And whether this poem is satirical or serious, nevertheless Dickinson writes over and over of the energy and power that emerge not from exterior sources of light, but from interior ones, from darkness.[16] Her strategic poetics, her "Gem-tactics," emerge from a *seemingly* "still – Volcano – life," – a "quiet – Earthquake style – / Too subtle to suspect," a "solemn – Torrid – Symbol" with "lips that never lie – / Whose hissing Corals part – and shut," causing even cities to "ooze away" (Fr 517, J 601). The ultimate in fiery fluidity, hidden within the mountain, the volcano has only to speak, and the houses of prose, the containers of civilization's decrees are transformed, their lineations, the grids of their streets, their labels and containers reduced to ashes, bits that float in the wind.

Adrienne Rich was the first to argue that it serves as an image for the poet herself, her own "Vesuvius at Home,"[17] a grassy "meditative spot" that "the general thought" would assume only to be "an acre for a Bird." But, the poet asserts,

> How red the Fire rocks below
> How insecure the sod
> Did I disclose
> Would populate with awe my solitute
> (Fr 1743, J 1677)

The power underground. The subconscious, the uncivilized, the primal, the "raw" – what lies under the surface of small talk, of prose, what lies beneath the socially defined seeming shapes of things, the reality beyond this daily reality – these are what interested this poet. A "Gem," from rock that has been dug from underground, sold and cut, faceted and polished, can be lost in the prosy winds of day – with its demands, its judgments of those who might not fit societal definitions of "normal" or "sane." But not volcanic fire, its rivers of fluid lava running underground. It is in fact that which lies underground, under the surface, below external appearances, that Dickinson most values. Over the gem, over the sun which allures yet burns or spurns, Dickinson values the source of creativity – the possibility of the raw material, the ore before it is cut, before it is rigidified into object, into something that can be lost. She preferred to "Work for Immortality," unlike the "Chiefer part," or the "Majority," who worked "for Time." Ordinary clock time, the pacing of broad daylight, resulted in "Money," but the other, "Immortality," was the result of "the mine" (Fr 536, J 406), the ore underground, not yet surfaced, from the dark.

* * *

As revolutionary as her contemporary Walt Whitman, Dickinson broke the bounds of nineteenth-century verse form, refusing the confines of conventional poetics. And like Whitman, she too wrote of the difficulties of being someone not cut out of dimity, someone who did not fit within the comfortable definitions of gendered behavior. Never marrying, eschewing the role of wife and mother to remain sister, next-door-neighbor, friend, and daughter, she retained her "Gem" by metaphorically constructing a place from which she could write her "Titanic Opera":

> I send two sunsets –
> Day and I – in competition – ran –
> I finished Two, and several Stars
> While He – was making One –
>
> (Fr 557, J 308)

These first four lines of this eight line poem show the poet clearly identifying with night, or the dark, as she wins this contest, even more triumphant than when she insists in "They shut me up in Prose" that she abolishes her captivity. And not only are the poet's creations more numerous than "Day's" "ampler" single creation, they are "more convenient," as the poet wryly comments "to a friend," more able to be enjoyed by actual human beings. Able to be carried "in the Hand," they are reminiscent of the "Gem" whose loss the poet laments in "I Held a Jewel in my fingers," but these creations are beyond the reach of any "prosy" winds. The "several Stars" of night's creating may of course be suns themselves for other planets. There is more than one "light" by which to view "reality," Dickinson seems to suggest.

"Broad daylight," the "clear" light of day caused all things to be viewed according to the definition agreed upon by the majority. Tenuous and precious though it must have been at least during winter months, the sunlight of a sensible New England day allowed no room for meditations on multiple perspectives for this poet, seeming to flatten things to their "normal" proportions. Quite literally, bright sunlight can flatten perspectives and erase fine distinctions (like freckles), as good photographers know. Like Nathaniel Hawthorne, whose fiction Dickinson followed, they prefer the shadowy times of late afternoon, and early morning, when subtle differentiations and gradations of shadings are more visible.[18] And this is a poet who reveled in the finest of subtleties, in varying points of view, who refused to pin down her writing to tidy endings, who delighted in ambiguity and exulted in "negative capability." As Sharon Cameron has shown, Dickinson chose not to choose.[19]

It is the very formlessness, the dark of the underground life that generates possibility:

> So from the mold,
> Scarlet and Gold,
> Many a bulb will rise
>
> (Fr 110, J 66)

The lily, writes Dickinson, "passes sure" through "the Dark Sod," from which she then can swing "her Beryl Bell" in "Extasy – and Dell" (Fr 559, J 392). Easy as a star, abolishing captivity. That dwelling place with numerous windows and doors, entrances and exits, was not only "Another way – to see" (Fr 696, J 627), but it allowed limitless perspectives, uncurtained, unprettified and boxed by prosy convention. The poem "I dwell in Possibility" contains no images of a wilting, scorching sun, no directives, and no expectations. To be that wide open to the moment, oblivious to prosaic social demands and stultifying theological ones, is poetry, possibility, and perhaps even paradise.

NOTES

1 In quoting the poems themselves, I have relied upon Franklin's editing, and in all cases, for simplicity's sake, use the first variant he cites.

2 Barbara Antonina Clarke Mossberg, *Emily Dickinson: When a Writer is a Daughter* (Bloomington: Indiana University Press, 1982), p. 172.

3 An alternative version reads: "Abolish his Captivity" (J 613).

4 See Cristanne Miller, *Emily Dickinson: A Poet's Grammar* (Cambridge, MA, and London: Harvard University Press, 1987) for a discussion of the influence of common meter and the hymns of Isaac Watts and on Dickinson's metrics. See especially pp. 141–3.

5 Mossberg, *When a Writer*, pp. 117–18.

6 For a discussion of the relation to Dickinson of food with language, see Mossberg, *When a Writer*, pp. 135–46.

7 Margaret Homans, *Women Writers and Poetic Identity: Dorothy Wordsworth, Emily Brontë, and Emily Dickinson* (Princeton University Press, 1980), pp. 171, 173.

8 See L I: 30, L I: 31, L II: 185, for a few examples. See also my discussion of the poet's conflict with cultural expectations in *Lunacy of Light: Emily Dickinson and the Experience of Metaphor* (Carbondale: Southern Illinois University Press, 1987), especially pp. 43–5.

9 See Mossberg, *When a Writer*, for an extended study of the role of daughter as a defining one in Dickinson's poetry.

10 S. P. Rosenbaum, ed., *A Concordance to the Poems of Emily Dickinson* (Ithaca and London: Cornell University Press, 1964).

11 See Albert Gelpi, *Emily Dickinson: The Mind of the Poet* (Cambridge, MA: Harvard, University Press, 1965), pp. 1–6; John Cody, *After Great Pain: The Inner Life of Emily Dickinson* (Cambridge, MA: The Belknap Press of Harvard University Press, 1971), p. 120; and Sandra M. Gilbert and Susan Gubar, *The Madwoman in the Attic: The Woman Writer and the Literary Imagination* (New Haven: Yale University Press, 1979), p. 596, for a few examples.

12 See Barker, *Lunacy of Light* for an extended analysis of Dickinson's metaphoric rejection of light and all it represents (including masculine values and forces) and her embracing of and inspiration from darkness and its associations (including a sense of a female nurturing space, protected from the intruding "eye" of a partriarchal "light").

13 See Martha Nell Smith, *Rowing in Eden: Rereading Emily Dickinson* (Austin: University of Texas Press, 1992), for an extensive discussion of the poet's relationship to Susan Huntington Dickinson. See also Ellen Louise Hart and Martha Nell Smith (eds.), *Open Me Carefully: Emily Dickinson's Intimate Letters to Susan Huntington Dickinson* (Ashfield, MA: Paris Press, 1998), for a collection of the life-long correspondence between Emily and Susan.

14 *The Poetics of Space* (Boston: Beacon Press, 1969), p. 39.

15 See Jack Capps, *Emily Dickinson's Reading, 1836–1866* (Cambridge, MA: Harvard University Press, 1966), for a detailed discussion of Dickinson's books and reading. See also Barker, *Lunacy of Light*, especially pp. 12–30.

16 See Barker, *Lunacy of Light*, pp. 74–133.

17 "Vesuvius at Home: The Power of Emily Dickinson," in Sandra M. Gilbert and Susan Gubar (eds.), *Shakespeare's Sisters: Feminist Essays on Women Poets* (Bloomington and London: Indiana University Press, 1979), pp. 99–121.

18 See the introduction to *The Scarlet Letter*, where Hawthorne describes the perfect climate for the imagination as a combination of moonlight and coal-fire. But he also equates darkness with knowledge distorted, grown monstrous and destructive. See Barker, *Lunacy of Light*, pp. 15–16.

19 *Choosing Not Choosing: Dickinson's Fascicles* (University of Chicago Press, 1992).

GUIDE TO FURTHER READING

Barker, Wendy. *Lunacy of Light: Emily Dickinson and the Experience of Metaphor.* Carbondale: Southern Illinois University Press, 1987.

Cameron, Sharon. *Choosing Not Choosing: Dickinson's Fascicles.* University of Chicago Press, 1992.

Capps, Jack. *Emily Dickinson's Reading.* Cambridge, MA: Harvard University Press, 1966.

Cody, John. *After Great Pain: The Inner Life of Emily Dickinson.* Cambridge, MA: The Belknap Press of Harvard University Press, 1971.

Gelpi, Albert. *Emily Dickinson: The Mind of the Poet.* Cambridge, MA: Harvard University Press, 1965.

Gilbert, Sandra M. and Susan Gubar. *The Madwoman in the Attic: The Woman Writer and the Nineteenth-Century Literary Imagination.* New Haven: Yale University Press, 1979.

eds. *Shakespeare's Sisters: Feminist Essays on Women Poets.* Bloomington and London: Indiana University Press, 1979.

Homans, Margaret. *Women Writers and Poetic Identity.* Princeton University Press, 1980.

Miller, Cristanne. *Emily Dickinson: A Poet's Grammar.* Cambridge, MA, and London: Harvard University Press, 1987.

Mossberg, Barbara Antonina Clarke. *Emily Dickinson: When a Writer is a Daughter.* Bloomington: Indiana University Press, 1982.

Smith, Martha Nell. *Rowing in Eden: Rereading Emily Dickinson.* Austin: University of Texas Press, 1992.

5

FRED D. WHITE

Emily Dickinson's existential dramas

[handwritten annotation:] existential: human subject is acting / feeling / living human individual.

I

It is always tempting to regard Dickinson as a confessional poet – one whose poems, for all their innovative brilliance, are nonetheless outpourings of her own private feelings toward love, death, nature, and immortality. A closer look at her vast poetic project, however, reveals a far more complex artistic purpose, one that revels in both the possibilities and the impossibilities of language to evoke the experiences of life and mind. Dickinson, I wish to argue, constructs scenarios in verse, dramatizes the predicaments or states of mind or perceptions of imagined speakers, *personae*. "When I state myself, as the Representative of the Verse," she explains to her "preceptor" Thomas Wentworth Higginson in an early letter, "it does not mean – me – but a supposed person" (L 268). The distinction is exceedingly important for she is presenting herself not as a sentimental "poetess" but as a Woman of Letters with an artistic agenda of profound scope and vision, reflecting what Matthew Arnold would term "high seriousness." In that same letter to Higginson she proclaims, "My Business is Circumference": a wonderfully compact way of asserting that her poetic project embraces concerns that are relevant to the entire human sphere, not just to herself.

I shall also argue that Dickinson's world-view is *existential*, which is to say that her personae regard the individual self, and not any divine agency, as solely responsible for the events that shape their lives, which are intrinsically limited, flawed, and separate from nature. The existentialist values longing over gratification, the journey over the destination, the creative process over its finished products. Anguish, doubt, penury, striving are of greater value than comfort, certainty, wealth, attainment – for the former intensify experience while the latter tend to numb it. The existentialist will rail against panaceas and anodynes, whether in word or deed:

> They say that "Time assuages" –
> Time never did assuage –

> An actual suffering strengthens
> As Sinews do, with age –
> (J 686, Fr 861)

For Dickinson, the poet is the supreme existentialist for she "Distills amazing sense / From ordinary meanings" – and the echo from John Newton's hymn, "Amazing Grace," is quite deliberate: The poet also can create grace, however limited or ephemeral, as well as "scalp your naked Soul" (J 315, Fr 477). Dickinson's poetry, as Inder Nath Kher states, displays "a fundamental concern for existence itself as seen through the power of the creative imagination."[1] For the existentialist, the power to imagine, to shape experience out of language, is as close as human beings can get to achieving salvation.

Dickinson articulates her existential world-views in both a dramatic and a dramatistic manner, the latter being Kenneth Burke's term for language that performs rhetorically and dialectically, and does more than express feelings or convey knowledge. A text is dramatistic when it generates tensions or dialectical relationships (Burke calls them ratios)[2] among five elements – purpose, setting, act, actor, and agency (i.e., means of perpetrating the act). Dickinson's poems are often highly dramatistic because of the ingenious, far-reaching dialectical relationships that they generate among this "pentad" of discourse elements. Let's see how they operate in one of Dickinson's well-known quatrains:

> Surgeons must be very careful
> When they take the knife!
> Underneath their fine incisions
> Stirs the Culprit – *Life*!
> (J 108, Fr 156)

Superficially, the *scene* evoked is an operating room where surgeons (*agent*), scalpels in hand (*agency*) are about to cut into a patient (*act*) for the *purpose* of healing the patient. But they must proceed cautiously because life is so precarious. On this superficial level, the point is patently obvious; and if that were all there was to the poem, it would be promptly brushed aside as a mere trifle. However, the exclamatory tone of the speaker, the startling use of "culprit" to modify "*Life*" – and finally the intense emphasis on the word "*Life*" triggers a different level of reading, together with a more complex interplay of the dramatistic elements. The speaker – who seems to be an adult speaking in a child's voice – is the underlying agent, who uses her innocent childhood demeanor to admonish an overly rational adult society (the underlying scene) to put less faith in their surgical techniques – i.e., positivistic science (the underlying agency) – and to be more respectful of the unpredictable, wily, inscrutable nature of life, which tends not to yield its secrets when the knife of reason is brought to it.

Dickinson's poems also are dramatic in the conventional sense of the word – not just in the way they depict personae engaged in dramatic mono-logue or dialogue, but in the way they construct a virtually Aristotelian problem/situation-crisis/climax-denouement progression. Instead of directly conveying the poet's own thoughts and feelings about the subject, Dickinson prefers the aesthetically richer indirection of a dramatic rendering, whereby characters – personae – speak in their own disparate voices, thereby creating a richer and more complex work of art.

Elizabeth Phillips points out that Dickinson's imagination was naturally "histrionic," that "she changes point of view, role, situation, genre, language, and style with remarkable speed and adroitness."[3] Phillips cites, as an exam-ple, Dickinson's use of a child persona arguing with God in "Papa above! / Regard a mouse / O'erpowered by a Cat! / Reserve within thy kingdom / A 'Mansion' for the Rat!" (J 61, Fr 151).

Often, though, the dramatic rendering can be subtle and multi-leveled. Let us consider this popular poem of hers as a case in point:

> I never hear the word "Escape"
> Without a quicker blood,
> . . .
> I never hear of prisons broad
> By soldiers battered down,
> But I tug childish at my bars
> Only to fail again!
>
> (J 77, Fr 144)

The poem dramatizes an artist's recognition of one of life's central para-doxes: the mind, which contemplates and yearns for boundless freedom, is bound forever in a mortal body. The speaker, giddy with the possibility of escape – perhaps through books or play or dreaming – feels that she could simply spread her wings and fly away from her real-world confinement. Even before we get to the second stanza, it is apparent from the very first line that the speaker is aware that she has experienced this feeling many times, and that the "flying attitude" can only be momentary.

In the second stanza – Act Two, as it were – the speaker's thoughts shift rad-ically from the thrill of escape to its futility; dramatically speaking, problem leads to crisis. She envisions a prison and a battlefield, scenes of nightmarish confinement – tropes for the tragic self-confining tendencies of a violent and bellicose society – as an analogue to her own "bars" against which she tugs futilely and *childish*(ly) – a key word that triggers a dialectical reversal from the child*like* idealism of the first stanza. For all her imaginative powers, the speaker discovers, by virtue of her humanness, that she must suffer the same flaws and limitations as anyone else; those prisoners and soldiers symbolize *all* humanity. (Crisis reaches climax and denouement.) Here, then, in a mere eight lines, Dickinson has wrought a Blakean innocence-to-experience existential drama.

Dickinson's existentialist sensibility has much in common with that of the Danish philosopher Soren Kierkegaard (1813–55). For Kierkegaard, life must be accepted for what it is – as a finite (that is, non-universal) existence. Kierkegaard refutes Hegel's universal synthesis because it ignores reality at the individual level. Individual existence is flawed and filled with suffering and limitations (both physical and mental), but that defines life's authenticity. Kierkegaard criticizes the Romantic poets for using their powers of creative imagination to escape into inauthentic realms of their own making. Thus, they live "in a totally hypothetical and subjunctive way,"[4] which causes them to lose touch not only with the authentic world but with themselves.

Aside from Kierkegaard, whose ideas probably had not yet spread beyond Europe in Dickinson's day, a kind of proto-existentialist thought can be detected in America via Calvinist and Presbyterian Christianity, which advocated deep learning and self-discovery. The Presbyterian minister Charles Wadsworth, one of Dickinson's spiritual mentors (aside from the rumored possibility that she was in love with him), asserted from the pulpit that "Man's business on this sublunary platform is to work out his hidden character in the face of the universe" – this he proclaimed in his sermon "Development and Discipline." (Note the similarity between this statement and Dickinson's "My business is Circumference.") Self-reliance was also behind Mary Lyon's rigorous curriculum at the Mt. Holyoke Seminary for Women – it placed heavy emphasis on the natural sciences. Studying nature was an important prerequisite to becoming a good Christian; a sure path to God was through intense study of His creations. Henry David Thoreau, whom Dickinson had probably read, for she mentions him in a letter, advocated self-knowledge and self-betterment through deliberate intimate knowledge of the physical world and learning "to live deliberately, to front only the essential facts of life."[5] And of course, the plays of Shakespeare, her most beloved author, are filled with existential moments, from Macbeth's "sound and fury" anguish over the meaninglessness of human destiny to Hamlet's bitter assessment of human nature ("What a piece of work is a man! how infinite in faculty . . . in apprehension how like a god! the beauty of the world! the paragon of animals! And yet, to me, what is this quintessence of dust?"). And Shakespeare would certainly have agreed with Dickinson's speaker's claim that "'Hamlet' to Himself were Hamlet – / Had not Shakespeare wrote – " (J 741, Fr 776). Quite clearly, then, Dickinson had sufficient exposure to existentialist thinking for it to have influenced her at least indirectly.

Dickinson's poems are existential for yet another reason: their speakers
seldom feel secure in the promise of – or refuse to take refuge in – a transcendent reality as do the speakers in so much of Romantic poetry. Dickinson's
speakers ironically are *most* secure with the doubts and uncertainties of
their flawed and finite existence – a disposition that John Keats, a proto-
existentialist Romantic (whose immortality questing personae eventually
confront their mortality), termed "negative capability." There may exist an
infinity of possible realms – Heaven itself among them – that beckon to be
explored, but they never can be *escaped* into. The speaker can never venture
beyond "circumference," the word in this context effectively conveying the
paradoxical human predicament of being both free and confined: free to
explore while at the same time confined by the inescapable forces of gravity,
mortality, and the limitations of individual human perception. Thus in the
poem "I saw no Way – the Heavens were stitched – ," all the speaker needs
to do is "touch the Universe – "

> . . .
> And back it slid – and I alone –
> A Speck upon a Ball –
> Went out upon Circumference –
> Beyond the Dip of Bell –
> (J 378, Fr 633)

This little poem – ironic even in its smallness, for its scope is epic – can
be read as a drama of the Christian speaker's discovery of her decidedly un-
Christian plight: possessed with the desire to learn the secrets of the heavens,
she soon realizes that such a discovery cannot be made. And yet, the very act
of exploring – of venturing out "upon Circumference" despite her being a
mere Speck upon the earth – is what makes her life purposeful and – paradoxically – more meaningful than before. To examine one's life unflinchingly and
learn to accept it for what it really is – the prime existential directive – is to
liberate oneself from such inflexible directives as church dogma ("the Dip of
Bell") that present themselves as the sole path to salvation. For her, a mortal
woman whose paradigm of reality consists of domestic objects like thread
and needle, the fabric of heaven can never appear more than "stitched."
In another poem the speaker proudly proclaims, "The Queen discerns like
me – Provincially – " (J 285, Fr 256). The existentialist thus learns to accept
her intrinsically restricted reality, just as the speaker in the following poem
progresses from an enthusiastic expectation of reaching heaven to an enthusiastic acceptance of disbelief in that very expectation. Notice how skillfully

Dickinson dramatizes the lapse of childlike faith as an existential awareness of the consequences of maintaining such faith takes hold:

> Going to Heaven!
> I don't know when –
> Pray do not ask me how!
> Indeed I'm too astonished
> To think of answering you!
> Going to Heaven!
> How dim it sounds!
> . . .
> Perhaps you're going too!
> Who knows?
> If you should get there first
> Save just a little space for me
> Close to the two I lost –
> The smallest "Robe" will fit me
> And just a bit of "Crown" –
> For you know we do not mind our dress
> When we are going home –
>
> I'm glad I don't believe it
> For it would stop my breath –
> And I'd like to look a little more
> At such a curious Earth!
> I'm glad they did believe it
> Whom I have never found
> Since the mighty Autumn afternoon
> I left them in the ground.
>
> (J 79, Fr 128)

Like a three-act stage play, this three-stanza dramatic monologue captures the speaker's dawning skepticism toward the Christian promise of an afterlife, a skepticism that leads her to a triumphant existential rejection of that afterlife. *Act One*: The speaker is highly agitated; she keeps exclaiming, "Going to Heaven!" too astonished by the concept either to believe or disbelieve that it's true. It's as if she has, for the first time in her life, dared to question the promise of heaven. As we soon realize, she is attending a funeral where everyone apparently is reassuring her that her recently deceased friends are most assuredly on their way to heaven. *Act Two*: The speaker's tone shifts from astonishment to sarcasm: Well, if heaven is such a great place, you must be getting ready to go there yourself! If so, be sure to save a space for me – which shouldn't be a problem because I'm so small.

Like the speaker in "I saw no way the Heavens were stitched," this speaker ironically equates space in heaven with ordinary domestic space: why should it be otherwise? Also, why should I dress any differently than I would for home? The comparison pokes fun at the uncritical acceptance of heaven as "up there," taking up actual space, inhabited by departed souls wearing white robes. *Act Three*: The speaker's tone changes from sarcasm to a triumphant, almost Nietzschean bravado in not only expressing disbelief in the heaven myth, but in equating it with annihilation of self – for if the myth were true, it would mean losing the world – the "*mighty* Autumn afternoon" – forever.

Faced with the resulting isolation and finitude, the individual must direct his or her own life with great deliberateness, despite the fact that there is no certainty of behavior, no divinely sanctioned moral code. As Kierkegaard asserts, "Fulfillment is always in the wish," and "Doubt is a cunning passion."[6] Now lest the individual be overwhelmed by hopelessness and despair, Kierkegaard posits a way out, and that is to abandon reason and make a pure leap of faith across the unbridgeable gulf to God. As we shall see, Dickinson's speakers do not make such a leap. They may be poised to do so, just as Dickinson herself had been poised to receive Christ during her student days, but they are unable to take that final step toward becoming a Christian.

In Dickinson's case, her love of earthy things was a major deterrent: "It is hard for me to give up the world" (L 23) she states flatly to her close friend Abiah Root in 1848. More seriously, like the speaker in "Going to Heaven!" it was her inability to conceive of the existence of an afterlife that kept her from embracing Christianity. In 1846, when she was a mere fifteen years old, she wrote to Abiah, "I am continually putting off becoming a Christian ... Does not Eternity appear dreadful to you. I often get thinking of it and it seems so dark to me that I almost wish there was no Eternity ... I cannot imagine with the farthest stretch of my imagination my own death scene" (L 10). That last statement helps us to understand what is going on in poems like "I died for Beauty" (J 449, Fr 448), in which the speaker converses from inside her tomb with one "who died for Truth," buried in the tomb beside her – or in her most famous poem, "Because I could not stop for Death" (J 712, Fr 479), in which the presumably dead speaker is merely being *driven* to heaven without ever arriving there – or in "I heard a Fly buzz – when I died" (J 465, Fr 591) in which the moment of death is occupied by a buzzing fly instead of the king who would escort her into heaven. One literally cannot transcend one's own life, these poems argue dramatically; so long as there is consciousness, earthly existence must continue.

2

T. Z. Lavine in *From Socrates to Sartre*, identifies six themes in existentialism: (1) Existence precedes, and is superior to, essence; (2) Awareness of the nothingness at the heart of our existence produces anguish; (3) Existence is inexplicable and absurd; (4) Sciences, philosophies, or religions that argue for universal systems are invalid; (5) Death, like the sword of Damocles, hangs over our heads every moment of our lives, and for that reason must be acknowledged and confronted; (6) The individual is alienated from society, from the natural world, from the cosmos.[7] Dickinson gives dramatic poignancy to each of these existentialist themes in her poems, as I shall now attempt to show.

Existence precedes and is superior to essence

This is the foundation of existentialist thought. Whereas *essential being* is timeless and selfless and linked inseparably to all creation (the Transcendentalist view), *existence* is bound by temporality, individual limitation, and isolation. The existentialist chooses existence over essence because the self has no empirical means of apprehending a transcendent realm. The best we can do is define the timeless, the heavenly, in terms of the temporal and earthly – but to do that is to champion the existential over the transcendent! Dickinson dramatizes this principal existential condition in at least three different ways. One way is to show her speakers meditating upon their limited, isolated, time-bound natures, as in "I tie my Hat":

> Life's little duties do – precisely –
> As the very least
> Were infinite – to me –
>
> I put new Blossoms in the Glass –
> And throw the old – away –
> I push a petal from my Gown
> That anchored there – I weigh
> The time 'twill be till six o'clock
> ...
> And yet – Existence – some way back
> Stopped – struck – my ticking – through –
> We cannot put Ourself away
> As a completed Man
> Or Woman – When the Errand's done
> We came to Flesh – [u]pon –

There may be – Miles on Miles of Nought –
Of Action – sicker far –
To simulate – is stinging work –
To cover what we are
From Science – and from Surgery –
Too Telescopic eyes
To bear on us unshaded –
For their – sake – not for Ours –
. . .
Therefore – we do life's labor –
Though life's Reward – be done –
With scrupulous exactness –
To hold our Senses – on –

(J 443, Fr 522)[8]

The speaker begins by reflecting upon the details comprising a typical day in her life. They consist of mundane chores, but she tends to them with care, as if they were of "infinite" importance. The ultimate irony of the poem is that they *are* of infinite importance because, existentially speaking, human experience is all there is; the finite self, for all practical purposes, is infinite for the self can never experience its own cessation (death).

The poem captures the speaker's struggle to reconcile the received wisdom that life has ultimate purpose with more empirically based suspicion that there is no such purpose, that life's path consists only of "Miles on Miles of Nought." Whatever the case, there is nothing we can do about it! To keep our sanity we must not be persuaded by the scientific image of the human organism – science serves its own needs, not our deepest human needs – but continue to do our life's work "to hold our Senses – on" – a richly resonant phrase that suggests keeping our sanity as well as believing in our human senses enough to forego the need for a supernatural *raison d'etre*.

Another way to dramatize the superiority of existence over essence is to compare the ironic richness of impoverished, finite life with the poverty of riches in the conventional sense. In the dramatic monologue, "Your Riches – taught me – Poverty" (J 299, Fr 418) the speaker asserts to her beloved, "To have a smile – for a mine – each day – / How better, than a Gem!" The poem escapes being a mere conventional analogy between spiritual (or amatory) and material riches, however, when the speaker discloses the true basis for her poverty:

At least, it solaces to know
That there exists – a Gold –
Although I prove it just in time
It's distance – to behold!

The speaker obtains proof that the loved one is "Gold" only when they are apart. As in the famous "Wild nights" monologue (J 249, Fr 269), the speaker only imagines her ecstasy while in a state of isolated longing. "*Were* I with thee / Wild nights should be / Our luxury!" (emphasis mine).

A third way that Dickinson's speakers dramatize the superiority of existence over essence is by capturing the intensity of living from moment to moment – precarious yet thrilling – "It tingles in the Mind" (J 1175, Fr 1247) as one of her personae asserts. Life is most interesting when it is most uncertain, as when the speaker in Poem J 875/Fr 926 steps cautiously "from Plank to Plank":

> I knew not but the next
> Would be my final inch –
> This gave me that precarious Gait
> Some call Experience.

The key word in this poem is *precarious* – not just "uncertain," but, in the context of the poem, an uncertainty leading to self-confidence bordering on faith. The word is etymologically related to prayer (*precari*) – a nuance that almost certainly did not escape Dickinson, who knew Latin and who once told Higginson that her lexicon "was my only companion" (L 261). The connotation of self-confidence is further enhanced by the word *Gait*, which calls to mind the stately cantering or prancing of a horse. So in this existentially dramatic moment we envision the speaker stepping across the planks of her life slowly and cautiously but confidently, never fearfully, never assuming that she has more than another "inch" of life left – and all the while keenly aware of all that is going on about her, the way a responsible artist must be.

In a similar but more ominous poem, the speaker's precarious stepping deteriorates from Planks to Blanks:

> From Blank to Blank –
> A Threadless Way
> I pushed Mechanic feet –
> To stop – or perish – or advance –
> Alike indifferent –
>
> If end I gained
> It ends beyond
> Indefinite disclosed –
> (J 761, Fr 484)

The prancing gait of the first poem has become a blind groping across an indecipherable setting – indecipherable because it does not matter whether the speaker stops, advances, or dies. We are almost in the paralyzed milieu of a Samuel Beckett play. Life must go on. There is nowhere to go.

Awareness of nothingness produces anguish

For Dickinson, even more than for most later existentialists, anguish is "transporting" (J 148, Fr 146), "sovereign" (J 167, Fr 178), "reward" (J 614, Fr 447), "joy" (J 1420, Fr 1450). Anguish, pain, suffering, and longing, rivet us to the here and now; they rapidly douse idealistic flights of fancy. The anguish one suffers from discovering that life is devoid of any "higher" meaning than itself, that the universe is a void, is anguish *in extremis*, yet it is the necessary first step toward taking charge of our respective destinies. In the following dramatic monologue, the speaker suffers the anguish that comes from the growing fear that the universe may be devoid of God or divine purpose.

> I know that He exists
> Somewhere – in Silence –
> He has hid his rare life
> From our gross eyes.
> 'Tis an instant's play
> 'Tis a fond Ambush –
> ...
> But – should the play
> Prove piercing earnest –
> Should the glee – glaze –
> In Death's – stiff – stare –
>
> Would not the fun
> Look too expensive!
> Would not the jest –
> Have crawled too far!
>   (J 338, Fr 365)

The speaker of this monologue startles us by how rapidly her faith in God's existence degrades to bitter skepticism and anguish. The opening proclamation of faith is instantly compromised by the qualifying "Somewhere – in Silence." That in turn leads her to wonder if God might just be playing a cruel game of cosmic hide and seek with her. Death will decide just how gleeful this game is – and the speaker's caustic tone in the last stanza suggests she is quite certain that the jest will have gone too far.

Existence is inexplicable and absurd

The problem with attempting to "explain" existence is that the explainer inevitably resorts to divine revelation or some idealistic metaphysical system that cannot be empirically authenticated. In the following poem, the speaker compares two views of a sinking boat: a human one, represented by a sailor's perspective, and an angelic one:

> Adrift! A little boat adrift!
> . . .
> Will *no* one guide a little boat
> Unto the nearest town?
>
> So Sailors say – on yesterday –
> Just as the dusk was brown
> One little boat gave up its strife
> And gurgled down and down.
>
> So angels say – on yesterday –
> Just as the dawn was red
> One little boat – o'erspent with gales –
> Retrimmed its masts – redecked its sails –
> And shot – exultant on!
>
> (J 30, Fr 6)

Compared with the sailor's view, which merely reports on the boat's sinking after being overpowered by the storm, the angelic view reads like a gross euphemistic platitude – made especially ludicrous by the final image of the now celestial boat being jettisoned into heaven.

In "Of Course – I prayed – "(J 376, Fr 581) the speaker lashes out against a God who cared about her concerns "as much as on the Air / A Bird – had stamped her foot – / And cried 'Give Me' – ," concluding that it would have been better to be insensible in the tomb than to experience "This smart Misery." Human existence, lacking the comfort of God's palpable presence, is indeed miserable, the speaker seems to imply; but the only alternative is non-existence.

An even bleaker vision is dramatized in "Four trees upon a solitary acre" (J 742, Fr 778), in which objects in the natural world appear to be "Without Design / Or Order"; they acquire a transitory significance only in relation to each other. As for possible speculation upon their larger purpose, the only thing the speaker can say is "Unknown – " Gary Lee Stonum has called attention to the dramatic contrast between the randomness of objects depicted and the meticulous way in which the speaker/poet arranges them in the poem.[9]

Sciences, philosophies, or religions that argue for universal systems of truth are invalid

For Dickinson, abstract knowledge is most meaningful when it is subsumed by poetry; philosophical reasoning and religious belief are no exceptions.

Poetry, one might say, brings knowledge and faith into the sphere of experience. Thought is made palpable to the senses.

In the following poem, the speaker attempts to dismantle the Emersonian-transcendentalist premise that the soul of nature and the human soul are emanations from a universal oversoul. The speaker's tone, however, is more naïve than analytical – as if she is convinced that she can find proof of the Eternal just by sifting through phenomena. While not quite denying the existence of such a truth, the speaker nevertheless is rendered speechless when it comes to bodies awaiting resurrection.

> Some things that fly there be –
> Birds – Hours – the Bumblebee –
> Of these no Elegy.
>
> Some things that stay there be –
> Grief – Hills – Eternity –
> Nor this behooveth me.
>
> . . .
>
> Can I expound the skies?
> How still the Riddle lies!
> (J 89, Fr 68)

"The currents of Universal Being circulate through me," Emerson rhapsodizes in *Nature*.[10] But for Dickinson's speaker in the above poem nature is the ineffable Other, defying all efforts to pinpoint her essence, even though the riddle lies motionless before her eyes. Although Emerson confesses that "language and thought desert us, and we are as helpless as fools and savages" (p. 215), when we try to apprehend God, he nevertheless proclaims that "the mind is part of the nature of things," and "we learn that the highest [truth] is present to the soul of man, that the dread universal essence, which is not wisdom, or love, or beauty, or power, but all in one . . . is that for which all things exist" (p. 216). For Dickinson, however, word and world – mind and nature – are separated by an unbridgeable gulf.

Death's overhanging presence must be confronted squarely

"Death in earnest," Kierkegaard writes, "gives life force as nothing else does; it makes one alert as nothing else does."[11] Dickinson gives dramatic poignancy to the idea:

> Death sets a Thing significant
> The Eye had hurried by
>
> . . .
>
> To ponder little Workmanships

In Crayon, or in Wool,
With "This was last Her fingers did" –
Industrious until –

The Thimble weighed too heavy –
The stitches stopped – themselves –
And then 'twas put among the Dust
Upon the Closet shelves –

A Book I have – a friend gave –
Whose Pencil – here and there –
Had notched the place that pleased Him –
At Rest – His fingers are –

Now – when I read – I read not –
For interrupting Tears –
Obliterate the Etchings
Too Costly for Repairs

(J 360, Fr 620)

The eye in the first stanza could very well be Emerson's "transparent eyeball,"[12] now placed into an existential confrontation with the finite. What has grown significant are things the dead person has left behind: her "little Workmanships," the miniscule pencil markings that the speaker's friend had made in a gift book.[13] The seeming insignificance of these items reminds us how utterly removed from life the dead person becomes. One comes to terms with the reality of Death by regarding the emptiness left in its wake. Through death's "departing light / We see acuter, quite / Than by a wick that stays" (J 1714, Fr 1749).

Reading Dickinson's poems as existential dramas, both in the sense of staged scenarios and as dramatistic "language events," – poems in which philosophical and religious ideas are delineated, not just expressed – gives us a better sense of the scope and complexity of her project. Dickinson's poetry exemplifies what Kenneth Burke calls sensuous apprehension of form. For all her metaphoric brilliance, her thematic and stylistic complexity, she is most of all a poet of the deliberately lived moment, of physical presence, of life's unstoppable movement.

NOTES

1 Kher, *The Landscape of Absence: Emily Dickinson's Poetry* (New Haven: Yale University Press, 1958), p. 2.
2 Burke, *A Grammar of Motives* (New York: Prentice-Hall, Inc., 1945).

3 Phillips, *Emily Dickinson: Personae and Performance* (University Park: Penn State University Press, 1988), p. 78.

4 Kierkgaard, *The Concept of Irony, with Continual Reference to Socrates* (1841), in Howard V. Hong and Edna H. Hong (eds.), *The Essential Kierkegaard* (Princeton University Press, 2000), pp. 20–36.

5 Thoreau, *Walden* (1854), in Carl Bode (ed.), *The Portable Thoreau* (New York: Viking Penguin, 1975), p. 343.

6 Kierkgaard, *Practice in Christianity* (1850), in *Essential Kierkegaard*, pp. 373–84.

7 Lavine, *From Socrates to Sartre: The Philosophic Quest* (New York: Bantam Books, 1984), pp. 330–4.

8 The Johnson variorum edition includes a five-line stanza, immediately preceding the concluding stanza, that the Franklin variorum edition omits. Franklin had determined (*The Editing of Emily Dickinson: A Reconsideration* [Madison: University of Wisconsin Press, 1967] pp. 40–6) that the manuscript copy of the stanza belonged to another poem. See also Franklin's note at the end of the poem in vol. I, p. 531.

9 Stonum, *The Dickinson Sublime* (Madison: University of Wisconsin Press, 1990), p. 17.

10 Emerson, R. W. *Nature* (1836), in William H. Gilman (ed.), *Selected Writings of Ralph Waldo Emerson* (New York: NAL, 1965), p. 189.

11 Kierkegaard, *Three Discourses on Imagined Occasions* (1845), in *Essential Kierkegaard*, p. 166.

12 From *Nature*: "Standing on the bare ground, my head bathed by the blithe air, and uplifted into infinite space, all mean egotism vanishes. I become a transparent eyeball; I am nothing; I see all." This passage inspired the contemporary editorial cartoonist Christopher Cranch to draw a caricature of Emerson as a giant eyeball on long stick-legs, gazing heavenward.

13 One could argue that Dickinson is speaking autobiographically in this poem's last two stanzas – i.e., that she is recalling the time when her dear friend Benjamin Newton (her "dying Tutor" as she referred to him in a letter to Higginson) presented her with a copy of Emerson's *Poems*. I would argue, however, that Dickinson's persona in this poem just happens to have had an experience similar to her own – an experience that plays an important role in developing the theme of the poem.

GUIDE TO FURTHER READING

Burke, Kenneth. *A Grammar of Motives*. New York: Prentice-Hall, Inc., 1945.

Emerson, R. W. *Nature* (1836). In William H. Gilman, ed. *Selected Writings of Ralph Waldo Emerson*. New York: NAL, 1965.

Kher, Inder Nath. *The Landscape of Absence: Emily Dickinson's Poetry*. New Haven: Yale University Press, 1958.

Kierkegaard, Soren. *The Concept of Irony, with Continual Reference to Socrates* (1841). In Howard V. Hong and Edna H. Hong, eds. *The Essential Kierkegaard*. Princeton University Press, 2000, pp. 20–36.

Imagined Occasions (1845). In Howard V. Hong and Edna H. Hong, eds. *The Essential Kierkegaard*. Princeton University Press, 2000, pp. 164–9.

Phillips, Elizabeth. *Emily Dickinson: Personae and Performance*. University Park: Penn State University Press, 1988.

Stonum, Gary Lee. *The Dickinson Sublime*. Madison: University of Wisconson Press, 1990.

Thoreau, Henry David. *Walden* (1854). In Carl Bode, ed. *The Portable Thoreau*. New York: Viking Penguin, 1975, pp. 258–572.

Wadsworth, Charles. *Sermons* (1869). Philadelphia: Presbyterian Publishing Co., 1883.

6

SUZANNE JUHASZ AND CRISTANNE MILLER

Performances of gender in Dickinson's poetry

[handwritten: Standard way of opening an essay]

I

This essay discusses how poet and reader perform gender in Dickinson's poetry. Our discussion depends on a two-pronged general argument: first, that both gender and the lyric poem in and of themselves constitute performances and, second, that reading a lyric poem interpretively – that is, reading it seriously – also constitutes a performance. These general propositions, which borrow from performance and reader-response theories, support our more particular claims that Dickinson's poetry and the reading of gender in Dickinson's poetry constitute intersecting performances even beyond the level generic to lyric poetry. Specifically, Dickinson both constructs alternatives to a traditional, fixed binary gender system (woman/man) and opens opportunities for the reader to perform alternative genderings. Moreover, she implies that the woman poet herself cannot be conventionally gendered. Despite the fact that Dickinson's work is frequently literally performed and many critics have commented on the extent to which it demands active response from its readers,[1] the ways in which textual performance underscores Dickinson's writing has not been examined. In this essay we outline the principles supporting our argument and then analyze performances of gender in and of Dickinson's poems to show that her variant performances of gender are crucial to the general construction of her poetry.

Our thinking about performance and poetry is influenced by current social constructionist theories of performance that question the very existence or truth of identity, as well as the notion of gender as a fixed, stable, or interior aspect of something called a self. These theories propose that everything about us is constructed by the social conditions and ideologies in which we exist. Identity may be understood as a "performance," or the composite of performances that we enact to indicate, and hence possess, gender and other markers of identity. This is the contention of, for example, Judith Butler in many publications as well as her pathbreaking *Gender Trouble: Feminism and the Subversion of Identity* (1990). She points out that identity categories might be productions that create the effect of the natural, the original, and the inevitable, but that rather than being *origin* and *cause*, those identity categories are in fact the *effects* of institutions, practices, and discourses.[2]

The position that identity is "a compelling illusion"[3] has been both enthusiastically embraced and contested – the latter from, for example, the point of view of much contemporary psychoanalytic theory which, while postmodern in sympathy, nevertheless wishes to posit the reality of subjectivity or self-identity. Lynne Layton in *Who's That Girl? Who's That Boy?* for example, observes that in the paradigm of relational psychoanalytic theory "core" does not have to mean "innate" or "fixed" or even "unified." "But 'core,'" she notes, "does imply something internal that recognizably persists even while it may continuously and subtly alter, and there are real differences between theorists for whom a constructed interior relational world motivates behavior and those, like Butler . . . for whom interiority is an appearance, an effect of discourse."[4] In Dickinson's poetry there are indeed many instances where interiority is invoked: a sense of subjectivity that reveals a "continuity of going-on-being," in the words of the psychoanalyst D. W. Winnicott.[5] Dickinson's words for this entity are "soul" or "heart" or "mind." In this essay, however, we wish to focus on that other kind of identity, one that is created by performance and by, as Layton notes, discourse. To this end we have found in Butler's ideas a particularly helpful and apt theory of the *textual construction* of identity and, in particular, of gender. For the poem incarnates identity in the way that Butler understands identity to be constructed in the person, as we can see by substituting the word "poem" for her word "body" in the following description: "the *poem* is understood to be an active process of embodying certain cultural and historical possibilities" ("Performative Acts," p. 272). Even as one is not simply a body but rather one *does* one's body, so the speaker of a lyric poem is not so much a self as a self that is done – enacted, performed by the reader.

2

In order to understand Dickinson's poetic construction of identity or gender, it is necessary first to attend to the general characteristics of the lyric poem. As a genre, the lyric was historically linked with song, hence implicitly with a singer. Since the Renaissance, it has largely ceased to be sung and has instead come increasingly to be identified with personal self-expression or subjectivity. For example, in the nineteenth century, Wordsworth defined the lyric as "the spontaneous overflow of powerful feelings," and Hegel described the lyric as intensively subjective and personal.[6] This identification seems to us both accurate and misunderstood. On the one hand, the lyric always has a speaker, and the process of speaking always establishes a subjective presence or implied subjectivity. On the other hand, subjectivity in the lyric inheres not in the transmitted personal feelings of an autobiographical speaker or in any natural coherence of the speaking position as such, but in the fact that poems are made up of words. Hence, the construction of an apparently sincere or authentic lyric voice or speaker is still a construction. It is not the relation of the "I" to the poet or to any other established "self" but the use of words in the context of speech that implies a perspective or subjectivity in some form. The lyric, in other words, always implies an "I," but that subjective position does not refer to an identity outside the poem. One could say that the poem's language is both the stage on which its "I" performs and the script constituting that subjectivity or "I."

While one could perhaps claim that every instance of writing constitutes performance, the speaking position of the lyric poem is especially performative in the sense that the subjectivity it stages is distinct from both the "I" of everyday speech and the speakers of fiction or drama. In everyday life, there is an assumed – perhaps fictional – actuality or stabilizing core to the innumerable codes of selfhood we perform. In fiction or drama, there are multiple developed, embodied, and for the most part consistent "characters," recognizably distinguishable from other characters in the same fictional world. In the lyric poem, in contrast, there is for the most part no description of who is speaking, no embodiment, no development, no introduced "character."[7] For example, Dickinson's various personae or self-positionings as "Earl," "Wife" or "Queen" (Fr 451, 225, 596) are known either only by the tone and manner of the text or by self-naming within the poem's text. Dickinson's speakers exclaim "A Wife – at Daybreak – I shall be – " (Fr 185) or mention having been "a Boy and Barefoot" (Fr 1096) or a "Bernardine Girl" (Fr 211), but the poem provides no corroboration of these identity markers. Dickinson neither describes her speakers in narrative terms nor describes their positions as separate from herself, except in the single cryptic comment to Thomas Wentworth Higginson, "When I state myself [that is, use "I"] as the Representative of the Verse – it does not mean me – but a supposed person" (L 268).

Both as an instance of the lyric and because of its own characteristics, Dickinson's poetry constitutes a liminal space where various aspects of performance and identity collide. At the level of genre, this space is ambiguously grounded; as explained above, because the lyric "I" is bound only by the language and structures of the poem, it cannot have the kind of one-to-one identification assumable with any ordinarily spoken voice or role-playing, per se. At the level of Dickinson's poetry specifically, the grounding of this subjectivity is even more liminal. As has frequently been discussed, the majority of her poems are "sceneless," without specific narrative, historical, geographical, or situational frame.[8] They begin *in media res* – "Of Course – I prayed – " (Fr 581) with no reference to why the speaker might be praying – or address abstract issues: "Drama's Vitallest Expression is the Common Day" (Fr 776). Dickinson's poems take to an extreme the inclination of the lyric genre toward the constructed liminality of its subjective presence, the outline of a self in an unplaced moment. Hence the reader is even more than usually required to enact the contours of the speech-act or moment in interpretation, an enactment that constitutes performance in that the poem provides the only text for that implied subjectivity.

Not only, however, does a Dickinson poem constitute a particular kind of performance. Dickinson indicates in several poems that she thinks of life, of communal interactions, and of writing poetry all as performances, or at least as involving elements of performance. While the broadest of these claims is not related specifically to the poet's inscribing gender in her poems, it is useful to see the terms in which Dickinson imagines life as drama. For example, "Drama's Vitallest Expression is the Common Day," contrasts the professional drama enacted in theaters with that of ordinary life, suggesting that the longest lasting and "Vitallest" theater is that which occurs without an audience and without a formal stage: "This – the best enact / When the Audience is scattered / And the Boxes shut – " (Fr 776). The drama of professional theater "Perish[es] in the Recitation" – it lasts only as long as it takes to say the lines and then is dead. In contrast, the drama of ordinary life never perishes at all. As the poem concludes, any "Hamlet" or "Romeo" would live out his drama even if "'Romeo' left no Record" or "Had not Shakespeare wrote." While this poem on the one hand voices the common thought that "life is a stage" and its play closes only with death, it also suggests (anticipating Butler) that a life may consist of particular dramas that are continuously replayed, and that even death does not close the heart's "Theatre." As the poem ends, the drama is "infinite enacted" not in a particular individual's but in "the Human Heart," known to all of "Us." Hence the drama of a life is both private, of the "Heart," and broadly "Human" – or a part of communal understanding and, to some degree, participation.

Dickinson contrasts the unending life of "Drama" with mere mortality, more clearly highlighting the interactive nature of such theater, in the macabre poem "We dream – it is good we are dreaming – " (Fr 584). Here an unidentified "It" "would hurt us – were we awake," but the speaker dismisses this danger:

What harm? Men die – Externally –
It is a truth – of Blood –   [Fact]
But we – are dying in Drama –
And Drama – is never dead –   [seldom]

Here not only is drama "never dead" but its action consists of mutual "Cautious" attempts to discover just what the reality of this play might be and whether the "Phantasm" of dreaming is more or less real than the banal "truth – of Blood." Should we "open [our] eyes" and discover the dream mistaken, the "livid Surprise" might:

Cool us to Shafts of Granite –
With just an age – and name –
And perhaps a phrase in Egyptian –   [latin inscription]
It's prudenter – to dream –
                  (Fr 584, stanzas 2 and 4)

In reading this poem, the reader enters into its drama, into the cautious testing of interpretive and psychological boundaries, into the speaker's pact to continue the performance of "dream" rather than submitting to mere physiological "truth" – or, as a variant for this word, "Fact"– of blood. Such fact, for Dickinson, apparently leads straight to the cemetery, with its "Shafts of Granite" marked by words "Egyptian," or hieroglyphic, in their mysterious difference from the life of internal "Drama." Facts or truths not "of Blood" are the vital ones, according to Dickinson, and it is these that humans perform in their private theaters.

In contrast to the infinitely enacted drama of "the Human Heart," Dickinson writes elsewhere of natural phenomena as mere "Theatricals of Day." For example, a sunset is applauded by "Universe," a "Crowd" and even "God" in the poem "Like Mighty Foot Lights – burned the Red" (Fr 507); or, in "Whole Gulfs – of Red, and Fleets – of Red," another sunset is staged by "appointed Creatures" who appear "In Authorized Arrays – / Due – promptly – as a Drama – / That bows – and disappears – " (Fr 468). According to these poems, even the most magnificent natural spectacles, like professional theater, "Perish in the Recitation." Yet while the theatrical sunset passes, the poem written in response to its spectacle both constitutes a new and more vital performance and provides a script for the perception of a sunset that requires ongoing enactment on the part of its readers. Nature, human life, and poetry all constitute performances, but Dickinson constructs a clear hierarchy between them. Nature provides extraordinary but brief spectacles; human life at its most vital constitutes "infinite enacted" "Drama." It is the poem, however, that stages or scripts these performances for the reader, and it does so through its construction of a liminal subjectivity positioned in the lyric as the poem's speaker. It is here that the drama of the poem intersects with the performance of gender – both thematically in the poem's claims and through the identity positioning of the speaker, as interpreted by the reader.

Butler
Gender - subversive/repitition - Scripted / F = subordination

3

Gender is so important because it serves as one of the most crucial factors in the social and psychic construction of identity. The women's movements of the nineteenth and twentieth centuries, followed by what we now label "gender studies" in the academy, attests to this fact as well as to the uneven distribution of power that has historically tended to accompany definitions of gender for both individual persons and for societies at large. Certainly, for Emily Dickinson in nineteenth-century America, her position as a person gendered "woman," especially in its relation to her identity as a writer of poems, was of the utmost concern, as many contemporary scholars have pointed out. Using Butler as our guide in contemplating how gender may be constructed in lyric poetry, we note how the performance of gender might be "a corporeal style, an 'act'" ("Performative Acts," p. 272). For Butler, gender is not intrinsic but constructed in each person by means of a compulsory repetition of subjectivating norms ("performances"), and "this repetition constitutes the temporalized scene of gender construction and destabilization."[9] Gender is therefore "an identity constituted through a stylized repetition of acts": it is "the mundane way in which the bodily gestures, movements, and enactments of various kinds constitute the illusion of an abiding gendered self." Indeed, gender performance, says Butler, requires an audience to believe it and give it meaning; this audience, like the readers of a poem, "come[s] to believe and to *perform* in the mode of belief" ("Performative Acts," pp. 270, 271, our italics).

Gender can also, as Butler further proposes, be transformed – that is, not represented in a purely conventional manner – because if the ground of gender identity is the stylized repetition of acts through time and not a seamless identity, then the "arbitrary relation" that exists between such acts allows for the possibility of a different sort of repeating, by way of the "breaking or subversive repetition of that style" ("Performative Acts," p. 271). In "Critically Queer" she sees "the gaps opened up in regulatory norms" as producing potential gender transformation (p. 22). Certainly this possibility exists in the language act of the poem. Dickinson, of course, is famous for linguistic gaps supplied by syntax, elision, figures of speech and sheer omission.[10] Such gaps create a space that functions analogously to Butler's arbitrary relation between performative acts, and can be sites for a break in stylized gender

gender can be redood in different ways due to the changing of these acts

or a subversive repetition of it. Dickinson also opens conceptual gaps between variant constructions of gender – in individual poems and from poem to poem. In these spaces between conventional constructions of gender she presents modifications, diversions, and conditions that are contentious or problematic, and in this fashion she skews and alters gender identities.

With the exception of the occasional introductory line like "A solemn thing – it was – I said – /A Woman – white – to be" (Fr 307), Dickinson is rarely overt and frequently not literal about gender as inflecting the identity of her speaker. However, her poems are replete with conventional performative signs for indicating that gender is present: costumes, settings, and actions. Indeed, gender signs are always conventional; that is the point about the cultural construction of gender. It perpetually and ritually seeks a generic set of denominators, if only to cover the manifold possibility for variation that exists in people. We cannot recognize performances of alterity without the markers of the normative. Dickinson provides conventional gender signs in, for example, "I felt my life with both my hands" (Fr 357), where not only does the speaker check out the existence and nature of her identity by looking in a mirror (a stereotypic feminine activity), but in the course of her perusal "push[es her] dimples by" to see if they "twinkled back." This speaker may well be a ghost, or an angel (she is dead), but she is a feminine one. In "I sing to use the Waiting" (Fr 955), a speaker waiting for a traveling companion has but her bonnet to tie and then shut the door to her house before she embarks: we know by the bonnet that her gender is feminine. In "I'm ceded – I've stopped being Their's – " (Fr 353) the speaker's childhood is characterized by dolls and a string of spools. Referring to this speaker as "she" seems justified because of the girlish toys with which she played. In many other poems as well, when the speaker ties her hat and creases her shawl (Fr 522) or goes out with her basket to pick berries (Fr 358), we see evidence of feminine gender by way of its cultural conventions.

In similar fashion, qualities and characteristics of the implied speaker can be identified as feminine. For example, the speaker in "I was the slightest in the House – " (Fr 473), with her smallest room and little lamp, who never speaks unless addressed and then speaks "brief and low" – who cannot bear, indeed, "to live – aloud," evinces the modesty and self-effacement that stereotypically characterized a nineteenth-century lady. The speaker incarnates these qualities in language: or, more properly, in her claimed unwillingness to use it. Frequently linguistic signifiers indicate the proper configurations of the feminine. These include *lack* of agency, initiative, and power – that is, passivity, receptivity, and powerlessness – along with the many subsidiary qualities and characteristics that develop from this condition. Such signifiers are apparent in phrases like "To lose thee – sweeter than to gain / All other hearts I knew" (Fr 1777), "and how I just said 'Please'" (Fr 923), or even "Come slowly – Eden!" (Fr 205).

Readers attuned to Dickinson's gender performances rarely think of her, or her speakers, as contentedly feminine. Nonetheless, Dickinson's gender bending requires the context (even if it is a pretext) of conventionality. Thus, when Dickinson begins a poem with the phrase, "I'm 'wife,'" she establishes a traditional femininity for her speaker: "I'm 'wife' – I've finished that – / That other state – " (Fr 225). Her following declaration, however, disrupts this context: "I'm Czar – I'm 'Woman' now." Indeed, both of the femininely inflected words, "wife" and "Woman," are presented in quotation marks. Further, the "Woman" of line three is linked, by way of a dash – or gap – to the masculinely inflected czar, *not* in quotation marks. If the speaker, according to the first stanza, has achieved the status of wife by finishing "That other state," which is identified in the second stanza as "the Girl's life," then wifedom may turn out to be something other than conventional womanhood.

This poem is about achieving the culturally appropriate gender situation – wifedom – so safe and comfortable, perhaps, because it *is* culturally mandated. However, the element of czarness in wifedom, as well as the indication of constructedness that those opening quotation marks create, alert us to gender complication rather than security. The wife goes on to identify her situation as a "soft Eclipse," a kind of "Heaven" in comparison to the "Earth" of the girl's life; from this perspective, wifedom looks "safer" and girlhood looks "odd." Assigning "comfort" to wifedom turns "That other kind," by means of a dichotomous comparison, into "pain." "But Why compare?" the speaker asks: "I'm Wife! Stop there!" Yet the poem is all about the comparison. Certainly her depiction of heavenly comfort as "soft Eclipse" is a little alarming in its connotations of obscuration and dimming by way of proximity to some other celestial body, perhaps someone like the "Man of Noon" to whom she refers in a letter about matrimony (L 93). Girlhood in its very singularity or vitality may seem "odd" only to a woman lulled by convention into a half-life.

Curiously, the czar is generally elided in readings of this poem.[11] A czar is a male monarch, a person having great power. If a wife can be likened to a czar, then there is something other than eclipse involved in her condition as Dickinson presents it: the *power* of conventional positionality or as Butler puts it, the *activeness* of "inducing the body to become a cultural sign" ("Performative Acts," p. 273). This achievement of heterosexual privilege makes the wife paradoxically more "masculine" than the girl who, in her unattached and unsubordinated state (which may seem to be manly), is in some important way essentially feminine. She, at any rate, has no quotation marks around her. In this poem the purpose of introducing the masculine signifier in the gaps of conventional gender performance seems not so much to create an alternative gender as to query or destabilize attitudes about conventional femininity itself.

In contrast, in the berry-picking poem referred to earlier (Fr 358), the radical activities of the speaker, set in and poised against the context of everyday gender-related activities, do indicate a transformation of the concept of the feminine. In this poem the reader hears both gender-appropriate modesty and hesitation – "Perhaps I asked too large" – and gender-inappropriate assertiveness and claims of importance – "I [did] ask too large." The speaker, in fact, not only asked but took: "no less than skies." She explains that "Earths, grow thick as / Berries, in my native Town – ." Indeed, her basket holds just "Firmaments," which dangle "easy" on her arm.

Taking skies, announcing your "native Town" to be more conducive to growing earths than berries, and finding your basket more suited to holding firmaments than the berries for which it was designed – these acts are unconventional. Yet because they are enacted within the context of the conventionally feminine – the firmaments are contained by a basket, not, say, a lasso – the speaker performs herself as a "girl" who dares to be different. This indicates that her native town might be understood as something like her mind or imagination, her terrain of choice the skies, a way of expanding but not exiting altogether the usual life of the girl, whose smaller bundles, for this speaker, "Cram." This is gender-bending: altering or transforming the range of femininity but not turning it into anything we would call masculinity or even something as contemporary as transgendered identity. Poems such as these offer examples of how poetic language and structure highlight that arbitrary relation between gendered acts of which Butler speaks, those gaps of which Dickinson is so fond. In these gaps she cultivates the possibilities for gender critique and transformation.

Dickinson's feminine speakers use their gender to construct and deconstruct their own identities as well as to discuss the performative nature of gender. In "I tie my Hat" (Fr 522) gender turns out to be an act of simulation.

> I tie my Hat – I crease my Shawl –
> Life's little duties do – precisely –
> As the very least
> Were infinite – to me –
>
> I put new Blossoms in the Glass –
> And throw the Old – away –
> I push a petal from my Gown
> That anchored there – I weigh

> The time 'twill be till six o'clock –
> So much I have to do –   [I have so much]

This speaker is an adept performer of the "little duties" of gender conventions. She ties her hat, creases her shawl, and brushes petals from her gown so as, she says in the poem's final line, "To hold our – Senses – on – ." These are acts of simulation, she explains, because for her "existence – some way back – / Stopped – struck – my ticking – through – ." Yet even after some terrible occurrence that might make any of us feel as if "the errand's done / We came to Flesh – opon," we cannot "put Ourself away / As a completed Man / Or Woman – ," observes the speaker, thus pointedly connecting identity to gender. This cryptic remark seems to mean that her "life" is over, if life is the errand we came to flesh upon. Yet after "life" is finished, the speaker does not cease. She keeps going – "There may be – Miles on Miles of Nought – / Of Action – sicker far – ," and therefore she must simulate.

> To simulate – is stinging work –
> To cover what we are
> From Science – and from Surgery –
> Too Telescopic eyes
> To bear on us unshaded –
> For their – sake – Not for Our's –

It is significant that what is simulated is gender, in this way covering "what we are." For the sake of others, then, we go on with the charade of gender, which is what makes us seem human. Yet there is something in the performance of gender for the actor as well as the audience. Doing these daily acts, "With scrupulous exactness," enables us "To hold our Senses – on – ." The poem specifies gender as the act that keeps us in culture. It gives us an identity: it makes of us a "Man" or "Woman." Simulating may be "stinging work," but it provides this protection, this coverage.

This poem, however, further asserts a subjectivity that is without or beyond or beneath the simulations of gender. We can be, the poem maintains, "unshaded": existing but without gender. Doing "life's labor" of gender occasions both comfort (it takes up the time till six o'clock) and suffering (it is stinging work). Unshaded, however, we are still there, albeit (at the very minimum) culturally deviant. This poem has often been read as the soliloquy of an acculturated woman who plays her social role even though the real woman within is lost or angry or both. In this sense role playing is in no way a postmodern concept. Our more constructionist reading attests to Dickinson's understanding of an identity that is complex enough to sustain both performance and essence.

Ed uses poetic techniques to produce a variety of ways to perform femininity

4

Viewing gender as a performance reveals how Dickinson both uses and disrupts conventional gender codes in the language of her poems. Seeing the act of reading as a performance – or as one element of the poem's cumulative performance – clarifies the degree to which interpretation participates in the gendering of the poem's speaker, even when that implied presence carries no obvious gender markings and does not call attention to itself with an explicit "I." Just as our discussion of gender performance borrows from performance theory, our contentions about reading are indebted to reader response theory of the 1970s. Here, however, we believe that understanding the basic tenets of reader-response theory in terms of performance extends its possibilities, as well as bringing us closer to the particular nuances of Dickinson's poetry. Stanley Fish, Michael Riffaterre, Wolfgang Iser, and others have written at length about the interactive process through which a reader perceives or receives a text, and about specific elements of knowledge or competence that a reader brings to a text in understanding it.[12] By conceiving the reading process as not just interactive but performative, we want to stress that readers make repeated specific and singular choices in the process of interpretation, even while they may recognize multiple contingencies of reading and the plurality of meaning in a given text. Performance implies particular enactment. A thorough interpretation of a poem, for example, might involve fluid negotiation of multiple possibilities of meaning, but each aspect of interpretation or meaning is itself fixed. It is in that sense analogous to performance, which must be enacted in a single way even though there are infinite possibilities for enactment. Thinking of the performance of meaning as vocalizing the poem clarifies this claim: while a poem may be read in a multitude of ways, each vocal performance can give voice to only a limited range of these ways. Currently, all critical theories acknowledge interpretation as multiplicitous. Surprisingly, however, the choice of how to gender a poem's speaker continues to be unacknowledged or unarticulated and represented as monolithic. Understanding reading as an act of performance foregrounds the extent to which even a reader's unthinking assumption of gender, or unconscious registering of implied and subtle gender codes, may influence other aspects of interpreting a poem.

The standard practice for gendering a speaker in poetry criticism is, to our knowledge, untheorized. It proceeds thus: a poet writes a lyric poem in which an "I" speaks. If that "I" is not specifically and obviously gendered in a way contrary to the author's apparent gender, the "I" is assumed to share the author's gender. Hence, all Emily Dickinson's unmarked speakers are referred to as "she"; all Robert Frost's as "he." Even in anti-voice or

markers & assumptions

highly abstract lyric poetry, the practice is to refer to the language of the poem in terms of the poet's gender. When the speaker introduces herself with the lines "Title divine, is mine. / The Wife without the Sign – " (Fr 194), this assumption has obvious point. Here the reader's role is minimal: the reader understands conventional gender codes from ordinary life and so can recognize and enact them immediately when encountering them in a poem. In lyric poems that present an idea or proposition, however, the presence of a first-person speaker is downplayed to the extent that most readers have no sense of making or encountering gender distinctions in interpreting the poem.

The poem "Drama's Vitallest Expression is the Common Day" provides an interesting example of such a propositional and apparently non-gendered presence. As indicated earlier, this poem suggests that a life lived vitally has the same kind of universal power as great plays by Shakespeare, hence that its drama constitutes a definingly "Human" set of circumstances or crises, "infinite enacted / In the Human Heart." By distinguishing "Vitallest" from other forms of "Expression," Dickinson suggests that people may choose not to play a role in life's drama, or at least not to perform a vital role; they may choose instead to be a part of "the Audience" awaiting the next spectacle, or someone else's drama. The poem, however, positions the reader specifically as one of "Us," one familiar with Shakespeare's Hamlet and Romeo and, hence suggestively, one of "the best" – those who need no audience to enact their truest dramas, which are internal. So far so good: no gender markers are required. Yet these distinctions provide a key to the reader's role in interpreting gender in the poem.

The work of the *poem* is to position the reader. The reader, in turn, must position the speaker, the tone, the implications, the desires implied in the poem, working only from clues provided by style, metaphor, vocabulary, and the general grammatical and cultural competencies familiar to us from reader-response theory. Because this poem is propositional, it calls attention to no aspects of a speaker's personality or individual bearing. And yet any interpretation of the poem assumes characteristics of its speaker of necessity – even if the assumption is simply that "Dickinson" speaks here in transparent representation of her own perceptions. For example, the reader might well perform this speaker as male: it identifies with the characters Hamlet and Romeo rather than Queen Gertrude or Juliet; further, the speaker identifies with Romeo as the one who might leave a "Record / Of his Juliet" – that is, Romeo as not just lover but writer, a metonym for Shakespeare, the archetypal (male) poet. Similarly, it refers to the individual as the "Owner" of its individual "Theatre" – a legal position associated in the mid-nineteenth century with men. Throughout, the tone is assured, authoritative, "masculine" in conventional codes. These are characteristics of the speaking position acknowledged by the reader only if the question of gender arises, and because the interest of this poem does not lie in the assumed or implied attributes of its speaker the question is not likely to arise. Nonetheless, these are obvious assumptions to make and they involve familiar conventions for constructions of gender. Without identifying what leads to this assumption, the reader may well refer to this speaker as "he." Moreover, to the extent that the reader performs the speaker as authoritative, an "Owner," a "Hamlet" or "Romeo," the reader also positions "himself" as sharing in these characteristics as one of "Us."

To perform the poem differently – for example, as spoken by a woman positioning herself as masculine – requires a different interpretive frame, different assumptions about the poem's relation to the world in which it is set, and a more complex sense of the poem's speaking position as performatively gendered. In such a reading, for example, the poem's quotation marks around "Hamlet" and "Romeo" might signal the *lack* of (gender) congruence between the (feminine) speaking actor, poet, lover on the one side and Shakespeare's (male) heroes on the other. While generally the script of this poem itself provides no gaps between alternative conventions of gender, the quotation marks might be read as marking gender tension, although such a clue is at best slight and subtle. It is more likely that the reader who performs a gender-conscious reading of this poem approaches the poem already with general assumptions about the likelihood of encountering gender ambiguity, whether those assumptions are born of feminist training, acquaintance with Dickinson's many other gender-bending poems, or both. By the same token, the reader unconscious of gender in the poem also approaches it with assumptions about gender construction – most likely, assumptions either that it is irrelevant in this case or generally unimportant to Dickinson. The performance of the speaker's gender, then, stems equally from the poem's script and from the reader's assumptions about gender construction and about Dickinson.

Returning to the sunset poem, "Whole Gulfs – of Red, and Fleets – of Red" (Fr 468), we see here again that the reader is a more active part of the staging of the scene than at first appears and brings gender assumptions to her or his performance. The reader must first find the sunset in the metaphoric "Gulfs" and "Fleets of Red / And Crews – of solid Blood – " that apparently without a superior agency "place [themselves?] about the West – Tonight / As 'twere specific Ground – ." Whether the poem's terms are cinematic, industrial, or naval, it is clear that an idiosyncratic speaker perceives and describes the scene, imagining colors in the sky as crews, fleets, blood, actors, and so on. The reader must then identify that idiosyncrasy: is it melodramatic, macabre, playful? As in "Drama's Vitallest Expression," the speaker appears ungendered. Following one conventional coding, a reader might interpret the excessive dashes and high melodrama of the poem as suggesting a feminine perspective, as well as the lack of specificity about what these "Crews" of "Blood" actually do. Similarly, one could note the contrast between the bloody "Crews" initially referred to and the coyly distanced later reference to "appointed Creatures," reducing these horrific workers to obedient and harmless actors on some vast stage, almost house-wifely. On the other hand, imagining this language and imaginative vision as proceeding from a masculine speaker might make him seem oratorical and highly mannered – not breathless, melodramatic, and naive but a calcu-lating and manipulative actor setting up the drama of a sunset gruesomely and mysteriously only to transform it into an instance of almost military order: crews of blood marching in "Authorized Arrays." One reading moves from the gruesome to the almost coy, the other from the gruesome to the perhaps equally frightening inhumanity of military precision and obedience. As suggested earlier, such interpretation, and gendering, may be performed in alternative, perhaps multiple or contradictory ways, given the many con-ventions for coding and enacting gender. Each coding, however, entails a distinct interpretive posture: one may read a speaker as potentially mascu-line or feminine, or as undercutting conventions of gender coding, but the speaker cannot be both male and female at once.

The Dickinson poems requiring the most obvious and, perhaps also for that reason, most interesting gender performances are those in which direct address of an "I" to a "you" demands the reader's two-fold interaction with the speaker, both as the "you" addressed and as the agency performing the "I," whether or not the poem provides conventional gender markers for this enactment. "You've seen Balloons set – Hav'nt You?" (Fr 730) is one such poem. Like the poems "Whole Gulfs – of Red" and "Like Mighty Foot-lights," "You've seen Balloons" involves a literal performance and audience described by a speaker and, again, the poet does not gender the speaker in obvious ways. An uncoded speaker addresses an unidentified "you" in telling a story about the ways balloons first "ascend" like "Swans," and then "set."

> Their Ribbons just beyond the eye –
> They struggle – some – for Breath –
> And yet the Crowd applaud, below –
> They would not encore – Death –

> The Gilded Creature strains – and spins –
> Trips frantic in a Tree –
> Tears open her imperial Veins –
> And tumbles in the Sea –
> (Fr 730, stanzas 3 and 4)

Perhaps most striking in this poem is that the speaker foregrounds the descent, not the rising, of a balloon, and that the descending balloon is feminine. This surprising focus is underlined by the speaker's opening reference to plural "Balloons" and then abrupt switch to the singular "Gilded Creature" at the precise moment of the narration in which the balloon both initiates its fall and is gendered: while ungendered balloons ascend "spurn[ing] the Air, as 'twere too mean / For Creatures so renowned – ," the lonely "Gilded Creature . . . Tears open her . . . Veins – / And tumbles in the Sea – ." Also striking is that the speaker seems as interested in the audience as in the event – as in the poem "The Show is not the Show / But they that go" (Fr 1270). Between the lines describing ungendered plural ascent and singular female fall, the speaker describes the crowd's response, and the conjunctions, "And yet," introducing the crowd's applause, demonstrate the disjunction between her or his expectation and the clerks': apparently, unlike the speaker, they cheer, then "retire with an Oath," dismissively observing "'Twas only a Balloon."

The poem presents the reader with many *obvious* puzzles. Among them is not the question of the speaker's gender. Perhaps, then, the reader must work backwards, through the performance of other aspects of this poem to the question of gender. For example, one reading might begin with the speaker's sympathy for the death of the "Gilded" feminine being – apparently a painted woman, suggesting the extremes of prostitute or actress, but perhaps also any woman whose livelihood depends on reputation or public respect, and who would hence feel obliged to hide her flaws or weaknesses through gilding. In the era of middle-class womanhood as "the angel in the house," this could be understood as the position of most women Dickinson knew. The poem may describe the progress of a woman's life as an undifferentiated communal childhood of swanlike ascent abruptly terminated by an adulthood of isolated vulnerability and disaster. This plot line is well known in popular mid-nineteenth-century fiction: good girl grows up, succumbs to temptation, and falls. In such a reading, the speaker's empathy might mark her as female, aghast at the unfeeling response of the applauding and indifferent clerks who, apparently, see only spectacle, just another balloon. Similarly, the speaker's implied difference from the masculine "Clerks" may mark her position as female.

In another reading, however, the speaker's tone could imply comic distance from both the clerks and the balloon. The exaggerated stateliness and nobility attributed to the balloon's initial ascent suggests a masculine idealization of feminine beauty and purity: in this well-known discourse, women were indeed "creatures" fabled to live in an atmosphere of such refined delicacy that even "Air" would be "too mean" for them. As feminist criticism has long shown, it is only logical that manipulators of this dehumanizing discourse would also condemn those who "struggle – some – for Breath" at this imagined, idealized elevation. "Creatures" who can't bear the height – in the light of such bipolar, patriarchal judgment – must be merely gilded, impure, and unworthy of masculine idealization; they deserve the metaphorical and literal fall described by the speaker – first melodramatically as torn veins and then casually with the phrase "And tumbles in the Sea." In such a reading, the reader might (like Betsy Erkkila) position the speaker (representing Dickinson?) as elitist, condemning the fallibility of more vulnerable women in reconstructing the clerk-like, masculinist relegation of women to either pedestalled purity or a fall.[13] Or, following the same tonal and coded reading of the poem, the reader might (as we are more inclined to do) see the speaker as critiquing the limited vision of such a patriarchal discourse through repeated reference to the attitude of the clerks. Or in another reading, the speaker may be trying to signal alternatives to this gender polarity by pointing to conventions of both feminine ("balloon") and masculine ("Clerk") behavior or perception. Perhaps the speaker tries to displace gender fixity here through questioning such norms. The reader's perception of the speaker's gender, then, is linked directly to the reader's perception of Dickinson's likely range of responses to the conventions of gender, apparently coded in the rise and fall of the balloon, the clerks' applause, and the general tone of the poem.

The fact that the poem itself focuses on the interpretation of female behavior typologically presented (the balloon), suggests that all questions of gender may be significant here and hence encourages the reader to attend to her own gender perceptions and choices. Our point, furthermore, is that such choices are virtually inevitable, and performative. Just as one does not dress, eat, walk, or talk thinking at every second that one is coding oneself as masculine or feminine, one makes assumptions about a speaker's tone, positionality, perspective, realm of discourse, and so on without necessarily recognizing such assumptions as participating in the performance of gender. Becoming conscious of these assumptions in relation to Dickinson's poems almost always alters, at least subtly, the attitude the reader can imagine of the speaker to the topic and language of the given poem.

performance – how to perform

5

in g of

What does the performance of a poem look like? To this point we have theorized an admittedly complex process. We would now like to present a reading, as the reading "I" performs the written "I" of "I would not paint – a picture – " (Fr 348). This poem overtly addresses the processes of reading and writing, and this reader's performance discovers how gender is importantly imbricated in their relationship. In the act of exploring the interaction between an initially feminized audience (reader) and a masculinized artist (poet), the poem and its own reader discover a critique and realignment of these dichotomized and eroticized gender positions, which is what enables the speaker, in the end, to imagine herself as *both* poet and reader.

As the reader, "I" find myself playing the speaker who identifies as what we will call a "reader." Since the poem progresses in parallel stanzas from the topics of painting to music to poetry, it seems both fair and useful to see the other arts as analogues for writing, which becomes the subject of the final stanza. And, since this all takes place in a poem, its artist is a poet. In the same way, then, "reader" here becomes a generic term for one who responds to art. As a whole, this well-known poem offers a passionate case for the powers of reading, except that at the end it springs a surprise. For suddenly it imagines reader and writer as not distinct from one another but as the same being.

"I would not paint – a picture – ," the poem begins. "I'd rather be the One / It's bright [fair] impossibility / To dwell – delicious – on – ." The poem's gendering of the artistic process, the relationship between writer and reader by way of the poem, helps to prepare for and explain the speaker's final desire to be the whole shebang herself – "herself" because, by the end of the first stanza, I, the reader, am identifying the speaker as feminine and performing her experience as such. I do this because the conventional gender markers of active/passive, agential/receptive seem to adhere, as the poem begins, to a masculinized artist and a feminized reader, whose feelings are "evoked" by the painter and the painting. She wonders "how the fingers feel / Whose rare – celestial – stir – / "Evokes [Provokes] so sweet a torment – / Such sumptuous – Despair – ." Her sufferings remind me of a heroine in a Gothic romance. So, as I perform the "viewing" experience that she describes, I see her/me in a white gown – as Emily Dickinson?

And yet this heroine is anything but passive, I discover as I act her script. She "dwell[s] – delicious" on the "bright impossibility" that is the painting; she herself performs, putting herself in the place of, the fingers that made the painting, imagining their "rare – celestial – stir –." What I find myself performing, in fact, is an erotic act – for those fingers are sparking in me (as reader twice over) the most intense of feelings: an extreme torment and despair that are not ladylike at all, so "delicious," "sweet," and "sumptuous" are they. The act of reading – a painting in this case – turns out to be anything but passive, I discover. So if I am a woman reader, the script is leading me down the garden path of agency / "masculinity," an experience that I find intriguing and enjoyable.

In stanza two, wherein the speaker "would not talk, like Cornets –" but would rather be the one "Raised softly to the Ceilings [Horizons] – / And out, and easy on [by] – ," the listener/reader of music gets busier yet, although again art is the agent of my experience. The journey that I enact as a kind of hot air balloon (a round, soft, feminine form) takes me to the ceiling and on through villages of ether into the skies of the imagination.

> Myself endued Balloon   [upborne/upheld/sustained]
> By but a lip of Metal –
> The pier to my Pontoon –

By the end of *this* stanza the musical instrument is not only the prompt or springboard for the important activity, my journey, but a lip or a pier to my pontoon. Again, I cannot ignore the erotic feelings stirring in me, especially as occasioned by that skillful lip. By the time I get to the third and final stanza, my own performance has been unconventionally feminine in its activity, expressiveness, and eroticism.

The third stanza purports to mirror the opening two: "Nor would I be a Poet – / It's finer – Own the Ear – ." I feel now that I am at the climax of the poem and of my readerly experience. Then why am I characterized suddenly as "Enamored – impotent – content," possessing but "The License to revere"? I may be enamored, but I certainly have been neither impotent nor content. As an actor, I can only play this *ironically*, as a reference to the kind of femininity I do not possess, the way the world might have understood the feminine reader before they saw my performance. I do adore the poem, and by way of it, the poet, but my reverence is an active thing, a privilege that is *awful* in its connotations of a reverence so strong as to invoke fear.

> A privilege so awful   [luxury]
> What would the Dower be,
> Had I the Art to stun myself
> With Bolts – of Melody!

Given the variant femininity that the poem has enabled me to enact, along with the demonstrated importance of the reading experience to this poem, what would the dower (gift of bride to husband, gift from the estate of dead husband to wife, or more simply, endowment or talent) be, if I possessed the art of arts – to be both poet and reader? The imagery is autoerotic now, an orgasmic moment that combines the phallic "Bolts" with the more feminine (in its pleasing tunefulness) "Melody." However, my performance itself has broken down these dichotomous positions. For the poet is always her own reader, performing her poem as she writes it; and the reader always becomes akin to a poet, in that her performance is a kind of re-"writing" of the poem. So this very poem, spoken by a persona who calls herself reader, is "really" spoken by a poet imagining herself as reader. Poetry and reading are both performances, after all. The writer of this poem is a woman who first presents her speaker as a reader, a reader whose femininity is interestingly inflected with masculine attributes. She then presents her speaker as hypothetical poet, whose gender by this point in the poem cannot be conventionally masculine. In other words, there is no "man" involved here but rather a series of bent gender positions for a woman to take, as Dickinson also intimates in "Drama's Vitallest Expression" with her "Romeo" or "Hamlet." A woman poet and/or reader, this poem suggests, can never be conventionally feminine. Most of Dickinson's plays on gender alterity take us ultimately to this starting place. By scripting gender experience into her poetic performances, she enables her readers as well to experience that uneasy but "delicious" experience.

Emily Dickinson was a nineteenth-century American woman poet who chose to write lyric poetry, a genre that highlights the performative in both its structures of language and its demands on the reader. Her fascination with the performance of gender, in particular, has much to do with her life as well as her art. As many have shown, to write poetry as a woman is itself a gender-bending act. In her life, Dickinson was not a political feminist. She generally adhered to gender conventions in dress and behavior appropriate to her class and race, although we should note, as many have done, that her various exaggerations and omissions can themselves be seen to constitute critique and alteration of these same conventions. In her writing, however, she played faster and looser with the forms and acts that might designate "woman," when "woman" is aligned with "poet." Her performances of gendered identity, both subtle and bold, utilize the gaps between acts of gender to enable the possibility for the breaking or subversive repetition of gender styles. She seems aware that these possibilities exist, enabling her to present such altered or even radical performances of gender.

And yet, although we have described and learned from these aspects of her performances, we do not want to characterize Dickinson as thoroughly postmodern. A woman of her time, she also posits an interior subjectivity: a "soul" or "heart" or "mind," such as the "Human Heart" of "Drama's Vitallest Expression" or the "unshaded" existence in "I tie my Hat – I crease my Shawl." For Dickinson, gender and other attributes or categories of personal identity, such as class, race, and sexuality, may well be socially constructed, but they are constructed upon a core of self that "goes on being," even though it might change its outer configurations in various fashions across time and experience. In lyric poetry, in particular, the gender of a speaker can be bent, varied, altered, challenged, or transformed as well as enforced, for poetry is a world dedicated to *living* "in Drama."

NOTES

1 While Elizabeth Phillips addresses performance in *Emily Dickinson: Personae and Performance* (Pennsylvania State University Press, 1988) she understands this concept as having to do with discrete, chosen moments of theatricality differentiable from non-theatrical behavior. All other work written on performance has to do with theatrical representations of Dickinson, primarily *The Belle of Amherst*. On theatricalizations of Dickinson's poetry, see Jonnie Guerra's "Dickinson Adaptations in the Arts and Theatre" in Gundrun Grabher, Roland Hagunbüchle, and Cristanne Miller (eds.), *Emily Dickinson Handbook* (Amherst: University of Massachusetts Press, 1998). On the importance of the reader's gender, see Robert McClure Smith's *The Seductions of Emily Dickinson* (Tuscaloosa: University of Alabamba Press, 1996).

2 Butler, *Gender Trouble: Feminism and the Subversion of Identity* (New York: Routledge, 1990), pp. x, xi.

3 Butler, "Performative Acts and Gender Constitution: An Essay in Phenomenology and Feminist Theory," in Sue-Ellen Case (ed.), *Performing Feminisms: Feminist Critical Theory and Theatre* (Baltimore: Johns Hopkins University Press, 1990), p. 271.

4 Layton, *Who's That Girl? Who's That Boy?: Clinical Practice Meets Postmodern Gender Theory* (Northvale, NJ: Jason Aronson Inc., 1998), p. 25.

5 S. W. Winnicott, *The Maturational Processes and the Facilitating Environment: Studies in the Theory of Emotional Development* (Madison, CT: International Universities Press, 1965), p. 60.

6 James William Johnson, "Lyric Poetry," in Alex Preminger, Frank J. Warnke, and O. B. Hardison, Jr (eds.), *Princeton Encyclopedia of Poetry and Poetics* (Princeton University Press, 1965; enlarged 1974), p. 461.

7 Cristanne Miller develops this idea at greater length in her essay "Subjectivity as 'Voice' in the Lyric Poem," in Paul Geyer, Monika Schmitz-Emans, Roland Hagenbüchle, and Claudia Junke (eds.) *Kritische Theorie des Subjekts im 20. Jahrhundert* (Würzburg: Königshausen & Neumann, forthcoming 2002).

8 See Robert Weisbuch, *Emily Dickinson's Poetry* (University of Chicago Press, 1975).

9 Butler, "Critically Queer," *Gay and Lesbian Quarterly*, 1 (1993): 17–32, here 22.

10 See Cristanne Miller, *Emily Dickinson: A Poet's Grammar* (Cambridge, MA: Harvard University Press, 1987).

11 Martha Nell Smith's reading of the poem, for example, in *Rowing in Eden*, emphasizes the disappointment of a woman who "finds that her new state of existence pales beside that promised by the seductive romances formulated by a

suitor." Smith notes the quotation marks around "wife" and "Woman," seeing them as sarcastic reminders to readers that they are appellations only, but does not comment on the presence of the word "Czar" (*Rowing in Eden: Rereading Emily Dickinson* [Austin: University of Texas Press, 1992], p. 186).

12 See, for example, Wolfgang Iser's *The Act of Reading: A Theory of Aesthetic Response* (Baltimore: Johns Hopkins University Press, 1978); Stanley Fish's *Is There a Text in this Class: The Authority of Interpretive Communities* (Cambridge, MA: Harvard University Press, 1980); and Michael Riffaterre's *Semiotics of Poetry* (Bloomington: University of Indiana Press, 1978).

13 See Betsy Erkkila, "Emily Dickinson and Class," *American Literary History* 4, 1 (Spring 1992): 1–27.

GUIDE TO FURTHER READING

Butler, Judith. *Gender Trouble: Feminism and the Subversion of Identity.* New York: Routledge, 1990.

"Performative Acts and Gender Constitution: An Essay in Phenomenology and Feminist Theory." In Sue-Ellen Case, ed. *Performing Feminisms: Feminist Critical Theory and Theatre.* Baltimore: Johns Hopkins University Press, 1990, pp. 270–282.

Fish, Stanley. *Is There a Text in this Class: The Authority of Interpretive Communities.* Cambridge, MA: Harvard University Press, 1980.

Flynn, Elizabeth A. and Patrocinio P. Schweickart, eds. *Gender and Reading: Essays on Readers, Texts, and Contexts.* Baltimore: Johns Hopkins University Press, 1986.

Guerra, Jonnie. "Dickinson Adaptations in the Arts and Theatre." In Gudrun Grabher, Roland Hagenbüchle, and Cristanne Miller, eds. *Emily Dickinson Handbook.* Amherst: University of Massachusetts Press, 1998.

Iser, Wolfgang. *The Act of Reading: A Theory of Aesthetic Response.* Baltimore: Johns Hopkins University Press, 1978.

Johnson, James William. "Lyric Poetry." In Alex Preminger, Frank J. Warnke, O. B. Hardison, Jr., eds. *Princeton Encyclopedia of Poetry and Poetics.* Princeton University Press, 1965, enlarged 1974.

Juhasz, Suzanne, Cristanne Miller, and Martha Nell Smith. *Comic Power in Emily Dickinson.* Austin: University of Texas Press, 1993.

Layton, Lynne. *Who's That Girl? Who's That Boy?: Clinical Practice Meets Postmodern Gender Theory.* Northvale, NJ: Jason Aronson Inc., 1998.

Miller, Cristanne. *Emily Dickinson: A Poet's Grammar.* Cambridge, MA: Harvard University Press, 1987.

"Subjectivity as 'Voice' in the Lyric Poem." In Paul Geyer, Monika Schmitz-Emans, Roland Hagenbüchle, and Claudia Junke, eds. *Kritische Theorie des Subjekts im 20. Jahrhundert.* Würzburg: Könighausen & Neumann, forthcoming 2002.

Phillips, Elizabeth. *Emily Dickinson: Personae and Performance.* Philadelphia: Pennsylvania State University Press, 1988.

Riffaterre, Michael. *Semiotics of Poetry.* Bloomington: University of Indiana Press, 1978.

Roman, Camille, Suzanne Juhasz, and Cristanne Miller, eds. *The Women and Language Debate: A Sourcebook*. New Brunswick, NJ: Rutgers University Press, 1994.

Smith, Martha Nell. *Rowing in Eden: Rereading Emily Dickinson*. Austin: University of Texas Press, 1992.

Smith, Robert McClure. *The Seductions of Emily Dickinson*. Tuscaloosa: University of Alabama Press, 1996.

Weisbuch, Robert. *Emily Dickinson's Poetry*. University of Chicago Press, 1975.

Winnicott, D. W. *The Maturational Processes and the Facilitating Environment: Studies in the Theory of Emotional Development*. Madison, CT: International Universities Press, 1965.

7

SHIRA WOLOSKY

Emily Dickinson: being in the body

> I am afraid to own a Body –
> I am afraid to own a Soul –
> Profound – precarious Property –
> Possession, not optional –
>
> Double Estate – entailed at pleasure
> Upon an unsuspecting Heir –
> Duke in a moment of Deathlessness
> And God, for a Frontier.
>
> (J 1090/Fr 1050)

In this poem Emily Dickinson seems at her furthest remove from Walt Whitman. His "I am the poet of the Body and I am the poet of the Soul . . . The first I graft and increase upon myself, the latter I translate into a new tongue" (Song 21)[1] in its inclusive, expansive energy poses the most extreme counterpoint to Dickinson's exclusions, retractions, and renunciations. I wish to argue, however, that Dickinson's work addresses cultural forces and challenges in ways continuous with Whitman's, although ultimately with a difference in cultural position from his, that remains fundamental.

The body, or rather the problem of embodiment, which this poem proposes, is a central figure, or site, in Dickinson's work. It intersects a range of forces or concerns both powerful and colliding. This begins with questions of identity that almost obsessively concern her. Such questions are multiple. They include her identity as a poet, where the very possibility of, or desire for, embodiment in a text and as language is highly ambivalent; her identity as a woman, both in terms of inhabiting a woman's body and of womanhood as

Poems 1050 and 788 are reprinted here by permission of the publishers and the Trustees of Amherst College from The Poems of Emily Dickinson, *Ralph W. Franklin, ed., Cambridge, MA: The Belknap Press of Harvard University Press, Copyright ©️ 1998 by the President and Fellows of Harvard College. Copyright ©️ 1951, 1955, 1979 by the President and Fellows of Harvard College.*

a figure for the body; her religious identity, in a broad metaphysical context of ambivalence towards material and temporal embodiment; and finally, her identity as an American, in terms of definitions of selfhood as these have peculiarly taken shape within the history of the United States.

In this poem, what must first be emphasized is the difficulty and obduracy of the text. Indeed, as often occurs in Dickinson, the text becomes more recalcitrant and opaque the longer one works with it. This textual obduracy is, in many ways, in itself a central Dickinsonian subject. Dickinson poems require the closest textual attention. They cannot easily be cited as evidence in an argument, since closer textual work almost always uncovers further readings and implications not easily resolved or subsumed into a summary statement. This is the case both within and between Dickinson texts. It is one of the first tasks of Dickinson criticism exactly to acknowledge and consider this textual multiplicity in Dickinson's work, but less as indeterminacy or open-ended ambiguity or (only) aesthetic play than as the deployment and mutual confrontation between personal and cultural forces that are deeply at stake for her.

What often occurs, as here, is that the texts propose a number of figural systems, on a number of different levels. These include sets of images, syntactic and formal relationships, off-rhyme and other complex prosodic patterns, and multiple senses or usages of individual words, each of which acts as a place of intersection between several possible references. The result is a highly structured text of extreme density. On the one hand, Dickinson's poems invite or promise a complex orchestration of the different figural levels she deploys. However, close attention to her language often discloses that the figural levels ultimately do not fully correlate with one another. A process that might be called figural mismatch, or slippage, instead occurs. The text, that is, promises to set up elaborate metaphorical analogues, reminiscent of the intercrossing figural levels of Renaissance metaphysical poetry. Different levels of experience seem to be images or metaphors for each other, to represent each other in an architectonic structure. This promise or implication of systematic, tight, even highly ornate correspondences, however, is then stymied. Instead, what is experienced is a resistance to just such correspondences. Figural correlation becomes figural slippage.

This figural slippage poses firstly a formal and textual challenge. In the case of "I am afraid to own a Body," the challenge unfolds through complications of analogy. The (fear of) owning a body and/or soul – and it is important that the soul is not privileged here, that Dickinson does not prefer to own a soul without a body – is, in itself, proposed as a metaphysical or religious topic. But it is developed in a language that is also economic: property, possession, and estate. At the same time, the structure of economy becomes increasingly gendered. Entailment is a specifically male form of inheritance; and "Heir" and "Duke" are both specifically male forms of inheritor. But of course "entailed" is at the same time a philosophical term, continuous with the poem's metaphysical opening, and resumed explicitly in the concluding reference to "God."

The poem thus introduces three levels to start: a metaphysical one, an economic one, and a gendered one. And, in the familiar structure of metaphorical transfer or analogy, we expect that these three will be brought into a relationship of mutual representation. But such correlation or transference does not fully occur. The poem's conclusion, for example, is peculiar. It oddly obtrudes spatial imagery for a God that by definition is spaceless, indeed, is utterly without and beyond body. This, of course, is unique neither to this poem nor to Dickinson. As Geoffrey Hartman remarks on a poem with certain similarities to this one ("Our Journey had Advanced," J 615), "the very idea of Eternity . . . cannot be represented by space and time categories [although] this does not explain why Emily Dickinson is haunted by a conception impossible to depict."[2]

In J 1050, too, the spatial imagery, while seemingly an attempt at locating God or locating the speaker in relation to God, at least in metaphor, is in effect no less dislocating, or dissolving into illocality. For the conclusion points, as Dickinson so often does, in at least two incompatible directions: "And God, for a Frontier." God as a frontier in one sense promises consolation, as the boundary or bounding principle giving shape or reference to a life. In another sense, this frontier-God or God as frontier may be bounding as a menace – inescapable, limiting, imprisoning. An American usage enters here. As Sacvan Bercovitch points out, the frontier only acquired its meaning of unlimited and expansive possibility in an American context; in Europe it had meant a fixed and inexorable boundary.[3] The poem plays on both senses. The second, limiting possibility recalls that the poem opens with the fear of owning a body and/or a soul, a fear tied to just these questions of imprisonment or limiting definition. Terms of hesitation or discomfort then continue throughout the text, with its sense of "precarious" property, imposed ("not optional") on one unprepared for it ("unsuspecting"). And yet, this language of hesitation appears alongside, or may itself comprise, expressions of exuberance. The property is also "Profound." In this sense its fragility (as "precarious") may be precious. "Unsuspecting" may suggest something unearned, but therefore all the more gracious, or unhoped for, in humility. These double possibilities come to special focus in the line, "Duke in a moment of Deathlessness." The title "Duke" may be a kind of play on Dickinson's own name, a sign of her nobility. And "Deathlessness" suggests just that immortality or transcendence or sublimity that the property, as precious inheritance, could bestow. And yet, this "Deathlessness" lasts but a moment; and "Duke" is a title that excludes Dickinson's gender, and that is alien to American social structures and laws of inheritance.[4] Indeed, the whole structure of property she evokes is one that doubly does not apply to herself: as a woman and as an American.

Dickinson seems to take away with one hand what she offers with the other. Economy and history remain in the poem, however, as figural representations of the text's initial (and then final) terms. These are terms of religion although, as we will see, not exclusively so. The poem almost encapsulates Dickinson's stance towards her religious inheritance in general, including its hierarchy of body and soul, or soul against body. That is, she is profoundly torn regarding her own inheriting of this tradition. There is an extent to which the Christian metaphysical tradition inevitably informs her work, and indeed never ceases to do so. Dickinson never entirely divests herself of the Christian, and specifically Calvinist, context in which she grew up in Amherst, although her relation to it is often one of rebellion and contention. The very fact that poems of more or less definite religious displacement or conflict take their place alongside poems of more or less religious devotion and conformity (and the arrangement is not simply chronological: there is no clear evolution in Dickinson's work from one stance definitively into another) argues for a continuous metaphysical pressure on her. This would not make Dickinson a "religious poet," nor is conversion from deprivation to transcendence in art, if not religion, her fundamental and overarching poetic structure. She is, instead, a poet of religious engagement, whose very criticism of religion reflects her deep involvement in it.[5] Adopting the trope of this poem, Dickinson's work as a whole may be called a "Double Estate," double and indeed contradictory in its orientation. It at once asserts a possible faith and, no less painfully, questions and denies such faith. This is the case in Dickinson not only regarding religion. The question is: what is at issue in her acceptance or her rejection, in her conformity and her resistance? What is her fear, and what is her desire?

We have come to that crux of doubling, of texts as somehow at odds or at cross-purposes in their internal structures and their mutual relationships, with which every Dickinson commentator ultimately must grapple. Dickinson texts, as here, both say and unsay, claim and disclaim, desire and decline, offer and retract, assert and deny, gain and lose, define and circumvent definition.[6] Whatever stance a poem seems to pursue, by the end it seems no less to unravel. Or, oppositional forces, or commitments, which are brought into headlong confrontation, seem to demand exclusive choices and sacrifice, often painfully, and almost always at great cost. In my own reading of this characteristic doubling or ambivalence, I see Dickinson's as a powerful agonistic voice, caught between incompatible visions, assertively critical of each of them, unable to resolve their contradictions nor yet able to reside comfortably in any of their competing claims. It is a poetry of anger, dissatisfaction, and critique; also of mocking, even wicked wit; and of sublimity, although often at painful cost. Attempts to reconcile Dickinson's dualities as though she desires not to desire, or as though she successfully converts restrictions and losses into a means of grace, therefore, do not do justice to the profound conflicts which Dickinson's verse dramatizes.[7] Dickinson cannot really have things both ways. Nor do her doublings coexist in a kind of suspended judgment or passive uncertainty, or as a detached contemplation of abstract possibilities, or even as aesthetic strategies, although her stances do strongly implicate a theory, or role, for art.

This aesthetic interest enters as a further level of figuration in J 1090. The body and soul that Dickinson on the one hand retreats from, but on the other hand longs for, also can suggest her literary inheritance, as it becomes embodied in her language. Such imagery of the embodiment of her own writing is proposed, obliquely or directly, in many poems. As she writes in one famous instance (in ways too complicated to explore here), the "Word" is made "Flesh" in poetry (J 1651/Fr 1715).[8] But Dickinson's stances toward textual, as toward other embodiments, tend to be, as in "I am afraid to own a Body," profoundly agonistic, or contesting. In another poem with much cross-imagery with "I am afraid," she writes, "To own the Art within the Soul" is "to entertain/ with Silence as a Company" (J 855/Fr 1091). True art is associated with silence. In this privileging of silence, there is an element of the Romantic sublime such as Roger Shattuck has discussed, in which Dickinson's resistance to full realizations in both expression and experience may reflect less a default than a "banquet of abstemiousness," a feast of moderation or abstinence. Within the tenets of a Romantic imagination, what is not always exceeds what is, with poetry a dwelling in such further "possibility" (J 657/Fr 466).[9] This structure of Romantic imagination as abstemiousness, or to follow Harold Bloom's anatomy of it, as one that makes the negation of nature or experience into the ground for poetic creativity,[10] is a vital force in Dickinson. But Dickinson's poetry further brings out the complicated relation between Romantic imagination and more traditional metaphysical structures. Romantic imagination in its own way continues to privilege an unrealized sublimity over concrete realization or embodiment, including embodiment in language. This Romantic privilege, however, refers not to a divine or dogmatic eternity, but to the further power and potential of the human imagination. The art work stands then as a positive sign to its own further productions, a promise that will never be completely fulfilled but which will ever open into still greater creative possibilities.

Dickinson's verse also invokes and asserts such a Romantic sublimity, not unlike Whitman's. But in her case the possibilities of artistic imagination are chastened, as are its resources in the self, by gender and by metaphysical scruple. For one thing, the body and soul she fears and desires to inherit in "I am afraid to own a Body" is that of a woman, who cannot be entailed heir to a ducal title. To be born into a woman's body is to be barred from such social resources of power. It is also to be precariously placed in metaphysical tradition; to be, if not barred, then subordinated within hierarchies of spiritual power, where the female has been long associated with body and emotion, as against a spirituality and reason represented as male.[11] But to enter into her embodied estate is generally to come under the liability of death, that frontier Dickinson so perpetually met with face to face, whether defined by God or by nothingness. Against more ordinary usage, "estate" here is not immortality but mortality. Yet to enter the mortal estate is also a kind of birth. The "Double Estate" is, in effect, nothing other than selfhood, which the terms "Property" and "Possession" also evoke. The self is oneself proper, one's self-possession, one's self as one's own. But this double estate as body and soul situates Dickinson's self precariously indeed. Fear, or ambivalence, at owning a body with a soul resonates with centuries of metaphysical hierarchy, or suspicion, according to which embodiment in the material and temporal world somehow threatens, if it does not betray, essential nature defined as intelligible, or spiritual, or eternal.[12] Being in the body is in this context a kind of philosophical pun, or paradox. For in the philosophical tradition, body has stood as opposite to being, although also as its sign, if only in a partial, attenuated and to some extent treacherous way. Within metaphysical hierarchy, the two are not equally legitimate resources for her, nor are they necessarily or entirely mutually confirming.

Here we glimpse some of the strained asymmetries that become evident in Dickinson's work. First, the ideologies of selfhood that Whitman or Emerson might pursue are different for Dickinson simply because of her gender. As Joyce Appleby remarks, liberal individualism in many of its strictures presumes "the human personality [to be] male."[13] For a woman within nineteenth-century culture, to achieve one's selfhood is also to subordinate it, as daughter and wife (motherhood seems to me to have its own distinctive structure and authority).[14] This would frame a general ambivalence to achievement, poetic as otherwise, which can be located in restrictive gender roles for nineteenth-century women. Dickinson's poetic, as indeed her biographical reclusion, reflects in complex ways (at once conforming to and contesting) social norms requiring women to be modest, retiring, or, as Dickinson suggests, hidden.

But these gendered positions also reach beyond the social into the religious realm. The kinds of identification with the divine possible for Whitman or Emerson is from the outset impossible for Dickinson. Her self cannot be a figure for God in the same way as theirs can, if only by virtue of a differently sexualized relationship, with all that this implies regarding authority and subordination, self-fulfillment and self-denial. And both the social and religious economies in turn implicate material ones. "Estate" is itself, in the poem, a metaphysical/material pun, while the property structure implicit in the poem reaches beyond selfhood to ownership (another pun that underscores their intimate relationship, especially in America). It is worth noting that several of the poems immediately surrounding this one in its fascicle set explicitly focus on economic imagery. In one, a "letter" from the world reports the stock market's "advance and Retrograde" (J 1089/Fr 1049). In another, Dickinson again equates her self- "Possession" as "Me" with the "Riches I could own" in "Dollars," an "Earldom," and "Income" (J 1093/Fr 1053). The poetic prospect opens toward questions of how far a self owns itself under God, how far a woman owns herself in relation to man, and also, how far identity in America is established through ownership, possession, and inheritance.

There remain, finally, questions of her own art, in consonance or contrast with the other forms of owning the poem may invoke. Dickinson is extremely self-conscious of the religious residue in Romantic language claims, and of its complicating effects. This is evident in any number of her texts, in which true art, and indeed truth itself, is aligned with silence as the sign of spirit as against the body of language. In a series of interrelated poems, a pun on "Mines" associates selfhood with valuable property, and in turn with true art as unspoken word, against a language that is told aloud, as when the word that "fails" is "A Rapture as of Legacies – / Of introspective Mines" (J 1700/Fr 1689). The same pun appears in "To own the Art within the Soul," where the truly owned art of "Silence" becomes an image of nakedness or disembodiment ("unfurnished Circumstance"), and also an image of spiritual property and selfhood: "Possession is to One / As an Estate perpetual / Or a reduceless Mine" (J 855/Fr 1091).

Dickinson in such texts brings together, but also breaks apart, the multiple levels of her identity, in terms of gender, art, religion, and history. Not every Dickinson poem brings all of these constructions together or situates them in the same ways. Sometimes gender is the prevailing structure, sometimes art, sometimes metaphysics. History is almost always brought to bear in a tangential fashion, often through an imagery of economy that is surprisingly pervasive. But, while Dickinson gathers into her texts these different engagements, seeming to promise they will serve as figural correlatives for each other, what often occurs instead is that they come into collision through ambivalent or contradictory representations. Instead of correlation, there is slippage. That the body, as in "I am afraid to own a Body," should be a peculiar crossing-point for these correlations and collisions accords with its equivocal status within the traditions of her culture. Both Dickinson's biography and her art are strangely marked with this equivocation. Her acts of reclusion – of herself in her house and her white dress, and of her poems, in her refusal to publish them, while nevertheless writing and collecting them in her fascicles – can be seen as acts of profound ambivalence towards owning a body and a soul, a way of being in the worlds of time and text, and yet withholding herself from them. These issues and images are reassembled, and also disassembled, in another well-known text that focuses on the body, but that makes questions of writing and publication its primary topic:

> Publication – is the Auction
> Of the Mind of Man –
> Poverty – be justifying
> For so foul a thing
>
> Possibly – but We – would rather
> From our Garret go
> White – Unto the White Creator –
> Than invest – Our Snow –
>
> Thought belong to Him who gave it –
> Then – to Him Who bear
> Its Corporeal illustration – sell
> The Royal Air –
>
> In the Parcel – Be the Merchant
> Of the Heavenly Grace –
> But reduce no Human Spirit
> To Disgrace of Price –
>
> (J 709/Fr 788)

Without entering into all the complexity of this text, I would like briefly to identify some of its basic figural constructions. First, there is a peculiar gendering, in that Dickinson on the one hand generalizes her statement in terms of "the Mind of Man," but also includes specifically feminine, biographical markers in her imagery of reclusion in "Our Garret" and of being "White," recalling her own habit of white dress. There is also a suggestion of gendering in the poem's imagery of prostitution, which, however, is not restricted to sexual sale. Rather, it becomes part of a second figural level involving economic language, in which selling is a betrayal of purity or fidelity or commitment. That this is offered as imagery of metaphysical alignments, where Grace as opposed to the dis-grace of "Price" has its own cultural history. Representing divine things in economic terms is a rhetoric that reaches back, in America, to the Puritan Fathers. This rhetoric was, perhaps, always unstable. Instead of subordinating material things to sacred ones, it risks doing the obverse. Terms of analogy may, after all, be converted in either direction. That very risk is what Dickinson exposes here. For here, instead of attempting a consistent analogy in which this world is a sign for the next world and material success a sign for spiritual grace, Dickinson's text suggests cracks or inconsistencies in the relationship between the terms. Economic gain becomes spiritual betrayal. To sell the "Royal air" is to debase it.

The economic, gendered, and metaphysical imagery are brought into further relation through the poem's imagery of the body. This in turn is developed through the poem's topical concern, publication. The poem's major site of ambivalence concerns its own production, or at least its status in a public, as opposed to a private, realm (where public and private are themselves gendered spaces in nineteenth-century discourse, with women restricted to the latter). To put her work before the public corresponds in the text's economic imagery to a foul auction, and in its gendered imagery to a kind of prostitution, a (sexual) betrayal of white purity. This corresponds in turn to religious imagery aligning publication with a betrayal of the next world (the "White Creator") for this one. And all of these come together in bodily imagery that is itself highly charged and highly conflicted. Publication is made a figure of embodiment: it is the "Corporeal illustration" of a "Thought" aligned with the spiritual and the divine. Such incorporation hence takes on all the valence of foul betrayal associated with auction, sexuality, and worldliness. But it corresponds also with the poem's own existence, at least as it becomes embodied in the text we are reading.

In this poem, Dickinson mediates these tensions to some extent by leaving open the possibility of some intermediate state between published embodiment and a textuality that is written, but not made public. Her fascicle mode of not publishing might represent just such a compromise, or mediating effort. Despite this compromise, or rather, in response to its riveting peculiarity, the poem remains precariously balanced between its callings. Dickinson remains torn, and dissatisfied with each of her options. It is as if Dickinson wants both to find a linguistic body for her poetry and yet also not to limit it; just as, in her white dress, she wants both to be in the body and to be bodiless; to be gendered and yet to be genderless; to be in the world and yet to be in the spirit, where these two remain in some sense antithetical. This recalls "I am afraid to own a Body," with its fear of owning a body or soul. There, too, Dickinson seems at once to negate and to affirm ownership, selfhood, God, and art. She hopes to inherit a precious (male) legacy; she fears to inherit a precarious estate. God is a sublime frontier of ever-opening possibility or desire; God is a repressive boundary. Language is positive embodiment; language is betrayal, liability, and confinement.

These counterposing directions represent severe and often painful conflicts – those that are not only personal to Dickinson, but also broadly reflecting her culture. Dickinson's texts are scenes of cultural crossroads, situated within the many and profound transitions taking place around her. These include the changing, indeed the tremendously dynamic, status of women in nineteenth-century America;[15] the no less dynamic countercrossing between religious tradition and secularizing forces; and emerging re-definitions of selfhood, both in art and in society, through complex intellectual, social and economic changes as the century evolves. The Civil War, during which Dickinson experienced a great burst of poetic energy and production, is a highly volatile moment in which such cultural tensions exploded.[16] This historical connection must be made against a resistance to history so often observed in critical discussions of Dickinson's poetry, responding no doubt to the poetry's own obliqueness. While it is impossible to elaborate this complex cultural moment here, I do wish to argue one specific point of context. The figural orders that Dickinson so forcefully evokes and interrupts in her poetry are those basic and precious to her surrounding culture. Their origins may be traced to the specific modes of Puritan religious and natural typologies, where the events of history and the world were interpreted as signs of divine intention. This figural or typological impulse did not simply die in the nineteenth century, but rather underwent transformations whereby the events of American life continued to be understood as moments in a universal drama of redemption, even if such redemption was increasingly claimed for history rather than eternity.[17] Not least, figural orders continue to structure a highly metaphorical Romantic art, through a typology of nature and the imagination, centered in the self but whose circumference extends infinitely through spiralling images and tropes of productive power and creativity. As Emerson writes in "Circles," using Pauline language: "We learn that God IS; that he is in me; and that all things are shadows of him."[18]

Dickinson inherits this figural order and method of interpreting her world, with its implicit claims that the various levels of experience and of identity are mutually confirming and culturally coherent. This is the case for Whitman as well. Whitman, in his stupendous and extravagant figural energy, is intent on creating a poetry, and indeed an America, in which each aspect of experience can serve as a figural transformation, or as he calls it, translation, of each. Material prosperity is a sign of spiritual possibility. The self is a sign of a community of love; the American world is a constantly evolving figure of worlds to come. Each poem generates and transforms into further poetries of Romantic imagination. And the body is an articulate sign for the soul, so that he declares, "I am the poet of the Body and I am the poet of the Soul... The first I graft and increase upon myself, the latter I translate into a new tongue" ("Song" 21). Yet in Whitman, this figural project is far from secure. Indeed, it is haunted by a fearful skepticism that such a figural poetics of America is not quite the case, that these ongoing correlations do not in fact hold.

In the case of Dickinson, such skepticism dominates and intrudes directly into the figural construction. She too ranges across a variety of levels of language and experience, in a textual architecture that seems to correlate one with the other. But then the correspondences slip, or break apart, or contradict, or misalign. Or, they realign, but only at the cost of one of their commitments. To inherit as duke is not to inherit as woman. God is welcomed, but also shunned, as frontier. Sublime imagination, or religious immortality, is announced, but not necessarily as coherent figures for each other, and elusively, for only a moment, seeming to be produced by language construction, as if "Deathlessness" comes into being through the abstract compounding of its word. The bodies of the self and of language are both claimed and feared. These analogical slips are not, however, signs of a loss of linguistic control or of mere incoherence. They, rather, textually enact a kind of cultural slippage in which a female gender complicates or contradicts assertions of an American or Romantic selfhood; material progress in the world subverts or opposes, rather than realizes spiritual longings; self-fulfillment contests self-denial; and body remains in tension with soul, including poetic embodiment as against some pure artistic essence. There are many entries into Emily Dickinson's verse: psychobiography, Romantic aesthetics, philology, formalist and theoretical issues, history, religion, and gender. Her work indeed encompasses each of these. But it particularly does so in ways that expose the complex and often tense relationships between these various concerns. The result is a work that remains at once formally explosive and culturally engaged.

NOTES

1 Walt Whitman, *The Complete Poems*, (New York: Penguin, 1975), p. 83.
2 Geoffrey Hartman, "The Voice of the Shuttle," in *Beyond Formalism* (New Haven: Yale University Press, 1970), p. 349.
3 On the American as against European meanings of frontier, see Sacvan Bercovitch, *The Rites of Assent* (New York: Routledge, 1993), p. 51.

4 Carl Degler, *Out of Our Past* (New York: Harper and Row, 1959), p. 103; 3-4; 44-5. Cf. Marshall Harris, *Origin of the Land Tenure System in the United States* (Ames: Iowa State College Press, 1953), p. 373. Although entailment structures of inheritance were officially outlawed in the United States Constitution, in 1791, they had never taken root in the New World, although some attempts were made in the South to establish a British structure of landed gentry. What of course took root in the South instead of fuedal forms of inherited nobility was the plantation system of slavery.

5 For this view of Dickinson, see Jane Donahue Eberwein's *Dickinson: Strategies of Limitation* (Amherst: The University of Massachusetts Press, 1985), p. 40.

6 See, for example, Suzanne Juhasz's article, "Reading Dickinson Doubly," in S. Juhasz and C. Miller (eds.), *Emily Dickinson: A Celebration for Readers* (New York: Gordon and Breach, 1989), pp. 217-21; also Barbara Packer's essay in the same collection, "Emily Dickinson's Riddles"; and Gary Lee Stonum, *The Dickinson Sublime* (Madison: University of Wisconsin Press, 1990).

7 See, for example, Sharon Cameron, *Choosing Not Choosing* (University of Chicago Press, 1992); and Eberwein's *Strategies*.

8 For further discussion, see Shira Wolosky, *Emily Dickinson: A Voice of War* (New Haven: Yale University Press, 1984).

9 Roger Shattuck, "Banquet of Abstemiousness," *New York Review of Books*, 20 June 1966, pp. 55-9.

10 See, for example, Harold Bloom, "The Central Man," in *The Ringers in the Tower* (University of Chicago Press, 1971).

11 There are many discussions of this association of woman with body. See Elizabeth Spelman, "Woman as Body," *Feminist Studies*, 8, 1 (Spring: 1982); R. H. Bloch, "Medieval Misogyny," *Representations*, 20 (Fall: 1987) 1-24; Judith Butler, *Gender Trouble* (New York: Routledge, 1990), etc.

12 For a full history of this ambivalence against the body and specifically its implications for attitudes toward language, see Wolosky, *Language Mysticism* (Stanford University Press, 1994).

13 Joyce Appleby, *Liberalism and Republicanism in the Historical Imagination*, (Cambridge, MA: Harvard University Press, 1992), p. 1.

14 Most feminist readings of Dickinson focus on this point of subordination, either as a gendering of artistic power (see Joanne Feit Diehl, *Dickinson and the Romantic Imagination*, [Princeton University Press, 1981]) or in the context of nineteenth-century culture (see Joanne Dobson, *Dickinson and the Strategies of Reticence* [Bloomington: Indiana University Press, 1989]).

15 For a comparison between our own time and the nineteenth century as periods of transition and backlash, see Susan Bordo, *Unbearable Weight: Feminism, Western Culture and the Body* (Berkeley: University of California Press, 1993).

16 For a discussion of Dickinson's relationship to cultural issues in the Civil War, see Wolosky, *A Voice of War*.

17 For the continuity and transformations of figural interpretation in American culture, see Bercovitch, *The Puritan Origins of the American Self* (New Haven: Yale University Press, 1975); and *Rites of Assent*.

18 Ralph Waldo Emerson, *Selections*, ed. Stephen Whicher, (Boston: Houghton, Mifflin 1960), p. 172.

GUIDE TO FURTHER READING

Appleby, Joyce. *Liberalism and Republicanism in the Historical Imagination.* Cambridge, MA: Harvard University Press, 1992.

Bercovitch, Sacvan. *The Puritan Origins of the American Self.* New Haven: Yale University Press, 1975.

The Rites of Assent. New York: Routledge, 1993.

Bloom, Harold. "The Central Man," *The Ringers in the Tower.* The University of Chicago Press, 1971.

Bordo, Susan. *Unbearable Weight: Feminism, Western Culture and the Body.* Berkeley: University of California Press, 1993.

Butler, Judith. *Gender Trouble: Feminism and the Subversion of Identity.* New York: Routledge, 1990.

Degler, Carl. *Out of Our Past.* New York: Harper and Row, 1959.

Diehl, Joanne Feit. *Dickinson and the Romantic Imagination.* Princeton University Press, 1981.

Dobson, Joanne. *Dickinson and the Strategies of Reticence: The Woman Writer in Nineteenth-Century America.* Bloomington: Indiana University Press, 1989.

Eberwein, Jane Donahue. *Dickinson: Strategies of Limitation.* Amherst: University of Massachusetts Press, 1985.

Emerson, Ralph Waldo. *Selections,* ed. Stephen Whicher. Boston: Houghton, Mifflin 1960.

Harris, Marshall. *Origin of the Land Tenure System in the United States.* Ames: Iowa State College Press, 1953.

Hartman, Geoffrey. "The Voice of the Shuttle." In *Beyond Formalism.* New Haven: Yale University Press, 1970.

Juhasz, Suzanne. "Reading Dickinson Doubly," in S. Juhasz and C. Miller (eds.). *Emily Dickinson: A Celebration for Readers.* New York: Gordon and Breach, 1989, pp. 217–221.

Packer, Barbara. "Emily Dickinson's Riddles," in S. Juhasz and C. Miller (eds.). *Emily Dickinson: A Celebration for Readers.* New York: Gordon and Breach, 1989.

Stonum, Gary Lee. *The Dickinson Sublime.* Madison: University of Wisconsin Press, 1990.

Whitman, Walt. *The Complete Poems.* New York: Penguin, 1975.

Woloky, Shira. *Emily Dickinson: A Voice of War.* New Haven: Yale University Press, 1984.

Language Mysticism. Stanford University Press, 1994.

8

DANEEN WARDROP

Emily Dickinson and the Gothic in Fascicle 16

To enter into the experience of reading a Dickinson manuscript is to relinquish previous notions about the effect of her poetry. The manuscripts of Emily Dickinson provide a playground for this singular poet who wished to experiment with word variants, framing of stanzas, idiosyncratic enjambment, and dashes that ascend, descend, shorten and lengthen.[1] Studying any one Emily Dickinson fascicle, the reader begins to notice the dialogues that the poems carry on with each other. They carom off each other, and the movement doesn't stop, so that when the reader returns and reopens the book, the voices still vibrate. This is the case for Fascicle 16, a grouping of poems that demonstrates a skillful interplay of Gothicism and the problems inherent in identity formation. The fascicle supplies all the accouterments of Gothic effects – apparitions, mirrors, windows, smoke, ghosts, things that wink in the gloaming, lightning, a funeral, repetitious beating sounds, and eerie depths – but it also widens out in other poems to encompass larger questions of the unity of identity.[2]

In Fascicle 16 we can see particularly well how Dickinson works within the conventions of an established genre, Gothicism, which by this time she was accustomed to using, in order to turn to more difficult questions of how an identity is formed. The experience of a disjunctive identity, one of the hallmarks of modernism and postmodernism, is an area Dickinson pioneered. While this essay does not range far from the conventional wisdom of Dickinson studies in claiming her as the foremother of modernist and postmodernist poetry, it does find a new avenue for her modernism by tracing it through Gothicism.[3] The Gothic poems of Emily Dickinson function as extremely effective works that, like classic Gothic novels, titillate, frighten, and inspire dread in the reader. Dickinson's poems represent prime specimens of the genre; in addition, however, Dickinson utilizes her Gothic proclivities in order to give physical, palpable verity to the pressing questions of selfhood in latter nineteenth-century America. She needed to feel her way through to a modernist breakthrough, and Gothicism provided the instrument of breakthrough.

Inaugurating a concern with the process of identity or subject formation, Dickinson predates the concerns of poets writing in the decades after her. When the status of the subject becomes confounded, to the point of becoming fractured or even indistinguishable, needless to say, the identity of the "I" is in jeopardy. This jeopardized "I" thoroughly informs modernist and postmodernist works of the twentieth and twenty-first centuries. Julia Kristeva, in discussing modernism, characterizes the modernist text as one that fragments reality and often, in so doing, shatters itself. She identifies the new element in the modernist text as the position of the "splitting subject in conflict who risks being shattered."[4] This splitting, conflicted, shattering subject forms the primary concern of writers of the last century preoccupied with demonstrating the vagaries of a modernist or postmodernist existence that endangers the unity of the speaker. The dangers posed to the speaker prove thoroughgoing, constituting changes "in the *status of the subject* – his relation to the body, to others, and to objects" (p. 15). Kristeva understands language, ruptured as it is in the modernist text, as threatening to the unity of the individual, and while it is not the purview of this essay to explicate Kristeva's theories on subjectivity, her basic notions of modernism, including the shattering of the speaking self, highlight Dickinson's movement toward the modernist poem. Dickinson's co-optation of Gothicism allows her the leeway to apprehend this new notion of subjectivity. Gothicism, with its inherent dissolution of identity, provides a natural segue to a consideration of the splitting subject.

The first part of this essay will examine Gothic conventions, and the second part will turn to the vexed condition, as Dickinson sees it, of modern subjectivity, all within the purview of Fascicle 16, which not only demonstrates Gothicism and modernist identity, but also provides a showcase for some of the reasons we should read Emily Dickinson in manuscript form. Encountering a fascicle in Franklin's *Manuscript Books* leads a reader to reassess involvement with Dickinson's poems. The handwriting squirms on the page. The dashes so uniform and nearly regulatory in Johnson's print editions become less like scaffolding. In the manuscripts the dash instead seems to destabilize the lines, goring and tossing language about. The white space so prominent in print versions of Dickinson's poems shrinks, so that in the manuscripts the lens enlarges and the handwriting dominates the page. Fascicle 16 registers for the reader all of these impressions and some intriguing features in addition, including two deletions, a blank page, and a flap attached to the end of the final poem. One of the shorter fascicles, it contains eleven poems that play off each other in engaging ways, and our investigation of Gothicism and subjectivity will include an appreciation of the distinctive facets of Dickinson's handwritten manuscripts.

The Gothic heart of Emily Dickinson's Fascicle 16 encompasses the lurid, secret, ghostly, and deathly. Poem Fas 16.6, "'Tis so appalling – it Exhilarates – " (Fr 341), is the sixth poem of the eleven, with five poems on either side, in the exact center of the fascicle.[5] I have termed the poem elsewhere "metagothic," a condition in which a work defines Gothicism even as it conveys Gothic effects. Dickinson could not have been unaware that she placed this poem at the heart of Fascicle 16. These opening lines, as follow, purvey an excellent example of the dichotomy at the core of Gothicism: *appalling exhilaration*:

> 'Tis so appalling – it Exhilarates –
> So over Horror, + it half Captivates –
> The Soul stares after it, secure –
> + To know the worst, leaves
> No dread more –

Dickinson plays the opposites of the appalling and the exhilarating against each other in good Gothic fashion. Gothicism, as identified by Sigmund Freud's notion of the uncanny in his article *"Das Unheimliche,"* depends upon the melding, or even mistaking, of oppositions.[6] The German word for "uncanny," *das Unheimliche*, means, interestingly, both home and homely. In other words, the meaning of the word rests precisely upon its opposite, both what is comfortable and homey, and what is uncomfortable, eerie, and decidedly un-homey. The twist of the Gothic inheres in the psychological fact that what can scare the most remains what is closest. What happens right in the home – especially the dynamics of family, and even more especially, what has been repressed within the family – is what makes for the most thrilling scare. Dickinson proves herself skillful at purveying such frights, for she finds the Freudian twist in her oxymorons – the appalling exhilaration so to speak, the captivating horror, the liberating fright, the freeing terror.

She couldn't have captured the definition of Gothicism better. Her metagothic poems exemplify the oscillating nature of Gothicism; they seem to rest on one side of the oxymoron – say, what is exhilarating – only to turn at a moment's notice to the other – what is appalling. This Gothic dread is compounded by reading Dickinson poems in the manuscript versions. There are several ways in which the fascicle version of the poem can help us appreciate the Gothic flavor of Dickinson's poetry more than print versions can. For instance, Dickinson's handwritten enjambment causes more clipped lines in the poem than the print arrangement, so that we discern the last line of the first stanza, "No dread more – " as deserving of attention on its own. It is worth noting, of this line, that in the Johnson reader's edition (the long-accepted and conventional version of Dickinson poems), Johnson opted for "A Sepulchre, fears frost, no more – " (J 281), instead of "To know the worst, leaves/ No dread more – ." As Johnson's edition does not supply variants, the poem appears finished and finally edited with that line, and hence that version has become the staple. While both lines are Gothically evocative, I find the fascicle version, with its metagothic emphasis on the relationship between knowing and dread, worth, at the least, equal consideration. Moreover, the fascicle's line draws attention to the verb, "leaves," a word of loss, which hangs in suspense.

That Dickinson has a premium on suspense can be seen in the metagothic description of suspense as a kind of sawing: "Suspense kept sawing so – ." The activity of sawing describes a constant back-and-forth motion, the same back-and-forth dynamic essential to causing goosebumps in the best suspense stories. Even the directors of C-grade movies know suspense comes from the kind of relentless sawing that Dickinson describes. Indeed, the poet delivers such intensive "sawing" that she follows the bald, cold truth with a hint of relief in prayer (which doesn't help), and the dread of death, with a moment of relief when she seems to toss us a pillow for our cheek. Such comfort is not lasting, of course, because the saw must slide in the opposite direction, hence the effects of horror once more intensify:

> Others – Can wrestle –
> Your's, is done –
> And so of Wo, bleak dreaded –
> come,
> It sets the Fright at liberty –
> And Terror's free –
> Gay, Ghastly, Holiday!
>
> (Fr 341)

The word, "come," in the final stanza, demands a line to itself in the fascicle. As a one-word line it proclaims its potency, a plenary word that plays on erotic expectation as well as suspenseful *dénouement*. It announces that the worst has happened. The worst has come.

Almost the worst: the most macabre and frightening enjambment occurs in the penultimate stanza, with the two-word line, "your Cheek." Less emphatic in print versions that incorporate the two words into a more tame, seven-word line, the fascicle renders the line as follows:

> Looking at Death, is Dying –
> Just let go the Breath –
>
> And not the pillow at
> your Cheek
> So Slumbereth –   (Fr 341)

Interestingly, the page break occurs after "Just let go the Breath – ," an instance in which the physical rendering of the poem on the page underscores the activity endorsed. The fact that the activity is frightening, perhaps hinting at suicide, makes the physical representation all the more mortifying. I want to emphasize, though, the two-word line, "your Cheek," which even more emphatically afflicts the reader with Gothic chills. The line gathers its punch because the poem has abruptly made an about-face from the first-person plural ("we" in the third stanza) to the second person, which the line, "your Cheek," announces. The second person point of view in Dickinson proves very rarely to be friendly, often pointing a finger, and in this case it proves as cold and as bald as the truth the poem finds. The two-word line registers powerfully this unsettling change in point of view, using a kind of horrific syntax. In fact, near the middle of the poem that occupies the center of the fascicle, Dickinson suddenly puts the onus of the fear in "your" hands – literally, in your bed, if we take the pillow seriously. The poet could not get much closer to the reader. In an *Unheimliche* way, the poet cannot scare much closer to home.

Dickinson carries the second person point of view into the final stanza, where the reader's dilemma ("Your's" [sic]) is finally, and very personally imaged; that is, it too engages the second person. That second "yours" renders the "Gay, Ghastly, Holiday!" of the final line, replete with exclamation mark, ineluctably the reader's. Dickinson has thrown the Gothic in our lap, and we're stuck in the center with it. Moreover, the word "holiday" carries overtones of the *Unheimliche* oxymoron. A holiday, or holy day, gains resonance from the mention of prayer earlier, in the third stanza. That Dickinson makes her holy day ghastly can only put our sense of security as readers into further jeopardy. In some important ways Dickinson pits what we know as the cold, bald truth against what some might pray for, to the extent that they allow hope to enter. The gay, ghastly holiday finds a moment of certain knowing, and what is known is that terror is free to do its insidious work. In the middle of the comma-stumbling "Gay, Ghastly, Holiday!" exist many reversals of oxymoronic fear, and it is all yours, reader.

As Dickinson pits the opposites that constitute Gothicism against each other in the middle poem, Fas 16.6, she does so in the fascicle-at-large, too. A well-known poem in Fascicle 16, "I like a look of Agony," (Fr 339),

Fas 16.4, captures precisely this conundrum of opposites existing *in toto*. Dickinson captures the homey/homely paradox succinctly with the phrase, "homely Anguish" a condition she applauds in the poem. "I like a look of Agony" further offers the metagothic insight that the Gothic operates on bodily reflexes – convulsions and throes, and the beads of sweat on the forehead. As Dickinson's condition for poetry predicates itself upon bodily reaction, her attraction to the jitters and hair-raisings caused by Gothicism is easy to comprehend. Dickinson wrote to Higginson the following: "If I read a book [and] it makes my whole body so cold no fire ever can warm me I know *that* is poetry. If I feel physically as if the top of my head were taken off, I know *that* is poetry. These are the only way I know it. Is there any other way" (L 342a).

There is not any other way – at least not in these poems. Not at the heart of Fascicle 16, not as we are left with a pillow to clutch, and nothing to know except that which is dreadful and ghastly. What we know includes the ability "To scan a Ghost" (Fas 16.6), which is faint, ethereal and otherworldly, and the best we can hope is that suspense might be superseded by death, which Dickinson describes as "Easy" by comparison. In this way she designates Gothic "sawing" as the most macabre and torturous of states. In the "sawing," too, she locates an important pun. In that we speak of seeing as understanding and comprehending, we can observe Dickinson figuring both kinds of seeing plentifully in this central poem (stares, know, scan, grappling, truth, hold, sure, show, know, looking, wrestle), so that the "sawing" must incorporate an ungainly pun for both what has been seen and what has been known. As the sawing motion cuts back and forth it becomes harder than ever for the reader to know what is seen and what is known. Here Dickinson provides the ultimate suspense of the Dickinsonian Gothic.

That suspense inheres throughout other poems in the grouping, especially on either side of the sixth, middle poem. For instance, the poem immediately preceding the middle poem, "'Tis so appalling – it Exhilarates – ," is the well-known, "I felt a Funeral, in my Brain," (Fr 340), Fas 16.5. The Gothic maneuvers herein are manifold: a Poesque repetition found in the beating sounds of words, a grisly suspense building in the syntax and parataxis ("and then, and then"), numbness, altered consciousness, after-death experience, the victimized female subject, and severe uncertainty on the part of the speaker. The poem also privileges the aural, a staple of Gothic texts, in which the visuals become so dim and obscured that the reader feels blind, and must rely on a finely attuned sense of hearing. We traverse through "I felt a Funeral, in my Brain," relying heavily upon our hearing so that, like the speaker, in the next to last verse, we feel our beings have become an ear.

Along with the speaker, we feel the fragility of experience that no longer depends on seeing (knowing) but upon hearing (what might finish knowing, at least as we have experienced it).

Another strange dissonance emerges when we study the fascicle manuscript – we can see the relatively rare occasion of a word crossed out. "I like a look of Agony," immediately preceding "I felt a Funeral," evidences another deletion, with the crossing out of the phrase, "Death, comes," just before the beginning of the second stanza. The experience of reading these two words that Dickinson struck through with three lines is a major part of the experience of reading the manuscripts that is lost in print culture, and reinforces the sense that the poem is elastic, in process, a workshop entity, and alive. The struck words form the most visually prominent part of the manuscript poem.

In "I felt a Funeral, in my Brain," Dickinson substituted the word, "Soul," for the crossed-out word, "Brain," in the third stanza, but the substitution does not indicate a multiple choice, as do the variants, which are indicated by cross marks. The intention in the case of this third stanza is clear (I use caret marks here to show the deleted word):

> And then I heard them
> lift a Box
> And creak across my <Brain>
> Soul
> With those same Boots of
> Lead, again,
> Then Space – began to toll, . . .

Dickinson may have decided upon the deletion so as to avoid the repetition of "Brain" from the first line, but this seems unlikely, as she doesn't flinch from repetition elsewhere in this poem or others. More likely, there exists a kind of equation of brain and soul, a kind of thinking in God, or prayer in cognition, that underlies her notion of what it is to be a conscious human being. Perhaps, too, this strange equation accounts for the stoppage of knowing at the poem's unresolved finish.

Accordingly, another feature of the fascicle poem involves the appearance of word variants directly subsequent to the last line of the poem, so that the variants appear to be the last line. The variants add a valency of indeterminacy to an already highly indeterminate ending. In all the other poems of Fascicle 16 the word variants appear after a definitive spacing, obvious indentation, or slash drawn between the end of the poem and the list of variants. Such relatively definitive formatting does not occur with the word variants of "I felt a Funeral, in my Brain." In this case the final line and the line of variants appear in such a way as to be indistinguishable by formatting, as follows:

> And + Finished knowing – then –
> Crash – + Got through –

With the same value, visually, the two lines in conjunction with each other tempt us to read them, at least upon first perusal, as lines of equivalent value in the poem. Such a temptation renders further disruptions and permutations of knowing, more than the poem has already been understood to contain in print versions. Further, the word, "Crash," proves startling, especially given that the poem has induced in us an already highly sensitized sense of hearing.

Directly following the middle poem, "How noteless Men, and" (Fr 342), Fas 16.7, also turns the tables on our sensory perceptions. Bookended with, and in contrast to, "I felt a Funeral, in my Brain," it seems to ask us to defray our sense of hearing in order to privilege the visual. We see this in the first stanza, in which notelessness is invoked, a lack of the aural, in favor of the "sudden sky" that might reveal something. The privileging of the visual, though, is suggested only to be snatched away:

> How noteless Men, and
> Pleiads, stand,
> Until a Sudden sky
> Reveals the fact that
> One is rapt
> Forever from the Eye –

The subject of the above, "How noteless Men, and," is the "Members of the Invisible," a revealing topic, given that the eye offers so significant a sense for the reader here. We strain to see what cannot be seen, what becomes "rapt" from the eye. It is telling that in the 1929 publication of this poem, editors altered the word "rapt" to read, "wrapt." Dickinson's word, "rapt," opens up the possibility of an implicit pun on what is hidden and what is open, whereas the editorial "wrapt" fails to encourage such a double-edged meaning. The rapt/wrapt nature of revelation is, curiously, one of the major themes of the fascicle.

The pith of the rapt/wrapt nexus demonstrates the means by which faith can turn to Gothic despair, light to murkiness, revelation to secret: one is *rapt* with transcendence; one is *wrapt* with secret.[7] It demonstrates the means by which the *Unheimliche* can creep into the soul, turning a spiritual phenomenon into something cryptic. Further, a nexus can appear to us even more prominently when we read the manuscript poems because of

Dickinson's placement of the poems within the fascicle. For instance here in Fas 16.7, the speaker, throughout the course of the poem, seems to hope to hear word of the invisible people, but in the last line the heavens pass by "Without a syllable – ." Both sight and hearing are confounded, both religious and Gothic expectations. Both the experience of death and that of the after-life finish with an annihilation of knowing. The annihilation of knowing constitutes the anti-resolution of both poems directly enclosing the center poem of Fascicle 16.

The eleven works of Fascicle 16 are organized around a Gothic gore, with "'Tis so appalling – it Exhilarates – " at the center, and the poem, "How noteless Men, and" following it, and "I felt a Funeral, in my Brain" preceding it. It may be that such a metagothic work as Fas 16.6 and such a frightening full-blown Gothic work as Fas 16.5 provide a sort of grounding in bodily sensation and a touchstone of fear (after all, Dickinson likes agony because she knows it's true) so that she can undertake experimentations in subjectivity on either side of that center. Further, a similar pattern inheres in the entire fascicles before and after Fascicle 16. In Fascicle 15, the dead-center poem, "If I may have it, when its"' (Fr 431), exemplifies perhaps the most grisly of all Dickinson's Gothic poems, describing the yearning to possess and stroke a corpse. In Fascicle 17, the center poem is "If Anybody's friend be dead" (Fr 354), which arguably includes necrophilia, and the poem immediately following it constitutes another of Dickinson's most gruesome productions, "It was not Death, for" (Fr 355), a surreal Gothic landscape of dread and despair. Such an overview, accounting for the inter- and intra-arrangements of fascicle materials argues for the need to read Dickinson's poems in manuscript form as well as in print versions.

I do not believe such a stellar poet as Emily Dickinson consciously designated artificial patterns that she wished her poems to uphold by manipulating the order of her poems. Dickinson, in fact, is famous for eschewing order, as can be seen in a letter she wrote to Higginson claiming that "when I try to organize – my little Force explodes – " (L 271). I do believe, however, that when a poet sits down with her works the poems suggest, by their own integrity, an associative placing or shuffling found by propinquity and kitty-corneredness and unaccountable sparkings that occur when poems' boundaries begin to chafe against each other. Moreover, characterizing such an associative placement can be useful in seeing yet one more radius of meaning through the poems of Emily Dickinson, and hence the necessity for fascicle study.

I turn now to poems in which we will examine subjectivity, poems that form a volatile world in which identity remains always in process, where syntax consumes itself, where oppositions dissolve and intermingle.

Dickinson's work in the Gothic form allowed her more leeway to explore new avenues of consciousness, and ironically, by utilizing the somewhat clunky apparatus of the Gothic, she enabled herself to achieve new effects. She pursued not just the standard creepy-crawly effects, but the more delicate ontological questions of subjectivity. She extended the freedom advanced in the supernatural elements of the Gothic to enter into issues that have come to characterize modernism and postmodernism, such as what constitutes the individual self and the other self. Some of the strategies Dickinson employs to explore subjectivity include the following: a punning on the word "eye" to parallel the "I," an offering of dimness as opposed to lightness as constitutive of self-knowledge, the repetition of "mine" providing the insistent syntactic scaffolding for a poem, the "I" divested of the material world finding itself in isolation, the phasing of consciousness that appears especially in her vexed pronoun usage, and the trading of perspectives (between the dead and the alive, between the male and the female) which constitutes the condition of looking the "*other way.*"

In the technique of looking so as to see the "other way" Dickinson's Gothic style culminates, and it is from this vantage that she can begin her modernist and postmodernist exploration of the disintegrating, problematic subject. I offer a postmodernist, long view of the fascicle by way of looking at the first two poems of Fascicle 16 in juxtaposition with the final two. Finally, I will investigate the closing poem of the fascicle, Fas 16.11, to see the ways in which Dickinson problematizes gender so as to illuminate the uncanny construction of subjectivity. In this final poem she practices reverse gendering, an experiment in the dislocation of self that shows discrepancies in male and female behavior codings.

The initial poem of Fascicle 16, "Before I got my Eye put out – " (Fr 336B), Fas 16.1, announces that its topic targets individual consciousness, with both the "I" and its homonym, "Eye," prominent in the first line. The ostensible topic is vision, but the topic actually announces the lack of vision after having been able to see before, hence suggesting the Gothic penchant for dimness and obscurity. Words of light and seeing are again legion: eye put out, see, Eyes (know no), sky, stars, Noon, eyes, Lightning's jointed Road, look at, Window pane, eyes, Sun. It is no coincidence that the editors of the 1891 *Poems* entitled it "Sight." Yet, the artificial 1891 title provides only the faintest glimmer of what occurs in the poem. What takes place constitutes nothing less than the speaker's introduction of a new way of seeing – a way of seeing without the eye (and sometimes, frighteningly, without the "I"). Dickinson broaches the contrast between dimness and vision, harking to the contrast between the wrapt and the rapt, in the first line of the first poem of Fascicle 16, where light and darkness defy the boundaries of opposition.

From the very outset of the world of Fascicle 16 the greatest vision results from the most darkness.

The poem inaugurates the issue of self, the "I" that stands behind the insistent repetition of "mine." For the speaker, conventional sight is tantamount to possession; when she could see, before, the entire world was "mine" – the meadows and mountains and forests and stars. In fact, the repetition of "mine" sets up the syntax for three of the poem's five stanzas. One of these, the fourth stanza, shows not only the thrill but the danger of looking, when seeing is commensurate with being:

> The Motions of the Dipping
> Birds – + Morning's Amber Road –
> The + Lightning's jointed Road –
> For mine – to look at when
> I liked,
> The News would strike me dead –

Looking is owning, to a transcendentalist, but Dickinson turns this transcendentalist truism on its ear. For instance, the transcendentalist Emerson ascribed ownership to looking; because he could see the view of his neighbor's property, he owned it. Dickinson seems to consider the Emersonian way only to reject it at the end of this poem. Such viewing, rich as it may be, proves to be too much for the speaker, for she finds demise in such excess. Emerson accrues vision to himself; Dickinson limits it so as to claim the wealth of strangeness inherent in the action of limitation.

The stanza above warrants interest additionally because of the proposed variant that is present not as postscript to the poem but within the very workings of the stanza itself. Johnson chose the phrase " + Morning's Amber Road – " for his reader's edition to the exclusion of the phrase seemingly preferred in the fascicle, " + Lightning's jointed Road – ." The fascicle offers both phrases, with the first phrase, probably a variant, jotted above the second. While my transcription here cannot make obvious the prominence of "Lightning's jointed Road – ," a look at the fascicle manuscripts will confirm its primacy. Probably Johnson made the choice of "Morning's Amber Road – " because he worked from a version sent in a Higginson letter rather than from the fascicle. As a result of Johnson's choice, "Morning's Amber Road – " has become the standard version, and the phrase, " + Lightning's jointed Road – " relatively overlooked. The phrase concerning lightning goes much further to emphasize the fear of sight: the flash that can blind, or the jointedness of a road seen in such sudden light, or the forked journey of duality, or the consciousness that must consider dichotomy and consider it in a moment's apprehension. The phrase, " + Lightning's jointed Road – ," hence, proves important to the twin considerations of dimness and vision. And, the news that would strike the speaker dead commensurates with the fearful powers of lightning.

The point is that Dickinson's speaker would rather use her soul than her eyes; she would rather intuit with the sight given to her soul than have the full light of reason:

> So safer – guess – with just
> my soul
> Upon the window pane
> Where other creatures put
> their Eyes –
> Incautious – of the Sun –

Some things we see better in the dark. The line, "my soul," underscores the decision the speaker makes in this poem: the speaker would rather see with her soul. (The two-word line, "my soul," recalls, in its choice of soul over knowledge, the poem, "I felt a Funeral, in my Brain," in which Dickinson favored the word, "Soul," over the crossed-out word, "Brain.") The usual boundaries of self drop away in this final verse of "Before I got my Eye put out – " so that all that remains is a bodiless soul against a window pane – surely a divested "I" in the usual sense of "I."

The second poem of the fascicle, "Of nearness to her sundered" (Fr 337), continues with the meditation of the divested self. The self in this poem, too, has lost everything that a material world might use to define the "I" and, similarly, the self is the soul. In addition, this poem contemplates the powers of dimness and vision:

> Of nearness to her sundered
> Things
> The Soul has special times –
> When Dimness – looks the Oddity –
> Distinctness – easy – seems –
>
> The Shapes we buried, dwell
> About,
> Familiar, in the Rooms –
> Untarnished by the Sepulchre,
> + The Mouldering Playmate Comes –
>
> In just the Jacket that he
> wore –
> Long buttoned in the Mold
> Since we – old mornings,

> Children – played –
> Divided – by a world –
> The Grave yields back her
> Robberies –

At this point, at which the grave yields her robberies, the manuscript page ends – inviting the sawing suspense that arises as we expect the ghost to arrive from the dead – before the stanza proceeds to deliver exactly that apparition on the next page. We find undeniably Gothic elements in the poem in the forms of dimness, shapes, burial rooms, mouldering, mold, grave, robberies, apparitions. Indeed, the "Mouldering Playmate," a gruesome phrase, harkens straight from a lineage that can be traced from before to after Dickinson, from the eighteenth to the twentieth century, Horace Walpole to Edgar Allan Poe to Wes Craven.

The point of view of the poem designates the consciousness of one who is dead and has returned home, to the things of her material existence that no longer belong to her now that she is incorporeal. The soul's sight, in one of the "special times," can apprehend earthly things clearly. The vision of the soul seems to prompt and grant the special vision of the speaker in the second stanza, who speaks from the point of view of "we," the living. The poem's uncertainty delays this first-person-plural point of view until the final stanza, however. The entire back-and-forth phasing of perspective between the third person and the first-person plural proves unsettling, to say the least, and the bridge between the bodiless and the embodied soul appears to be the body of the mouldering playmate. Through this playmate's body that, in grisly fashion, has been "Long buttoned in the Mold," the two parties conjoin in an uncertain time reference and uncertain ontological status.

I call this perspective a phasing of consciousness, and Dickinson uses it as an uncanny way to elicit chilling effects, as well as a Gothicized way to elicit the problems of self-identity. One of the means by which Dickinson intensifies self-and-other disjunction is by utilizing exacerbated pronoun shiftings. She accomplishes this phasing of consciousness in many poems, and the Gothic repercussions are palpable; more than ever we become disoriented, such disorientation providing the mounting fear that saturates Gothicism. The modernist implications likewise mount, the self-and-other disjunction marking exactly the uneasy territory of the last century of poetry. Two excellent examples of such pronoun disjunctions, the odd constructions "themself" and "ourself," occur in the final stanza of the above poem, "Of nearness to her sundered":

> As we – it were – that perished –
> Themself – had just remained

till we rejoin them –
And 'twas they, and not
ourself
That mourned.

_____ _____ _____

+ Our

In this stanza we see Dickinson utilize "Themself" and "ourself," both compound pronominal constructions exemplifying her employment of plural words in the first syllable and singular words in the second syllable of the constructions. Such conflation of plural and singular elements in a word that designates the self can only prove highly disconcerting.

We can corroborate our sensations of reading discomfort by seeing that the editors of the *Atlantic Monthly* changed Dickinson's pronoun constructions. The refamiliarized constructions in the 1929 *Atlantic* version of the poem read "Themselves" and "Ourselves." Dickinson's macabre constructions, however, were no mistake: they serve to highlight the strangeness of being an "I," when "them" and "our" intrude into the self. Indeed, the entire poem describes this strangeness of perception that includes both one and another at the same time, re-merging and dividing in a way that resists articulation by any rational means.

Just so, the mourning is not of the living for the dead, but the *other way*. In many aspects, Fascicle 16 targets, precisely, the condition of perceiving in the other way, when self becomes other and other becomes self, and the boundaries of identity prove emphatically permeable. If we turn now to the back of the fascicle, we can see in Fas 16.9, "'Twas just this time, last" (Fr 344), a similar phasing of consciousness, an exacerbation of self and other, and an encomium of seeing the other way. This poem follows directly the fascicle's blank page – appropriately so – as the poem is spoken by one who has died. That the speaker might have had to pass through a page of nothing in order to find her voice in the text seems fitting. Her voice echoes the voice in "Of nearness to her sundered," except that the earlier voice speaks in the third person, whereas this voice speaks in the first person and more immediately. Like the earlier returning soul, this one sees clearly the people and things of the material world, and misses them. Also as in that poem, the dead grieve the living instead of the living grieving the dead. The speaker decides to think in this manner she calls the other way:

But this sort, grieved myself,
And so, I thought the other
way,
How just this time, some

perfect year –
Themself, should come to me –

In this poem, too, the wonderful, spooky, ragtag, and by now, familiar pronoun "Themself" was changed by editors to the more tidy "themselves" in the 1896 *Poems*. Another significant editorial change involves the important second and third lines of the verse, "And so, I thought the other/way." In 1896 the two lines were revised and condensed to one: "I thought how it would be." Scandalously inept, the tame revision doesn't come close to capturing the disordered and brilliant consciousness of a dead speaker who turns the tables on expected ways of thinking and being, who in the sweep of two short lines can turn "they" into me, and "I" into "them."

The divergent usages of pronouns occur so often throughout Dickinson's work as to suggest that she used one voice against another voice in order to attain a multivocal effect.[8] In particular, we can identify in Fascicle 16 oscillating, or phasing, pronominal strategies, that shift and shift again, from first person singular to first person plural. Within the course of the eleven poems of the fascicle the point of view oscillates between "I" and "we" and "you" many times, offering multivocal possibilities that comment on a radically unstable self. The speaker's original situation does not satisfy her so she changes not her situation but her way of thinking about it; she phases it, so that upside-down becomes inside-out, way becomes other. In addition, the radical enjambment of the fascicle's "other/way" only underscores the otherness of the mode of perceiving and being.

Finally, let's turn to the resolving poem in Fascicle 16.[9] In "He showed me Hights I" (Fr 346B), Fas 16.11, a male character shows the speaker heights she never saw. We automatically remember the strange seeing of the first poem, so that the fascicle circles back on itself. The poem Fas 16.11 proposes an exacerbated way of seeing that forms a primary attribute, as we have noted, for both Gothic and modernist patterns throughout Fascicle 16. The enjambment in the fascicle version renders the first line so that the oppositions of "he" and "I" bolster either end of the line. As we will see, this poem in its different versions allows us to consider not only severe pronoun disjunction but a powerful example of looking the *other way* in terms of gender.

Dickinson offers in "He showed me Hights I" the distinctive feature of the use of dialogue. This is not unheard of in Dickinson's poems, but it is not the rule, and the dialogical approach unfolds and elucidates this final poem whereby Dickinson delineates oppositional and phasing positions. The two positions for the conversation in "He showed me Hights I" elucidate gender dynamics, power dynamics, considerations of the after-life, techniques of rhetoric and communication and, in the final stanza, the epiphanic result of such positionings. The first stanza begins in dialogue:

> He showed me Hights I
> never saw –
> "Woulds't climb" – He said?
> I said, "Not so".
> "With me – " He said –
> "With Me"?

First of all, the two-word line, "never saw," recalls the primary topic of vision and "sawing," especially as "never saw" is echoed by "not so" two lines following, so that the condition of what one sees and the condition of what is rival each other at the outset. The phenomenon of "sawing" has governed the texture of Fascicle 16 throughout, and the trope demands return in this culminating poem. Further, to add to the manifold ways of seeing, this poem presents a way of seeing that can reach altitudes, in heights the speaker has never seen before. Yet she demurs to climb these heights, rejecting his offer.

The reader detects a slightly menacing tone in the seducer's voice, in his insistence and persistence in offering climactic ascension. His repetition ("with me, with me") recalls the Gothic thrumming and echoing in "I felt a Funeral, in my Brain" near the center of the fascicle ("treading – treading – ," and "beating – beating – ,"). Supercilious, he seems to exhibit disbelief that she might choose not to respond to him, that she might choose not to climb given what he sees as the irresistible condition of himself as guide. His language is persuading; hers, with the clipped "Not so," the more measured. He continues his sexual overtures, as described by her:

> He showed me secrets –
> Morning's nest –
> The Rope the Nights were put
> across –
> "And now, Woulds't have me
> for a Guest"?
> I could not find my "Yes".

He tries to induce her compliance by showing her secrets, perhaps a prelude to sexual secrets. The first image is sweet, maternal, domestic. The second recalls the tactics of Radcliffean Gothic, in accord with the eighteenth-century novels of Gothic author Ann Radcliffe, who would inevitably explain away all her uncanny effects in the last chapter. Here the secret of

night is simply a circus trick, a magic show, a ludic moment that need not
be fear-inducing at all. Provocatively, the manuscript arrangement argues for
a sexual interpretation, given the line break after the proposal, "Woulds't
have me." That she responds the way she does makes it seem as if she con-
siders answering affirmatively, but cannot find it in herself, or cannot find it
in language, to do so.

What happens next in the fascicle demonstrates a wonder of suspenseful
posturing, and it seems impossible that Dickinson did not understand that
she manipulated the physical text in this way. The fascicle, as an entity
stitched together, finishes with two lines, but after that, a small, pinned-on
flap carries through with the final lines. Below are the two lines, after which
I indicate the break between fascicle proper and fascicle flap by adding a
space after the two lines:

> And then – He brake His Life –
> And lo'
>
> A light for me, did
> solemn glow –
> The + steadier, as my
> face withdrew
> And could I further
> "No"?
> + larger –

In the printing of Johnson's 1955 three-volume edition of poems, he reported
the second part of this poem still missing, and supplied the lines after "lo"
in brackets, assuming their existence because of another version of the poem
sent to Susan Gilbert Dickinson.

Franklin explains the flap by suggesting that Dickinson "pinned it as a
verso" (Fr, p. 334). A writer cannot possibly use material text to greater
effect in heightening suspense. The false ending of, "And lo'" recalls the
climaxing use of the last word, "then – " in "I felt a Funeral, in my Brain,"
after the repetition of "and then." "Lo'" carries no dash or comma after it,
which lends heightened anticipation. Literally, we must hold our breath after
the "lo" at the bottom of the page – Johnson must have had to hold his
breath for many years – until we find the pinned flap and can continue in
this poem that quests for heights. Once we reach the flap, we behold the
light promised throughout the fascicle, in solemn glow. The ending light derives both from the vocabulary of religion and the vocabulary of Gothicism.
Dickinson again plays the trick of reversed perspective: a light shouldn't
glow steadier as one recedes, of course; it should grow dimmer. Such a light
can be seen as both inspired faith and uncanny, Gothic apparatus.

The primary question of the last poem, however, remains, "And could I further/'No'?" To "further no" uses memorable syntax to ask if the speaker can further her discourse of no, a kind of other-world of negative perceptions. Does a woman ensnared in a seductive circumstance reach a point at which it seems there is no way to win, no way to further her refusal by continuing to say no? This interchange suggests an awful – and horrific – reality, for the question of the speaker locates the dilemma for those in the speaking position of women in our culture.

The "No," moreover, possesses a line of its own, and because elsewhere Dickinson states that "no" is the "wildest word," we can see dual possibilities for no – both horror-filled and, paradoxically, freeing. The wild "no" indicates a negative capability, where "Terror's free – ," and where we might find a gay, ghastly holiday. Kristeva's modernist, revolutionary poetics are furthered by rejection, by the no, by the nothing that rankles; such revolutionary poetics reverses the positioning of the subject. Kristeva asserts that the modern text had to "take up the entire economy of the subject . . . and reverse it" (*Revolution*, p. 187). In other words, modernist literature takes the precepts of self-identity and switches them – sees them the other way. In "He showed me Hights I," Dickinson demonstrates how the economy of the subject, the I, is affected by the need to reject, as in the rejection of seducer by seduced (the quintessential Gothic relationship between master and young woman). Also, the speaker rejects language as it proceeds in the conventional expectations we have for it – that is, well-behaved pronouns in predictable subject positions.

Kristeva emphasizes the reversal – the revolutionary text that takes up the entire system of the subject expressly in order to "*reverse* it." As if Dickinson hasn't reversed enough expectations for her poetics, in this finale, with the reverse effect of the light for instance, she gives us an additional, exciting opportunity to see reverse gender tactics, when we compare this poem with another version of the poem. The other version, "I showed her Hights she never saw – " (Fr 346A), does not appear in the fascicle but, as noted earlier, was sent in a letter to Dickinson's sister-in-law and good friend, Susan Gilbert Dickinson, and signed, "Emily – ."[10] In this letter version of the poem, the seducer is the speaker, a female, speaking from the point of view of the first person. The seduced is also female: "I showed her Hights she never saw – /'Would'st Climb,' I said?/She said – 'Not so' – /'With *me*' – I said – 'With *me*?'" By contrasting the two versions we can revisit our understandings of the subject's identity.[11] Herein lies a tour de force of pronoun interactions that, in a significant way, question gender relations.

Some of the major differences between the two versions include the lack of capitalization for the two females in the second version, whereas the male pronoun in the fascicle poem is capitalized. The capitalized "He" may indicate that the male character is God, or that he represents a secular master figure, or simply that the man-seducer is perceived by the woman as powerful. Unlike the fascicle seduction poem, the letter version of two females contains no stanza breaks, a difference that delivers the poem all in one breath, hence rendering it less measured and clipped in tone. In addition, the poem of female-female seduction includes copious usages of italicization (four instances, as opposed to none in the fascicle version). The italicization brings the tone of the personal into the poem, italics heralding the diction of emphasis and possibly passion. Perhaps it even intimates private jokes between the two women. The italics may afford an emotional vulnerability to the voice of the female seducer (now the "I") that the male seducer lacks. In the letter version both instances of the word "*me*" have been accorded stress, so that the speaker sounds nearly desperate. She also stresses the word "*now*," which appears after she has shown the woman she addresses the morning nest and night ropes and before she renews her case. While pressing her case, this female speaker's use of italics causes her to seem aware of and perhaps even frightened of her own temerity. The italics may also indicate that she remains more aware of how invested she is in response, which the male speaker doesn't parallel, remaining more distant.

These may appear subtle distinctions, given a capitalized letter here and an italic there, but let's examine in detail a part of the poem to determine the effect of the voice that, similar in words, reads very differently in diction given such delicate discrepancies in voicings. Here I will cite the final four lines of the female-female seduction poem:

> And then, I brake my life – And Lo,
> A Light, for her, did solemn glow,
> The larger, as her face withdrew –
> And *could* she, further, "No"?

Here the speaker loses the one she desires, whose face withdraws even as the lovelight of the speaker grows, a perspective on the light divergent from the fascicle version. In the fascicle the speaker reports the light growing steadier, presumably as she imagines it in the mind of the seducer. In the letter poem, the speaker herself can report firsthand that the light grows larger. The italicized "*could*" of the letter version can seem melancholic, despondent, unrequited. In the letter version, the female seducer has the final say, so that our sympathies might be more prone to stay with the desperate seducer, as opposed to the fascicle version, where the seduced has the final say, hence claiming our sympathies. The commas placed in the last line of the letter version slow the pace and add pathos to the ending question, once again inducing our sympathy with the seducer. The female-female dynamic may describe a relationship of more equal power, at least on the emotional level at which the character can claim the reader's sympathies.

Thus, the poem in its two versions proves far from definitive, far from certain, far from leaving any speaker in any fixed speaking position. It is just like Dickinson to *reverse* the entire equation, telling the story from a radically different gender positioning, which of course does not tell the same story at all. Whereas in the more conventional male-female story, the female must be at all times circumspect about power differential, and hierarchy remains a structure that both parties constantly maneuver to situate and understand themselves from within, in the same-sex story, the relationship suggests diffused authority and responsibility rather than hierarchy. The same-sex relationship offers the possibility that it remains parallel as opposed to laddered, eschewing dichotomy, and interpenetrating.

These considerations elucidate just some of the ways that we can appreciate the reading experience afforded by Dickinson's poems. While I have strayed outside Fascicle 16 here to observe the peculiarities of a version that can be paired with "He showed me Hights I," the peculiarities of the fascicle itself have led me to look at the particular themes of this pair. Dickinson's cross-gendering of the poem's versions severely calls into question the expectations for subjectivity of nineteenth- and, for that matter, twentieth- and twenty-first-century readers. She manipulates our readings so as to show the revolutionary workings of Kristevan *reverse* that shatter our comfortable expectations about the unity of identity. Through reversal, Dickinson writes revolutionary, modernist poetry that shakes our sense of subjectivity, and makes us wonder if identity may, after all, be recuperated in such a world where modulations never cease, and phasings continually rearrange the self. She makes us feel it in a way that we can't deny. It's hard to shake off such trenchant lessons in thinking the other way.

Grappling with some of the concepts we have come to see as modernist and postmodernist – in particular struggling with the concept of the "I" as tenuous, transitory, undefinitive, ruptured, and sometimes difficult to distinguish from another – proves difficult yet, by now, familiar terrain for us. For Dickinson, though, such concepts of fractured ontology were pioneering and iconoclastic. In exploring such new and dangerous territory, she may have needed a guide, and she used the conventions of the Gothic to steer her to her new "I." The Gothic came as close as any established form could come to purveying a sense of disintegration of the world, the reversal of reality. Dickinson brought that sense of disintegration and reversal to the self, as we can see illustratively in "I felt a Funeral, in my Brain." Here we encounter the "I" both dead and alive, both knowing and not, both controller and victim of the story's telling. Kristeva's positing of a shattered subject serves well to indicate my reading experience of Dickinson, where I, as a reader, feel constantly in danger of disintegration, just as the "I" of the speaker dissolves and resolves itself into new pronoun formations. Dickinson's Gothicism jump-starts her modernism, and Fascicle 16 shows us the workshop of her attendant explorations, moving from macabre Gothic milieu to exploded modernist self.

NOTES

1 Sharon Cameron's *Choosing Not Choosing: Dickinson's Fascicles* (University of Chicago Press, 1992) brilliantly identifies these and many other characteristics of the manuscripts. In the fascicles, Dickinson gathered artistic power by having it all ways, as Cameron asserts, both choosing and not choosing variants. Other early proponents of reading the manuscripts on their own terms include Susan Howe, *The Birth-Mark: Unsettling the Wilderness in American Literary History* (Hanover: University Press of New England, 1993), and Martha Nell Smith *Rowing in Eden: Rereading Emily Dickinson* (Austin: University of Texas Press, 1992). More recently critics have contributed manuscript studies as, for example, those by Marta Werner, *Emily Dickinson's Open Folios: Scenes of Reading, Surfaces of Writing* (Ann Arbor: University of Michigan Press, 1995), and Dorothy Huff Oberhaus, *Emily Dickinson's Fascicles: Method and Meaning* (University Park: Pennsylvania State University Press, 1995). See also Domhnall Mitchell's "Revising the Script: Emily Dickinson's Manuscripts," *American Literature* 70 (1998), 705–37, assessing Dickinson manuscript studies.
2 Any observations about Dickinson's Gothicism stem from my work, *Emily Dickinson's Gothic: Goblin with a Gauge* (University of Iowa Press, 1996).
3 David Porter's *Dickinson: The Modern Idiom* (Cambridge, MA: Harvard University Press, 1981), argues that Dickinson exists as the exemplar of American modernism. Porter, by the way, does not expressly discuss Gothicism as a catalyst for finding modernist effects.
4 Julia Kristeva, *Revolution in Poetic Language*, trans. Margaret Walker (New York: Columbia University Press, 1984), p. 187.
5 I provide my own transcriptions of the fascicle poems from the Franklin *Manuscript Books* (Fas), rendering as well as print culture will allow the original line breaks, word variants, etc. When I first mention the poem, however, I will give the poem number according to Franklin variorum numbering.
6 "The Uncanny," in *The Complete Psychological Writings of Sigmund Freud*, trans. James Strachey (London: Hogarth Press, 1953), vol. XVII, pp. 217–56.
7 Mark Edmundson might be understood to see a kind of rapt/wrapt nexus in his exciting study of Gothicism, *Nightmare on Main Street: Angels, Sadomasochism, and the Culture of the Gothic* (Cambridge, MA: Harvard University Press, 1997). Edmundson sees the Gothic as imbedded in American culture; whereas in earlier centuries the Gothic would have operated in opposition to religion, current popular

culture values horror as it operates in opposition to transcendence. He pits the twentieth-century Gothic against what he calls a culture of facile transcendence, exemplified by TV talk shows such as Oprah Winfrey's, wherein participants find easy self-revelation.

8 Paul Crumbley argues for Dickinson's heteroglossia of voices in his book, *Inflections of the Pen: Dash and Voice in Emily Dickinson* (Lexington: University Press of Kentucky, 1997).

9 While I do not discuss in detail every poem in Fascicle 16, the few omitted poems also resonate with the themes and techniques of the ones discussed, including different types of vision, indeterminacy of the self, and the interweavings of the perspective of speakers before and after the grave.

10 Prominent among those who have argued for Susan Gilbert Dickinson as Emily Dickinson's artistic confidante and possible lover is Martha Nell Smith in her fine book, *Rowing in Eden: Rereading Emily Dickinson* (Austin: University of Texas Press, 1992), and also Smith and Ellen Louise Hart in *Open Me Carefully* (*OMC*). Notably, Paula Bennett (*Emily Dickinson: Woman Poet* [University of Iowa Press, 1991]) and Lilian Faderman (*Surpassing the Love of Men: Romantic Friendship and Love Between Women from the Renaissance to the Present* [New York: Morrow, 1981]) have also discussed lesbian imagery in Dickinson's poetry.

11 Vivian Pollak, for instance, identifies several Dickinson poems along with Fr 346 (Fr 57, Fr 277, Fr 1242, and Fr 1602) in which "alternate versions change the genders of pronouns" in *Dickinson: The Anxiety of Gender* (Ithaca: Cornell University Press, 1984) p. 136.

GUIDE TO FURTHER READING

Bennett, Paula. *Emily Dickinson: Woman Poet.* University of Iowa Press, 1990.

Cameron, Sharon. *Choosing Not Choosing: Dickinson's Fascicles.* University of Chicago Press, 1992.

Crumbley, Paul. *Inflections of the Pen: Dash and Voice in Emily Dickinson.* Lexington: The University Press of Kentucky, 1997.

Edmundson, Mark. *Nightmare on Main Street: Angels, Sadomasochism, and the Culture of the Gothic.* Cambridge, MA: Harvard University Press, 1997.

Faderman, Lillian. *Surpassing the Love of Men: Romantic Friendship and Love between Women from the Renaissance to the Present.* New York: Morrow, 1981.

Freud, Sigmund. "The Uncanny." In *The Complete Psychological Writings of Sigmund Freud.* Trans. James Strachey. London: Hogarth Press, 1953. Vol. XVII, pp. 217–56.

Howe, Susan. *The Birth-Mark: Unsettling the Wilderness in American Literary History.* Hanover: University Press of New England, 1993.

Kristeva, Julia. *Revolution in Poetic Language.* Trans. Margaret Walker. New York: Columbia University Press, 1984.

Oberhaus, Dorothy Huff. *Emily Dickinson's Fascicles: Method and Meaning.* University Park: Pennsylvania State University Press, 1995.

Pollak, Vivian R. *Dickinson: The Anxiety of Gender.* Ithaca: Cornell University Press, 1984.

Smith, Martha Nell. *Rowing in Eden: Rereading Emily Dickinson.* Austin: University of Texas Press, 1992.

Wardrop, Daneen. *Emily Dickinson's Gothic: Goblin with a Gauge.* University of Iowa Press, 1996.

Werner, Marta. *Emily Dickinson's Open Folios: Scenes of Reading, Surfaces of Writing.* Ann Arbor: University of Michigan Press, 1995.

CULTURAL CONTEXTS

9

DAVID S. REYNOLDS

Emily Dickinson and popular culture

Although the myth of Dickinson's alienation from her society is slowly dissolving, it has not been sufficiently recognized just how open she was to forces within her surrounding culture. In some ways, of course, Dickinson was the quintessentially *private* poet. It is also important to note, however, that she had a keen eye on American popular culture and drew poetic sustenance from it.

Indeed, there is evidence that she had a deep, frustrated desire for popularity. As a family acquaintance, Mrs. Ford, wrote to Mabel Todd, "I think in spite of her seclusion, she was longing for poetic sympathy and renown, and that some of her later habit of life originated in this suppressed and ungratified desire for distinction." Dickinson herself did at times express this desire for fame, as when she remarked to her sister-in-law Sue, "Could I make you and Austin – proud – sometime – a great way off – 'twould give me taller feet – '" (*LED*, p. 378). She once recalled that she and her cousin Louise Norcross had "in the dining-room decided to be distinguished. It's a great thing to be great, 'Loo,'" she remarked. Although she could adopt a pose of literary shyness before the *Atlantic Monthly* editor Thomas Wentworth Higginson, writing to him that publication was as "foreign to my thought, as Firmament to Fin," the fact remains that she sent this leading man of letters six poems in response to his call for pieces from "new or obscure contributors" (*LED*, pp. 378, 539). Her thirst for fame and popularity sometimes surfaces in her poems, as when she writes that her "Holiday" will be "That They remember me," and her "Paradise" will be "the fame – / That They – pronounce my name –" (J 431).

If fame was the "Paradise" she fantasized about, then she was destined for paradise. Time would prove that her poetry could have strong appeal for the mass audience. When her *Poems* were posthumously published in 1890, the first edition went through six printings in as many months and eleven editions in the first two years, a remarkable sale for a poetry volume, then or now. While it is true that this volume's strong sale is partly explained by the editors' careful tailoring of her poetry for the masses – by regularizing its punctuation and so forth – the later rediscovery and reprinting of the original fascicles, in all their awkward glory, in no way diminished Dickinson's popularity, among critics as well as general readers.

A major reason for her enduring popularity is that she was extraordinarily receptive to the popular literature and culture of her own time. She was thoroughly familiar not only with classic literary sources – especially the Bible, Shakespeare, Keats, the Brontë sisters, Elizabeth Barrett Browning, Emerson, and Thoreau – but also with many popular contemporaries that have since fallen from view. Her poems and letters reveal that she was a highly receptive witness of many phenomena in nineteenth-century popular culture, including imaginative sermons, reform movements, penny newspapers, best-selling novels, and women's literature. She was unique among American women of her day in the breadth of her awareness of the most experimental tendencies in contemporary American culture. Much of her poetry can be viewed as an individualistic adaptation of popular literary strategies.

For example, she felt the impact of the widespread shift in popular religious discourse from the doctrinal to the imaginative. Between 1800 and 1860, popular sermon style, which had in Puritan times been characterized primarily by theological rigor and restraint of the imagination, came to be dominated by diverting narrative, extensive illustrations, and even colloquial humor.

Many of the central tensions in Dickinson's poetry result from the collision between the old and the new sermon styles. She was well positioned to feel every tremor produced by the collision. Her father, Edward Dickinson, was an avowed devotee of the old-style doctrinal preaching: he typically called a well-reasoned sermon by the conservative David Aiken "an intellectual feast," while he branded an imaginative sermon by the more liberal Martin Leland as "Unclean-unclean!" (YH I, p. 53; L II:251–2). Edward Dickinson also had a puritanical distaste for light literature. Emily recalled that her father read "lonely & rigorous books" and advised his children to read only the Bible (L II:475).

She had a particularly vivid memory of her brother Austin coming home one day with Longfellow's novel Kavanagh, hiding it under the piano cover, and making hand signs to Emily about the book. When the children later read the novel, their father was incensed. While it may seem strange that so apparently innocent a novel as Kavanagh should provoke such a storm, we should recognize how revolutionary the novel was, given the strict doctrinal standards of Edward Dickinson. Longfellow's novel dramatizes the collapse of theological preaching, represented by the departing Rev. Pendexter, and the ascendancy of imaginative religion, embodied in the handsome young preacher Arthur Kavanagh. Kavanagh's piquant pulpit illustrations and stories lead one character to exclaim, "Such sermons! So beautifully written, so different from old Mr. Pendexter's."[1] Emily Dickinson mentioned the novel often in her letters and felt a special kinship with the novel's heroine, Alice Archer, a gloomy, dreamy girl who sublimates her hopeless infatuation for Kavanagh in poetic visions – in much the same way that Emily herself may have been driven to a kind of poetic frenzy by her unrequited passion for a real-life Kavanagh, the Rev. Charles Wadsworth.

Critics have long pondered the Wadsworth-Dickinson relationship, hard evidence of which is frustratingly slim. It is known that while visiting Philadelphia in 1855, during her only trip outside of Massachusetts, Emily most likely was taken to hear Wadsworth preach at Arch Street Presbyterian Church. It is also known that Wadsworth later visited her at least twice in Amherst, that two volumes of his sermons were given to her, that she probably read many of his other sermons in newspaper reprintings, and that she developed strong feelings toward him. Some believe that Emily's great "terror" in 1862 and her incredible poetic productivity that year was a response to Wadsworth's removal to Calvary Church in San Francisco (hence the double pun involved in Emily's description of herself as "the Empress of Calvary"). Intriguing as the relationship is, the much-debated issue of Emily's feelings for Wadsworth is perhaps less relevant than the fact that in the mid-1850s, just at the moment when she was beginning to write serious poetry, she was deeply moved by a preacher who must be regarded as one of the antebellum period's foremost innovators in American sermon style.

Her response to Wadsworth had been prepared for by her increasing preference for imaginative preaching, often against her father's wishes. In 1851 she probably went to hear the popular Henry Ward Beecher, who was visiting Amherst giving a lecture, significantly, on "Imagination." By 1853 she could go into raptures over a notably anecdotal sermon on Judas and Jesus given by the visiting preacher Edwards A. Park, a sermon whose secular emphasis she later described: "It was like a mortal story of intimate young men" (YH I, p. 287). The Martin Leland sermon that her father dismissed as "unclean" was imaginatively liberating for her, as she mimicked Leland's theatrical manner and repeated sections of the sermon aloud. Also in the early 1850s, she befriended the popular author and editor Josiah G. Holland, whose liberal religious views were criticized by one conservative paper as "creedless, churchless, ministerless Christianity" (YH I, p. 296). By aligning herself with several of the most progressive religious stylists of the day, Emily Dickinson was launching a silent but major rebellion against the doctrinal tradition valued by her father.

Her excitement about Wadsworth, therefore, can be viewed as a natural outgrowth of her increasing attraction to the new religious style. One newspaper compared Wadsworth to an earlier pulpit innovator, John Summerfield, but stressed that "Wadsworth's style ... is vastly bolder, his fancy more vivid, and his action more violent ... [His topics are] peculiar, and quite out of the usual line"; he is typically "rapid, unique and original, often startling his audience ... with a seeming paradox."[2] Mark Twain would also be struck by the uniqueness of Wadsworth's pulpit manner, noting that he would often "get off a first-rate joke" (*YH* II, p. 112) and then frown when people started laughing. In short, Wadsworth's style was adventurous, anecdotal, and very imaginative, with a tendency to the startling and paradoxical. Emily Dickinson once praised his "inscrutable roguery" and seemed to copy his impish style in many poems and in her message to J. G. Holland: "Unless we become as Rogues, we cannot enter the Kingdom of Heaven" (L II:901, 703). The jocular familiarity with which she generally treats divine and biblical images doubtless owes much to the new sermon style that Wadsworth perfected.

It is helpful to know that such imaginative revisions of religion were going on around Dickinson and that she was extraordinarily responsive to them. By her own confession, she came to detest theological preaching ("I hate doctrines!" she declared after one old-fashioned sermon), and she devoured every example of the new religious style that came within her rather limited purview. She once commented that the only way to tell if a poem is good is to ask whether, after reading it, you feel like the top of your head has been taken off. She seemed to apply the same rule to the sermons she attended and the books she read. A religious work, in her eyes, must possess both striking imagery and a sense of ultimacy; theology or moralizing is secondary to the work's *effect* upon the imagination. For instance, she disdained three Baptist tracts about "pure little lives, loving God, and their parents, and obeying the laws of the land" – purely secular pious stories that, in her words, "dont *bewitch* me any" (L I:144). In contrast, even though she was skeptical about Christian doctrines, she could revel in the Rev. Aaron Colton's "enlivening preaching,... his earnest look and gesture, his calls of *now today*" (L I:120). Similarly, she could be totally captivated by "a splendid sermon" from Edwards A. Park, which left the congregation "so still, the buzzing of a fly would have boomed out like a cannon. And when it was all over, and that wonderful man sat down, people stared at each other, and looked as wan and wild, as if they had seen a spirit, and wondered they had not died" (L I:272). The combined imagery here of the fly, death, and religion seems to anticipate Dickinson's famous poem "I heard a Fly buzz – when I died." At any rate, we should note that in both the poem and her letter describing Park's sermon, it is not theology or Christianity that counts but rather the existential impact of a momentous situation.

What new religious stylists like Wadsworth and Park had finally taught Emily Dickinson is that religion could be freely applied to many secular situations and expressed through startling imagery. Because of Dickinson's extensive use of witty conceits, many critics have likened her to the meta-physical poets of the Renaissance or to the American Puritan poet Edward Taylor. There is, however, a crucial difference between the metaphysicals and Dickinson: all their creative flights are finally confined by Christian doctrine, whereas she soars adventurously beyond doctrine by mixing the sacred and the secular, the Christian and the pagan. And she had been taught how to achieve this mixture by her popular religious culture.

One of her poetic responses to the new religious style was the redefinition of church, sermons, and worship along totally secular lines. Witness the reduction of religious images to the world in the following stanzas:

> Some keep the Sabbath going to Church –
> I keep it, staying at Home –
> With a Bobolink for a Chorister –
> And an Orchard, for a Dome –
> . . .
> God preaches, a noted Clergyman –
> And the sermon is never long
> So instead of getting to Heaven, at last –
> I'm going, all along.   (J 324)

This poem may be regarded as a clever adaptation of the antebellum religious style: not only does it shift worship from the church to nature and sing praise to short sermons, but it actually converts God into an entertaining preacher obviously trained in the new sermon style. A similar fusion of the sacred and the secular is visible in the poem that begins "To hear an Oriole sing / May be a common thing – / Or only a divine" (J 526), in which the last phrase arrests the reader with its offhandedly casual treatment of the holy. Sometimes this casualness is taken to playful extremes, as when she refers to God as "Papa above!" watching down upon a "mouse," who asks for the privilege of living forever "Snug in seraphic Cupboards" (J 61). Among the many other Dickinson poems that daringly reapply sacred imagery are: "These are the days when Birds come back – " (J 130), "There's a certain Slant of light" (J 258), and "Mine – by the Right of the White Election!" (J 528). In these poems such images as Holy Communion, sacrament, hymns, and the doctrine of election are detached totally from their sacred referents and fused with either nature or the human psyche. In still other poems she displays a jaunty freedom with the Bible, as in "The Bible is an antique Volume" (J 1545), which includes a series of secular re-enactments of sacred imagery, such as calling Eden "the ancient Homestead," Satan "the Brigadier," and sin "a distinguished Precipice/Others must resist."

Another fertile seedbed of imagery for Dickinson was temperance literature, which also stimulated many other writers of the American Renaissance, including Whitman, Melville, Thoreau, and Poe. No reform movement had as widespread an influence in antebellum America as temperance. To combat America's extraordinarily high alcohol consumption, which by 1830 reached the staggering amount of around ten gallons of absolute alcohol per adult citizen annually, waves of temperance orators and writers swept the country between 1835 and 1860.

Although much temperance literature was didactic in a straightforward way, an increasing proportion of it, capitalizing on the popularity of sensational fiction, was lurid and violent in its renderings of alcohol's ravages. With the rise of the Washingtonians, an organization of reformed drunkards who thrilled the public with their graphic anecdotes about battles with the bottle, the temperance movement became riddled with contradictions and ambiguities. Notorious instances of backsliding – particularly that of the Washingtonian leader John Bartholomew Gough, who in 1845 disappeared for a week and then was found in a whorehouse recovering from an alcoholic binge – gave rise to the oxymoronic character of the "intemperate temperance advocate," a staple figure of ridicule in subversive popular fiction. George Lippard in his best-selling reform novel The Quaker City sneered at "intemperate Temperance lecturers," caricaturing them in his portrait of the Rev. F. A. T. Pyne, who snickers, "We temperance folks must have some little excitement after we have forsworn intemperance. When we leave off alcohol, we indulge our systems with a little Opium."[3] Likewise, George Thompson in Life in Boston and New York presents the hypocritical temperance reformer Bob Towline, who boasts that "for over a year I lectured in public, and got drunk in private – glorious times!"[4] In fiction, the intemperate temperance stereotype eventually produced Mark Twain's Dauphin, the bald-pated con artist who runs temperance revivals in order to raise funds to buy whiskey.

In verse, this popular character was creatively reworked in the persona of one of Dickinson's most famous poems, J 214 ("I taste a liquor never brewed – "), which shows the poet adopting and transforming images and themes of popular temperance reform. This transforming process is visible in the opening verse, where she presents an "I" who is a wonderfully fresh avatar of the intemperate temperance advocate. The speaker is both completely drunk and completely temperate. She can exult in her drunkenness because hers is a liquor "never brewed," filling tankards "scooped in Pearl," an image suggesting the pearl-like whiteness of the air she loves and the extreme preciousness of her love of nature.

Having immediately revised the ironic trope of the intemperate temperance advocate, in the next two verses Dickinson gambols with it, revising several other popular images in the process:

> Inebriate of Air – am I –
> And Debauchee of Dew –
> Reeling – thro endless summer days –
> From inns of Molten Blue –
>
> When "Landlords" turn the drunken Bee
> Out of Foxglove's door –
> When Butterflies – renounce their "drams" –
> I shall but drink the more!

This speaker is not the hypocritical intemperate temperance advocate, publicly sober but privately debauched, but the exultantly open one, proclaiming a debauchery that is allied with the highest form of temperance. Dickinson, who was fully aware of antebellum popular culture in all its dimensions, seems to be intentionally playing on well-known temperance images. A central sequence in Timothy Shay Arthur's 1854 temperance best-seller *Ten Nights in a Bar-room* involves a landlord, Simon Slade, who kicks out of his saloon the drunken Joe Morgan, who later renounces alcohol due to the ministrations of his dying daughter. Dickinson uses similar imagery in her references to " 'Landlords' " who turn drunks out their doors and to alcoholics who "renounce their 'drams.' " Her use of quotation marks underscores the fact that she is "quoting," or borrowing, images from others – specifically, from temperance writers like Arthur. But she uses these images only to transform them. The drunkard being dismissed here is a bee that has extracted nectar from a flower. The renouncers of drams are butterflies that are leaving their resting places and fluttering through the air. And the "I" watching this beautiful spectacle only gets more and more drunk for having enjoyed it.

Dickinson has carried popular temperance images to a truly new, transcendent space, a fact she enforces in the poem's closing conceit of seraphs and saints celebrating the "little Tippler" for her intoxication over nature's bounty emphasizes the poem's metaphysical dimension. The playful oddity of the hat-swinging angels, the gaping saints, and the girl leaning against the sun gives the poem a metaphorical energy that leaves the reader intoxicated, as it were, with the poet's imaginativeness.

Dickinson's creative toying with temperance images continues in poem J 230 ("We – Bee and I – live by the quaffing – "). Once again, the "I" is the transformed intemperate temperance advocate, who can openly say that she lives "by quaffing" since her drinking companion is the bee and her "ale" and "burgundy" are beautiful things of nature. When Dickinson writes, 'Tisn't *all Hock* – with us – /Life has its *Ale* – ," she is again adopting a popular trope: the italicized "*all Hock*" was a common phrase used at temperance meetings to urge all present to pledge ("hock") themselves to sobriety. When the "I" says that she and the bee don't use the "*all Hock*" prompt, she is saying that pledges against alcohol are unnecessary for those who understand that life itself "has its *Ale.*"

Dickinson's adaptation of popular sources continues to the end of the poem:

> Do we "get drunk"?
> Ask the jolly Clovers!
> Do we "beat" our "Wife"?
> I – never wed –
> Bee – pledges *his* – in minute flagons –
> Dainty – as the tress – on her deft Head –
>
> While runs the Rhine –
> He and I – revel –
> First – at the vat – and latest at the Vine –
> Noon – our last Cup –
> "Found dead" – "of Nectar" –
> By a humming Coroner –
> In a By-Thyme!

The quotation marks used around several phrases are strategic, for Dickinson is quoting extensively from popular culture. The common temperance trope of the drunken husband who brutalizes his wife is cited in the rhetorical questions "Do we 'get drunk'?" and "Do we 'beat' our 'Wife'?" The sensationalists' association of alcohol with death is repeated in the reference to the drunkard "'Found dead'" by a coroner. The taking of the temperance pledge is recalled in the phrase about one who "pledges *his.*"

But all of these standard temperance images are couched in paeans to ordinary natural phenomena – bees, clover, nectar, and noontime – that redirect temperance rhetoric toward an affirmation of life itself. The bee and the persona get drunk in their mutual enjoyment of clovers. They revel in "the Rhine," a pun that associates drinking famous German wine with a love of beautiful landscapes like that of the River Rhine. The standard image in temperance literature of destructive all-day binges is recreated in the persona's boast of being "First – at the vat – and latest at the Vine – ," while another popular theme, the deadly effects of alcohol, is redirected in the images of drinking the "last Cup" of noon, being killed by "Nectar," and being found by a "humming Coroner," the bee. By manipulating popular temperance imagery, Dickinson joyously expresses her sense of the intoxicating nature of common experience.

Another popular genre that influenced Dickinson was popular sensational literature, ranging from the crime-filled penny newspapers that arose in the 1830s to the sensational pamphlet fiction that flooded America in the 1840s and 1850s. The antebellum public was fed on an increasingly spicy diet of horror, gore, and perversity in both mass newspapers and the closely allied genres of trial pamphlets and paper-covered adventure novels. Emerson complained that his countrymen spent their time "reading all day murders & railroad accidents" in newspapers.[5] Thoreau, similarly, spoke of the "startling and monstrous events as fill the daily papers."[6] Although sensational literature was not uniquely indigenous, American sensationalists gained a worldwide reputation for special nastiness and grossness. Whitman noted, "Scurrility – the truth may as well be told – is a sin of the American newspaper press."[7] In 1842 a British journalist wrote, "*Our* press is bad enough . . . But its violence is meekness and even its atrocities are virtues, compared with the system of *brutal and ferocious outrage* which distinguished the press of America," a sentiment echoed by the British traveler Emily Faithfull, who declared that "the American newspaper very often startles its more cultured readers with extraordinary sensational headings and the prominence it gives to horrors of all kinds – murders, elopements, divorces, and wickednesses in general."[8]

Competing with the penny newspapers were sensational pamphlet novels (often called "romances") featuring rollicking adventure and outcasts such as pirates, freebooters, and all kinds of criminals. Frequently published in garish yellow covers emblazoned with melodramatic woodcuts and eye-catching black lettering, this action-filled pamphlet fiction, priced cheaply and hawked in street book stalls, caused increasing alarm among conservative commentators. Surveying the sudden popularity of "Yellow Jacket Literature," one author complained in 1855 that "the popular press is teeming with works of vapid or unhallowed fiction, or grossly immoral books and prints," noting that in this fiction "the murderer, robber, pirate, swindler, the grog-shop tippler, the lady of fashion, the accomplished rake and libertine, are meritorious characters, held up in a spirit of pride and levity, and surrounded by a 'halo of emulation.'"[9]

Dickinson was profoundly aware of these darker dimensions of the American popular mind. It is notable that when she wrote poetry about popular culture, she was inevitably preoccupied with its violent, disorienting elements, as in poem J 1226 ("The Popular Heart is a Cannon first"). Dickinson recognizes that the "Popular Heart" can be best described in violent images pertaining to war, weapons, drinking, ditches, and prison. The popular culture she perceives is fluid and ever changing, having been torn from both the future ("Not a Tomorrow to know it's name") and from historical memory ("Nor a Past to stare"). It is associated with the muddy realm of ditches, and it thrives on diverting crime ("Ditches for Realm and a Trip to Jail/For a Souvenir").

Her letters of the 1850–3 period show that she was fascinated by sensational literature. The increasing space given in American newspapers to crimes and tragedies was a great source of amused interest to her. In an 1853 letter to Josiah Holland of the *Springfield Republican*, she declared that the lurid contents of his paper had changed her into a quirky disturber of the peace. "One glimpse of *The Republican*," she wrote, "makes me break things again – I read in it every night. Who writes those funny accidents, where railroads meet each other unexpectedly and gentlemen in factories get their heads cut off quite informally? The author, too, relates them in such a sprightly way, that they are quite attractive" (L 1:264). Always hungry for sensational news, she elsewhere thanked her brother Austin for a juicy news clipping about a manslaughter and asked him to send "anything else that's *startling* which you may chance to know – I dont think deaths or murders can ever come amiss in a young woman's journal" (L 1:114). Her tone in these letters captures precisely the combined grossness and offhand levity of sensational newspaper reporting.

The open admission into her consciousness of several popular sensational elements prepared the way for the haunted themes and broken style of her poetry. In a poem written around 1858 (J 8), she creates a horrific atmosphere by describing a wooded road haunted by banditti, a wolf, an owl, a serpent, screaming vultures, and beckoning "satyrs fingers." A similarly straightforward, monovocal use of sensational images occurs in these verses:

> I never hear the word "escape"
> Without a quicker blood.
> (J 77)

or,

> Had I a mighty gun
> I think I'd shoot the human race
> And then to glory run!   (J 118)

or,

> We like a Hairbreadth 'scape
> It tingles in the Mind . . .
> Like paragraphs of Wind
>
> (J 1175)

Such poems barely rise above the pedestrian sensationalism of penny papers and pamphlet novels. They are full of standard sensational images, including hairbreadth escapes, war, guns, murder, and accidents. Although they bear witness to Dickinson's fertile imagination, as when she compares the tingling effect of an escape to that of "paragraphs of Wind," they resemble popular pamphlet fiction in that they revel in action and adventure without pretending to probe deeper meanings.

More characteristically, Dickinson does with sensational literature what she did with religious and temperance rhetoric: she radically personalizes it by redirecting it toward quotidian experience and private emotion. Innovatively, she points out that all of us carry within ourselves narratives more exciting than the most sensational popular romances:

> No romance sold unto
> Could so enthrall a Man
> As perusal of
> His Individual One –
>
> (J 669)

She regularly uses the sensational to freshly illuminate themes related to nature, human psychology, and the poetic process. For instance, poem J 11 is a kind of "yellow novel in verse," featuring sensational images of pirates, buried treasure, and murder threats. Dickinson utilizes these common images not to concoct some adventurous plot but to sing praise to the beauty of a sunset:

> I never told the buried gold
> Upon the hill – that lies –
> I saw the sun – his plunder done
> Crouch low to guard his prize.

In this poem the sun is presented as a pirate who leaves on a hill plundered treasure enjoyed by the first person speaker, who assumes the persona of a hidden onlooker. To sustain the mood of excitement, Dickinson develops the pirate conceit over five verses. After shaking off a momentary fear of being killed by the pirate-sun, the onlooker marvels over the pirate's "wondrous booty" (the sunlight on the hill), consisting of "the fairest ingots / That ever kissed the spade!" Playfully, the onlooker wonders whether to "keep the secret" of the pirate treasure or reveal it, worrying that, as she tries to decide,

"Kidd will sudden sail" (the sun will depart). She ends by trying to come up with a suitable division of the spoils between herself and Kidd, the more famous pirate:

> Could a shrewd advise me
> We might e'en divide –
> Should a shrewd betray me –
> Atropos decide!

If here her persona is that of a pirate's co-conspirator, elsewhere it is that of a criminal. In poem J 23, she poses as a thief:

> I robbed the Woods –
> The trusting Woods. . . .
> I scanned their trinkets curious –
> I grasped – I bore away!

Through such pointed redirection of sensational images, Dickinson suggests that criminality is exciting not for its own sake, as a source of mere diversion or fantasy, but for its usefulness as a vehicle for wresting beauty and meaning from everyday experience. If here she "robs" nature, elsewhere she poses as the victim, rather than the perpetrator, of crime. In poem J 42, for instance, nature is the invasive criminal threatening the speaker, who cries, "A Day! Help! Help! Another Day!"

Dickinson's most successful applications of sensational images occur where she directs such images inward, using them as metaphors for the recesses of the psyche. If popular novelists terrified readers with vividly described horrific settings, she took the new step of reminding readers that the scariest rooms lay within. "One need not be a Chamber – to be Haunted – ," she writes. "The Brain has Corridors – surpassing/ Material place" (J 670). It's far safer, she continues, to meet at midnight an "External Ghost" or to be chased galloping through an abbey by some would-be assassin than to confront "That Cooler Host, . . . one's a'self." The most appalling terrors spring from the fantasies and aggressions lurking within:

> Ourself behind ourself, concealed –
> Should startle most –
> Assassin hid in our Apartment
> Be Horror's least.

This theme of the horror within the mind is echoed in several other Dickinson poems, as when she describes "The Loneliness whose worst alarm / Is lest itself shall see" (J 777). Internalizing adventure imagery, she writes elsewhere,

Adventure most unto itself
The Soul condemned to be –
Attended by a single Hound
It's own identity.   (J 822)

By finding psychological equivalents of sensationalism, Dickinson fashions vistas more horrifying than anything in popular fiction. This becomes clear when we compare a gory image in sensational fiction with a similar one in Dickinson's poetry. In the quintessential sensation novel, George Lippard's 1845 best-seller *The Quaker City*, the villainous protagonist, Devil Bug, gleefully dashes out the brains of an old woman by swinging her body like a hammer on a brass andiron. The scene is described in typically graphic fashion. "The brains of the old woman," Lippard writes, "lay scattered over the hearth, and the body which Devil-Bug raised in the air, was a headless trunk, with the bleeding fragments of a face and skull, clinging to the quivering neck" (p. 241). As ghastly as this scene is, it lacks the resonant painfulness of Dickinson's poem "I felt a Cleaving in my Mind" (J 937).

In Lippard's handling, the dashing out of brains is external to the reader's consciousness, because it results from the perverse criminality of a murderous character. Dickinson converts the dashing out of brains into a metaphor for losing one's mind. Recalling a bewildering psychological episode, the speaker describes a "Cleaving" in her mind, "As if my Brain had split." The unclear referent of "I tried to match it – Seam by Seam – ," where "it" could refer both to the mind and the brain, casts ambiguity over the remaining lines, in which the mind's unraveling, "Like Balls – upon a floor," has gory overtones of a brain being splattered. But the image of the splattered brain is far more excruciating in Dickinson than in Lippard, since it connotes severe mental trauma, not just aberrant criminal activity.

A similar psychological reinterpretation of sensational images occurs in the famous poem that begins, "I felt a Funeral, in my Brain" (J 280). Again, a comparison with Lippard's *The Quaker City* reveals Dickinson's improvements on the sensational mode. Lippard had taken sensationalism to new extremes of irrationalism, going beyond even his friend Poe in his exploration of the distortions of time and space caused by the excited fancy. For example, his description of Devil-Bug's dystopic dream of the future of Philadelphia begins with a nightmarish vision of "a hazy atmosphere, with coffins floating slowly past, and the stars shining through the eyes of skulls, and the sun pouring his livid light straight downward into a wilderness of new-made graves which extended yawning and dismal over the surface of a boundless plain." Next Devil-Bug sees the sun assume the shape of a skeleton-head, surrounded by stars, "each star gleaming through the orbless socket of a skull, and the blood-red moon went sailing by, her crescent face, rising above a huge coffin which floated through the livid air like a barque from hell" (p. 370). Pre-surrealistic in its oddness, Lippard's novel resembles its main setting, Monk Hall, a labyrinthine structure riddled with trap doors that are always opening beneath the reader's feet, sending him tumbling "down, down, down" (in Devil-Bug's oft-repeated words) into another dimension.

Dickinson experiments with a similar range of imagery, involving death, coffins, time/space distortion, and headlong plunges into other dimensions. But by gathering all these Lippardian phenomena into the consciousness of a first-person speaker, she gives them entirely fresh connotations. The fact that the speaker "*felt* a Funeral, in my *Brain*" [my italics] points the poem in two directions simultaneously: first, toward a delineation of an actual funeral service, followed by passage into the after-life; and second, toward a description of a descent into madness, followed by the collapse of reason. The "I" of the poem, like the personae of several other Dickinson poems, could be recalling her own funeral, with mourners "treading – treading –," sitting down at a service, and finally carrying out the coffin, at which point the speaker's soul passes alone into the silent, infinite other world described in the last two verses. At the same time, the "I" could be reliving a terrifying time when it felt as though she were losing her mind. This psychological interpretation is reinforced by a succession of phrases – "in my Brain," "My Mind was going numb –," "creak across my Soul" – that point to the possibility that the "Funeral" here signifies the death of the speaker's rationality and normalcy. In this light, the last two verses, in which the speaker feels "Wrecked, solitary" as "a Plank in Reason, broke," point to the utter alienation and confusion of the insane person.

The last three lines,

> And I dropped down, and down –
> And hit a World, at every plunge,
> And Finished knowing – then –

bring the poem's two major themes to apt culmination. As a conclusion to a death poem, these lines portray the soul, cast into the unknowable after-life, hurtling into infinite space and time. As an end to a psychological poem, they suggest the mind plunging without direction toward chaos, until the speaker has "Finished knowing" – i.e., lost the ability to understand anything. On both levels of meaning, the image of dropping "down, and down" and hitting "a World, at every plunge" has far more resonance than does Lippard's account of people falling "down, down, down" through the trap doors of the multilayered Monk Hall. For Lippard, the arch-sensationalist, the downward plunge of the murder victim is one more bloody plot twist designed to amuse thrillseekers. For Dickinson, the explorer of death and the human mind, the downward plunge of the speaker is a frightening tumble into ineffable mysteries.

Having surveyed a number of the cultural elements that fed into Dickinson's poetry, it is fitting to conclude by considering her in light of other American women writers, whose best works constituted a real literary flowering between 1858 and 1866, the very years that were by far her most productive as a poet. These years saw, on the one hand, the temporary diminution of the organized women's rights activity that had begun at Seneca Falls, New York in 1848 and, simultaneously, a search for more literary ways of expressing women's rage and fantasies. It was a period of extreme self-consciousness about the proliferation of varied women's roles in American culture. Mary Louise Hankins's *Women of New York* (1860) described no fewer than thirty-two kinds of American women – including, significantly, the confidence woman, who could playfully act out all the other women's roles with devilish ease. The variability Hankins perceived was enacted by women writers who took pride in literary acts of self-transformation and manipulation. In characterization, this pride was projected in characters like Medora Fielding in Lillie Devereux Blake's *Southwold* (1859) or Jean Muir of Louisa May Alcott's *Behind a Mask* (1866), canny heroines who avenge women's wrongs by feigning virtue. In plot, it produced broken narrative patterns. In theme, it was evidenced by a growing preoccupation with doubt and negativity. In style, it gave rise to minimalism, ellipsis, and compaction. Intrinsic to this women's literature was a belief in the tormented but dauntless core self of the woman artist, lying below all gender roles and regulating them at will, asserting its power through waspish imagery and daring to tackle universal themes that lay beyond myth or gender. Given the extreme fertility of this historical moment in American women's culture, it is perhaps understandable that fully sixty-two percent of the almost 1,800 poems Dickinson was to write in her lifetime were produced in the 1858–66 period.

Dickinson had special affinities with the authors of the so-called "literature of misery," the genre named and described by Samuel Bowles, the energetic editor she knew well.[10] If the women authors of the literature of misery sought to establish an artistic middle ground between the effetely conventional and the openly feminist, so Emily Dickinson explicitly rejected the "Dimity Convictions" of traditionalists and the public methods of women's rights activists, while she made the era's boldest quest for specifically artistic exhibitions of woman's power. If other women writers typically hid behind shifting literary masks, Dickinson played so many roles, from the childlike "Daisy" to the regal "Empress," that it becomes difficult to identify her actual, biographical self. If they often shifted tone and perspective in successive sketches or chapters, Dickinson regularly did so in successive verses, lines, and even words. If their experimental style was attacked as crude and formless, so was Dickinson's, as is most famously evidenced by Thomas Wentworth Higginson's complaint about her "spasmodic" style. If their work grew principally from the severe inward pain that gave the literature of misery its name, some of Dickinson's best poetry had a similar source, as suggested by verses in which she describes grief or pain as exhilarating: one thinks especially of the poem "I can wade Grief – / Whole pools of it – "(J 252). If along with this pain went a heady confidence in the creative act as the American woman's surest means of self-assertion, Dickinson too was nourished by this confidence, inherited partly from her father (an advocate of women's education and an outspoken admirer of the pioneering woman writer Catharine Sedgwick) and manifested continually by Dickinson's unparalleled poetic innovations. If they had redirected radical-democrat energies toward a search for a gender-free literary reality, Dickinson consummated this search in poetry that strains always toward the universal, poetry that reflects her great radical-democrat declaration: "My Country is Truth . . . It is a very free Democracy."[11]

In addition to these overall affinities between Emily Dickinson and other American women writers, there are more specific connections in the area of imagery and themes. Her repeated use of volcano imagery, for instance, is very much in the vein of the literature of misery. A basic assumption of this literature is that since women's energies were allowed no viable outlet, they gathered in upon themselves and lay burning inwardly, always threatening to erupt through a placid exterior. The heroines of the literature of misery often looked like sweet moral exemplars but raged inwardly with the ferocity of women victims bent on revenge. This fusion of docile and fiery qualities is summed up by a character in Sara Parton's *Ruth Hall* (1856), who generalizes, "Whenever – you – see – a – blue-eyed – soft-voiced – gentle – woman, – look – out – for a hurricane. I tell you that placid Ruth is a smouldering volcano."[12] In Blake's *Southwold*, the author describes Medora Fielding in a typical moment: "No one could have guessed that the calm indifference of her manner concealed a volcano of rage and scorn."[13] The heroine of another novel, *L'eoline*, declares, "A woman made reckless by wrongs, is without compassion," since beneath her gentle exterior lies "a spirit fearless and relentless as the untamed tigress."[14] Even the style of the literature of misery was a kind of dormant volcano, frequently muted and quietly imagistic but always with explosive implications.

Dickinson brought a full self-consciousness to the use of volcano imagery, recognizing that it applied both to women's lives and to women's literary style. Her sensitivity to these interrelated levels of meaning is powerfully captured in the first lines of the successive verses of poem J 601:

> A still – Volcano – Life –
> . . .
> A quiet – Earthquake Style –
> . . .
> The Solemn – Torrid – Symbol –

These lines are a highly compressed, self-reflexive enactment of the thematic and stylistic polarities of American women's literature. Dickinson's irregular prosody, with its ubiquitous dashes and caesurae, shows rhythm and structure being shattered by the pressure of vehement emotion brought under severe restraint, a stylistic feature common in the literature of misery (witness, for example, the pre-Dickinsonian pauses in the above-quoted passage from *Ruth Hall* on "a – blue-eyed – soft-voiced – gentle – woman, – "). In Dickinson's case, there is evidence that confirms the connection between volcano imagery and women's issues. At a key moment in the longest of her three "Master" letters she communicates the extreme tensions created by her buried feelings as follows: "Vesuvius dont talk – Etna – don't – " (L II:374). Although most generalizations about her character and personal life are tentative at best, the one that certainly holds true is that her extraordinary passional and intellectual powers were inevitably repressed and deflected, gaining full expression only in cryptic, loaded metaphors. It appears, therefore, that there is personal and gender-specific import in such famous Dickinson images as "Vesuvius at Home" (J 1705), "the reticent volcano" (J 1748), and "On my volcano grows the grass" (J 1677). We might be tempted to look for specific biographical sources for Dickinson's volcano imagery (such as the much discussed issue of a possible homoerotic attraction to her sister-in-law Susan Gilbert Dickinson), but more significant than such psychoanalytic guesswork is the realization that, whatever the personal motivations behind individual poems, Dickinson frequently discovered new applications for the volcano, one of the most common images in American women's writings.

Those who focus narrowly on a few Dickinson poems that seem directly feminist or on particular personality quirks that make Dickinson appear to be a nineteenth-century madwoman do not truly account for her stature as a paradigmatic American woman writer. Her real representativeness lies in her incomparable flexibility, her ability to be, by turns, coy, fierce, domestic, romantic, protofeminist, antifeminist, prudish, and erotic. She militantly asserted her creativity through ingenious metaphorical play and through brash imaginings of a gender-free literary reality. In this sense, of course, she was much like other authors of the American Women's Renaissance who evaded simple gender categories by freely combining the stereotypes generated by their culture, just as she shared their philosophical adventurousness and devotion to technique. But in Dickinson these common principles are so greatly exaggerated and intensified that they produce a wholly new kind of literature. Other women writers' manipulations of female stereotypes pale beside her endless adaptations and truly innovative fusions of these stereotypes. Their questions about religion and philosophy seem timid next to her leaps into an indefinite realm beyond all religion and philosophy. Their affirmations of women's creativity through stylistic experimentation are tentative when compared with her unremitting quest for the startling metaphor, the unusual rhyme, the odd caesura.

Even when she deals directly with gender issues, clear statement on these issues is abrogated on behalf of jaunty stylistic gamesmanship, signaled by tonal fusions and shocking images. Take the poem "I'm 'wife' – I've finished that" (J 199; c. 1860). Some critics have interpreted this as a wry, anti-marriage poem extremely unusual in a day when marriage was extolled as the highest good. The fact is that American women's wrongs literature had long portrayed the suffering of wives. Indeed, the year before Dickinson wrote the above poem there had appeared a dark women's novel, *The Autobiography of a Married Woman*, whose heroine becomes so disillusioned with marriage that she exclaims, "O, mothers! Train your daughters to self-reliance, and not to feel that they are to marry simply because everybody does marry. ... There are very few happy marriages; there can be but few, where interest and self-love form the tie." [15]

Dickinson's poem stands out not for any new statement about marriage it might contain but for its playful fusion of the opposing views on marriage that were circulating in American culture. One view, related to the conventional ethos of domestic fiction, was that marriage was a state of heavenly bliss and of remarkable power for women. In Dickinson's own life, this idealization of domesticity was reflected in her well-known enjoyment of housekeeping activities and in certain statements in her letters, such as her 1851 message to Susan Gilbert: "Home is a holy thing – nothing of doubt or distrust can enter it's blessed portals" (L 1:150). In the poem, this view is enforced by the images of the home as heaven and the wife as "Czar" and "Woman" – images that invest the marriage relation with both bliss and power for women. The contrasting view, related to the outlook on marriage held by many suffragists and women's wrongs authors, saw marriage as an unequal state in which women suffered a range of ills, from economic deprivation to loss of independence. In Dickinson's life, this hostility to marriage was reflected in her indomitable spinsterhood and in direct cries of protest in letters, such as her exclamatory note to Abiah Root, "God keep me from what they call *households*," or her early comment to Susan Gilbert that their unmarried state must seem enviable to "the *wife*,...sometimes the *wife forgotten*" (L 1:99, 210). In the poem above, the anti-marriage view is crystallized in subtle images, such as "soft Eclipse" and "Stop there!" suggesting the termination of a woman's independence in marriage.

Dickinson was not the first American writer to incorporate both positive and negative views of marriage. Sara Parton, the author whose "spicey passages" Dickinson had read to her father,[16] had done this in successive sketches in *Fern Leaves*, and many women writers of the 1850s had studied tensions between womanly independence and heterosexual love. Dickinson was perhaps the first, however, to fuse contrasting views in a single text and in individual metaphors. The literary fusion enables her to achieve a far more complete view of marriage than was advanced by either the pro-marriage or anti-marriage groups. The message, if any can be gleaned, is that marriage is a heavenly state of power in which women gain safety and comfort but, at the same time, lose the painful but exhilarating self-sufficiency of maidenhood. More important than the poem's message, however, is its stylistic power. How concisely Dickinson communicates the treatment of wife as the husband's objective possession through the quotation marks around "wife" and "Woman"! How subtle are the tonal shifts in the poem, as the persona wavers between enthusiasm and skepticism about marriage! How potently does the phrase "soft Eclipse" communicate that cushioned banality she envisages in marriage! As always in Dickinson's poetry, the greatest triumphs here are stylistic.

Given Dickinson's literary aims, it is not surprising that she directly rejected women's rights and was notably inconsistent on women's issues. In the course of her close relationship with Thomas Wentworth Higginson she never showed interest in one of his favorite reforms, women's rights, and when the progressive popular novelist Elizabeth Stuart Phelps wrote to her in 1872 asking for her aid in the women's cause, she burned Phelps's letter and mailed her a flat refusal. This indifference to political feminism was part and parcel of serious authorship during the American Women's Renaissance. It is no accident that Dickinson's most productive literary period was in the early 1860s, for this was the moment when all women's rights activity was suspended. As early as 1858, outside opposition and internal dissension had created a notable diminution of suffrage activity, and the Civil War brought a complete cessation of women's conventions between February 1861 and May 1866. Dickinson's earliest (and many of her best) poems were written between 1858 and 1866, precisely the years that produced some of the finest works of Lillie Devereux Blake, Elizabeth Stoddard, Rebecca Harding Davis, Louisa May Alcott, Alice and Phoebe Cary, and Harriet Prescott Spofford. Was Dickinson conscious that she was a member of this pioneering literary sisterhood? Little evidence survives to give us a sure answer, but her comments about one of these authors – Harriet Prescott Spofford – show that she was more moved by contemporary American women's writing than by any other favorite classic authors, even Shakespeare. After she finished the last installment of Spofford's story "The Amber Gods" (in the February 1860 issue of the *Atlantic)* she begged her sister-in-law to send her everything Spofford wrote. "The Amber Gods," an imaginative tale involving mysterious amber beads and frustrated love, elicited this high compliment from Dickinson: "It is the only thing I ever read in my life that I didn't think I could have imagined myself" (*YH* ii, p. 6) She was even more affected by Spofford's "Circumstance" (1860), a story about a woman alone in the Maine woods who fends off a half-human "Indian beast" by singing to him. Dickinson was so haunted by the story that she wrote to Higginson in 1862: "I read Miss Prescott's 'Circumstance,' but it followed me, in the Dark – so I avoided her – " (L ii:404). Coming from a woman who believed that literature should be bewitching and devastating, this was high praise.

Whatever cross-influences between Dickinson and the other women writers may have existed, it is certain that she absorbed their overall goal of depoliticizing women's discourse and shifting creative energy away from monolithic expression toward flexible impersonation. She took to a new extreme the liberating manipulation of female stereotypes. In successive poems she assumed with ease an array of shifting personae: the abandoned woman ("Heart! We will forget him!" J 47); the loving wife ("Forever at His side to walk – " J 246); the fantasist of erotic ecstasy ("Wild Nights – Wild Nights!" J 49); the acerbic satirist of conventional women ("What Soft – Cherubic Creatures – / These Gentlewomen are – ," J 401); the expectant bride on the eve of her wedding ("A Wife – at Daybreak I shall be – ," J 461); the sullen rejecter of a lover ("I cannot live with You," J 40).

This is, of course, only a small sampling of other countless poses. We should not be concerned that these poses frequently contradict each other and that several of them seem far more conservative or obsequious to males than might be expected from the strongest woman poet in the English language. Instead, we should recognize her elusiveness as the major ingredient of her artistry and of her representativeness as a writer of the American Women's Renaissance. If Sara Parton's "Floy" showed her power by sending impossibly mixed signals to baffled male reviewers, if Blake's Medora Fielding and Alcott's Jean Muir took vindictive pride in never showing a true face to men, if the "confidence woman" in Hankins's *Women of New York* proudly impersonated every female stereotype, Dickinson outdid them all by donning an unparalleled variety of masks behind which the core self lay as an ever-present but always invisible manipulator. Even in letters to confidants, Dickinson was quick to hide behind personae and to point up the totally fictive nature of other poetic poses. As she wrote to Higginson in 1862, "When I state myself, as the Representative of the Verse – it does not mean me – " (L II:412). For Dickinson, all women's stereotypes become matters of literary theater and metaphorical play.

A result of this endless capacity for manipulation was her unusual fusion of female stereotypes, which is particularly visible in "My Life had stood – a Loaded Gun – " (J 754). A common stereotype in popular fiction was the adventure feminist, the tough woman who could survive extreme physical peril and outbrave men in battle. We have seen that another image associated with women, the volcano, was commonly used in the literature of misery to represent the quiet but inwardly explosive woman who was denied a viable outlet for her energies. The first stereotype enacted fantasies of power; the second reflected the realities of repression and powerlessness. In her poem Dickinson takes the wholly original step of fusing these contrary images. On the one hand, the "I" of the poem is the ultimate adventure feminist, the omnipotent aggressor who does all the hunting and speaking for her master and always guards him from danger. On the other hand, she has a "Vesuvian face" that signals the total repression of her aggressions in deference to him. Whether or not the man here referred to as "Owner" is the intended recipient of Dickinson's pained "Master" letters, the poem makes it clear that Dickinson is conjuring up an adventure-feminist fantasy and, simultaneously, suggesting the suspicion that this imagined power is an illusion. A loaded gun is not useful until it is fired, just as the "I" of the poem gains power only when carried off by her master. The fantasies and frustrations the "I" embodies, however, are secondary to the potency of the poem itself. This ingenious fusion of contradictory female stereotypes sets off a string of lively metaphorical associations that themselves constitute the aggressiveness of the woman writer.

Dickinson's most sophisticated poems are those in which she permits imagery from radically different cultural arenas to come together in an explosive metaphorical center. In some other women's writings of the 1850s, such as Parton's *Ruth Hall* and Cary's *Married, Not Mated*,[17] disparate cultural images are *juxtaposed* in single texts, creating a certain density and stylistic innovativeness. In Dickinson's poetry, such contrasting images are consistently *fused* in single stanzas, even in single words, so that they radiate with fresh suggestions – and create intriguing puzzles for would-be interpreters.

Notice the poetic fusions in the famously cryptic poem "Mine – by the Right of the White Election!" (J 528). In this poem, negative images reminiscent of sensational literature ("Scarlet prison," "Bars," "Veto," "Grave's Repeal") are fused with affirmative, ecstatic religious imagery ("White Election," "Vision," "Confirmed," "Delirious Charter!"). The lack of a clear referent for "Mine" points up the radical open-endedness of meaning that results from the creative fusion of opposing cultural elements. Dickinson had profited immensely from her earlier awareness of different progressive phenomena in popular culture: on the one hand, the sensational writings that had featured prisons, death, and blood; on the other hand, relaxed religious discourse, which suddenly became available for creative recombination with secular imagery. Dickinson grafts together the two kinds of imagery and retains the ultimacy of vision that had long governed her ponderings of large issues. Dickinson's wholly original fusion of contrasting types of images in dense poetry truly distinguishes her. If, as many critics believe, "Mine" refers to the poetic gift, it may be said that Dickinson is fully justified for the boasting, assertive tone of this poem. Through reconstructive fusion, she had managed to create a poem that salvages both the sensational and the religious by bringing them together and infusing them with a new emotional intensity and metaphysical resonance.

A similar intensification through poetic fusion occurs in one of her most famous love poems, "Wild Nights – Wild Nights!" (J 249). It is not known whether Dickinson had read any of the erotic literature of the day or if she knew of the stereotype of the sensual woman.[18] Given her fascination with sensational journalism and with popular literature in general, it is hard to believe she would not have had at least some exposure to erotic literature. At any rate, her treatment of the daring theme of woman's sexual fantasy in this deservedly famous poem bears comparison with erotic themes as they appeared in popular sensational writings. The first stanza of the poem provides an uplifting or purification of sexual fantasy not distant from the effect of Walt Whitman's cleansing rhetoric, which was consciously designed to counteract the prurience of what he called the "love plot" of much popular fiction. Dickinson's repeated phrase "Wild Nights" is a simple but dazzling metaphor that communicates wild passion – even lust – but simultaneously lifts sexual desire out of the scabrous by fusing it with the natural image of the night. The second verse introduces a second nature image, the turbulent sea and the contrasting quiet port, which at once universalizes the passion and purifies it further through abstract metaphor. Also, the second verse makes clear that this is not a poem of sexual consummation but rather of pure fantasy and sexual impossibility. Unlike popular erotic literature, the poem portrays neither a consummated seduction nor the heartless deception that it involves.

There is instead a pure, fervent fantasy whose frustration is figured forth in the contrasting images of the ocean (the longed-for-but-never-achieved consummation) and the port (the reality of the poet's isolation). The third verse begins with an image, "Rowing in Eden," that further uplifts sexual passion by yoking it with a religious archetype. Here, as elsewhere, Dickinson capitalizes nicely on the new religious style, which made possible such fusions of the divine and the earthly. The persona's concluding wish to "moor" in the sea expresses the sustained intense sexual longing and the simultaneous frustration of that longing. In the course of the poem, Dickinson has communicated great erotic passion, and yet, by effectively projecting this passion through unusual images of nature and religion, has rid it of even the tiniest residue of sensationalism.

It is fair to generalize from these and other letters that Dickinson was unique among American women of her day in the breadth of her awareness of the most experimental tendencies in contemporary American culture. Her excitement over press reports of tragedies, her attraction to the new religious style, and her interest in women's writing all reveal a sensibility that was absorbing various kinds of popular images. Dickinson recognized the need for an artistic form that would serve to control and fuse these often contradictory elements. She appropriated the iambic rhythms and simple verse patterns of English hymnody, which had been famously utilized in the Isaac Watts hymns she knew from childhood, as controlling devices to lend structure and resonance to these disparate themes.

In her poetry, therefore, Dickinson was both inscribing her culture and personalizing it. She was that rare oxymoronic being, a _private-public_ poet.

NOTES

1 _Kavanagh_ (1849; rpt., _Hyperion and Kavanagh_ [Boston: Houghton Mifflin, 1886]), pp. 325–6.
2 _Springfield Republican_, October 22, 1850; reprinted from the _New York Evening Post_.
3 Lippard, _The Quaker City; or, The Monks of Monk Hall_, ed. David S. Reynolds (1845; rpt., Amherst: University of Massachusetts Press, 1995), pp. 201, 291.
4 Thompson, _City Crimes; or, Life in Boston and New York_ (New York: William Berry, 1849), p. 121.
5 _Emerson in His Journals_, ed. Joel Porte (Cambridge, MA.: Harvard University Press, 1982), p. 433.
6 _The Journal of Henry David Thoreau_, ed. Bradford Torrey and Francis H. Allen (New York: Dover, 1962), vol. IV, p. 267.
7 _Brooklyn Daily Eagle_, 26 February 1847.
8 _Foreign Quarterly Review_ (London), October 1842, and E. Faithfull, _Three Visits to America_ (Edinburgh: David Douglas, 1884), p. 336.

9 Anonymous, *Confessions and Experience of a Novel Reader* (Chicago: William Stacy, 1855), p. 73.

10 *Springfield Republican*, 7 July 1860.

11 Quoted in Richard B. Sewall, *The Lyman Letters: New Light on Emily Dickinson and her Poetry* (Amherst: University of Massachusetts Press, 1965), p. 71.

12 Sara Parton, *Ruth Hall: A Domestic Tale of the Present Time* (New York: Mason Brothers, 1855), p. 133.

13 L. D. Blake, *Southwold: A Novel* (New York: Rudd & Carleton, 1859), p. 47.

14 *The Una*, June 1855.

15 Anonymous, *The Autobiography of a Married Woman. No Girlhood* (New York: S. A. Rollo & Co., 1859), p. 155.

16 Millicent Todd Bingham (ed.), *Emily Dickinson's Home: Letters of Edward Dickinson and his Family* (New York: Harper & Brothers, 1955), pp. 312–13.

17 Phoebe Cary, *Married, Not Mated, or, How They Lived at Woodside and Throckmorton Hall* (New York, 1856).

18 See David S. Reynolds, *Beneath the American Renaissance: The Subversive Imagination in the Age of Emerson and Melville* (New York: Knopf, 1988), ch. 7.

GUIDE TO FURTHER READING

Bingham, Millicent Todd, ed. *Emily Dickinson's Home: Letters of Edward Dickinson and his Family.* New York: Harper & Brothers, 1955.

Reynolds, David S. *Beneath the American Renaissance: The Subversive Imagination in the Age of Emerson and Melville.* New York: Knopf, 1988.

Sewall, Richard B. *The Lyman Letters: New Light on Emily Dickinson and her Poetry.* Amherst: University of Massachusetts Press, 1965.

10

DOMHNALL MITCHELL

Emily Dickinson and class

I

In 1881, Emily Dickinson wrote to her friend Elizabeth Luna Chapin Holland, including news of her brother Austin's having hired a day-laborer to help with work around the family property.[1] Since the death of their father, Edward, in 1874, Austin had been responsible for running both the Homestead in Main Street that Emily lived in with her sister Lavinia and their mother, and the Evergreens next door, occupied by himself, his wife, Susan Gilbert Dickinson, and their children:[2]

> We have a new Black Man and are looking for a Philanthropist to direct him, because every time he presents himself, I run, and when the Head of the Nation shies, it confuses the Foot –
> When you read in the "Massachusetts items" that he has eaten us up, a memorial merriment will invest these preliminaries.　　　　　　(L 721)

Together, these two short paragraphs serve as a convenient introduction to the compound of issues that are central to this essay. At one level, they seem undeniably racist: the man is identified by his colour only; Dickinson associates him with the lowest part of the body and herself with the higher mind; and she jokes about him being a primitive cannibal. In addition, she pokes fun at philanthropists, or anyone whose political agenda includes wanting to help people who are economically, ethnically, politically, sexually, or socially disadvantaged. The writing also enables fairly precise co-ordinates of class to be traced. The laborer is referred to as a "Foot," and such a term (however ironically deployed) derives some of its force from a long tradition in conservative thinking whereby parts of the human body were used to illustrate and justify hierarchical relations in society.[3] The head thinks, the foot walks and works: each has its own function, designed by nature (which is designed in turn by God). Since the parts of the body were fixed, and could not be moved around, they supported the argument that the members of the body politic ought similarly to remain in the class to which they were born. "What if the foot," asked Pope, "ordain'd the dust to tread,/ Or hand to toil, aspir'd to be the head?" And he continued, "Just as absurd for any part to claim/ To be another, in this gen'ral frame:/ Just as absurd, to mourn the tasks or pains/ The great directing MIND of ALL ordains."[4] In short, what the letter tells us is something less obvious than that the Dickinsons were sufficiently privileged to be able to employ people to work physically on their behalf (thus freeing Emily to do other things, such as to write amusing letters about those whose service freed her). It tells us further that she described herself to friends in ways that uncritically accepted the propriety of this stratification.

At the same time, "confusing the foot" can be thought of less literally as an appropriate way of describing Dickinson's formal and linguistic practices as a poet, as a person who writes in meter (or feet). Dickinson has long been thought of as a literary subversive, someone who disrupts language in order to further subvert authority and reason. Her rejection of conventional meter, rhyme, punctuation and grammar; her refusal to publish (in the conventional sense of committing her work to distribution in printed editions); and her elimination of dates and titles are familiar elements of claims to non-conformity made on her behalf. The critic L. C. Knights is representative when he observes that Dickinson's "frequent use of dashes, instead of the conventional punctuation ... has the effect of breaking down categories with their implication of fixed meanings and relations."[5] To what extent this challenge to poetic or linguistic orthodoxy can be formulated as a radical social and *political* stance may be a matter of debate. For some, Dickinson's comfortable and uncontested status as a member of one of Amherst's leading families does not fit seamlessly with descriptions of her either as a discursive revolutionary or as a lyric spokeswoman for liberal egalitarianism. Whereas the nineteenth century in America is characterized by, among other things, the aggregated emergence of women as a public, political but non-institutional pressure group, Dickinson's life is characterized by withdrawal and non-intervention. Whereas Dickinson's friend, Helen Hunt Jackson, involved herself in the plight of the Native Americans of Southern California, castigating Federal policy towards them first in *Century of Dishonor*, and subsequently in *Ramona*, Dickinson concentrated on poems of the subjective imagination. Whereas for some middle-class women of northern European descent prose fiction functioned as an extension of other reform activities, lyric poetry was the genre most removed from social and political engagement.

And yet, indifference can be formulated as a political relation or act, the absence of any serious treatment of social subjects a sign that these things were regarded as unimportant or irrelevant to a life of reasonable privilege. If the poetry can be accused *implicitly* of being the expression of a literary consciousness that seems distant from considerations of economic necessity and the antagonisms of class and ethnicity, the letters (and not just the early ones) show a similar indifference to current affairs. On the rare occasions when Dickinson does speak to such issues, she is dismissive or whimsical. "Do you know of any nation about to besiege South Hadley?" she wrote from Mount Holyoke Seminary (L 16).[6] Such comments betray a characteristic attitude to political unrest or upheaval, a confidence in history's failure to interrupt the important aspects of an advantaged life. Like the excerpt from the letter above, the tone of Dickinson's comments about the lives of servants, immigrants, condemned prisoners, the victims of industrial accidents and the fatally ill children of the poor is generally comic, and this is significant in itself. At least traditionally, comedy is the genre of the low, the non-serious, while tragedy, the higher genre, is reserved elsewhere for the circumstances of her own life and the lives of those she cared about.

> I have just seen a funeral procession go by of a negro baby, so if my ideas are rather dark you need not marvel.... (L 9)

> Father remarks quite briefly that "he thinks they have found their master," mother bites her lips, and fears you "will be *rash* with them" and Vinnie and I say masses for poor Irish boys souls. So far as *I* am concerned I should like to have you kill some – they are so many now, there is no room for the Americans, and I cant think of a death that would be more after my mind than *scientific destruction, scholastic dissolution*, there's something lofty in it, it smacks of *going up*! (L 43)[7]

> It rains in the Kitchen, and Vinnie trades Blackberries with a Tawny girl – Guess I wont go out. My Jungle fronts on Wall St. (L 320)

> Poor fellow, how he warmed when I gave him your message! The red reached clear to his beard, he was so gratified; and Maggie stood as still for hers as a puss for patting. The hearts of these poor people lie so unconcealed you bare them with a smile. (L 337)[8]

> Dick's Maggie is wilting. Awkward little flower, but transplanting makes it fair. (L 367)[9]

> Of Miss P—— I know but this, dear. She wrote me in October, requesting me to aid the world by my chirrup more ... I replied declining. She did not write to me again – she might have been offended, or perhaps is extricating humanity from some hopeless ditch. (L 380)[10]

> I am glad that you are not hung – like the "Mollie Maguires," tho' doubtless heinous as themselves – in a sweet way – (L 589)

Vinnie is far more hurried than Presidential Candidates – I trust in more distinguished ways, for *they* have only the care of the Union, but Vinnie the
Universe – (L 667)

Catalogues such as this are misleading, of course, for by removing statements
from their epistolary and biographical contexts one exaggerates and distorts
their proportion and significance. The attitudes expressed are unpleasant,
but not everyone who casually repeats stereotypes to close friends would
necessarily endorse or promote these seriously otherwise. But the above list
is nonetheless useful in allowing us to formulate the premise of a remarkable
and fairly consistent lack of political correctness in Dickinson's epistolary
writings. Generally speaking, it is true to say that Emily Dickinson was
contemptuous of progressive movements and unconcerned by the social in-
equalities they attempted to redress, uninterested in the plight of Native and
African-Americans, hostile to the Irish who did not work for her family (and
patronising to those who did). She jokes about the hanging of the Molly
Maguires (a secret organization of Irish miners in Pennsylvania, members of
which were executed at various stages between June 1877 and January 1879),
and compares the death of a flower with the death of a servant's child.[11] In
a famous comment to Thomas Wentworth Higginson, she disparaged those
townspeople going past the Homestead as unthinking masses (L 342a). She
completely ignored the largest mass execution in the legal history of the
Unites States, in 1862, when thirty-eight Santee Sioux Indians were hanged
in Mankato, Minnesota, for their roles in an uprising sparked by chronic
shortages in food, clothing, and fuel. This list of slights and oversights is
by no means comprehensive, but it usefully illustrates what Dickinson is
uninterested by: ethnic injustices, martial and political conflict, urban and
industrial conditions, and the real lives and deaths of the lower classes.

There is no reason, of course, why Dickinson should have been reform-
minded, or more politically sound – no reason either why she should have
written about the Civil War, or economic and ethnic parity. Nonetheless,
these were perfectly respectable and even popular subjects for women writers. This is important, because one of the reasons forwarded for Dickinson's
alleged indifference to political and economic issues lies less with her class
than with her gender. At this point, it might be useful to return to the
excerpted letter with which this essay began. Although Emily and Lavinia
Dickinson lived alone in the Homestead with their invalid mother, it was
Austin who had responsibility for the financial management of their household. Like his father and grandfather before him, Austin worked as a lawyer,
sat on the Town Council at various periods, was associated with Amherst
College, and involved himself with important civic projects, such as helping

to design Amherst Common and the Wildwood Cemetery. His movements and opinions were often matters of public record and reported in local newspapers. Emily, according to the Censuses that coincided with various periods of her life, was "at home," and her movements and opinions were visible mainly to close members of her family, recorded (if at all) in private correspondence.

In short, one can hardly blame the disenfranchised for feeling unable, or refusing, to take seriously historical events and experiences from which they were largely excluded. Indeed, another explanation for the egregiously comic tone of comments made about occurrences that are not obviously comic in themselves might simply be that, as a woman, Dickinson had never been encouraged or expected to discourse authoritatively on happenings of that kind. Such topics lay outside the sphere of a woman's influence or interest as these were defined by nineteenth-century, middle- and upper-class white society, so that the absence of seriousness may be a symptom rather than a cause. That is to say, Dickinson wrote lightly because she had been brought up to expect her opinions about these matters not to be taken or expressed seriously. The comedy may be conditioned or defensive, then: it is the most appropriate genre for people – including women – who felt that they had no right to involve themselves with such subjects in the first place.

Any evaluation of Dickinson's political position involves recognizing that she rejects the conventional role of the spiritual, sentimental woman even as she appears to accept the freedom her economic status afforded her of remaining largely unaffected by public affairs. Dickinson's writing can simultaneously be seen as a site of political resistance and reaction.[12] Nevertheless, it is difficult to accept the image of Dickinson as a champion of *women's* rights because there is so little direct evidence that she had any sympathy whatsoever for the plight of other women. Again, the absences in her writing have fairly clear implications. There are no references, for example, to the 1848 Seneca Falls Woman's Rights Convention, or to industrial disputes such as the one in February 1860, when 800 women operatives and 4,000 workmen marched for higher wages during a shoemaker's strike in Lynn, Massachusetts. In addition, the men she corresponded with outside her family were leading and socially conservative figures whose views she never openly challenged: Josiah Gilbert Holland, founder of *Scribner's Monthly* and an opponent of publication by women, for example.

Samuel Bowles, another friend and correspondent, and editor of the *Springfield Republican*, was politically conservative, in the sense that he supported the Whigs until their collapse in 1854. But he was a progressive on women's issues, and a man with a close circle of women friends, including Maria Whitney, a foreign language instructor at Smith College, an early reformist, and another of Dickinson's many correspondents. He promoted the work of local women writers, and appointed a woman as literary editor to the *Republican* after (and probably because) Holland left the paper. The point to make is that Bowles would have made a sympathetic audience for any discussion of women's rights, but Dickinson never availed herself of the opportunity. Instead, she ridiculed women who involved themselves in public affairs, so much so that she once apologized to Bowles in writing for having satirised Florence Nightingale and Elizabeth Fry in his presence (L 223). Her letters to Bowles generally discuss literature and questions of faith, but not politics. Thus, though it is fair to say *in theory* that Dickinson's gender may have complicated her class allegiances, in practice there seems little evidence of frustration at the lack of institutional opportunities for greater participation in public affairs. With Dickinson, it seems that her class outweighed her gender when it came to such considerations: writing to friends of her own station and background, her jokes are typical in that they enact and emphasise exclusiveness more than a sense of exclusion.

What is more, Dickinson's letters coincide with the kinds of attitudes expressed by Austin when he took a six-week trip through the South and West in 1887, a year after her death. Mingling with both the emergent and lower classes, the self-made men and the poor, Austin felt "dizzy and bewildered."[13] The alien landscape and values of its inhabitants forced him to reconsider and define the nature of his superiority to "niggers, poor whites, and other trash." He was grateful – like the speaker of Fr 285 – that he was "born in New England," and his reactionary politics eventually found solace in a flight to culture:

> Money, land, cattle, corn, railroads, sudden futures, are all that is talked of in the west, or thought of. A man is a man for the cunning or chance by which he has siezed upon more than his part of the heritage of this world. It is unnutritious to me, and it is repulsive. I would[nt] give a volume of Emerson for all the hogs west of the Mississippi. (Longsworth, *Austin and Mabel*, p. 300)

"What makes a few of us so different from others?" wrote Emily in 1853, taking up again the theme of a letter sent to Austin earlier, where she had expressed a keen sense of their "being unlike most everyone" (L 114, 115). For both Dickinsons, their sense of uniqueness has its foundations in tradition, which makes New Englanders of their class superior to people of different ethnic, social, and even geographic backgrounds. The opposition between "heritage" and "fortune" is significant, suggesting unease but also outrage at patterns of social diversity and mobility. Social conditions were changeable and varied during the middle decades of the nineteenth century.[14] Since property and wealth were no longer reliable guides to a person's birthright and pedigree, the Dickinsons fell back on the aesthetic as an alternative form of capital, a possession and a privilege that money could neither dislodge nor buy. A predilection for culture became the distinguishing mark of a rejected intelligentsia, which felt that it had social merit, but not the power of influence.

II

How do we reconcile the Dickinson rightly celebrated in anthologies and critical works as an imaginative force, a writer of extraordinary sensitivity and depth, with the Dickinson of the excerpted letters – someone who celebrates social differences by conveying dubious and sometimes offensive stories about ethnic minorities? We can try to work through these issues by looking at one of Dickinson's best known poems, "I'm Nobody! Who are you?" paying particular attention to what I take to be the class dimensions of Dickinson's preference for observation above involvement.

> How dreary – to be – Somebody!
> How public – like a Frog –
> To tell your name – the livelong June –
> To an admiring Bog!   (Fr 260A)

"I'm Nobody! Who are you?" is often sentimentalized as a kind of apologia for the oppressed and marginal, partly on the grounds that the banishment referred to in the fourth line of the first stanza is traditionally one of the punishments for dissent against tyranny. Such liberal readings of the poem are complicated – though not fully denied – by the inclusion of "Bog" at the end of the poem, for the word was associated derogatively with the Irish in nineteenth-century Massachusetts. Rather than expressing sympathy for the disenfranchised, the speaker expresses both anxiety and contempt for the democratic system that gives "bog-trotters" access to political and cultural influence. "Nobody" is emphatically not of Tom Paine's party, nor for the promotion of universal suffrage and the rights of man. Rather, he or she is closer to the Captain Farrago of Hugh Henry Brackenridge's *Modern Chivalry* (1804), horrified at the prospect of the illiterate Irish servant Teague O'Regan being elected to office:

The Captain coming up, and finding what was on the carpet, was greatly chagrined at not having been able to give the multitude a better idea of the importance of a legislative trust; alarmed also, from an apprehension of the loss of his servant. Under these impressions he resumed his address to the multitude. Said he, this is making the matter still worse, gentlemen: this servant of mine is but a bog-trotter, who can scarcely speak the dialect in which your laws ought to be written; but certainly has never read a single treatise on any political subject; for the truth is, he cannot read at all. The young people of the lower class, in Ireland, have seldom the advantage of a good education; especially the descendants of the ancient Irish, who have most of them a great assurance of countenance, but little information, or literature.[15]

The poem might be said further to align itself with the disdain of particular images deployed by William Cullen Bryant in *The Embargo; or, Sketches of the Times*, his poetical garrotting of Thomas Jefferson, then (in 1809) the outgoing President of the United States. Bryant urges Jefferson to:

> Go, search with curious eye, for horned frogs,
> Mid the wild wastes of Louisian bogs;[16]

The image of Jefferson as a naturalist is double-edged: the couplet (in itself a sign of Augustan sophistication) judges him not as a scientist but as a deliberate exploiter and misleader of his supporters, who are illiterate, stupid, and provincial. By extension, Dickinson's speaker deftly distinguishes her secret communiqué (which is oblique, codified, figurative, private, and *cultured*) from those of the frog (which are crude, vulgar, unrefined, public, and *natural*).[17] The implication of both poems is that the deployment of political rhetoric in the pursuit of power demeans the user, bringing him down to the animal state of the lower orders whose support he depends on. (Interestingly, Amherst Common, which from 1750 was occasionally used for political meetings and which was not far from the Dickinson Homestead on Main Street, lay adjacent to a large frog pond.)[18]

This is not to say that Dickinson was alluding to Brackenridge or Jefferson in her poem, but that her language situates her in an American tradition of thought and writing that responds with alarm to the dangers perceived as latent in a democratic system.[19] Banishment itself is a sign of this speaker's caste: those who belong to the lower orders, and rebel in any kind of way, suffer harsher punishments. The choice of term is informed by class, then, and it is interesting that the listener (in the third and fourth lines of the poem) is prohibited from further imparting the information that there is more than one "Nobody." One senses here a redefinition or reversal of the normal equations: the consolation for not having one's worth publicly recognized is the assurance that being a "name" is socially debasing. Being popular was a sure sign of one's vulgarity: in 1851 Herman Melville wrote privately to Evert A. Duyckinck that the true "test of distinction is getting to be reversed; and, therefore, to see one's 'mug' in a magazine, is presumptive evidence that he's a nobody."[20] Read in this way, the poem can be seen as profoundly reactionary and anti-egalitarian, for it establishes a hierarchy whereby public speakers of any kind are ridiculed at the expense of the restricted, privileged company of the retiring writer and her private reader. What marks the poem is not a sympathetic bonding of the politically disadvantaged, but a contemptuous dismissal of any explicitly public utterance – political or cultural.

III

Many of Emily Dickinson's poems are read, perhaps mistakenly, as being more politically generous than they actually were.[21] "Publication – is the Auction/Of the Mind of Man" is another (what follows here are the final two stanzas of the poem).

> Thought belong to Him who gave it –
> Then – to him Who bear
> It's Corporeal illustration – sell
> The Royal Air –
>
> In the Parcel – Be the Merchant
> Of the Heavenly Grace –
> But reduce no Human Spirit
> To Disgrace of Price –   (Fr 788)

Written in 1863, the poem has benefited from the historical accident of its proximity in time to the Civil War. The references to auctions, the buying and selling of human souls, and the "Corporeal illustration" in line 11 (like a brand), accumulate to suggest a parallel between the merchandising of literature and the barbarism of slavery. In this reading, the potential abuse of the dark print mirrors the actual abuses inflicted on the coloured victims of the slave system, and this fits in with the poem's ostensible message, which strongly resists the idea that human worth can be calculated or measured in financial terms.

In fact, the tensions in the poem may be more strongly related to class. As biographers have pointed out, the Dickinson family history was overshadowed by her paternal grandfather's loss of fortune and forced sale of the family property during the 1820s. The poem alludes to the practice whereby a bankrupt's possessions were seized by the court and sold at auction for the partial relief of debt. Such auctions were advertised in local newspapers, and Dickinson's language is redolent of the shame and degradation associated with them. The point to be made here is that publication for Dickinson is equivalent to a public stripping of assets and dignity, in the sense that it calls into question the social and/or literary status of the person doing the publishing/selling. Refusing to print, then, becomes a way of authorizing one's work, imparting to it a kind of stability and permanence at a period in American history when the power and influence of established New England families was beginning to decline (sometimes abruptly, as a result of failed investments and speculation), and when the reputation of a writer was in part dependent on a volatile literary economy. When the Dickinson Homestead was repurchased (in 1855), the *Hampshire and Franklin Express* congratulated the family for restoring the house to its rightful owners. The mere fact that the newspaper could make such a comment demonstrates how anxieties about ownership were the shared concerns of a social class.[22]

The poem above is an excellent example of how a conservative motive for writing (the encroachment of trade on a previously noble or genteel activity) can coincide with an apparently more radical agenda (a plea for the abolishment of *all* slavery). In this context, it is worth pointing out that Dickinson's brother Austin paid for a substitute to take his place during the Civil War; whatever his motives, the fact that he could afford and want the choice of not taking an active part in the conflict provides an interesting glossary on the poem. When Dickinson's father, Edward, wrote (again in 1855) that "by the help of Almighty God, not another inch of our soil *heretofore consecrated* to freedom, shall *hereafter* be polluted by the advancing tread of slavery...," his comments are (by the standards of progressive thought at the time) conservative (*LED*, p. 536). He is not calling for an end to slavery: he is demanding that slavery not be allowed in Massachusetts, which is a different thing. Edward Dickinson belonged to the discredited and dying Whig Party, which tore itself apart over the issue of slavery. In 1860, he ran for Lieutenant Governor of Massachusetts on behalf of the Constitutional Union Party, which on the eve of the War was still trying to compromise with the Southern states, allowing them to maintain slavery.

Such matters aside, the poem's association of "whiteness" with virtue ("Possibly – but We – would rather/ From Our Garret go/ White – Unto the White Creator – / Than invest – Our Snow") complicates any liberal approach to its contents. Although Dickinson seems (barely, in lines three and four) to admit that certain economic conditions might justify publishing for money, it is clear that she sees this as socially demeaning. Publication compromises the class status of the speaker, reducing her to a mere cipher in a scheme of economic exploitation. In other words, it is not slavery *per se* that the speaker objects to, as much as her potential contamination through entrance into a system of evaluative relations appropriate to separate, and lower, social spheres. At one level, of course, one infers from the poem that in an ideal world everyone should have the right to control each aspect of the circumstances of their existence. But there is a disparity to the imagery of the second stanza: it is precisely Dickinson's ignorance of the actual trauma of historical exploitation and poverty that enables her speaker to claim she would never sell her work. Her cultural heroism as an unacknowledged observer of (and in) an age of philistinism is predicated on her economic segregation from need. Dickinson did not have to compromise her artistic integrity, bluntly, because she could afford not to: her class position protected her from "so foul a thing." For the truth is that being bought and sold, like starvation itself, is rarely a choice: that the poem advances such an extreme position unjustly shames all of those for whom writing was a professional necessity – who published in order to survive. It further degrades those men and women who were forced to work for a living generally, because it suggests that death or negation would have been nobler choices.

Issues of ownership, property, racial and class status, and literary integrity are all bound up together in this poem. On one level, the poem may be thought of as a lament for the loss of the patronage system, an important aspect of the social hierarchy in earlier centuries. Because the patron afforded protection, economic and political, to the writer, this allowed her or him the necessary financial freedom to concentrate on work. The poem is based on the conservative perception that the conditions for literary excellence had been more favorable in the past. Technological advances in methods of printing and distribution, as well as increases in the population, levels of literacy, and standards of living, had dramatically augmented the demand for literary products. Whereas 109 works of American fiction were published during the 1820s *in their entirety*, for example, the number had risen to 1,000 in 1850 alone.[23] Authorship had been transformed from a leisured pastime into a profession subject to the competitive laws of the market. For Dickinson, however, writing remained a spiritual calling, not a commercial occupation, and the goods she produced were shared with friends, rather than sold.

The encroachment of trade, the lower cost of producing paper, the improvements in print technology, the rise of the canals and railways, the greater numbers and buying power of readers: these factors rapidly altered the literary field. There were more authors selling in greater numbers than ever before. In a literary culture where success was often defined in commercial terms, those who did not, or would not, sell, felt aggrieved and alienated. Dickinson's poem derives much of its force from the premise that literature cannot have both a commodity *and* a cultural value, and that artistic integrity would be undermined by the appeal of the dollar. For her, the professionalisation of culture was a crisis of inestimable proportions, since ownership of the self was an absolute precondition of imaginative merit. Writ large in her poetry is the assumption that any relation of dependence on, or profit from, publication would compromise literary standards. If one extends the logic further, the implication is that truly great literature remained the prerogative of a particular class – those who were financially self-possessed, or freed from necessity in one way or another.

IV

Emily Dickinson published approximately ten poems in her lifetime. Elizabeth Chapin Holland, however, was one of a select few who received autographed poems – thirty-one of them, between 1854 and 1884 (Fr 1553). Many critics see Dickinson's practice of circulating manuscripts in her correspondence as denying literature's status as commodity: crafted by hand, and sent to friends and relatives, a poem derived its significance as part of a culture of exchange embedded in a local economy of individual relations. For others, Dickinson's refusal to publish proves that her messages conflicted with prevailing ideologies. Betsy Erkkila sees such limited circulation as a sign that Dickinson wrote poems and addressed themes that appealed to a very limited circle within a privileged social class. For her, Dickinson's privatised writings promote the lyric as bourgeois ornament – both an object to be admired and hidden from more general view, and an object that promotes a culture of detached aesthetic enjoyment.

It may be that both these views are true: Dickinson is *both* a literary innovator *and* a political conservative. It may also be that one can be said to inform the other: in an age of professed democracy and association, Dickinson was a disassociated and disaffected exile – an outsider, an ironic commentator on, and interrogator of, social discourses. She would not, of course, be the first to be artistically great and politically elitist. Think of T. S. Eliot, Ezra Pound, and William Butler Yeats, and one is confronted with a paradox: some of the previous century's most innovative and challenging writing was by men attracted by the forces of ideological reaction and retreat. There is a similar paradox in nineteenth-century American literature: its leading canonical practitioners complained about precisely the absence of raw materials for writing in nineteenth-century America. James Fenimore Cooper was one of the first to grumble in his 1828 *Notions of the Americans*:

> There is scarcely an ore which contributes to the wealth of the author that is found here in veins as rich as in Europe. There are no annals for the historian; no follies (beyond the most vulgar and commonplace) for the satirist; no manners for the dramatist; no obscure fictions for the writer of romance; no gross and hardy offences against decorum for the moralist; nor any of the rich, artificial auxiliaries of poetry. The weakest hand can extract a spark from the flint, but it would baffle the strength of a giant to attempt kindling a flame with a pudding-stone.[24]

The tradition was continued by de Tocqueville (in *Democracy in America*, 1840) and Hawthorne (in his preface to *The Marble Faun*, 1860):

> No author, without a trial, can conceive of the difficulty of writing a Romance about a country where there is no shadow, no antiquity, no mystery, no picturesque and gloomy wrong, nor anything but a commonplace prosperity, in broad and simple daylight, as is happily the case with my dear native land.[25]

Thomas Wentworth Higginson joined the ranks of the disaffected in 1867:

> American literature is not yet copious, American scholarship not profound, American society not highly intellectual, and the American style of execution, in all high arts, yet hasty and superficial.[26]

Henry James famously expanded the list of absences in his *Hawthorne* of 1879:

> No State, in the European sense of the word, and indeed barely a specific national name. No sovereign, no court, no personal loyalty, no aristocracy, no church, no clergy, no army, no diplomatic service, no country gentlemen, no palaces, no castles, nor manors, nor old country-houses, nor parsonages, nor thatched cottages nor ivied ruins; no cathedrals, nor abbeys, nor little Norman churches; no great Universities nor public schools – no Oxford, nor Eton, nor Harrow; no literature, no novels, no museums, no pictures, no political society, no sporting class – no Epsom nor Ascot![27]

In all of these comments, there is a convergence of cultural, physical, and socio-economic dimensions: both Cooper and Hawthorne complain about the "commonplace," and James lists the missing institutions of rank and privilege. The following stanzas by Emily Dickinson derive some of their meaning from this tradition of literary anti-egalitarianism: or at least, the insertion of the verse into that complex of cultural codes yields interesting results.

> It sifts from Leaden Sieves –
> It powders all the Wood.
> It fills with Alabaster Wool
> The Wrinkles of the Road –
>
> It makes an even Face
> Of Mountain, and of Plain –
> Unbroken Forehead from the East
> Unto the East again –
>
> (Fr 291A)

This is not so much (or not only) a poem about the effects of snow on the landscape (after all, snow is never mentioned) as it is about an enervating climate of "it"ness (it and its are repeated eleven times in a total of twenty lines). A landscape of interesting differences and distinctions is reduced by the close to mediocrity – something "even," undistinguished, common. Significantly, the one human reference in the poem is to a Queen (in the final stanza): the stultifying sameness described by the speaker imparts a further socio-political dimension. At one level, this is death; at another, it is the dullness of democracy. And opposing both is the pastoral memory of a golden age that coincides with a burst of alliteration in line 13: though now "empty," summer's "Room" has yielded "Harvests" that are stored and recorded in the sounds and stanzas of poetry.

It seems difficult to avoid the possibility that the poem might have a political aspect, since it describes the relentless movement across the landscape of thousands, or millions, of small agents who, singly, amount to nothing but, collectively, threaten to overwhelm even the most powerful in society.[28] Written (it is conjectured) around 1862, the poem's images would appear to relate most easily to the Civil War that had begun the year before. And yet, the terms of the description seem to suggest a more elemental struggle, between traditional, hierarchical structures, and other forces of uncertain origin. An excerpt from another letter to Elizabeth Holland strengthens such an impression:

> The Snow is so white and sudden it seems almost like a Change of Heart –
> though I dont [sic] mean a "Conversion" – I mean a Revolution.   (L 678)

The poem would appear to meditate on the conflicting potentialities of American history in the middle of the nineteenth century. On the one hand, there is the promise of freedom represented by vast natural space. On the other, there is the fear that the sheer number of foreign immigrants attracted by this promise will destabilise, destroy, or diminish its fragile balance for those already living there. This is the lyric equivalent of Dickinson's earlier comment to Austin that "they are so many now, there is no room for the Americans" (L 43). In such a reading, the landscape embodies fears about a political system that was still in the process of evolving, and that hovered precariously between authority and anarchy. What I am suggesting here is an attitude of skepticism toward snow in all of its aspects – and that this includes the political. Nevertheless, the poem is not obviously or crudely about politics – even though the references to leaden sieves, headless crops, ransacked rooms, and the death of a monarch might suggest the violence of class conflict (which has personal ramifications, since Dickinson referred to herself as a New England Queen in F 285). What frightens the speaker – one imagines – is that the artisans of snow are literally unconscious of the havoc they wreak in the name of a force that is indifferent to them. Individually small and non-threatening, their gathering in a common cause enables them to devastate property (denoted by the rails and fences of the third stanza), order (denoted by the Queen), and tradition (denoted by the Harvest) – the entire history of aesthetic, economic, political, and social distinction. This is the irony of the poem: the artisans are simultaneously the fools and the tools of tyranny and vulgarity.

The snow is persistent, ubiquitous. It is possible that the direction it takes – past face (line 5) and forehead (line 7) to wrists (line 17) and down to ankles (line 18) – means that the speaker remains somehow protected. For if we work backwards from ankles to wrists and up to forehead and face, then it seems clear that if the head is affected first, it will cease to function. But the speaker of this poem does not cease, even if what she describes is obviously intimidating. Instead, she records the site of an apparently lost landscape: she remembers the location of rails and fences, breaks in the landscape, the grandeur of rooms and the distinction between an artisan and a Queen. It is her mind, her powers of observation, that preserves the knowledge of this landscape: to put it another way, mind, memory, perception – these are the counter weapons of a displaced intelligentsia. For the creative imagination can see beneath the surface to record patterns of continuity amidst change: the landscape of differences is seen as the natural one, the uniformity imposed by snow as an artificial obfuscation. And this landscape will return: it lies buried "from the East/Unto the East," but east is where the sun rises, and a rising sun will ultimately melt snow and restore the true geographical and political formations that are permanently there.

In many ways, the poem echoes middle-class ideas about nature as an agent of stability during times of social change: for Andrew Jackson Dowling, a landscape architect and friend of Dickinson's brother, nature was a powerful means of civilisation. Nature was perceived as having an insistent and pos-itive moral force, which is why the latter half of the nineteenth century was the age during which great landscaping projects such as Central Park in New York came about. At the same time, there was a vulnerability to intrusion.[29] Typically, the American middle-classes opened nature to the lower classes, but at the same time set up fences, railed paths, and erected signs saying "Keep off the Grass." They privileged perception and promoted a culture of viewing and not usage. Indeed, one of the more fascinating aspects of the poem is precisely the speaker's spectatorial relationship with the forces she describes. She seems able to witness change, but not to prevent it, and this suggests both an *unwillingness* to intervene and an *inability* to do so. In other words, her gaze reflects powerlessness and privilege at the same time. The speaker cannot act: at the same time, not acting is seen as a good thing. Once more, looking becomes the final refuge of a consciousness that is sufficiently leisured to be able to observe and report, but not to influence or alter.

V

It was Henry James who wrote that the "house of fiction has not one window, but a million – a number of possible windows not to be reckoned, rather."[30] His choice of terms echoes the first stanza of Dickinson's "I dwell in Possibility":

> I dwell in Possibility –
> A fairer House than Prose –
> More numerous of Windows –
> Superior – for Doors –
>
> (Fr 466A)

There is a wonderful alignment of economic and aesthetic dimensions here. At a very literal level, more windows mean more space: and the bigger the house, the greater the resources of the people living inside it. In the nineteenth century, windows were potential objects of display, signs of status: they more easily allowed heat out and cold in, and therefore indicated to passers-by that one could afford not to conserve heat during the winter. During the summer evenings, windows admitted more light, which was practical mainly for those families who were educated and leisured enough to be able to afford the production and consumption of materials for reading and writing. Windows also enabled the use of curtains, which were often as decorative as functional, and whose purpose included the preservation of privacy: thus, they allowed house-owners to make further statements about their taste and social position, depending on the quality of the textiles used.

When Edward Dickinson re-purchased his father's Homestead in 1855, he had a brick extension built on to the rear of the house, a cupola added to the roof, and a conservatory built for his wife and elder daughter, both of whom were botanical enthusiasts. A veranda was erected (on the western side), with French doors giving access to it. In a lithograph drawn in 1858 (from the east), one can make out approximately twenty-seven windows, in addition to the cupola and conservatory: there would have been around forty in total. Clearly, Edward wanted to send a message to his neighbours: after Samuel Fowler Dickinson's bankruptcy and exile (to Ohio in 1833), his family had not only re-established their social position, but enhanced it. Just as clearly, when Dickinson defines poetry's advantage over prose as a multiplicity of perspective, she is making a hierarchical claim on a literary level similar to the one made by her father on a social level.

Dickinson's description of poetry therefore tells us a great deal about her own position and priorities in life. The windows suggest plenty, an abundance of perspectives, and at the same time a desire to distinguish oneself from those with fewer means. They celebrate illumination, enlightenment, knowledge – and contrast these with those who live, by choice or necessity, in darkness. At the same time, the windows suggest someone who is both an observer *and* an outsider: many of Dickinson's speakers can look but are prevented from further participation. Dickinson's position as a female member of the provincial gentry in Amherst almost certainly contributed to the formation of a consciousness that felt special and even superior, but also excluded from the public spheres of action and power.[31] The result is the frequent promotion in her writing of non-involvement, strategic withdrawal, deferral, anonymity, and witness. Her emphasis on secrecy, sight and silence is a compensatory gesture, a form of consolation, for this combined sense of exclusiveness and exclusion. Henry James is useful here: in a letter to Mrs Humphrey Ward, he argued that overt political commentary makes one "sacrifice all sorts of blest freedoms and immunities, treasures of detachment and perception that make up, and more than make up, for the 'outsider' state."

A Marxist reading of this position would detect a class reflex at work here, the intelligentsia responding to a perceived failure to influence reality and retreating instead to the safety of observation and obscurity. A withdrawn sensitivity to imaginative issues rather than an active involvement with social topics becomes the defining characteristic of artistic excellence and integrity. For James, reviewing Hawthorne in 1872, what is important is the "*leisure* of attention"[32] that is synonymous with the "boundless freedom" mentioned in the letter to Mrs Ward. But as Christopher Benfey reminds us, "freedom and capacity require . . . a secure place, a room of one's own."[33] For Dickinson's speakers, one depends on the other, so that

> the very meaning of freedom . . . was unintelligible outside their notion of property: freedom . . . *was* property of one's own person in a market society where he who sold his capacities (his labour) ceased by . . . definition to be free.[34]

For the speaker of the poems under discussion, freedom is defined in a similar way: as the right to withdraw, to withhold, to witness. There is another dimension to this: many of Dickinson's poems were never published in the poet's own lifetime – at least, not in the conventional sense by which "publication" is equated with "print." Those that were circulated went only to a few friends and members of her family. The rest were collected in fascicles, or hand-sewn manuscript anthologies, found after her death. The fact that the poems did not appear in the mass media of the day prevented them from offering any kind of solace or support for the kinds of audiences that contemporary readers imagine her writing implies (since they were not transmitted into other social environments). This act of segregation further strengthens the impression of their integrity – they only observe, they do not appear or act in the world at all. It also promotes the idea of her literature as privately, even silently, produced and consumed. The works were rare, unknown, and their production unrelated to economic, moral or political imperatives, which made them self-sufficient, ludic, and liberated from the necessities of didactic, mimetic, or waged discourse. Dickinson's art derives its values from internal criteria – not from the causes it supports or addresses, but from their absences. Her writing remains independent of conditions outside its immediate field.

> The denial of economic interest ... finds its favourite refuge in the domain of art and culture, the site of pure consumption ... The world of art [is] a sacred island systematically and ostentatiously opposed to the profane world of production, a sanctuary for gratuitous, disinterested activity in a universe given over to money and self-interest ... [35]

The second point to make about "I dwell in Possibility," by way of moving towards a conclusion, is that poetry's doors are specified as being superior in terms of *quality* rather than quantity. They are a better kind of door, perhaps even an alternative to doors, rather than just bigger doors or a larger number of them. In order to understand the implications of this, it helps to remember that a door (according to Webster's 1828 *American Dictionary of the English Language*) is not only an "opening or passage into a house ... by which persons enter" but also "the frame of boards, or any piece of board or plank that shuts the opening of a house or closes the entrance into an apartment or any inclosure." Doors are also the markers of property: they enact the boundaries between self and society, private and public territories. Used figuratively, a door is not only a point of entry (to architectural and subjective interiors), but also a way of controlling and (if necessary) *barring* access. An important difference between poetry and prose, then, is that the former is less open, less obvious: its meanings are more difficult to reach. James and Dickinson are similar in this respect: the former prizes a "certain indirect and oblique view of [the] presented action"; the latter advises to "Tell all the Truth but tell it slant – / Success in Circuit lies" (Fr 1263).[36] This kind of strategic obfuscation suggests a link between circumlocution, culture, and gentility. Speaking directly, plainly, publicly, outright; inhabiting a common language – this is the downward, levelling trend that a democratic system or a competitive, commerce-driven literary economy forces the speaker or writer towards. In an 1898 letter to H. G. Wells about *The Turn of the Screw*, James claimed that "the difficulty itself is the refuge from vulgarity."[37] For Dickinson, too, one senses that her celebrated indeterminacy is a way of encoding and preserving her sense of distinction. In other words, poetry's traditionally more heightened and elliptical discourse is a means of guaranteeing that only a fraction of the nineteenth-century population can understand the nature of its (form, not content-based) appeal.

Like James, the complexity of style was a device for escaping national and temporal boundaries and guaranteeing cultural and intellectual legitimacy. Like James again, the quality and longevity of writing is further enhanced by a refusal to engage directly with political individuals, parties or trends. If the United States could not furnish the materials for literary excellence, one form of compensation was to ignore American subjects altogether, at least with regards to specific social and historical experience. But it is precisely this desire to avoid guilt by association (with a culture Dickinson and much of her generation perceived to be unexceptional) that enables her poetry to accommodate different interpretative viewpoints – including ones that she may have opposed in her writing to begin with. And this answers the question posed at the beginning of this essay: since Dickinson struggled (successfully) *not* to include contextual information in her writing – to erase all traces, in fact, of what she saw as the contamination of the contemporary, her work acquires an astonishing adaptability or flexibility of reference. As the poems are read at further and further removes from the particular alignment of social, historical, and material circumstances they originally emerged from and engaged with, different schemes and alignments of meaning are made available. In one way, the poems can be thought of as rogue satellites that alter direction and attach themselves to different interpretative orbits and centres of gravity. This is both the fate and gift of literature: to generate meanings across boundaries of time and space, class, and colour – and beyond even the control of the consciousness from which it originally emerged. "Nature," Dickinson once wrote, "is a Haunted House – but Art – a House that tries to be haunted" (L 459). Literature is a site about which there are competing or successive claims of ownership (those of author, performer, reader, scholar), and any composition set down on paper allows the possibility of perspectives that differ in emphasis from one's own. The spectres at the margins of Dickinson's pages include the readers of the present: we are somewhere between squatters, illegally occupying property at the time of its owner's absence, and tenants with fuller rights of residency. There is no need to overlook flaws, but over time we can learn to live with them, and to admire aspects of the view and the magnificent architecture of surmise.

NOTES

1 Such laborers were often referred to as hired hands: their situation had changed little since the days of William Langland's fourteenth-century *Piers Plowman*, where there is a line about "Laborerys that han no land bot liue on here handus" (p. 105). *Piers Plowman: The Z Version*, ed. A. G. Rigg and Charlotte Brewer (Toronto: the Pontifical Institute of Mediaeval Studies, 1983).

2 Emily Dickinson was born in 1830, the eldest daughter and second child of Edward Dickinson and Emily Norcross. Emily Norcross was the daughter of a well-to-do farmer. Edward was the son of a lawyer who would become a lawyer himself: he would be twice elected to the Massachusetts General Court (in 1838 and 1852), and to the United States Congress (in 1852). Emily's letters tell (in emphatically unimpressed terms) of serving tea and refreshments to Governor Banks and his wife, who were Edward's guests during commencement week for Amherst College, in August 1860. Edward Dickinson often had receptions for visiting dignitaries in his gardens; later, his daughter-in-law, Susan Dickinson, would host gatherings for Ralph Waldo Emerson and Harriet Beecher Stowe among others.

3 The Foot may also be thought of as a pun on "Footman." Alternatively, it may be an obscure local joke. According to the 1880 Amherst Census, John D. Thompson, aged thirty-five, was an African-American day-laborer, and the son of Henry Thompson and Martha Washington. Her nickname was "Wealthy Foot."

4 Alexander Pope, "An Essay on Man: Epistle One," in *The Poems of Alexander Pope*, ed. John Butt (London: Methuen, 1963), p. 514.

5 Knights, "Defining the Self: The Poems of Emily Dickinson," in Boris Ford (ed.) *The New Pelican Guide to American Literature*, vol. IX (Harmondsworth: Penguin, 1988), p. 159.

6 Emily was well-educated by the standards of women in her day: she attended the Amherst Academy from 1840 (after four years of primary school) and South Hadley Female Seminary (Mount Holyoke College) from 1847 to 1848.

7 Austin was teaching in Boston, and clearly wrote about having to use physical discipline to control his pupils. Despite modern assumptions to the contrary, corporeal discipline was not a given at the time: schools, and individuals, diverged in opinion and practice. For more on this, see Richard H. Brodhead, *Cultures of Letters: Scenes of Reading and Writing in Nineteenth-Century America* (University of Chicago Press, 1993), pp. 13–47.

8 The man referred to as an Irish laborer is identified (conjecturally) by Johnson as Tim Scannell, while "Maggie" is Margaret Maher, who worked for the Dickinsons. That Scannell might have been embarrassed in a negative way seems not to have occurred to Dickinson. "Maggie" is a generic name applied to Irish female servants. Irish women named Margaret are called Peggy by other Irish people. For more on this, see Johnson (L, p. 466).

9 Margaret Kelly, aged 17, the daughter of James and Ellen Kelly, died in July 1872 (L, p. 496).

10 The Miss P. referred to is identified in notes by Johnson as possibly being Elizabeth Stuart Phelps, an activist for women's rights and reform issues generally.

11 See also Joanne Dobson, *Dickinson and the Strategies of Reticence: The Woman Writer in Nineteenth-Century America* (Bloomington: Indiana University Press, 1989), pp. 78–9, for a discussion of many of the same letters and topics.

12 Feminist critics advance gender as the primary reason for withdrawal, though it may not be the only reason. Although nineteenth-century American women were citizens (as long as they weren't slaves or first-generation immigrants) without a vote, it did not follow that "they were not part of the political community." Women writers used literature as a means with which to influence public policy: Harriet Beecher Stowe is the best example, but Lydia Maria Child, Catharine Maria Sedgwick, and (most interestingly) Helen Hunt Jackson all used fiction as a forum for reform. Jackson was described by Emerson as America's greatest living novelist, and was immensely popular, as well as being Dickinson's correspondent for many years, and someone who urged her to publish. For a discussion of women and public life see Lois W. Banner "Elizabeth Cady Stanton: Early Marriage and Feminist Revolution" in Linda K. Kerber and Jane de Hart-Matthews (eds.), *Women's America: Refocusing the Past*, (New York and Oxford: Oxford University Press, 1987), p. 201.

13 Polly Longsworth, *Austin and Mabel: The Amherst Affair and Love Letters of Austin Dickinson and Mabel Loomis Todd*, (New York: Farrar, Straus, and Giroux, 1984), p. 301.

14 For more on the social terrain in Western Massachusetts at this time, see Christopher Clark, *The Roots of Rural Capitalism: Western Massachusetts, 1780–1860* (Ithaca: Cornell University Press, 1990).

15 *Modern Chivalry, or the Adventures of Captain Farrago and Teague O'Regan, his Servant, a Rough, Sharp Piece of Humourous Fiction, Partaking, to Some Extent of the Nature of an Autobiography* (Philadelphia: J. Conrad & Co., 1804), pp. 14–15.

16 Bryant, *The Embargo; or, Sketches of the Times. A Satire* (Boston: E. G. House, 1809), p. 12.

17 However, nineteenth-century Americans felt that free speech was a right inherent in human nature as well as republican citizenship. A classic statement of this view, which was known as the natural rights theory, is provided in the following passage by the Jeffersonian Republican lawyer St. George Tucker: "Liberty of speech and of discussion in all speculative matters, consists in the absolute and uncontrollable right of speaking, writing, and publishing, our opinions concerning any subject, whether religious, philosophical, or political; and of inquiring into and, examining the nature of truth, whether moral or metaphysical; the expediency or inexpediency of all public measures, with their tendency and probable effect; the conduct of public men, and generally every other subject, without restraint, except as to the injury of any other individual, in his person, property, or good name." See "Of the Right of Conscience; and of the Freedom of Speech and of the Press," in *Blackstones' Commentaries* (South Hackensack, NJ: Rothman Reprints, 1969), p. 11.

18 Dickinson's scorn for the populist speaker is opposed in Jennie Collins's *Nature's Aristocracy; or, Battles and Wounds in Time of Peace. A Plea for the Oppressed* (Boston: Lee and Shepard, 1871). Here the "frog agent" of the Mill is ridiculed by striking workers, who are superior to him by virtue, even as they are economically, ethnically and socially lower (pp. 262–3). The agent is called the frog because of his arrogance and conceit: Dickinson's frog is characterized by stupidity and lack of sophistication.

19 The Whig party which Edward Dickinson, the poet's father, belonged to, and which elected him in 1852 to the Congress of the United States, advocated essentially conservative policies: belief in strong central government; support for the established business concerns of the North East (such as industry and transport, the latter a particular interest of Edward Dickinson's, who succeeded in bringing the railway to Amherst); and resistance to the growing economical power and populism which they associated with the opening of the frontier.

20 *The Letters of Herman Melville*, ed. Merrell R. Davis and William H. Gilman (New Haven: Yale University Press, 1960), p. 121.

21 A notable exception is Betsy Erkkila. Her article on "Emily Dickinson and Class," *American Literary History* 4,1 (1992): 1–27 is highly recommended, as is her chapter on Dickinson in *The Wicked Sisters: Women Poets, Literary History, and Discord* (New York: Oxford University Press, 1992).

22 The *Hampshire and Franklin Express* was a Whig newspaper, as was the *Northampton Gazette* which Edward Dickinson began subscribing to in 1848, as an alternative to the *Northampton Courier*. The "pursuits and embarrassments" of Samuel Fowler Dickinson's career were followed also by the *New-England Inquirer*, and the public sale of his half of the house was advertised in the *Hampshire Gazette*.

23 Michael T. Gilmore, *American Romanticism and the Marketplace* (University of Chicago Press, 1985), p. 4.

24 Cooper, *Notions of the Americans*, ed. David Grimsted (New York: Braziller, 1970), pp. 108–9.

25 Nathaniel Hawthorne, *The Marble Faun: Or, the Romance of Monte Beni*, ed. Richard H. Brodhead (New York: Penguin, 1990), p. 3.

26 Higginson, "A Plea for Culture," *The Atlantic Monthly* 19, 111 (Jan 1867): 29–37.

27 *Hawthorne*, (Ithaca: Cornell University Press, 1987), p. 34.

28 A similar process is described in Alan Brownjohn's poem, "Snow in Bromley," where nature effaces the achievements and pretensions of the suburban middle class in England (in *The Railings* [London: Digby Press, 1961], p. 40). My thanks to Jeremy Hawthorn for bringing this poem to my attention.

29 Though the poem does not say so directly (because direct statement is in itself a sign of vulgarity), the process by which landscapes are transformed into mediocre sameness by an army of artisans surely has cultural as well as political implications. In an age of professed democracy, popular education, mass publication, and increasing numbers of museums and galleries as well as readers, landscapes had become too easily available, and as a consequence over-represented, exhausted of meaning, cheapened by their very accessibility. Walter Benjamin's "A Small History of Photography," in *One-Way Street and Other Writings*, trans. Edmund Jephcott and Kingsley Shorer (London: NLB, 1979) is relevant here: "The stripping bare of the object, the destruction of the aura, is the mark of a perception whose sense of the strangeness of things has grown to the point where even the singular, the unique, is divested of its uniqueness – by means of its reproduction." The landscape becomes a symbol for the cultural market that reproduces too many superficial images of landscape. America, the poem might be construed as saying, is drowning in worthless paper (p. 245).

30 James, Preface to *Portrait of a Lady* (Oxford University Press, 1995), p. 8.

31 Though her father was elected to the General Court of Massachusetts in 1873, his political career was largely a failure. By the end of the Civil War, the party he had belonged to no longer existed. One senses in Dickinson's poetry a desire to regain eminence for the family, but a recognition that influence was no longer possible.

32 James, "Passages from the French and Italian Note-Books: A Review in *The Nation*, 1872," in J. Donald Crowley (ed.), *Hawthorne: The Critical Heritage* (London: Routledge & Kegan Paul, 1970), p. 448.

33 Benfey, *Emily Dickinson and the Problem of Others* (Amherst: University of Massachusetts Press, 1984), p. 49.

34 Perry Anderson, "Components of the National Culture," in Alexander Cockburn and Robin Blackburn (eds.), *Student Power: Problems, Diagnosis, Action* (Harmondsworth: Penguin, 1969), p. 242.

35 Pierre Bourdieu, *Outline of a Theory of Practice* (Cambridge University Press, 1977), p. 197.

36 James, "Preface" to *The Golden Bowl* (Harmondsworth: Penguin, 1974), p. 7.

37 James, "To H. G. Wells (1898)," in Deborah Esch and Jonathan Warren (eds.), *The Turn of the Screw* (New York: Norton, 1999), p. 116.

GUIDE TO FURTHER READING

Anderson, Perry. "Components of the National Culture." In Alexander Cockburn and Robin Blackburn, eds. *Student Power: Problems, Diagnosis, Action.* Harmondsworth: Penguin, 1969.

Banner, Lois W. "Elizabeth Cady Stanton: Early Marriage and Feminist Revolution." In Linda K. Kerber & Jane de Hart-Matthews, eds. *Women's America: Refocusing the Past.* New York and Oxford: Oxford University Press, 1987.

Benfey, Christopher E. G. *Emily Dickinson and the Problem of Others.* Amherst: University of Massachusetts Press, 1984.

Benjamin, Walter. "A Small History of Photography." In *One-Way Street and Other Writings*, trans. Edmund Jephcott and Kingsley Shorer. London: NLB, 1979.

Bourdieu, Pierre. *Outline of a Theory of Practice.* Cambridge University Press, 1977.

Brackenridge, Hugh Henry. *Modern Chivalry, or the Adventures of Captain Farrago and Teague O'Regan, his Servant, a Rough, Sharp Piece of Humourous Fiction, Partaking, to Some Extent of the Nature of an Autobiography.* Philadelphia: J. Conrad & Co., 1804.

Brodhead, Richard H. *Cultures of Letters: Scenes of Reading and Writing in Nineteenth-Century America.* University of Chicago Press, 1993.

Brownjohn, Alan. "Snow in Bromley." In *The Railings.* London: Digby Press, 1961.

Bryant, William Cullen. *The Embargo; or, Sketches of the Times. A Satire.* Boston: E. G. House, 1809.

Collins, Jennie. *Nature's Aristocracy; or, Battles and Wounds in Time of Peace. A Plea for the Oppressed.* Boston: Lee and Shepard, 1871.

Cooper, James Fenimore, *Notions of the Americans* [1828], ed. David Grimsted. New York: Braziller, 1970.

Dobson, Joanne. *Dickinson and the Strategies of Reticence: The Woman Writer in Nineteenth-Century America.* Bloomington: Indiana University Press, 1989.

Erkkila, Betsy. *The Wicked Sisters: Women Poets, Literary History, and Discord.* New York: Oxford University Press, 1992.

Gilmore, Michael. T. *American Romanticism and the Marketplace.* University of Chicago Press, 1985.

Hawthorne, Nathaniel. *The Marble Faun: Or, the Romance of Monte Beni* [1860], ed. Richard H. Brodhead. New York: Penguin, 1990.

Hobbes, Thomas, *Leviathan.* London: Penguin Books, 1985.

James, Henry. "Passages from the French and Italian Note-Books: A Review in *The Nation,* 1872." In J. Donald Crowley, ed. *Hawthorne: The Critical Heritage,* London: Routledge & Kegan Paul, 1970.

Hawthorne, ed. Tony Tanner. London: Macmillan, 1967.

"To H. G. Wells (1898)." In *The Turn of the Screw,* eds. Deborah Esch and Jonathan Warren. New York: Norton, 1999.

"Preface" to *The Golden Bowl.* Harmondsworth: Penguin, 1974.

Knights, L. C. "Defining the Self: The Poems of Emily Dickinson." In Boris Ford, ed. *The New Pelican Guide to American Literature,* vol. IX. Harmondsworth: Penguin, 1988.

Langland, William. *Piers Plowman: The Z Version,* ed. A. G. Rigg and Charlotte Brewer. Toronto: The Pontifical Institute of Mediaeval Studies, 1983.

Longsworth, Polly. *Austin and Mabel: The Amherst Affair and Love Letters of Austin Dickinson and Mabel Loomis Todd.* New York: Farrar, Straus, and Giroux, 1984.

Melville, Herman. *The Letters of Herman Melville,* ed. Merrell R. Davis and William H. Gilman. New Haven: Yale University Press, 1960.

Pope, Alexander, "An Essay on Man: Epistle One." In *The Poems of Alexander Pope,* ed. John Butt. London: Methuen, 1963.

Tucker, St. George, "Of the Right of Conscience; and of the Freedom of Speech and of the Press." In *Blackstones' Commentaries.* South Hackensack, NJ: Rothman Reprints, 1969.

11

PAULA BERNAT BENNETT

Emily Dickinson and her American
women poet peers

While a host of feminist scholars, beginning in the 1970s, are principally responsible for Emily Dickinson's remarkable surge to the front ranks of major American authors, these same scholars have, for the most part, shown little interest in recuperating the poetry of other American women writers of Dickinson's day. Instead, by largely ignoring this sizable body of writing, they have helped maintain the *cordon sanitaire* that has, since the early decades of the twentieth century, cut the Amherst poet off from her peers. With only two exceptions – Cheryl Walker and Joanne Dobson – those Dickinson scholars who have touched on this subject, myself included, have done so largely at these other women poets' expense, setting them up not as authors in their own right but as so much prima facie evidence for Dickinson's genius and her ability to transcend the limits of her time, place, and gender. Thus, for example, the introduction to my 1990 study of Dickinson concludes, "At a period when, it seems, virtually every woman poet in the United States failed to rise above the limitations imposed on women's poetry by women's complicity in a system that oppressed them, Emily Dickinson sought 'taller feet.'"[1] This assertion, at which I shudder now, implicitly treats the discussion of Dickinson *qua* nineteenth-century American woman poet as a zero sum game. The less her women poet peers could be said to have achieved, the greater Dickinson's own accomplishment became. Conversely, anything one gave to them, took from her.

But the building of a literature is not and should not be treated as a zero sum game and when it is, both sides lose. Since the first publications of Dickinson's poetry in the 1890s, scholars, feminist and otherwise, have treated her as an anomaly, as she herself put it, "the only Kangaroo among the Beauty" (L 268). Even now, when the verse of other nineteenth-century American women poets is finally beginning to attract the serious attention

I wish to thank Vivian Pollak and Eliza Richards for their very careful and rigorous readings of this manuscript in its earlier stages.

it deserves, most Dickinson scholars show little interest in it or in exploring any possible influence it might have had on her work. Rather, they have continued to align her either with the "great" British women writers of her time (the Brontës, *et al.*) or with the male authors of the American Renaissance. Increasingly today, she is situated outside her own century altogether, effectively treated as a modernist in nineteenth-century dress, with no connection to her peers at all.

The consequence of these strategies has, among other things, been to leave intact the grounding of Dickinson's mythic status as isolate – her own self-chosen stance – in a monumental misreading of the poetry that other nineteenth-century American women wrote. As a literary equivalent of Foucault's "repressive hypothesis," the assumption that nineteenth-century American women poets ex-Dickinson never rose above their "complicity in a system that oppressed them" speaks more to our own projections onto "Victorian" women/society than it does to the actual circumstances under which these women wrote. At the least, the past two decades of research into Harriet Beecher Stowe and other antebellum sentimentalists has demonstrated that for many women the apparent "restraints" of nineteenth-century gender ideology, or "domestic ideology," as it is called, were in themselves sources of power not to be dismissed lightly.

Even more important where Dickinson is concerned, however, is that the Amherst poet was, in fact, living at a cultural moment when American women poets generally had come of age as artists, not as domestic ideologues. Indeed, by the last decades of the century, women poets were beginning to outpublish men even in the most exclusive and prestigious venues, – the *Atlantic Monthly, Scribner's Monthly,* and *Harper's New Monthly Magazine* – that is, the very magazines Dickinson read. As daughters of the first sizable generation of feminist activists, these writers were keenly aware of the social and economic impediments confronting them, but few, if any, exhibit the kind of deep-structured gender anxiety that Dickinson so notoriously manifests. On the contrary, the dominant mainstream women poets of the post-bellum/*fin de siècle* period – Frances Butler Kemble, Julia Ward Howe, Lucy Larcom, the Cary sisters, Rose Terry Cooke, Helen Hunt Jackson, Harriet Prescott Spofford, Celia Thaxter, Louise Chandler Moulton, Sarah Piatt, Elizabeth Stuart Phelps, Ella Wheeler Wilcox, Edith M. Thomas, and Lizette Woodworth Reese – were all consummate professionals, enjoying formidable public reputations. They did *not* hide themselves away in attics, nor did they necessarily give up marriage or children. Sarah Piatt, for example, my choice for the strongest woman poet in the century after Dickinson, bore eight children of whom six survived into adulthood, even while publishing more than 440 poems, many of them among the most powerful American political poems the century produced.

These are facts of no mean importance and, as Dobson insists, when approaching Dickinson, they need to be accounted for. Why did Dickinson so dramatically dis-identify with other American women poets; why, if they were not failed writers themselves, did she make so much of the limits of gender anyway? Why, that is, did she repeatedly figure herself as isolate, to use another of her favorite images, a spider working in the dead of night, dancing to itself alone? I am not, let me be clear, challenging the critical assumption that Dickinson was isolated. To a great extent she was, and the consequence of this isolation can be seen everywhere in her writing, poems and letters. Nor am I dismissing the anxieties she clearly felt because of her sex. But much like Dobson, I have come to see these matters, largely, as effects produced by Dickinson's own idiosyncratic self-construction.[2] That is, I see them as part of a positioning strategy that Dickinson herself deliberately adopted – just as she adopted the white dress and other accouterments of a Gothic persona. These behaviors were not thrust upon her, either by her situation as a gifted woman writer or by the putatively "Victorian" gender values of the society in which she lived.

Dickinson's refusal to identify with other American women poets of her day was undoubtedly overdetermined, a product of her unique response to the internal and external forces informing her life and art. In this essay, I will look at only one strand, that which is best illuminated by her ambiguous handling of a set of images around sewing, spinning, weaving, and knitting, that other nineteenth-century American women poets also habitually used. Comparing the way in which these other women treated these images to Dickinson's use of them helps reveal, I shall argue, a deep, abiding conflict within Dickinson's own poetic, one that led her to reject forcibly the poetry of her American women peers even while exploiting many of the same strategies and themes as they did. Like the mythical push-me-pull-you beast in Dr. Dolittle, Dickinson's poetics, in theory as well as in practice, faced in two opposite directions at once. On the one hand, aligning herself with the (largely, male) literary immortals, Dickinson wanted to write not for today but "for all time." As her letters to her "preceptor," Thomas Wentworth Higginson, make clear, literary immortality, like personal immortality, obsessed her. To this extent, one could say that Dickinson was indeed striving, literarily-speaking, for "taller feet" (L 238), since this was not, as we shall see, the primary goal driving most of her women peers to write.

On the other hand, however, despite her enormous literary ambitions, Dickinson lived a surprisingly narrow life, a life of "feminine" sequestration;

and it is within the terms of this highly regressive gender position, one pre-supposing female subordination, or, as I put it once, women's "complicity in a system that oppressed them," that her poetry takes shape. Her figures and concerns are drawn from the daily cycles of private life and her poems are set in largely domestic space – the kitchen, the garden, the parlor, the bedroom, or, at the furthest from home, her neighbors' houses, the street, the graveyard, and the church. As a result, strikingly *unlike* her women poet peers, politically speaking, Dickinson is no progressive in her verse. On the contrary, in her letters, she savagely mocks those women writers who are, scornfully referring to their efforts as attempts to "extricat[e] humanity from some hopeless ditch" (L 380). Although Dickinson scholars have recently tried to find intimations of more enlightened social attitudes in Dickinson's poetry, to do so they must read against the grain of the poetry itself, from which all allusions to history and to society have largely been excluded.

It is, I believe, Dickinson's singular determination to juggle her two basically incompatible positions – her utter immersion in domestic life and her obsessive quest for literary immortality – that made her such an anomaly in her own day, as in ours. Dickinson had an amazingly strong sense of literary agency, one that allowed her to wield words as only major writers, confident in their own place in literary history, dare do. At the same time, however, to a degree unmatched by any prominent woman writer on either side of the Atlantic, she appears to have lacked a sense of social and political agency altogether. By comparing how Dickinson uses the highly domestic imagery of textile manufacture (from ancient times, identified as, predominantly, a female form of labor) with how other American women poets of her period used it – women whose sense of social and political agency was far greater than her own – one can learn a great deal about what was truly distinctive, and even radical, in Dickinson's poetics, and what decidedly was not. Using male spiders to do her spinning for her, Dickinson was able to install domestic life within the logic of a (masculine) transcendence, making the latter's putative boundlessness "fit" within the highly circumscribed space of a woman's body/a woman's life and art. But for all its seeming libratory character, this double-sided poetics left traditional gender roles intact and Dickinson batting irresolutely between them. In the remainder of this essay, I will examine how this dilemma plays out in the contradictions of her verse and in her own uneasy self-positioning as artist.

Even a swift dip into Willis Buckingham's monumental history of Dickinson's reception in the 1890s supports the conclusion that most early readers of Dickinson's poetry did not dismiss her poetry or devalue it simply because its author was a woman. Neither, however, did they collapse her work into that of her female poet peers. On the contrary, they enthusiastically rhapsodize over Dickinson's many more masculine seeming virtues – in Buckingham's words, "her originality, strangeness, and force"[3] – even when, as often happened, they were uncomfortable with one or another of her formal innovations (most commonly her use of off- or slant-rhyme). Where these readers had difficulty rather was in knowing how to place her work. Again and again, they cite Higginson's comparison of her poems to flowers torn up by the roots; and they use words such as "weird," "spectral," and "ghostly" to articulate her poems' strangely disembodying effects, and the equally estranging gender ambiguity they projected.[4]

By relocating Dickinson's poetry in the material circumstances of her daily life, and in her social relations with others, a number of scholars, including Jay Leyda, Barton Levi St. Armand, Wendy Martin, Judith Farr, and myself, have sought to fill in what appears to be the empty space around and within Dickinson's poems, what Leyda cannily referred to as their "omitted center" (*YH* I, p. xxi) but which could also be called their omitted circumference – their context. Given as gifts, included in letters, passed around among family members, cherished by those who received them, Dickinson's poems – or, at any rate, a sizable number of them – did not in fact hang utterly unanchored in air. Rather, like the filaments that Walt Whitman's spider spins out of itself, they were ductile threads that she used to connect to others.

But while this is true, Dickinson herself rarely speaks of her writing in these terms. Rather, as those who first encountered her in print recognized, she depicts herself in her poetry as alone, a spider spinning delicate webs out of a secret self, a self known, finally, only to God. In invoking this highly restrictive yet supremely liberating scenario, Dickinson thus seems to confirm her early readers' view of her. Divorcing herself and her writing both from the work of her American contemporaries and from the historical, social, and material givenness of the world in which she lived, she writes, or seems to write, outside time and place in a private space of her own. In this space she enacts her poetry's central dematerializing gesture, transforming concretes into phantasms and lending phantasms the materiality of concretes, a process epitomized in the familiar and exquisite lines, "I dwell in Possibility – / A Fairer House than Prose – " (J 657, Fr 466). The nullification of the "real world" in such lines hardly requires unpacking. As one of her hostile early reviewers might have said – Andrew Lang, for example – one cannot "dwell" in "Possibility," nor is prose a "House."

In this essay I will look closely at two poems that deal explicitly with the space that Dickinson created in her poetry and with her self-presentation as an isolated writer, a writer who speaks out of a void: "The Spider holds a Silver Ball" (J 602, Fr 513), which she was never able to finish, and

"A Spider sewed at Night" (J 1138, Fr 1163), among her most powerful and purest renditions of the isolate theme. What I want to suggest is that the disembodiment Dickinson attributes to her art, especially in the second of these two poems, reflects her attempt to negotiate between the two competing and equally legitimate poetics that drove her verse. The first, found ubiquitously in prescriptive literature of the day, identified great writing with the transcendent and the sublime. In this poetics, the artist's goal was to achieve the kind of immortality that Dickinson attributes to Shakespeare in such hyperbolic statements as "While Shakespeare remains Literature is firm" (L 368) or, as she put it to Higginson, "she read Shakespeare & thought why is any other book needed" (L 342b). Dickinson's commitment to this conception of art can be seen in "The Poets light but Lamps – / Themselves – go out – " (J 883, Fr 930) and it runs through a number of similarly conventional poems that she wrote specifically on poetry, e.g., "This was a Poet – " (J 448, Fr 446), "The Martyr Poets – did not tell – " (J 544, Fr 665), and "I reckon – when I count at all – " (J 569, Fr 533). Although men were not the sole producers of this kind of art – for Dickinson there was always Emily Brontë, Elizabeth Barrett Browning, and George Eliot – she, like most readers of her day, seems to have identified the generic "great" artist as male; and it is probably for this reason that she frequently deploys masculine figures when treating writing abstractly.

Alternatively, however, there was a second, far more pragmatic approach to poetry in which Dickinson was also thoroughly steeped and which, in fact, she regularly practiced. In this approach, poetry did not aim at transcendent cultural expression but served as a social activity, a kind of "making" or quasi-material craft, typically motivated by economic considerations rather than the desire for lasting fame. Favored by a striking number of women writers, including Eliza Earle, Lucy Larcom, Rose Terry Cooke, Elizabeth Stoddard, Helen Hunt Jackson, and Harriet Prescott Spofford, in this poetics, artists, including poets, were identified with textile workers: weavers, knitters, seamstresses, etc., and they viewed their product as analogous to these other forms of makings. Taken thus, women's traditional roles as textile workers came to mediate their relationship as artists to the social world in which they lived, and for which they produced not just poems but clothing, shrouds, lace, and other artifacts of material culture, some necessary for life, some of more purely aesthetic or decorative value. "I send you only a Humming Bird," Dickinson wrote Mrs. Edward Tuckerman, enclosing "A Route of Evanescence" (L 627) and suggesting that her friend take gift, bird, and poem as one. Dickinson may be giving women's craftwork her own inimitable twist here, but she is treating her poem as equivalent to craftwork nonetheless.

In identifying her spider-artists as male isolates, working in a void, but in nevertheless attributing conventionally feminine material-centered activities – knitting, spinning, and sewing – to them, Dickinson was, I believe, both expressing and attempting to resolve the tensions that her waffling between these two antithetical poetics created in her work. On the one hand, she wanted immortality, that is, the status of the transcendent (male) artist. On the other, such use of her art as she made came (as it did for many nineteenth-century women) through her materially channeled connections to others. By nature a highly private and introspective person, Emily "had to think – she was the only one of us who had that to do," her sister Lavinia reported after Dickinson's death[5] – writing was her most important link to the external world. At the same time, however, insofar as she exploited her poems as material items, she risked undermining their claim to transcendence. How, that is, were her readers to distinguish an art that created humming birds in words from one that stuffed them in order to make decorative gift items – according to Elizabeth Barrett Browning in *Aurora Leigh* an accomplishment expected in well-bred young ladies, right along with spinning glass and modeling "flowers in wax."[6] Could one achieve "great" or immortal poetry while still using one's poems as surrogates for material items? Was a poem given as a gift or incorporated (literally) within the textual body of a letter, still a poem?

The degree to which Dickinson individuated this dilemma only becomes apparent when one compares her handling of imagery drawn from female hand-work with that of other American women poets of her period. The idiosyncratic nature of Dickinson's internal conflict over her poetic aims and the unacknowledged but crucially important class bias that lay at its core sets her strongly apart from her peers. For the latter poets, most of whom made their living by their literary efforts, women's textile work, in particular, was a multivalent symbol of their lifetime mingling of duties and art, the one inseparable from the other. They used images drawn from textile work to speak of women's political concerns, their labor in wartime, their delight in craft, their confinement within the home, the sacrifices they made for family, their relation to God, and their bonds to other women. Indeed, so ubiquitous are these textile figures, they become, as in Rose Terry Cooke's description of Harriet Prescott Spofford, the universal symbol of all forms of female labor, from nursing and teaching to authoring books:

> Women who are driven by the necessities of their lives to write, as others are to sew, to teach, or to nurse, do not cease their labors till the pen drops from their weary hand, and the exhausted brain refuses to feed the laboring fingers. "Work! Work! Work!!" is not only the "Song of the Shirt," but the song of the Woman, and under that stringent cry we reel off pages of fiction, overridden

by the dreamy facts of need, like the spider, spinning not only our dwellings, but our grave-clothes from our own breasts.[7]

For Cooke, who was at the bitter end of a long career when she wrote this paragraph, women did not engage in writing as a luxury, no more than they sewed or knit or wove for themselves alone. Such activities were labor and in grouping writing with them, Cooke was underscoring the pragmatic foundation upon which most women's aesthetic endeavors had traditionally been based, whether or not they actually received remuneration for them. Women might make beautiful quilts, but they made them for "everyday use," as Alice Walker points out in her well-known story of that name.

At the same time, textile manufacture also provided women writers with figures for their own relation to women's growing sense of social responsibility and agency in the nineteenth century. For example, in a poem published in 1836 in William L. Garrison's *Liberator*, "Lines, Suggested on reading 'An Appeal to Christian Women of the South,' by A.E. Grimke [sic]," the feminist abolitionist poet, Eliza Earle, a twenty-nine-year-old Quaker from Leicester, Massachusetts, uses weaving as a figure for an emerging female literary tradition of socially engaged writing. Reading the "speaking pages" of Grimké's anti-slavery tract helps this young woman grasp new political possibilities for herself as well:

> Well hast thou toiled in Mercy's sacred cause;
> And thus another strong and lasting thread
> Is added to the woof our sex is weaving,
> With skill and industry, for Freedom's garb.
> Precious the privilege to labor here, –
> Worthy the lofty mind and handy-work
> Of Chapman, Chandler, Child, and Grimke too.[8]

For Earle, the socially engaged "handy-work" of writers like Maria Weston Chapman, Elizabeth Chandler, Lydia Maria Child, and Angelina Grimké opened the way for women, otherwise forbidden to "lift [their] voices in the *public* ear," to exercise political agency without violating gender and class norms: "The pen is ours to wield, / The heart to will, and hands to execute" (*NAWP*, p. 406). No less than Dickinson, therefore, Earle understood writing as a form of power. But where Dickinson lodged writing's power in the sensational power of language itself, it was principles that made Earle feel "physically as if the top of [her] head was taken off" (L 342a) when reading Grimké's anti-slavery tract. What legitimated women's writing for this young Quaker woman was not the brilliant use of words but the social function they served.

A former Lowell mill girl, Lucy Larcom also develops textile metaphors in relation to social service. In the poem "Weaving," women's association with the manufacture of textiles (from L. *manu factus* made by hand and *texere* to weave) becomes an encompassing central figure not just for women's literary agency but for the ties that bind them to the nation's fate and that bind Northern white women and Southern black women together in a web of social responsibility. Staged in the mind of a mill girl working at her loom, Larcom's poem is an astonishingly complex treatment of art's relation to the polity. In her capacity as weaver, the speaker not only comes to understand that she cannot separate from the outside world, but she acknowledges that she must bear responsibility for what occurs within it even if she is not directly involved:

> "I weave, and weave, the livelong day:
> The woof is strong, the warp is good:
> I weave, to be my mother's stay;
> I weave, to win my daily food:
> But ever as I weave," saith she,
> "The world of women haunteth me."
> (*NAWP*, p. 115)

Bound to her loom by deep familial obligations, Larcom's speaker is haunted by the less immediately present obligations she also shares with other women, women who like herself live in a nation divided between slave and free, North and South, black and white. As the poem unfolds against this recognition, the speaker gradually realizes that the cloth she weaves is a poisonous "Nessus-robe" of war (*NAWP*, p. 116). Saturated with the blood of the slaves who picked the cotton from which it is made, this fabric now becomes a shroud that will be soaked in the blood of soldiers who die to make the slaves free. In the poem's final ironic gesture, Larcom's speaker, like Earle's, discovers in her weaving a "speaking page," one that tells her of the nation's self-chosen tragic fate and of her own complicity in the national blood-letting. Larcom's final stanza offers a stunning re-vision in women-oriented terms of one of the best-known passages in British devotional literature, John Donne's, "No man is an *Iland*."[9] Relocating the seventeenth-century divine's assertion of spiritual brotherhood among men in the specifically politicized space created by the bonds between black and white women, the mill girl accepts responsibility as the burden of her art:

> "Alas! the weft has lost its white.
> It grows a hideous tapestry,
> That pictures war's abhorrent sight: –
> Unroll not, web of destiny!

Be the dark volume left unread, –
The tale untold, – the curse unsaid!"

So up and down before her loom
    She paces on, and to and fro,
Till sunset fills the dusty room,
    And makes the water redly glow,
As if the Merrimack's calm flood
Were changed into a stream of blood.

Too soon fulfilled, and all too true
    The words she murmured as she wrought:
But, weary weaver, not to you
    Alone was war's stern message brought:
"Woman!" it knelled from heart to heart,
"Thy sister's keeper know thou art!"
                    (*NAWP*, pp. 116–17)

While abolitionist writers such as Earle and Larcom were primarily concerned with using their poetry as an open space in which to exercise social and political agency, other women writers like Elizabeth Stoddard and Harriet Prescott Spofford were more directly engaged in issues of literature itself, using their weaver-seamstress figures more as Dickinson used her spider to explore the limits of their art. Stoddard may seem particularly close to Dickinson insofar as she chafed mightily against what she viewed as the damaging restraints placed on her as a Victorian woman artist. In "Before the Mirror" (1860), Stoddard identifies her woman-weaver with Tennyson's Lady of Shallot. Imprisoned, presumably "for her own good," within a room she can never leave, and cut off from direct experience, Stoddard's protagonist fills her loom with the images of images, shadowy makings as empty, finally, as the life she leads:

For not with altar, tomb, or urn,
    Or long-haired Greek with hollow shield,
Or dark-prowed ship with banks of oars,
    Or banquet in the tented field;

Or Norman knight in armor clad,
    Waiting a foe where four roads meet;
Or hawk and hound in bosky dell,
    Where dame and page in secret greet;

            ...Nothing bright
Is woven here: the shadows grow
Still darker in the mirror's light!

And as my web grows darker too,
Accursed seems this empty room;
I know I must forever weave
These phantoms by this hateful loom.
(*NAWP*, p. 435)

But is the emptiness and lack of connection that Stoddard describes in this poem really like Dickinson's in the end? For Dickinson, "freedom" as she told her young niece Mattie, *was* the ability to lock others out, *was* the privilege to be alone in her own room.[10] For Stoddard's weaver, this same isolation kills. That is, unlike Dickinson's isolation, which stimulated the wealth of her imagination, Stoddard's holds only the shadows of what will never be. Unable to pull off the kind of epiphanic transformations that allowed Dickinson to find "Peru" in a carnation (J 1366, Fr 1462) or ascend to heaven with a robin's flight (J 328, Fr 204), Stoddard's woman artist is destroyed by the very situation that leaves Dickinson's speakers bursting with life. Put another way, Stoddard writes to protest women's sequestration. Dickinson thrives on it.

Unlike Stoddard, Harriet Prescott Spofford in "Pomegranate-Flowers" (1861) does have good things to say about isolation, but in the end, her take on the woman artist is no more like Dickinson's than is Stoddard's. A very much updated version of the *hortus conclusus* (enclosed garden) topos, Spofford's poem presents a seamstress figure who, unlike Stoddard's weaver, is able to redeem her solitude by creating plentitude where emptiness would otherwise be. Indeed, Spofford boldly compares her humble heroine to Daedalus, the archetypal maker of the Minoan labyrinth (*NAWP*, p. 218), as well as to Arachne, the mythical Greek weaver for whom spiders – or "arachnids" – are named as a biological class (*NAWP*, p. 220). But unlike Dickinson, who genders her artist figures ambiguously at best, Spofford never lets us lose track of the gender of her lowly female "hand-worker," nor the specifically feminine qualities of her art. Creating an artwork that is quintessentially "feminine" in its materiality as in its function – a wedding veil – Spofford's seamstress remakes her world through her imaginative responses to her own creative efforts. But her achievements are never presented as other than they are, the products of a time-bound and material art, an art of women:

Bent lightly at her needle there
In that small room stair over stair,
All fancies blithe and debonair
She deftly wrought on fabrics rare,

> All clustered moss, all drifting snow,
> All trailing vines, all flowers that blow,
> Her daedal fingers laid them bare.
> (*NAWP*, pp. 217–18)

Trapped within the web she weaves, "Arachnean in a silver snare" (*NAWP*, p. 220), Spofford's protagonist experiences her makings as a source of abundant and overflowing joy but by immersing herself in the material world, not by attempting to transcend it. From this world's sights, sounds, and smells, the seamstress makes her own kind of poetry, a poetry epitomized in her erotic/imaginative response to the pomegranate-flower decorating her window ledge. In a way that curiously anticipates the relationship between speaker and nature in Wallace Stevens's "Sunday Morning"– and that can also be found ubiquitously in Dickinson's flower poems – Spofford's protagonist rejects transcendence in favor of the orgasmically experienced "real":

> Now, said she, in the heart of the woods
> The sweet south-winds assert their power,
> And blow apart the snowy snoods
> Of trilliums in their thrice-green bower.
> Now all the swamps are flushed with dower
> Of viscid pink, where, hour by hour,
> The bees swim amorous, and a shower
> Reddens the stream where cardinals tower.
> Far lost in fern of fragrant stir
> Her fancies roam, for unto her
> All Nature came in this one flower.
> (*NAWP*, p. 218)

But at the same time, Spofford differs profoundly from both Stevens *and* Dickinson by simultaneously insisting on her seamstress's location in a social "real." Dickinson's and Stevens's speakers are women of leisure, free to meditate on Sunday mornings, or at other times of the week, on their responses to nature and to God. Their art can go, as Dickinson so slyly, and so problematically, put it, "White – unto the White Creator – " (J 709, Fr 788). In this sense they and their art are outside time and place for all their immersion in "nature." Spofford's protagonist, on the other hand, not only responds ecstatically to the material world. Insofar as she is identified not just as a woman but as a working-class woman (and, indeed, possibly a prostitute since many such seamstresses were),[11] she is the essence of materiality herself – and, as most nineteenth-century American women poets ex-Dickinson were – subject to the "Disgrace of Price" (J 709, Fr 788).

Although in the poems just cited neither Spofford nor Stoddard treat direct political engagement as openly as do Earle and Larcom, all these writers are deeply vested in their female artists' social positioning as well as in issues related to "women's complicity in a system that oppressed them." Indeed, they show a good deal more awareness of the social consequences of women's oppression than does Dickinson herself, who rarely, if ever, exhibits much sympathy where matters of class, let alone race, are concerned. Whether positively or negatively, moreover, these writers all assert the materiality of women's art, its connections to "handy-work" of various kinds, including, as in Stoddard and Spofford, the erotic and autoerotic. For better or worse, they treat their makings as an art of immanence, deeply connected to the social and physical bodies. And, perhaps, because they did, they might all have agreed with Rose Terry Cooke in her powerful poem "Arachne" that their art was not likely to outlive its makers.

Published in the 1881 *Atlantic*, Cooke's "Arachne" appeared at a time when the author knew that she herself – together with her writing – was going to be forgotten. Not only had her own great popularity waned but she had before her the fate of other well-known women writers, Lydia Sigourney and Frances Osgood, for instance, who by the 1880s had long since ceased to be read. Worn down by an unfortunate marriage made late in life that brought her two step-children and a feckless younger husband who burdened her with debt, Cooke expresses none of Earle's or Spofford's optimism. The webs her spider-poet weaves prove eventually the cere-clothe in which her corpse will be wrapped.

> Poor sister of the spinster clan!
> . . .
> I know thy heart when heartless hands
>   Sweep all that hard-earned web away,
> Destroys its pearled and glittering bands,
>   And leave thee homeless by the way.
>
>   . . .
> I know what thou hast never known,
>   Sad foresight to a soul allowed, –
> That not for life I spin alone,
>   But day by day I spin my shroud.
>   (*NAWP*, pp. 161, 162)

After a lifetime of making, both Cooke and her poems were headed toward literary history's dustbin.

In earlier stanzas of "Arachne," Cooke identifies her spider protagonist as, literally, a home-maker, who spins the necessities of daily living directly out of herself. Having begun her career "restless, bold, and unafraid," Cooke's

Arachne is finally worn out by the relentless need to provide; and "the pearled and glittering bands" which represent her "art" have no value for those who follow her. Like herself, they are swept away in the final stanzas in a scenario strikingly like that which Dickinson invokes in "The Spider holds a Silver Ball." And it is, I believe, precisely this scenario that Dickinson struggles to defend herself against in her own spider poems. Embodied on the page as gifts or incorporated into letters, used as substitutes for the "real thing" – a hummingbird here, a sunset there – Dickinson's poems might have participated in the continuum of women's traditional craftwork but, by that very token, they were potentially vulnerable to the fate that overtook all such time-bound workings by women. That is, they were unless she could find some way to position them and herself differently.

Dickinson may have been speaking truthfully when she told Higginson that she was not concerned with fame during her lifetime (L 265); but her poems and letters suggest that she worried obsessively about immortality after death – both her poetry's and her own. In ways quite unlike most women poets of her period, Dickinson did not write out of pressing social concerns or as with Stoddard, Spofford, and Cooke, for money. As Erkkila has argued, despite her radical poetics, the Amherst poet was politically conservative and she was very well-heeled.[12] She could afford therefore to dismiss publication as "the Auction / Of the Mind" and vow to go "White – unto the White Creator" (J 709, Fr 788), her poems free from the stains left by time, place, or the need to grub for cash. She could, in short, afford to write in a void and write the void into her poetry, cutting its links to the social world and to the material connections she shared with others; and, in the two spider poems I am about to discuss, this is precisely what she does – or, rather, tries to do.

Although Dickinson wrote many poems on the role of the artist and on the ontological status of art, ranging from the highly conventional "The Poets light but lamps" (J 883, Fr 930) to the superbly idiosyncratic, "Essential Oils are wrung" (J 675, Fr 772), a poem that touches on many of the issues discussed in this essay, the two spider poems I discuss here are among her most personal and tension-fraught works. They also present a striking contrast to each other. For where Dickinson never finished "The Spider holds a Silver Ball" (J 605, Fr 513), "A Spider sewed at Night" (J 1138, Fr 1163) is, arguably, among her most "finished" poems. At thirty-two words, nothing is wasted, every word and image in place, and, however ambiguously phrased, its theme is an assertion: this spider sews for immortality and immortality is what it sews.

Dated 1863 by Franklin, "The Spider holds a Silver Ball" exhibits none of this definitiveness. On the contrary, especially when read with its variants, its

densely layered, multivalent metaphoric structure is riddled with contradictions. The spider-artist's "Tapestries" are described both as "Continents of
Light" and as "Sophistries" or lies (deceptions, illusions). The spider's activities are valuable and substantive (silver ball, knits, etc.); and they are
"unsubstantial Trade," plying from "Nought to Nought" – in the economic
terms carried by the variant ("expends"), an excessive or wasteful expendi-
ture of the self. Even the spider is a model of ambiguity – "masculine" in
gender and in certain of its activities (trade, supplanting, rearing supreme)
yet stereotypically feminine in other ways (dancing softly, knitting). The
only unambiguous moment in this poem comes at the end when, whatever
their intrinsic value, the spider's webs fall victim to the housewife's broom.
Like the webs spun by Cooke's Arachne, this spider's "handy-work" fails to
outlive its maker – doomed by the very materiality out of which it is made,
despite the void that darkness and secrecy place around it:

> An Hour to rear supreme
> His +Continents of Light –
> Then +dangle from the Housewife's Broom –
> His +Boundaries – forgot –
>
> +Theories +perish by +Sophistries
> (Fr 513)[13]

As the final variants suggest, the "Boundaries" that protect the spider's
"Continents of Light" are, like the "Continents" themselves, illusions. In
the light of day – the embodied light of physical reality signified by the coming of the housewife – the spider's dreams collapse into the matter from
which they came and the speaker leaves them there in the final stanza,
"dangling" inertly from "the Housewife's Broom."

That Dickinson was suffering unresolved ambivalence respecting her art's
ontological status when she wrote "The Spider holds a Silver Ball" (J 605,
Fr 513) seems evident. As I have argued elsewhere, I do not believe that she
could finish this poem, nor do I believe that editors should take the liberty –
as both Johnson and Franklin do – of "finishing" it for her.[14] The poem is the
sum of its indecisions, indecisions that derived from Dickinson's ambivalence
over how she wanted to present herself as artist and how she should present
the defining qualities of her art, how, that is, she should position it and
herself vis à vis the "real" world, whether the material world of women
or the ineffable, transcendental world of the male literary tradition. When
Dickinson returned to the spider theme six years later, in "A Spider sewed
at Night" (J 1138, Fr 1163), she had, it seems, a much clearer notion of what
she was doing and how she valued what she did, to which this later poem's
hyper-completed state attests.

Dismissing the material aspects of her spider's art as essentially immaterial or irrelevant to its reading – "If Ruff it was of Dame / Or Shroud of Gnome / Himself himself inform – " – Dickinson places the spider directly in touch with eternity, signified by the "Arc of White" on which the spider "sews." Then she dives straight for what matters: the immortality of the poem/web that the spider/artist creates. This, as she puts it, is the spider's "strategy," and this is what the spider produces. Effectively, for this artist, nothing else counts but the face she/he draws – the face of God, which she identified with the face of her art:

> A Spider sewed at Night
> Without a Light
> Opon an Arc of White –
>
> If Ruff it was of Dame
> Or Shroud of Gnome
> Himself himself inform –
>
> Of Immortality
> His strategy
> Was physiognomy –
> (J 1138, Fr 1163)

Although the poem's last stanza is susceptible to different readings, each reading is folded within the other. Written in isolation and the void, outside time, outside place, outside history and society, the strategy of immortal art is to reproduce itself, its own face, its sublime "physiognomy." To enter the world of this poem is presumably to leave behind both materiality and social life as signaled by the transition from such dismissible material items as a "Ruff" or a "Shroud" – a shedding, as it were, of the outer garment, the flesh – to the final settling on the pure abstraction of "Immortality." Confronted, then, as Dickinson's first readers were, with such a poem, it is not surprising that they had difficulty placing both the poet and her enigmatic texts. Nor is it surprising that so many of her poems appear to shimmer in the void that surrounds them, a void filled only by God, the atemporal God of poetic immortality, the God with whom she identified her in some ways all too Emersonian self. "Behind Me – dips Eternity – / Before Me – Immortality – / Myself – the Term between – " (J 721, Fr 743), Dickinson's speaker boldly declares, mirroring the narcissistic self-referentiality of the Deity whom she labeled with no small amount of irony, the "Son of none" and "Duplicate divine." In merging her art with Godhead, Dickinson, the middle term, achieved the immortality for which she yearned, escaping the vortex ("Maelstrom" or whirlpool) of time:

'Tis Miracle before Me – then –
'Tis Miracle behind – between –
A Crescent in the Sea –
With Midnight to the North of Her –
And Midnight to the South of Her –
And Maelstrom – in the Sky –
(J 721, Fr 743)

In poems such as "I dwell in Possibility," "Behind Me – dips Eternity – ," and "A Spider sewed at Night," Dickinson absorbs the material into the transcendent, cutting her poetry's ties to historically contingent social life, the life she lived as a nineteenth-century woman. However, as the preceding discussion has demonstrated, these were not ties she had to cut – nor did the isolating effect, which resulted from their cutting, accurately record her *necessary* position as a woman writer in respect to language. Dickinson, for example, is virtually certain to have known Spofford's "Pomegranate-Flowers," not only because she was a regular reader of the *Atlantic* and admired Spofford's short stories, but also because Samuel Bowles evinced substantial enthusiasm for the poem, reprinting excerpts in the *Springfield Republican* and reading passages from it aloud to a gathering at Susan Gilbert Dickinson's house.[15] As a regular reader of the *Atlantic*, Dickinson would in fact have been familiar with a number of major nineteenth-century American women writers, including not just Spofford but Larcom, Stoddard, and Cooke, all of whom appeared regularly in the periodical's prestigious pages. As noted earlier, she was also very well acquainted with the work of Barrett Browning and George Eliot, both of whom she admired tremendously and spoke of as great women writers. No less than Earle, then, Dickinson had before her a sizable list of women on both sides of the Atlantic whose literary achievements established women's right to write and to assume authorial subjecthood.

Dickinson's decision nevertheless to present herself as an isolate and a victim of masculinist oppression demands therefore another explanation. Historically, this other explanation has tended to be located in Dickinson's putative pathology and a wide range of diseases both physical and mental has been attributed to her. Indeed, this range is so wide it tends to undermine itself, for it hardly seems possible that a poet, ill in so many different ways, could have gotten out of bed in the morning, let alone written as much as Dickinson did. As a result, although pathology may have been involved, I would suggest that Dickinson's isolation is best viewed as a "reading effect," one generated not by illness but by her desire to achieve transcendence in her poetry and by her need to disassociate herself from womanhood's more material aspects, presenting herself as, effectively, a Gothic sprite instead: "weird," "spectral," "ghostly," and, of course, like the "White Creator" himself, always dressed in white.

Despite Dickinson's participation in nineteenth-century American women's material culture and in spite of the hundreds of poems she sent as gifts, included in her letters, or, indeed, sent as letters themselves, I have come to believe that Dickinson wrote, finally, for only one reader. That reader was God, the God with whom she identified both poetic immortality and herself. She did not have to write this way or to dematerialize her art. Nor did she have to present herself in life or art as an isolate. She chose to. It was, I would suggest, the only way she could have her cake (use her poems to maintain her connections in the social world) and eat it (write transcendentally; achieve sublimity and immortality) too. "The Poets light but Lamps – ," she declared in one of her most conventional versions of her peculiar vision of poetry's "high calling":

> Themselves – go out –
> The Wicks they stimulate –
> If vital Light
>
> Inhere as do the Suns –
> Each Age a Lens
> Disseminating their
> Circumference –
> (J 883, Fr 930)

Emerson could not have said it better. "So I conclude that space & time are things of the body," Dickinson wrote to Joseph Lyman in about 1865, "& have little or nothing to do with our selves. My Country is Truth."[16] It was not a country she shared willingly with others, those presumably more limited and time-bound than herself.

If this sounds as if I am reverting at least partially to an older, pre-feminist approach to Dickinson, to some extent, I am. Certainly, I find the influence of Puritan self-examination and Emersonian transcendentalism far more pertinent to her poetry and in particular to her speaker's positioning than I was ever prepared to grant before. Recent attempts, however well-intentioned, to relocate Dickinson's poetry in history, although illuminating in themselves, run counter to Dickinson's own assiduous attempts to place her poems outside "space & time." As "Essential Oils" makes clear, especially when read with "This was a Poet," like Emerson, Dickinson saw the artist's primary task as extracting the eternal from the matter of daily life. Reading her against other American women poets of her period, her determination to purge her poetry of the specifically historical and social could not be more striking. "George Who?" she infamously asked in 1884, noting, "[t]hat sums all Politics to me" (L 950). At least where her poetry is concerned, the query, rings true.

But by identifying the tension in her work between these two alternative poetics – one of transcendence, the other of materiality – I also hope that I have clarified why different sets of readers can come up with such different readings of her situation and why someone like myself could end up offering two such very different interpretations of the poet in one lifetime, hers, and mine. Despite her best efforts, the fact is that Dickinson never fully eradicated the material or even the social from her art. On the contrary, in her sensuous imagery as in her energetic response to the natural world, Dickinson immersed her art in the body and by incorporating so many of her poems into her letters, she maintained, however tenuously, their connections to social life, grounding them in multiple ways.

Dickinson therefore never uprooted her poems to the degree that her nineteenth-century readers believed. Take, for example, "A Spider sewed at Night," which is assuredly among the purest and most terrifying visions she produced. Yet even here, Dickinson deploys traditional images from women's handicraft that put the poem's abstract, dematerialized status in an ambiguous light. Although the spider sews "Without a Light," *what* it sews – be it "Ruff . . . of Dame" or "Shroud of Gnome," – still has multiple referents in the "real world." Even more ironically, this poem also enjoys dense inter-textual relations with other women's writings, in particular those produced by Dickinson's American women poet peers – the very peers whose existence she (like later scholars) so resolutely refused to acknowledge. And of course, there is also an edge of mockery to this poem and to Dickinson's entire conceptualization of the poet qua *male* spider, that puts her project or, at any rate, my argument regarding it, at risk. If Dickinson was seeking to convey a pure Emersonian transcendence, she also, as Rob Wilson has admirably demonstrated, was cutting it down to size, incorporating it within the (grotesque) body of a gnomic avatar – her spider, her self.[17] In embodying the transcendental Emersonian poet in a spider, Dickinson skirts very close to parodying not just the Concord sage, but herself. But then, whatever else, Dickinson was a very witty woman.

As Emerson admitted when speaking of Shakespeare, writers are not, in fact, isolates, nor like spiders, do they draw the material for their art solely from inside themselves.[18] Equally to the point, written words have no meaning when utterly divorced from the material, social, and historical circumstances out of which they arise and to which they point. Post-structuralist theorizing to the contrary, language is not an entirely enclosed, self-referential system, even though there are language-oriented poets like Dickinson (and even more, like Gertrude Stein) whose writing appears to strive for such an entirely dematerialized linguistic state. For the sake of Dickinson's art as well as for the pleasures readers take in her texts, this is probably just as well; for stripped of all reference to the material and the social, and of all inter-textual connections with what other women wrote, and stripped of the comic point of view that time and again grounds what might otherwise be a very pretentious ambition, Emily Dickinson's poetry would make "*lonely* & *rigorous*" (L 342a) reading indeed and probably not very interesting reading at that.[19]

NOTES

1 *Emily Dickinson: Woman Poet* (Iowa City: University of Iowa Press, 1990), p. 23.
2 *Dickinson and the Strategies of Reticence: The Woman Writer in Nineteenth-Century America* (Bloomington: Indiana University Press, 1989), pp. 46–9.
3 *Emily Dickinson's Reception in the 1890s: A Documentary History* (University of Pittsburgh Press, 1989), p. xv.
4 See, for example, citations 34, 70, 75, 86, 114, 117, and 155.
5 As quoted in *Emily Dickinson's Home: Letters of Edward Dickinson and His Family*, ed. Millicent Todd Bingham (New York: Harper & Brothers, 1955), p. 414.
6 Elizabeth Barrett Browning, *Aurora Leigh and Other Poems*, ed. Cora Kaplan (London: The Women's Press, 1978), p. 51.
7 As quoted by Cheryl Walker in "*Legacy* Profile: Rose Terry Cooke," *Legacy: A Journal of Nineteenth-Century American Writers* 9 (Fall, 1992): 147.
8 [Eliza Earle], "Lines, Suggested on reading 'An Appeal to Christian Women of the South,' by A. E. Grimke," in *Nineteenth-Century American Women Poets: An Anthology*, edited by Paula Bernat Bennett (Oxford: Blackwell Publishers, 1998), p. 405. All subsequent references to poems in this volume will appear in the text parenthetically as *NAWP*, followed by the page number.
9 The complete quotation reads, "No man is an *Iland*, intire of it selfe; every man is a peece of the *Continent*, a part of the *maine*...any mans *death* diminishes *me*, because I am involved in *Mankinde*; And therefore never send to know for whom the *bell* tolls; It tolls for *thee*." See "Meditations from 'Devotions Upon Emergent Occasions,'" in *The Complete Poetry and Selected Prose of John Donne & The Complete Poetry of William Blake*, ed. Robert Silliman Hillyer (New York: The Modern Library, 1941), p. 332.
10 Martha Dickinson Bianchi, *Emily Dickinson: Face to Face: Unpublished Letters, with Notes and Reminiscences* (Boston: Houghton Mifflin, 1932), pp. 65–6.
11 See Helena Michie, *The Flesh Made Word: Female Figures and Women's Bodies* (New York: Oxford University Press, 1987), p. 67.
12 Betsy Erkkila, "Emily Dickinson and Class," *American Literary History* 4 (Spring, 1992): 1–27.
13 See *The Manuscript Books of Emily Dickinson*, vol. 1 (Cambridge, Mass.: The Belknap Press of Harvard University Press, 1981), p. 542.
14 *Woman Poet*, pp. 42–5.
15 See Appendix xiv in Bianchi, *Emily Dickinson: Face to Face*, p. 282. The excerpts from Stoddard's poem appeared in the *Springfield Republican*, 11 May 1861.

See Katharine Rodier, "'Astra Castra': Emily Dickinson, Thomas Wentworth Higginson, and Harriet Prescott Spofford," in *Separate Spheres No More: Gender Convergence in American Literature, 1830–1930*, ed. Monika M. Elbert (Tuscaloosa: University of Alabama Press, 2000), pp. 63–64.

16 See *The Lyman Letters: New Light on Emily Dickinson and Her Family*, ed. Richard Sewall (Amherst: University of Massachusetts Press, 1965), p. 71.

17 Rob Wilson, *The American Sublime: The Genealogy of a Poetic Genre* (Madison: University of Wisconsin Press, 1991), p. 119.

18 Emerson, "Shakespeare: or, The Poet," in *The Works of Ralph Waldo Emerson*, vol. IV (New York, Philadelphia, and Chicago: The Nottingham Society, n.d.), p. 173.

19 These are the terms that Dickinson used to describe her father's reading when speaking to Higginson during his 1870 visit. See L 528.

GUIDE TO FURTHER READING

Bennett, Paula. *Emily Dickinson: Woman Poet.* University of Iowa Press, 1990.

ed. *Nineteenth-Century American Women Poets: An Anthology.* Oxford: Blackwell Publishers, 1998.

Bianchi, Martha Dickinson. *Emily Dickinson: Face to Face: Unpublished Letters, with Notes and Reminiscences.* Boston: Houghton Mifflin, 1932.

Browning, Elizabeth Barrett. *Aurora Leigh and Other Poems.* Ed. Cora Kaplan. London: The Women's Press, 1977.

Buckingham, Willis J. ed. *Emily Dickinson's Reception in the 1890s: A Documentary History.* University of Pittsburgh Press, 1989.

Dobson, Joanne. *Dickinson and the Strategies of Reticence: The Woman Writer in Nineteenth-Century America.* Bloomington: Indiana University Press, 1989.

Emerson, Ralph W. "Shakespeare: or, The Poet" in *The Works of Ralph Waldo Emerson* IV. New York, Philadelphia, Chicago: The Nottingham Society, n.d. 173.

Farr, Judith, *The Passion of Emily Dickinson.* Cambridge: Harvard UP, 1992.

Hillyer, Robert Silliman. *The Complete Poetry and Selected Prose of John Donne & The Complete Poetry of William Blake.* New York: The Modern Library, 1941.

Martin, Wendy. *An American Triptych: Anne Bradstreet, Emily Dickinson, Adrienne Rich.* Chapel Hill: University of North Carolina Press, 1984.

Michie, Helena. *The Flesh Made Word: Female Figures and Women's Bodies.* New York: Oxford University Press, 1987.

Rodier, Katharine. "'Astra Castra': Emily Dickinson, Thomas Wentworth Dickinson, and Harriet Prescott Spofford." In *Separate Spheres No More: Gender Convergence in American Literature, 1830–1930.* Ed. Monika M. Elbert. Tuscaloosa: University of Alabama Press, 2000, pp. 50–72.

Sewall, Richard. *The Lyman Letters: New Light on Emily Dickinson and Her Family.* Amherst: University of Massachusetts Press, 1965.

St. Armand, Barton Levi. *Emily Dickinson and Her Culture: The Soul's Society.* Cambridge University Press, 1984.

Walker, Cheryl. *The Nightingale's Burden: Women Poets and American Culture before 1900.* Bloomington: Indiana University Press, 1982.

Wilson, Rob. *The American Sublime: The Genealogy of a Poetic Genre.* Madison: University of Wisconsin, 1991.

SELECT BIBLIOGRAPHY

Primary works

Dickinson, Emily. *Bolts of Melody: New Poems by Emily Dickinson*. Ed. Mabel Loomis Todd and Millicent Todd Bingham. New York: Harper and Brothers, 1945.

The Complete Poems of Emily Dickinson. Ed. Martha Dickinson Bianchi. Boston: Little, Brown, and Company, 1924.

The Complete Poems of Emily Dickinson. Ed. Thomas H. Johnson. Boston: Little, Brown, and Company, 1960.

Final Harvest: Emily Dickinson's Poems. Selection and Introduction by Thomas H. Johnson. Boston: Little, Brown, and Company, 1961.

Further Poems of Emily Dickinson Withheld from Publication by her Sister Lavinia. Ed. Martha Dickinson Bianchi and Alfred Leete Hampson. Boston: Little, Brown and Company, 1929.

The Letters of Emily Dickinson. 3 vols. Ed. Thomas H. Johnson and Theodora Ward. Cambridge, MA: The Belknap Press of Harvard University Press, 1958.

Letters of Emily Dickinson. 2 vols. Ed. Mabel Loomis Todd. Boston: Roberts Brothers, 1894.

The Manuscript Books of Emily Dickinson. 2 vols. Ed. R. W. Franklin. Cambridge: The Belknap Press of Harvard University Press, 1981.

The Manuscript Books of Emily Dickinson. 2 vols. Ed. Mabel Loomis Todd. Boston: Little, Brown, 1896.

New Poems of Emily Dickinson. Ed. William H. Shurr, with Anna Dunlap and Emily Grey Shurr. Chapel Hill: University of North Carolina Press, 1983.

Open Me Carefully: Emily Dickinson's Intimate Letters to Susan Huntington Dickinson. Ed. Ellen Louise Hart and Martha Nell Smith. Paris Press, 1998.

Poems. Ed. Martha Dickinson Bianchi and Alfred Leete Hampson. Boston: Little, Brown, and Company [1937] 1950.

The Poems of Emily Dickinson. Ed. Martha Dickinson Bianchi and Alfred Leete Hampson. Boston: Little, Brown, and Company, 1930.

The Poems of Emily Dickinson, Variorum Edition. 3 vols. Ed. R. W. Franklin. Cambridge, MA: The Belknap Press of Harvard University Press, 1998.

The Poems of Emily Dickinson. 3 vols. Ed. Thomas H. Johnson. Cambridge, MA: The Belknap Press of Harvard University Press, 1955.

Poems of Emily Dickinson. First series. Ed. Mabel Loomis Todd and Thomas Wentworth Higginson. Boston: Roberts Brothers, 1890.

Poems by Emily Dickinson. Second series. Ed. T. W. Higginson and Mabel Loomis Todd. Boston: Roberts Brothers, 1891.

Poems by Emily Dickinson. Third series. Ed. Mabel Loomis Todd. Boston: Roberts Brothers, 1896.

The Single Hound: Poems of a Lifetime. Ed. Martha Dickinson Bianchi. Boston: Little, Brown, and Company, 1914.

Unpublished Poems of Emily Dickinson. Ed. Martha Dickinson Bianchi and Alfred Leete Hampson. Boston: Little, Brown, and Company, 1935.

Secondary works

Agrawal, Abha. *Emily Dickinson, Search for Self.* New Delhi: Young Asia Publications, 1977.

Alfrey, Shawn. *The Sublime of Intense Sociability: Emily Dickinson, H. D., and Gertrude Stein.* Lewisburg, PA: Bucknell University Press, 2000.

Anderson, Charles R. *Emily Dickinson's Poetry: Stairway of Surprise.* New York: Holt, Rinehart and Winston, 1960.

Arensberg, Mary. *The American Sublime.* Albany: State University of New York Press, 1986.

Barker, Wendy. *Lunacy of Light: Emily Dickinson and the Experience of Metaphor.* Carbondale: Southern Illinois University Press, 1987.

Benfey, Christopher. *Emily Dickinson: Lives of a Poet.* New York: Braziller, 1986.

Emily Dickinson and the Problem of Others. Amherst: University of Massachusetts Press, 1984.

Bennett, Paula Bernat. *Emily Dickinson: Woman Poet.* Iowa City: University of Iowa Press, 1990.

My Life, a Loaded Gun: Female Creativity and Feminist Poetics. Boston: Beacon Press, 1986.

ed. *Nineteenth-Century American Poets: An Anthology.* Oxford: Blackwell Publishers, 1998.

Bianchi, Martha Dickinson. *Emily Dickinson Face to Face: Unpublished Letters, With Notes and Reminiscences.* Boston: Houghton Mifflin Co., 1932.

Bingham, Millicent Todd. *Ancestor's Brocades: The Literary Debut of Emily Dickinson.* New York and London: Harper & Brothers, 1945.

ed. *Emily Dickinson's Home: Letters of Edward Dickinson and His Family.* New York: Harper & Brothers, 1955.

Blake, Caesar R. and Carlton F. Wells, eds. *The Recognition of Emily Dickinson: Selected Criticism Since 1890.* Ann Arbor: University of Michigan Press, 1964.

Bloom, Harold, ed. *Emily Dickinson.* New York: Chelsea, 1985.

Brose, Nancy Harris, Juliana McGovern Dupre, Wendy Tocher Kohler, and Jean McClure Mudge. *Emily Dickinson: Profile of the Poet as Cook.* Amherst, MA: Hamilton Newall, 1976.

Buckingham, Willis, ed. *Emily Dickinson's Reception in the 1890s: A Documentary History.* University of Pittsburgh Press, 1989.

Budick, E. Miller. *Emily Dickinson and the Life of Language: a Study in Symbolic Poetics.* Baton Rouge: Louisiana State University Press, 1985.

Buell, Lawrence. *New England Literary Culture: From Revolution Through Renaissance*. Cambridge University Press, 1986.

Cady, Edwin H. and Louis J. Budd, eds. *On Dickinson: The Best From American Literature*. Durham: Duke University Press, 1990.

Cameron, Sharon. *Choosing Not Choosing: Dickinson's Fascicles*. University of Chicago Press, 1992.

  Lyric Time: Dickinson and the Limits of Genre. Baltimore: Johns Hopkins University Press, 1979.

Capps, Jack L. *Emily Dickinson's Reading, 1836–1886*. Cambridge, MA: Harvard University Press, 1966.

Carton, Evan. *The Rhetoric of American Romance: Dialectic and Identity in Emerson, Dickinson, Poe, and Hawthorne*. Baltimore: Johns Hopkins University Press, 1985.

Chase, Richard. *Emily Dickinson*. American Men of Letters Series. New York: Sloane, 1951.

Cody, John. *After Great Pain: The Inner Life of Emily Dickinson*. Cambridge, MA: Harvard University Press, 1971.

Conrad, Angela. *The Wayward Nun of Amherst: Emily Dickinson in the Medieval Women's Visionary Tradition*. New York: Garland Publishing, 2000.

Crumbley, Paul. *Inflections of the Pen: Dash and Voice in Emily Dickinson*. Lexington: University Press of Kentucky, 1997.

Danly, Susan, ed. *Language as Object: Emily Dickinson and Contemporary Art*. Amherst: University of Massachusetts Press, 1997.

Davis, Thomas M. *Fourteen by Emily Dickinson, With Selected Criticism*. Chicago: Scott, Foresman, 1964.

Dickenson, Donna. *Emily Dickinson*. Leamington Spa: Berg, 1985.

Dickie, Margaret. *Lyric Contingencies: Emily Dickinson and Wallace Stevens*. Philadelphia: University of Pennsylvania Press, 1991.

Diehl, Joanne Feit. *Dickinson and the Romantic Imagination*. Princeton University Press, 1981.

  Women Poets and the American Sublime. Bloomington: Indiana University Press, 1990.

Dobson, Joanne. *Dickinson and the Strategies of Reticence: The Woman Writer in Nineteenth-Century America*. Bloomington: Indiana University Press, 1989.

Donoghue, Denis. *Emily Dickinson*. Minneapolis: The University of Minnesota Press, 1966.

Doriani, Beth Maclay. *Emily Dickinson: Daughter of Prophecy*. Amherst: University of Massachusetts Press, 1996.

Eberwein, Jane Donahue. *Dickinson: Strategies of Limitation*. Amherst: University of Massachusetts Press, 1985.

Erkkila, Betsy. *The Wicked Sisters: Women Poets, Literary History, and Discord*. New York: Oxford University Press, 1992.

Farr, Judith, ed. *Emily Dickinson: A Collection of Critical Essays*. New York: Prentice Hall, 1995.

  The Passion of Emily Dickinson. Cambridge, MA: Harvard University Press, 1992.

Fast, Robin Riley, and Christine Mack Gordon, eds. *Approaches to Teaching Dickinson's Poetry*. New York: MLA, 1989.

Ferlazzo, Paul J., ed. *Critical Essays on Emily Dickinson*. Boston, MA.: G. K. Hall, 1984.

Emily Dickinson. Boston: Twayne, 1976.

Ford, Thomas W. *Heaven Beguiles the Tired: Death in the Poetry of Emily Dickinson*. Tuscaloosa: University of Alabama Press, 1966.

Franklin, Ralph W. *The Editing of Emily Dickinson: A Reconsideration*. Madison: University of Wisconsin Press, 1967.

Galvin, Mary E. *Queer Poetics: Five Modernist Women Writers*. Westport, CT: Praeger, 1999.

Garbowsky, Maryanne M. *The House Without the Door: A Study of Emily Dickinson and the Illness of Agoraphobia*. Rutherford, NJ: Associated University Presses, 1989.

Gelpi, Albert J. *Emily Dickinson: The Mind of the Poet*. Cambridge, MA: Harvard University Press, 1965.

The Tenth Muse: The Psyche of the American Poet [1975]. Cambridge University Press, 1991.

Gilbert, Sandra M. and Susan Gubar. *The Madwoman in the Attic: The Woman Writer and the Ninteenth-Century Literary Imagination*. New Haven: Yale University Press, 1979.

Grabher, Gundrun, Roland Hagenbuchle, and Cristanne Miller, eds. *The Emily Dickinson Handbook*. Amherst: University of Massachusetts Press, 1998.

Gray, Janet, ed. *She Wields a Pen: American Women Poets of the Nineteenth Century*. University of Iowa Press, 1997.

Griffith, Clark. *The Long Shadow: Emily Dickinson's Tragic Poetry*. Princeton University Press, 1964.

Guthrie, James R. *Emily Dickinson's Vision: Illness and Identity in Her Poetry*. Gainesville, FL: University Press of Florida, 1998.

Higgins, David. *Portrait of Emily Dickinson: The Poet and Her Prose*. New Brunswick, NJ: Rutgers University Press, 1967.

Homans, Margaret. *Bearing the Word: Language and Female Experience in Nineteenth-Century Women's Writing*. University of Chicago Press, 1986.

Women Writers and Poetic Identity: Dorothy Wordsworth, Emily Bronte, and Emily Dickinson. Princeton University Press, 1980.

Howe, Susan. *The Birth-Mark: Unsettling the Wilderness in American Literary History*. Hanover: University Press of New England, 1993.

My Emily Dickinson. Berkeley: North Atlantic Books, 1985.

Jenkins, MacGregor. *Emily Dickinson, Friend, and Neighbor*. Boston: Little, Brown, and Company, 1930.

Johnson, Greg. *Emily Dickinson: Perception and the Poet's Quest*. University, AL: University of Alabama Press, 1985.

Johnson, Tamara, ed. *Readings on Emily Dickinson*. Greenhaven Literary Companion to American Authors. San Diego, CA: Greenhaven Press, 1997.

Johnson, Thomas H. *Emily Dickinson: An Interpretive Biography*. Cambridge, MA: Harvard University Press, 1955.

Juhasz, Suzanne, ed. *Feminist Critics Read Emily Dickinson*. Bloomington: Indiana University Press, 1983.

The Undiscovered Continent: Emily Dickinson and the Space of the Mind. Bloomington: Indiana University Press, 1983.

and Cristanne Miller, eds. *Emily Dickinson: A Celebration for Readers: Proceedings of the Conference Held on September 19–21, 1986 at the Claremont Colleges.* New York: Gordon and Breach, 1989.

Cristanne Miller, and Martha Nell Smith. *Comic Power in Emily Dickinson.* Austin: University of Texas Press, 1993.

Keller, Karl. *The Only Kangaroo Among the Beauty: Emily Dickinson and America.* Baltimore: Johns Hopkins University Press, 1979.

Kher, Inder Nath. *The Landscape of Absence: Emily Dickinson's Poetry.* New Haven: Yale University Press, 1974.

Kimpel, Ben. *Emily Dickinson as Philosopher.* New York: E. Mellen Press, 1981.

Kirkby, Joan. *Emily Dickinson. Women Writers Series.* London: Macmillan, 1991.

Knapp, Bettina L. *Emily Dickinson.* New York: Continuum, 1989.

Lambert, Robert Graham, Jr. *A Critical Study of Emily Dickinson's Letters: The Prose of a Poet.* Lewiston, NY: Mellen University Press, 1966, 1997.

Emily Dickinson's Use of Anglo-American Legal Concepts and Vocabulary in Her Poetry. Lewiston, NY: Edwin Mellen Press, 1997.

Lease, Benjamin. *Emily Dickinson's Readings of Men and Books: Sacred Soundings.* New York: St. Martin's Press, 1990.

Leder, Sharon and Andrea Abbott. *The Language of Exclusion: The Poetry of Emily Dickinson and Christina Rossetti.* New York: Greenwood Press, 1987.

Leyda, Jay. *The Years and Hours of Emily Dickinson.* 2 vols. New Haven: Yale University Press, 1960.

Lilliedahl, Ann Martha. *Emily Dickinson in Europe: Her Literary Reputation in Selected Countries.* Washington, DC: University of America, 1981.

Lindberg-Seyersted, Brita. *Emily Dickinson's Punctuation.* University of Oslo, 1976.

The Voice of the Poet: Aspects of Style in the Poetry of Emily Dickinson. Cambridge, MA: Harvard University Press, 1968; Uppsala: Almquist and Wiksells, 1968.

Loeffelholz, Mary. *Dickinson and the Boundaries of Feminist Theory.* Urbana: University of Illinois Press, 1991.

Lombardo, Daniel. *Hedge Away: The Other Side of Emily Dickinson's Amherst.* Daily Hampshire Gazette, 1997.

Longsworth, Polly. *Austin and Mabel: The Amherst Affair and Love Letters of Austin Dickinson and Mabel Loomis Todd.* New York: Farrar, Straus, and, Giroux, 1984.

The World of Emily Dickinson. New York: Norton, 1990.

Loving, Jerome. *Emily Dickinson: The Poet on the Second Story.* Cambridge University Press, 1986.

Lowenberg, Carlton. *Emily Dickinson's Textbooks.* Lafayette, CA: 1986.

Musicians Wrestle Everywhere: Emily Dickinson and Music. Berkeley: Fallen Leaf, 1992.

Lubbers, Klaus. *Emily Dickinson: The Critical Revolution.* Ann Arbor: University of Michigan Press, 1968.

Lucas, Dolores Dyer. *Emily Dickinson and Riddle.* DeKalb: Northern Illinois University Press, 1969.

Lundin, Roger. *Emily Dickinson and the Art of Belief.* Grand Rapids, MI: William B. Eerdmans Publishing Company, 1998.

Martin, Wendy. *An American Triptych: Anne Bradstreet, Emily Dickinson, Adrienne Rich*. Chapel Hill: University of North Carolina Press, 1984.

McGann, Jerome. *Black Riders: The Visible Language of Modernism*. Princeton University Press, 1993.

McIntosh, James. *Nimble Believing: Dickinson and the Unknown*. Ann Arbor: University of Michigan Press, 2000.

McNaughton, Ruth F. *The Imagery of Emily Dickinson*. Folcroft, PA: Folcroft Library Editions, 1973.

McNeil, Helen. *Emily Dickinson*. London: Virago, 1986.

Messmer, Marietta. *A Vice for Voices: Reading Emily Dickinson's Correspondence*. Amherst: University of Massachusetts Press, 2001.

Miller, Cristanne. *Emily Dickinson: A Poet's Grammar*. Cambridge, MA: Harvard University Press, 1987.

Miller, Ruth. *The Poetry of Emily Dickinson*. Middletown, CT: Wesleyan University Press, 1968.

Mitchell, Domhnall. *Emily Dickinson: Monarch of Perception*. Amherst: University of Massachusetts Press, 2000.

Mossberg, Barbara Antonina Clarke. *Emily Dickinson: When a Writer is a Daughter*. Bloomington: Indiana University Press, 1982.

Mudge, Jean McClure. *Emily Dickinson and the Image of Home*. Amherst: University of Massachusetts Press, 1975.

Noble, Marianne. *The Masochistic Pleasures of Sentimental Literature*. Princeton University Press, 2000.

Oberhaus, Dorothy Huff. *Emily Dickinson's Fascicles: Method and Meaning*. University Park: Pennsylvania State University Press, 1995.

Oliver, Virginia H. *Apocalypse of Green: A Study of Emily Dickinson's Eschatology*. New York: Peter Lang, 1989.

Olney, James. *The Languages of Poetry: Walt Whitman, Emily Dickinson, Gerard Manley Hopkins*. Athens: University of Georgia Press, 1993.

Olson, Steven. *The Prairie in Nineteenth-Century American Poetry*. Norman: University of Oklahoma Press, 1994.

Orzeck, Martin and Robert Weisbuch, eds. *Dickinson and Audience*. Ann Arbor: University of Michigan Press, 1996.

Ottlinger, Claudia. *The Death-Motif in the Poetry of Emily Dickinson and Christina Rossetti*. New York: Peter Lang, 1996.

Paglia, Camille. *Sexual Personae: Art and Decadence from Nefertiti to Emily Dickinson*. New Haven: Yale University Press, 1990.

Patterson, Rebecca. *Emily Dickinson's Imagery*. Amherst: University of Massachusetts Press, 1979.

The Riddle of Emily Dickinson. Boston: Houghton Mifflin, 1951.

Petrino, Elizabeth. *Emily Dickinson and Her Contemporaries: Women's Verse in America, 1820–1885*. Hanover, NH: University Press of New England, 1998.

Phillips, Elizabeth. *Emily Dickinson: Personae and Performance*. University Park: Pennsylvania State University Press, 1988.

Pickard, John B. *Emily Dickinson: An Introduction and Interpretation*. New York: Holt, Rinehart and Winston, 1967.

Pollak, Vivian R. *Dickinson: The Anxiety of Gender*. Ithaca: Cornell University Press, 1984.

ed. *A Poet's Parents: The Courtship Letters of Emily Norcross and Edward Dickinson*. Chapel Hill: University of North Carolina Press, 1988.

Pollitt, Josephine. *Emily Dickinson: The Human Background of Her Poetry*. New York: Harper, 1930.

Porter, David T. *The Art of Emily Dickinson's Early Poetry*. Cambridge, MA: Harvard University Press, 1966.

Dickinson: The Modern Idiom. Cambridge, MA: Harvard University Press, 1981.

Power, Mary James, Sister. *In the Name of the Bee: The Significance of Emily Dickinson*. New York: Sheed & Ward, 1943.

Pritchard, William H. *Talking Back to Emily Dickinson and Other Essays*. Amherst: University of Massachusetts Press, 1998.

Reising, Russell J. *Loose Ends: Closure and Crisis in the American Social Text*. Durham, NC: Duke University Press, 1996.

Reynolds, David S. *Beneath the American Renaissance: The Subversive Imagination in the Age of Emerson and Melville*. New York: Knopf, 1988.

Faith in Fiction: The Emergence of Religious Literature in America. Cambridge, MA: Harvard University Press, 1981.

Robinson, John. *Emily Dickinson: Looking to Canaan*. Boston: Faber and Faber, 1986.

Rupp, Richard H. *Critics on Emily Dickinson*. University of Miami Press, 1972.

St. Armand, Barton Levi. *Emily Dickinson and Her Culture: the Soul's Society*. Cambridge University Press, 1984.

Salska, Agnieszka. *Walt Whitman and Emily Dickinson: Poetry of the Central Consciousness*. Philadelphia: University of Pennsylvania Press, 1985.

Sanchez-Eppler, Karen. *Touching Liberty: Abolition, Feminism, and the Politics of the Body*. Berkeley: University of California Press, 1993.

Sewall, Richard Benson, ed. *Emily Dickinson, a Collection of Critical Essays*. Englewood Cliffs, N. J.: Prentice-Hall, 1963.

The Life of Emily Dickinson. 2 vols. New York: Farrar, Straus, and Giroux, 1974. Rpt. 1980, 1996.

The Lyman Letters: New Light on Emily Dickinson and Her Family. Amherst: University of Massachusetts Press, 1965.

Sherwood, William. *Circumference and Circumstance: Stages in the Mind and Art of Emily Dickinson*. New York: Columbia University Press, 1968.

Shurr, William H. *The Marriage of Emily Dickinson: A Study of the Fascicles*. Lexington: University Press of Kentucky, 1983.

Sielke, Sabine, ed. *Fashioning the Female Subject: The Intertextual Networking of Dickinson, Moore, and Rich*. Ann Arbor: University of Michigan Press, 1997.

Small, Judy Jo. *Positive as Sound: Emily Dickinson's Rhyme*. Athens: University of Georgia Press, 1990.

Smith, Martha Nell. *Rowing in Eden: Rereading Emily Dickinson*. Austin: University of Texas Press, 1992.

Smith, Robert McClure. *The Seductions of Emily Dickinson*. Tuscaloosa: University of Alabama Press, 1996.

Sohn, Youngmi. *The Challenge of Temporality: The Time Poems of Emily Dickinson*. New York: Peter Lang, 2000.

Sprague, Rosemary. *Imaginary Gardens: A Study of Five American Poets*. Philadelphia: Chilton Book Co., 1969.

Stein, Rachel. *Shifting the Ground: American Women Writers' Revision of Nature, Gender, and Race*. Charlottesville: University Press of Virginia, 1997.

Stocks, Kenneth. *Emily Dickinson and the Modern Consciousness: a Poet of Our Time*. New York: St. Martin's Press, 1988.

Stonum, Gary Lee. *The Dickinson Sublime*. Madison: University of Wisconsin Press, 1990.

Taggard, Genevieve. *The Life and Mind of Emily Dickinson*. New York, London: A. A. Knopf, 1930.

Thackrey, Donald E. *Emily Dickinson's Approach to Poetry*. Lincoln: University of Nebraska, 1954.

Thota, Anand Rao. Foreword by Satyanarain Singh. *Emily Dickinson: The Metaphysical Tradition*. Atlantic Highlands, NJ: Humanities, 1982.

Thurman, Judith. *I Became Alone: Five Women Poets, Sappho, Louise Labe, Ann Bradstreet, Juana Ines De La Cruz, Emily Dickinson*. New York: Atheneum, 1975.

Tripp, Raymond P., Jr. *Duty, Body, and World in the Works of Emily Dickinson: Reorganizing the Estimate*. Lewiston. NY: Edwin Mellon Press, 2000.

The Mysterious Kingdom of Emily Dickinson's Poetry. Denver, CL: Society for New Language Study, 1988.

Untermeyer, Louis, ed. *Emily Dickinson, 1830–1886*. New York: Simon & Schuster, 1927.

Walker, Cheryl. *The Nightingale's Burden: Women Poets and American Culture Before 1900*. Bloomington: Indiana University Press, 1982.

Walsh, John Evangelist. *This Brief Tragedy: Unraveling the Todd-Dickinson Affair*. New York: G. Weidenfeld, 1991.

The Hidden Life of Emily Dickinson. New York: Simon and Schuster, 1971.

Ward, Bruce. *The Gift of Screws: The Poetic Strategies of Emily Dickinson*. Troy, NY: Whitson Publishing, 1994.

Ward, Theodora. *The Capsule of the Mind: Chapters in the Mind of Emily Dickinson*. Cambridge, MA: The Belknap Press of Harvard University Press, 1961.

Wardrop, Daneen. *Emily Dickinson's Gothic: Goblin with a Gauge*. Iowa City: University of Iowa Press, 1996.

Weisbuch, Robert. *Emily Dickinson's Poetry*. The University of Chicago Press, 1975.

Wells, Henry Willis. *Introduction to Emily Dickinson*. Chicago: Hendricks House, 1947.

Werner, Marta. *Emily Dickinson's Open Folios: Scenes of Reading, Surfaces of Writing*. Ann Arbor: University of Michigan Press, 1995.

Whicher, George Frisbie. *This Was a Poet: A Critical Biography of Emily Dickinson*. New York: Charles Scribner's Sons, 1938.

Wilson, Raymond Jackson. *Figures of Speech: American Writers and the Literary Marketplace: From Benjamin Franklin to Emily Dickinson*. New York: Knopf, 1989.

Wolff, Cynthia Griffin. *Emily Dickinson*. Reading, MA: Addison-Wesley, 1988.

Wolosky, Shira. *Emily Dickinson: A Voice of War*. New Haven: Yale University Press, 1984.

Wylder, Edith. *The Last Face: Emily Dickinson's Manuscripts*. Albuquerque: University of New Mexico Press, 1971.

Reference works

Boswell, Jeanetta. *Emily Dickinson: A Bibliography of Secondary Sources, With Selective Annotations, 1890 Through 1987*. Jefferson, NC: McFarland, 1989.

Buckingham, Willis J. *Emily Dickinson, an Annotated Bibliography: Writings, Scholarship, Criticism, and Ana, 1850–1968*. Bloomington: Indiana University Press, 1970.

Clendenning, Sheila T. *Emily Dickinson, A Bibliography, 1850–1967*. Kent, OH: Kent State University Press, 1968.

Dandurand, Karen. *Dickinson Scholarship: An Annotated Bibliography, 1969–1985*. New York: Garland Publishing, 1988.

Duchac, Joseph. *The Poems of Emily Dickinson: an Annotated Guide to Commentary*. Boston: G. K. Hall, 1979.

Eberwein, Jane Donohue, ed. *An Emily Dickinson Encyclopedia*. Westport, CT: Greenwood Press, 1998.

Hampson, Alfred Leete. *Emily Dickinson: A Bibliography*. Northampton: The Hampshire Bookshop, 1930.

MacKenzie, Cynthia. *Emily Dickinson: Concordance to the Letters of*. Boulder: University Press of Colorado, 2000.

Rosenbaum, Stanford P. *Concordance to the Poems of Emily Dickinson*. Ithaca: Cornell University Press, 1964.

INDEX

Ship To:

Ship From:

Jessica Russell
P.O. Box 6571 UM Box#1922
Montevallo, AL 351156571 USA

TEXTBOOKSNOW-AMAZON
8950 W PALMER ST
RIVER GROVE, IL 60171

Date: 01/05/2012

SKU	Qty	Condition	Title
4388617U	1	Used	Cambridge Companion to Emily Dickinson
			9780521001182 Refund Eligible Through= 2/7/2012

Page 1 of 1

Return Information (cut and attach to the outside of return shipment)

Order #: 104-9492806-2102645

TEXTBOOKSNOW-AMAZON
8950 W PALMER ST
RIVER GROVE, IL 60171

(Attn: Returns)

DT74056

Order #: 104-9492806-2102645

	Price	Total
	$ 15.90	$ 15.90

Sub Total	$	15.90
Shipping & Handling	$	3.99
Sales Tax	$	0.00
Order Total	**$**	**19.89**

Order #: 104-9492806-2102645

Refund Policy: All items must be returned within 30 days of receipt. Pack your book securely, so it will arrive back to us in its original condition. To avoid delays, please use the return section and label provided with your original packing slip to identify your return. Be sure to include a return reason. For your protection, we suggest using a traceable, insured shipping service (UPS or Insured Parcel Post). We are not responsible for lost or damaged returns. Item(s) returned must be received in the original condition as sold and including all additional materials such as CDs, workbooks, etc. We will initiate a refund of your purchase price including applicable taxes within 5 business days of receipt. Shipping charges will not be refunded unless we have committed an error with your order. If there is an error with your order or the item is not received in the condition as purchased, please contact us immediately for return assistance.

Reason for Refund/Return:
Condition   Incorrect Item Received   Incorrect Item Ordered   Dropped Class   Purchased Elsewhere   Other
Contact Us: For customer service, email us at customerservice@textbooksNow.com.
Page 1 of 1

This book is for
Robert Silvers
and for
Christopher Dickey

"All Europe contributed to the making of Kurtz; and by-and-by I learned that, most appropriately, the International Society for the Suppression of Savage Customs had intrusted him with the making of a report, for its future guidance. And he had written it, too. I've seen it. I've read it. It was eloquent, vibrating with eloquence. . . . 'By the simple exercise of our will we can exert a power for good practically unbounded,' etc. etc. From that point he soared and took me with him. The peroration was magnificent, although difficult to remember, you know. It gave me the notion of an exotic Immensity ruled by an august Benevolence. It made me tingle with enthusiasm. This was the unbounded power of eloquence—of words—of burning noble words. There were no practical hints to interrupt the magic current of phrases, unless a kind of note at the foot of the last page, scrawled evidently much later, in an unsteady hand, may be regarded as the exposition of a method. It was very simple, and at the end of that moving appeal to every altruistic sentiment it blazed at you, luminous and terrifying, like a flash of lightning in a serene sky: 'Exterminate all the brutes!'"

—Joseph Conrad,
Heart of Darkness

THE three-year-old El Salvador International Airport is glassy and white and splendidly isolated, conceived during the waning of the Molina "National Transformation" as convenient less to the capital (San Salvador is forty miles away, until recently a drive of several hours) than to a central hallucination of the Molina and Romero regimes, the projected beach resorts, the Hyatt, the Pacific Paradise, tennis, golf, water-skiing, condos, *Costa del Sol;* the visionary invention of a tourist industry in yet another republic where the leading natural cause of death is gastrointestinal infection. In the general absence of tourists these hotels have since been abandoned, ghost resorts on the empty Pacific beaches, and to land at this airport built to service them is to plunge directly into a state in which no ground is solid, no depth of field reliable, no perception so definite that it might not dissolve into its reverse.

The only logic is that of acquiescence. Immigration is negotiated in a thicket of automatic weapons, but by whose authority the weapons are brandished (Army or National Guard or National Police or Customs Police or Treasury Police or one of a continuing proliferation of other shadowy and overlapping forces) is a blurred point. Eye contact is avoided. Documents are scrutinized upside down. Once clear of the airport, on the new highway that slices through green hills rendered phosphorescent by the cloud cover of the tropical rainy season, one sees mainly underfed cattle and mongrel dogs and armored vehicles, vans and trucks and Cherokee Chiefs fitted with reinforced steel and bulletproof Plexiglas an inch thick. Such vehicles are a fixed feature of local life, and are popularly associated with disappearance and death. There was the Cherokee Chief seen following the Dutch television crew killed in Chalatenango province in March of 1982. There was the red Toyota three-quarter-ton pickup sighted near the van driven by the four American Catholic workers on the night they were killed in 1980. There were, in the late spring and summer of 1982, the three Toyota panel trucks, one yellow, one blue, and one green, none bearing plates, reported present at each of the mass detentions (a "detention" is another fixed feature of local life, and often precedes a "disappearance") in the Amatepec district of San Salvador. These are the details—the models and colors of armored vehicles, the makes and calibers of weapons, the particular methods of dismemberment and decapitation used in particular instances—on which the visitor to Salvador learns immediately to concentrate, to the exclusion of past or future concerns, as in a prolonged amnesiac fugue.

Terror is the given of the place. Black-and-white police cars cruise in pairs, each with the barrel of a rifle extruding from an open window. Roadblocks materialize at random, soldiers fanning out from trucks and taking positions, fingers always on triggers, safeties clicking on and off. Aim is taken as if to pass the time. Every morning *El Diario de Hoy* and *La Prensa Gráfica* carry cautionary stories. *"Una madre y sus dos hijos fueron asesinados con arma cortante (corvo) por ocho sujetos desconocidos el lunes en la noche"*: A mother and her two sons hacked to death in their beds by eight *desconocidos*, unknown men. The same morning's paper: the unidentified body of a young man, strangled, found on the shoulder of a road. Same morning, different story: the unidentified bodies of three young men, found on another road, their faces partially destroyed by bayonets, one faced carved to represent a cross.

It is largely from these reports in the newspapers that the United States embassy compiles its body counts, which are transmitted to Washington in a weekly dispatch referred to by embassy people as "the grimgram." These counts are presented in a kind of tortured code that fails to obscure what is taken for granted in El Salvador, that government forces do most of the killing. In a January 15 1982 memo to Washington, for example, the embassy issued a "guarded" breakdown on its count of 6,909 "reported" political murders between September 16 1980 and September 15 1981. Of these 6,909, according to the memo, 922 were "believed committed by security forces," 952 "believed committed by leftist terrorists," 136 "believed committed by rightist terrorists," and 4,889 "committed by unknown assailants," the famous *desconocidos* favored by those San Salvador newspapers still publishing. (The figures actually add up not to 6,909 but to 6,899, leaving ten in a kind of official limbo.) The memo continued:

> "The uncertainty involved here can be seen in the fact that responsibility cannot be fixed in the majority of cases. We note, however, that it is generally believed in El Salvador that a large number of the unexplained killings are carried out by the security forces, officially or unofficially. The Embassy is aware of dramatic claims that have been made by one interest group or another in which the security forces figure as the primary agents of murder here. El Salvador's tangled web of attack and vengeance, traditional criminal violence and political mayhem make this an impossible charge to sustain. In saying this, however, we make no attempt to lighten the responsibility for the deaths of many hundreds, and perhaps thousands, which can be attributed to the security forces. . . ."

The body count kept by what is generally referred to in San Salvador as "the Human Rights Commission" is higher than the embassy's, and documented periodically by a photographer who goes out looking for bodies. These bodies he photographs are often broken into unnatural positions, and the faces to which the bodies are attached (when they are attached) are equally unnatural, sometimes unrecognizable as human faces, obliterated by acid or beaten to a mash of misplaced ears and teeth or slashed ear to ear and invaded by insects. *"Encontrado en Antiguo Cuscatlán el día 25 de Marzo 1982: camison de dormir celeste,"* the typed caption reads on one photograph: found in Antiguo Cuscatlán March 25 1982 wearing a sky-blue nightshirt. The captions are laconic. Found in Soyapango May 21 1982. Found in Mejicanos June 11 1982. Found at El Playón May 30 1982, white shirt, purple pants, black shoes.

The photograph accompanying that last caption shows a body with no eyes, because the vultures got to it before the photographer did. There is a special kind of practical information that the visitor to El Salvador acquires immediately, the way visitors to other places acquire information about the currency rates, the hours for the museums. In El Salvador one learns that vultures go first for the soft tissue, for the eyes, the exposed genitalia, the open mouth. One learns that an open mouth can be used to make a specific point, can be stuffed with something emblematic; stuffed, say, with a penis, or, if the point has to do with land title, stuffed with some of the dirt in question. One learns that hair deteriorates less rapidly than flesh, and that a skull surrounded by a perfect corona of hair is a not uncommon sight in the body dumps.

All forensic photographs induce in the viewer a certain protective numbness, but dissociation is more difficult here. In the first place these are not, technically, "forensic" photographs, since the evidence they document will never be presented in a court of law. In the second place the disfigurement is too routine. The locations are too near, the dates too recent. There is the presence of the relatives of the disappeared: the women

17

who sit every day in this cramped office on the grounds of the archdiocese, waiting to look at the spiral-bound photo albums in which the photographs are kept. These albums have plastic covers bearing soft-focus color photographs of young Americans in dating situations (strolling through autumn foliage on one album, recumbent in a field of daisies on another), and the women, looking for the bodies of their husbands and brothers and sisters and children, pass them from hand to hand without comment or expression.

"One of the more shadowy elements of the violent scene here [is] the death squad. Existence of these groups has long been disputed, but not by many Salvadorans. . . . Who constitutes the death squads is yet another difficult question. We do not believe that these squads exist as permanent formations but rather as ad hoc vigilante groups that coalesce according to perceived need. Membership is also uncertain, but in addition to civilians we believe that both on- and off-duty members of the security forces are participants. This was unofficially confirmed by right-wing spokesman Maj. Roberto D'Aubuisson who stated in an interview in early 1981 that security force members utilize the guise of the death squad when a potentially embarrassing or odious task needs to be performed."

—*From the confidential but later declassified January 15, 1982 memo previously cited, drafted for the State Department by the political section at the embassy in San Salvador.*

The dead and pieces of the dead turn up in El Salvador everywhere, every day, as taken for granted as in a nightmare, or a horror movie. Vultures of course suggest the presence of a body. A knot of children on the street suggests the presence of a body. Bodies turn up in the brush of vacant lots, in the garbage thrown down ravines in the richest districts, in public rest rooms, in bus stations. Some are dropped in Lake Ilopango, a few miles east of the city, and wash up near the lakeside cottages and clubs frequented by what remains in San Salvador of the sporting bourgeoisie. Some still turn up at El Playón, the lunar lava field of rotting human flesh visible at one time or another on every television screen in America but characterized in June of 1982 in the *El Salvador News Gazette*, an English-language weekly edited by an American named Mario Rosenthal, as an "uncorroborated story . . . dredged up from the files of leftist propaganda." Others turn up at Puerta del Diablo, above Parque Balboa, a national *Turicentro* described as recently as the April–July 1982 issue of *Aboard TACA*, the magazine provided passengers on the national airline of El Salvador, as "offering excellent subjects for color photography."

I drove up to Puerta del Diablo one morning in June of 1982, past the Casa Presidencial and the camouflaged watch towers and heavy concentrations of troops and arms south of town, on up a narrow road narrowed further by landslides and deep crevices in the roadbed, a drive so insistently premonitory that after a while I began to hope that I would pass Puerta del Diablo without knowing it, just miss it, write it off, turn around and go back. There was however no way of missing it. Puerta del Diablo is a "view site" in an older and distinctly literary tradition, nature as lesson, an immense cleft rock through which half of El Salvador seems framed, a site so romantic and "mystical," so theatrically sacrificial in aspect, that it might be a cosmic parody of nineteenth-century landscape painting. The place presents itself as pathetic fallacy: the sky "broods," the stones "weep," a constant seepage of water weighting the ferns and moss. The foliage is thick and slick with moisture. The only sound is a steady buzz, I believe of cicadas.

Body dumps are seen in El Salvador as a kind of visitors' must-do, difficult but worth the detour. "Of course you have seen El Playón," an aide to President Alvaro Magaña said to me one day, and proceeded to discuss the site geologically, as evidence of the country's geothermal resources. He made no mention of the bodies. I was unsure if he was sounding me out or simply found the geothermal aspect of overriding interest. One difference between El Playón and Puerta del Diablo is that most bodies at El Playón appear to have been killed somewhere else, and then dumped; at Puerta del Diablo the executions are believed to occur in place, at the top, and the bodies thrown over. Sometimes reporters will speak of wanting to spend the night at Puerta del Diablo, in order to document the actual execution, but at the time I was in Salvador no one had.

The aftermath, the daylight aspect, is well documented. "Nothing fresh today, I hear," an embassy officer said when I mentioned that I had visited Puerta del Diablo. "Were there any on top?" someone else asked. "There were supposed to have been three on top yesterday." The point about whether or not there had been any on top was that usually it was necessary to go down to see bodies. The way down is hard. Slabs of stone, slippery with moss, are set into the vertiginous cliff, and it is down this cliff that one begins the descent to the bodies, or what is left of the bodies, pecked and maggoty masses of flesh, bone, hair. On some days there have been helicopters circling, tracking those making the descent. Other days there have been militia at the top, in the clearing where the road seems to run out, but on the morning I was there the only people on top were a man and a woman and three small children, who played in the wet grass while the woman started and stopped a Toyota pickup. She appeared to be learning how to drive. She drove forward and then back toward the edge, apparently following the man's signals, over and over again.

We did not speak, and it was only later, down the mountain and back in the land of the provisionally living, that it occurred to me that there was a definite question about why a man and a woman might choose a well-known body dump for a driving lesson. This was one of a number of occasions, during the two weeks my husband and I spent in El Salvador, on which I came to understand, in a way I had not understood before, the exact mechanism of terror.

Whenever I had nothing better to do in San Salvador I would walk up in the leafy stillness of the San Benito and Escalón districts, where the hush at midday is broken only by the occasional crackle of a walkie-talkie, the click of metal moving on a weapon. I recall a day in San Benito when I opened my bag to check an address, and heard the clicking of metal on metal all up and down the street. On the whole no one walks up here, and pools of blossoms lie undisturbed on the sidewalks. Most of the houses in San Benito are more recent than those in Escalón, less idiosyncratic and probably smarter, but the most striking architectural features in both districts are not the houses but their walls, walls built upon walls, walls stripped of the usual copa de oro and bougainvillea, walls that reflect successive generations of violence: the original stone, the additional five or six or ten feet of brick, and finally the barbed wire, sometimes concertina, sometimes electrified; walls with watch towers, gun ports, closed-circuit television cameras, walls now reaching twenty and thirty feet.

San Benito and Escalón appear on the embassy security maps as districts of relatively few "incidents," but they remain districts in which a certain oppressive uneasiness prevails. In the first place there are always "incidents"—detentions and deaths and disappearances—in the *barrancas*, the ravines lined with shanties that fall down behind the houses with the walls and the guards and the walkie-talkies; one day in Escalón I was introduced to a woman who kept the lean-to that served as a grocery in a *barranca* just above the Hotel Sheraton. She was sticking prices on bars of Camay and Johnson's baby soap, stopping occasionally to sell a plastic bag or two filled with crushed ice and Coca-

Cola, and all the while she talked in a low voice about her fear, about her eighteen-year-old son, about the boys who had been taken out and shot on successive nights recently in a neighboring *barranca*.

In the second place there is, in Escalón, the presence of the Sheraton itself, a hotel that has figured rather too prominently in certain local stories involving the disappearance and death of Americans. The Sheraton always seems brighter and more mildly festive than either the Camino Real or the Presidente, with children in the pool and flowers and pretty women in pastel dresses, but there are usually several bulletproofed Cherokee Chiefs in the parking area, and the men drinking in the lobby often carry the little zippered purses that in San Salvador suggest not passports or credit cards but Browning 9-mm. pistols.

It was at the Sheraton that one of the few American *desaparecidos*, a young free-lance writer named John Sullivan, was last seen, in December of 1980. It was also at the Sheraton, after eleven on the evening of January 3 1981, that the two American advisers on agrarian reform, Michael Hammer and Mark Pearlman, were killed, along with the Salvadoran director of the Institute for Agrarian Transformation, José Rodolfo Viera. The three were drinking coffee in a dining room off the lobby, and whoever killed them used an Ingram MAC-10, without sound suppressor, and then walked out through the lobby, unapprehended. The Sheraton has even turned up in the investigation into the December 1980 deaths of the four American churchwomen, Sisters Ita Ford and Maura Clarke, the two Maryknoll

23

nuns; Sister Dorothy Kazel, the Ursuline nun; and Jean
Donovan, the lay volunteer. In *Justice in El Salvador:
A Case Study*, prepared and released in July of 1982
in New York by the Lawyers' Committee for International Human Rights, there appears this note:

> "On December 19, 1980, the [Duarte govern-
> ment's] Special Investigative Commission reported
> that 'a red Toyota ¾-ton pickup was seen leaving
> (the crime scene) at about 11:00 P.M. on Decem-
> ber 2' and that 'a red splotch on the burned van'
> of the churchwomen was being checked to deter-
> mine whether the paint splotch 'could be the result
> of a collision between that van and the red Toyota
> pickup.' By February 1981, the Maryknoll Sisters'
> Office of Social Concerns, which has been actively
> monitoring the investigation, received word from
> a source which it considered reliable that the FBI
> had matched the red splotch on the burned van
> with a red Toyota pickup belonging to the Shera-
> ton hotel in San Salvador.... Subsequent to the
> FBI's alleged matching of the paint splotch and a
> Sheraton truck, the State Department has claimed,
> in a communication with the families of the
> churchwomen, that 'the FBI could not determine
> the source of the paint scraping.'"

There is also mention in this study of a young Salvadoran businessman named Hans Christ (his father was
a German who arrived in El Salvador at the end of
World War II), a part owner of the Sheraton. Hans
Christ lives now in Miami, and that his name should

have even come up in the Maryknoll investigation made many people uncomfortable, because it was Hans Christ, along with his brother-in-law, Ricardo Sol Meza, who, in April of 1981, was first charged with the murders of Michael Hammer and Mark Pearlman and José Rodolfo Viera at the Sheraton. These charges were later dropped, and were followed by a series of other charges, arrests, releases, expressions of "dismay" and "incredulity" from the American embassy, and even, in the fall of 1982, confessions to the killings from two former National Guard corporals, who testified that Hans Christ had led them through the lobby and pointed out the victims. Hans Christ and Ricardo Sol Meza have said that the dropped case against them was a government frame-up, and that they were only having drinks at the Sheraton the night of the killings, with a National Guard intelligence officer. It was logical for Hans Christ and Ricardo Sol Meza to have drinks at the Sheraton because they both had interests in the hotel, and Ricardo Sol Meza had just opened a roller disco, since closed, off the lobby into which the killers walked that night. The killers were described by witnesses as well dressed, their faces covered. The room from which they walked was at the time I was in San Salvador no longer a restaurant, but the marks left by the bullets were still visible, on the wall facing the door.

Whenever I had occasion to visit the Sheraton I was apprehensive, and this apprehension came to color the entire Escalón district for me, even its lower reaches, where there were people and movies and restaurants. I recall being struck by it on the canopied porch of a restaurant near the Mexican embassy, on an evening when rain or sabotage or habit had blacked out the city and I became abruptly aware, in the light cast by a passing car, of two human shadows, silhouettes illuminated by the headlights and then invisible again. One shadow sat behind the smoked glass windows of a Cherokee Chief parked at the curb in front of the restaurant; the other crouched between the pumps at the Esso station next door, carrying a rifle. It seemed to me unencouraging that my husband and I were the only people seated on the porch. In the absence of the headlights the candle on our table provided the only light, and I fought the impulse to blow it out. We continued talking, carefully. Nothing came of this, but I did not forget the sensation of having been in a single instant demoralized, undone, humiliated by fear, which is what I meant when I said that I came to understand in El Salvador the mechanism of terror.

"3/3/81: Roberto D'Aubuisson, a former Salvadoran army intelligence officer, holds a press conference and says that before the U.S. presidential election he had been in touch with a number of Reagan advisers and those contacts have continued. The armed forces should ask the junta to resign, D'Aubuisson says. He refuses to name a date for the action, but says 'March is, I think, a very interesting month.' He also calls for the abandonment of the economic reforms. D'Aubuisson had been accused of plotting to overthrow the government on two previous occasions. Observers speculate that since D'Aubuisson is able to hold the news conference and pass freely between Salvador and Guatemala, he must enjoy considerable support among some sections of the army.... 3/4/81: In San Salvador, the U.S. embassy is fired upon; no one is injured. Chargé d'Affaires Frederic Chapin says, 'This incident has all the hallmarks of a D'Aubuisson operation. Let me state to you that we oppose coups and we have no intention of being intimidated.' "

—*From the "Chronology of Events Related to Salvadoran Situation" prepared periodically by the United States embassy in San Salvador.*

"Since the Exodus from Egypt, historians have written of those who sacrificed and struggled for freedom: the stand at Thermopylae, the revolt of Spartacus, the storming of the Bastille, the Warsaw uprising in World War II. More recently we have seen evidence of this same human impulse in one of the developing nations in Central America. For months and months the world news media covered the fighting in El Salvador. Day after day, we were treated to stories and film slanted toward the brave freedom fighters battling oppressive government forces in behalf of the silent, suffering people of that tortured country. Then one day those silent suffering people were offered a chance to vote to choose the kind of government they wanted. Suddenly the freedom fighters in the hills were exposed for what they really are: Cuban-backed guerrillas. . . . On election day the people of El Salvador, an unprecedented [1.5 million] of them, braved ambush and gunfire, trudging miles to vote for freedom."

—President Reagan, in his June 8 1982 speech before both houses of the British Parliament, referring to the March 28 1982 election which resulted in the ascension of Roberto D'Aubuisson to the presidency of the Constituent Assembly.

From whence he shall come to judge the quick and the dead. I happened to read President Reagan's speech one evening in San Salvador when President Reagan was in fact on television, with Doris Day, in *The Winning Team*, a 1952 Warner Brothers picture about the baseball pitcher Grover Cleveland Alexander. I reached the stand at Thermopylae at about the time that *el salvador del Salvador* began stringing cranberries and singing "Old St. Nicholas" with Miss Day. "*Muy bonita*," he said when she tried out a rocking chair in her wedding dress. "*Feliz Navidad*," they cried, and, in accented English, "*Play ball!*"

As it happened "play ball" was a phrase I had come to associate in El Salvador with Roberto D'Aubuisson and his followers in the Nationalist Republican Alliance, or ARENA. "It's a process of letting certain people know they're going to have to play ball," embassy people would say, and: "You take a guy who's young, and everything 'young' implies, you send him signals, he plays ball, then we play ball." American diction in this situation tends toward the studied casual, the can-do, as if sheer cool and Bailey bridges could shape the place up. Elliott Abrams told *The New York Times* in July of 1982 that punishment within the Salvadoran military could be "a very important sign that you can't do this stuff any more," meaning kill the citizens. "If you clean up your act, all things are possible," is the way Jeremiah O'Leary, a special assistant to U.S. national security adviser William Clark, described the American diplomatic effort in an interview given *The Los Angeles Times* just after the March 28 1982 election. He was speculating on how Ambassador Deane Hinton might be dealing with D'Aubuisson. "I kind of picture him saying, 'Goddamnit, Bobbie, you've got a problem and . . . if you're what everyone said you are, you're going to make it hard for everybody.'"

Roberto D'Aubuisson is a chain smoker, as were many of the people I met in El Salvador, perhaps because it is a country in which the possibility of achieving a death related to smoking remains remote. I never met Major D'Aubuisson, but I was always interested in the adjectives used to describe him. "Pathological" was the adjective, modifying "killer," used by former ambassador Robert E. White (it was White who refused D'Aubuisson a visa, after which, according to the embassy's "Chronology of Events" for June 30 1980, "D'Aubuisson manages to enter the U.S. illegally and spends two days in Washington holding press conferences and attending luncheons before turning himself in to immigration authorities"), but "pathological" is not a word one heard in-country, where meaning tends to be transmitted in code.

In-country one heard "young" (the "and everything 'young' implies" part was usually left tacit), even immature"; "impetuous," "impulsive," "impatient," "nervous," "volatile," "high-strung," "kind of coiled-up," and, most frequently, "intense," or just "tense." Offhand it struck me that Roberto D'Aubuisson had some reason to be tense, in that General José Guillermo García, who had remained a main player through several changes of government, might logically perceive him as the wild card who could queer everybody's ability to refer to his election as a vote for freedom. As I write this I realize that I have fallen into the Salvadoran mindset, which turns on plot, and, since half the players at any given point in the game are in exile, on the phrase "in touch with."

"I've known D'Aubuisson a long time," I was told by Alvaro Magaña, the banker the Army made, over D'Aubuisson's rather frenzied objections ("We stopped that one on the one-yard line," Deane Hinton told me about D'Aubuisson's play to block Magaña), provisional president of El Salvador. We were sitting in his office upstairs at the Casa Presidencial, an airy and spacious building in the tropical colonial style, and he was drinking cup after Limoges cup of black coffee, smoking one cigarette with each, carefully, an unwilling actor who intended to survive the accident of being cast in this production. "Since Molina was president. I used to come here to see Molina, D'Aubuisson would be here, he was a young man in military intelligence, I'd see him here." He gazed toward the corridor that opened onto the interior courtyard, with cannas, oleander, a fountain not in operation. "When we're alone now I try to talk to him. I do talk to him, he's coming for lunch today. He never calls me Alvaro, it's always *usted*, *Señor*, *Doctor*. I call him Roberto. I say, Roberto, don't do this, don't do that, you know."

Magaña studied in the United States, at Chicago, and his four oldest children are now in the United States, one son at Vanderbilt, a son and a daughter at Santa Clara, and another daughter near Santa Clara, at Notre Dame in Belmont. He is connected by money, education, and temperament to oligarchal families. All the players here are densely connected: Magaña's sister, who lives in California, is the best friend of Nora Ungo, the wife of Guillermo Ungo, and Ungo spoke to Magaña's sister in August of 1982 when he was in California raising money for the FMLN–FDR, which is what the opposition to the Salvadoran government was called this year. The membership and even the initials of this opposition tend to the fluid, but the broad strokes are these: the FMLN–FDR is the coalition between the Revolutionary Democratic Front (FDR) and the five guerrilla groups joined together in the Farabundo Martí National Liberation Front (FMLN). These five groups are the Salvadoran Communist Party (PCS), the Popular Forces of Liberation (FPL), the Revolutionary Party of Central American Workers (PRTC), the People's Revolutionary Army (ERP), and the Armed Forces of National Resistance (FARN). Within each of these groups, there are further factions, and sometimes even further initials, as in the PRS and LP-28 of the ERP.

During the time that D'Aubuisson was trying to stop Magaña's appointment as provisional president, members of ARENA, which is supported heavily by other oligarchal elements, passed out leaflets referring to Magaña, predictably, as a communist, and, more interestingly, as "the little Jew." The manipulation of anti-Semitism is an undercurrent in Salvadoran life that is not much discussed and probably worth some study, since it refers to a tension within the oligarchy itself, the tension between those families who solidified their holdings in the mid-nineteenth century and those later families, some of them Jewish, who arrived in El Salvador and entrenched themselves around 1900. I recall asking a well-off Salvadoran about the numbers of his acquaintances within the oligarchy who have removed themselves and their money to Miami. "Mostly the Jews," he said.

> "In San Salvador
> in the year 1965
> the best sellers
> of the three most important
> book stores
> were:
> The Protocols of the Elders of Zion;
> a few books by
> diarrhetic Somerset Maugham;
> a book of disagreeably
> obvious poems
> by a lady with a European name
> who nonetheless writes in Spanish about our
> country
> and a collection of
> Reader's Digest condensed novels."

> —*"San Salvador" by Roque Dalton, translated by Edward Baker.*

The late Roque Dalton García was born into the Salvadoran bourgeoisie in 1935, spent some years in Havana, came home in 1973 to join the ERP, or the People's Revolutionary Army, and, in 1975, was executed, on charges that he was a CIA agent, by his own comrades. The actual executioner was said to be Joaquín Villalobos, who is now about thirty years old, commander of the ERP, and a key figure in the FMLN, which, as the Mexican writer Gabriel Zaid pointed out in the winter 1982 issue of *Dissent*, has as one of its support groups the Roque Dalton Cultural Brigade. The Dalton execution is frequently cited by people who want to stress that "the other side kills people too, you know," an argument common mainly among those, like the State Department, with a stake in whatever government is current in El Salvador, since, if it is taken for granted in Salvador that the government kills, it is also taken for granted that the other side kills; that everyone has killed, everyone kills now, and, if the history of the place suggests any pattern, everyone will continue to kill.

"Don't say I said this, but there are no issues here," I was told by a high-placed Salvadoran. "There are only ambitions." He meant of course not that there were no ideas in conflict but that the conflicting ideas were held exclusively by people he knew, that, whatever the outcome of any fighting or negotiation or coup or countercoup, the Casa Presidencial would ultimately be occupied not by *campesinos* and Maryknolls but by the already entitled, by a Guillermo Ungo or a Joaquín Villalobos or even by Roque Dalton's son, Juan José Dalton, or by Juan José Dalton's comrade in the FPL, José Antonio Morales Carbonell, the guerrilla son of José Antonio Morales Ehrlich, a former member of the Duarte junta who had himself been in exile during the Romero regime. In an open letter written shortly before his arrest in San Salvador in June 1980, José Antonio Morales Carbonell had charged his father with an insufficient appreciation of "Yankee imperialism." José Antonio Morales Carbonell and Juan José Dalton tried together to enter the United States in the summer of 1982, for a speaking engagement in San Francisco, but were refused visas by the American embassy in Mexico City.

Whatever the issues were that had divided Morales Carbonell and his father and Roque Dalton and Joaquín Villalobos, the prominent Salvadoran to whom I was talking seemed to be saying, they were issues that fell somewhere outside the lines normally drawn to indicate "left" and "right." That this man saw *la situación* as only one more realignment of power among the entitled, a conflict of "ambitions" rather than "issues," was, I recognized, what many people would call a conventional bourgeois view of civil conflict, and offered no solutions, but the people with solutions to offer were mainly somewhere else, in Mexico or Panama or Washington.

The place brings everything into question. One afternoon when I had run out of the Halazone tablets I dropped every night in a pitcher of tap water (a demented *gringa* gesture, I knew even then, in a country where everyone not born there was at least mildly ill, including the nurse at the American embassy), I walked across the street from the Camino Real to the Metrocenter, which is referred to locally as "Central America's Largest Shopping Mall." I found no Halazone at the Metrocenter but became absorbed in making notes about the mall itself, about the Muzak playing "I Left My Heart in San Francisco" and "American

Pie" ("... *singing this will be the day that I die ...*")
although the record store featured a cassette called
Classics of Paraguay, about the *pâté de foie gras* for
sale in the supermarket, about the guard who did the
weapons check on everyone who entered the supermarket, about the young matrons in tight Sergio Va-
lente jeans, trailing maids and babies behind them and
buying towels, big beach towels printed with maps of
Manhattan that featured Bloomingdale's; about the
number of things for sale that seemed to suggest a
fashion for "smart drinking," to evoke modish cock-
tail hours. There were bottles of Stolichnaya vodka
packaged with glasses and mixer, there were ice buck-
ets, there were bar carts of every conceivable design,
displayed with sample bottles.

This was a shopping center that embodied the future
for which El Salvador was presumably being saved,
and I wrote it down dutifully, this being the kind of
"color" I knew how to interpret, the kind of inductive
irony, the detail that was supposed to illuminate the
story. As I wrote it down I realized that I was no longer
much interested in this kind of irony, that this was a
story that would not be illuminated by such details,
that this was a story that would perhaps not be illuminated at all, that this was perhaps even less a "story"
than a true *noche obscura*. As I waited to cross back
over the Boulevard de los Heroes to the Camino Real
I noticed soldiers herding a young civilian into a van,
their guns at the boy's back, and I walked straight
ahead, not wanting to see anything at all.

"12/11/81: El Salvador's Atlacatl Battalion begins a 6-day offensive sweep against guerrilla strongholds in Morazán."

—*From the U.S. Embassy "Chronology of Events."*

"The department of Morazán, one of the country's most embattled areas, was the scene of another armed forces operation in December, the fourth in Morazán during 1981.... The hamlet of Mozote was completely wiped out. For this reason, the several massacres which occurred in the same area at the same time are collectively known as the 'Mozote massacre.' The apparent sole survivor from Mozote, Rufina Amaya, thirty-eight years old, escaped by hiding behind trees near the house where she and the other women had been imprisoned. She has testified that on Friday, December 11, troops arrived and began taking people from their homes at about 5 in the morning.... At noon, the men were blindfolded and killed in the town's center. Among them was Amaya's husband, who was nearly blind. In the early afternoon the young women were taken to the hills nearby, where they were raped, then

killed and burned. The old women were taken
next and shot. . . . From her hiding place, Amaya
heard soldiers discuss choking the children to
death; subsequently she heard the children calling
for help, but no shots. Among the children murdered were three of Amaya's, all under ten years
of age. . . . It should be stressed that the villagers
in the area had been warned of the impending
military operation by the FMLN and some did
leave. Those who chose to stay, such as the evan-
gelical Protestants and others, considered themselves neutral in the conflict and friendly with the
army. According to Rufina Amaya, 'Because we
knew the Army people, we felt safe.' Her husband,
she said, had been on good terms with the local
military and even had what she called 'a military
safe-conduct.' Amaya and other survivors [of the
nine hamlets in which the killing took place] accused the Atlacatl Battalion of a major role in the
killing of civilians in the Mozote area."

*—From the July 20 1982 Supplement to the
"Report on Human Rights in El Salvador"
prepared by Americas Watch Committee and
the American Civil Liberties Union.*

At the time I was in El Salvador, six months after
the events referred to as the Mozote massacre and a
month or so before President Reagan's July 1982 certification that sufficient progress was being made in
specified areas ("human rights," and "land reform,"
and "the initiation of a democratic political process,"

phrases so remote *in situ* as to render them hallucinatory) to qualify El Salvador for continuing aid, a major offensive was taking place in Morazán, up in the mean hill country between the garrison town of San Francisco Gotera and the Honduran border. This June 1982 fighting was referred to by both sides as the heaviest of the war to date, but actual information, on this as on all subjects in San Salvador, was hard to come by.

Reports drifted back. The Atlacatl, which was trained by American advisers in 1981, was definitely up there again, as were two other battalions, the Atonal, trained, like the Atlacatl, by Americans in El Salvador, and the Ramón Belloso, just back from training at Fort Bragg. Every morning COPREFA, the press office at the Ministry of Defense, reported many FMLN casualties but few government. Every afternoon Radio Venceremos, the clandestine guerrilla radio station, reported many government casualties but few FMLN. The only way to get any sense of what was happening was to go up there, but Morazán was hard to reach: a key bridge between San Salvador and the eastern half of the country, the Puente de Oro on the Río Lempa, had been dynamited by the FMLN in October 1981, and to reach San Francisco Gotera it was now necessary either to cross the Lempa on a railroad bridge or to fly, which meant going out to the military airport, Ilopango, and trying to get one of the seven-passenger prop planes that the Gutierrez Flying Service operated between Ilopango and a grassy field outside San Miguel. At San Miguel one could sometimes get a taxi willing to go on up to San Francisco Gotera, or a bus, the problem with a bus being that even a roadblock that ended well (no one killed or detained) could take hours, while every passenger was questioned. Between San Miguel and Gotera, moreover, there was a further problem, another blown bridge, this one on the Río Seco, which was *seco* enough in the dry months but often impassable in the wet.

June was wet. The Río Seco seemed doubtful. Everything about the day ahead, on the morning I started for Gotera, seemed doubtful, and that I set out on such a venture with a real lightening of the spirit suggests to me now how powerfully I wanted to get out of San Salvador, to spend a day free of its ambiguous tension, its overcast, its mood of wary somnambulism. It was only a trip of perhaps eighty miles, but getting there took most of the morning. There was, first of all, the wait on the runway at Ilopango while the pilot tried to get the engines to catch. "*Cinco minutos*," he kept saying, and, as a wrench was produced, "*Momentito.*" Thunderclouds were massing on the mountains to the east. Rain spattered the fuselage. The plane was full, seven paying passengers at ninety-five *colones* the round trip, and we watched the tinkering without comment until one and finally both of the engines turned over.

Once in the air I was struck, as always in Salvador, by the miniature aspect of the country, an entire republic smaller than some California counties (smaller than San Diego County, smaller than Kern or Inyo, smaller by two-and-a-half times than San Bernardino), the very circumstance that has encouraged the illusion that the place can be managed, salvaged, a kind of pilot project, like TVA. There below us in a twenty-five-minute flight lay half the country, a landscape already densely green from the rains that had begun in May, intensely cultivated, deceptively rich, the coffee spreading down every ravine, the volcanic ranges looming abruptly and then receding. I watched the slopes of the mountains for signs of fighting but saw none. I watched for the hydroelectric works on the Lempa but saw only the blown bridge.

There were four of us on the flight that morning who wanted to go on to Gotera, my husband and I and Christopher Dickey from *The Washington Post* and Joseph Harmes from *Newsweek*, and when the plane set down on the grass strip outside San Miguel a deal was struck with a taxi driver willing to take us at least to the Río Seco. We shared the taxi as far as San Miguel with a local woman who, although she and I sat on a single bucket seat, did not speak, only stared straight ahead, clutching her bag with one hand and trying with the other to keep her skirt pulled down over her black lace slip. When she got out at San Miguel there remained in the taxi a trace of her perfume, Arpège.

In San Miguel the streets showed the marks of January's fighting, and many structures were boarded up, abandoned. There had been a passable motel in San Miguel, but the owners had managed to leave the country. There had been a passable place to eat in San Miguel, but no more. Occasional troop trucks hurtled past, presumably returning empty from the front, and we all made note of them, dutifully. The heat rose.

Sweat from my hand kept blurring my tally of empty troop trucks, and I copied it on a clean page, painstakingly, as if it mattered.

The heat up here was drier than that in the capital, harsher, dustier, and by now we were resigned to it, resigned to the jolting of the taxi, resigned to the frequent occasions on which we were required to stop, get out, present our identification (carefully, reaching slowly into an outer pocket, every move calculated not to startle the soldiers, many of whom seemed barely pubescent, with the M-16s), and wait while the taxi was searched. Some of the younger soldiers wore crucifixes wrapped with bright yarn, the pink and green of the yarn stained now with dust and sweat. The taxi driver was perhaps twenty years older than most of these soldiers, a stocky, well-settled citizen wearing expensive sunglasses, but at each roadblock, in a motion so abbreviated as to be almost imperceptible, he would touch each of the two rosaries that hung from the rearview mirror and cross himself.

By the time we reached the Río Seco the question of whether or not we could cross it seemed insignificant, another minor distraction in a day that had begun at six and was now, before nine, already less a day than a way of being alive. We would try, the driver announced, to ford the river, which appeared that day to be running shallow and relatively fast over an unpredictable bed of sand and mud. We stood for a while on the bank and watched a man with an earthmover and winch try again and again to hook up his equipment to a truck that had foundered midstream. Small boys dove repeatedly with hooks, and repeatedly surfaced, unsuccessful. It did not seem entirely promising, but there it was, and there, in due time, we were: in the river, first following the sandbar in a wide crescent, then off the bar, stuck, the engine dead. The taxi rocked gently in the current. The water bubbled inch by inch through the floorboards. There were women bathing naked in the shallows, and they paid no attention to the earth-mover, the small boys, the half-submerged taxi, the *gringos* inside it. As we waited for our turn with the earthmover it occurred to me that fording the river in the morning meant only that we were going to have to ford it again in the afternoon, when the earthmover might or might not be around, but this was thinking ahead, and out of synch with the day at hand.

When I think now of that day in Gotera I think mainly of waiting, hanging around, waiting outside the *cuartel* ("COMANDO," the signs read on the gates, and "BOINAS VERDES," with a green beret) and waiting outside the church and waiting outside the Cine Morazań, where the posters promised *Fright* and *The Abominable Snowman* and the open lobby was lined with .50-caliber machine guns and 120-mm. mobile mortars. There were soldiers billeted in the Cine Morazán, and a few of them kicked a soccer ball, idly, among the mortars. Others joked among themselves at the corner, outside the saloon, and flirted with the women selling Coca-Cola in the stalls between the Cine Morazán and the parish house. The parish house and the church and the stalls and the saloon and the Cine Morazán and the *cuartel* all faced one another, across what was less a square than a dusty widening in the road, an arrangement that lent Gotera a certain proscenium aspect. Any event at all—the arrival of an armored personnel carrier, say, or a funeral procession outside the church—tended to metamorphose instantly into an opera, with all players onstage: the Soldiers of the Garrison, the Young Ladies of the Town, the Vendors, the Priests, the Mourners, and, since we were onstage as well, a dissonant and provocative element, the *norteamericanos*, in *norteamericano* costume, old Abercrombie khakis here, Adidas sneakers there, a Lone Star Beer cap.

We stood in the sun and tried to avoid adverse attention. We drank Coca-Cola and made surreptitious notes. We looked for the priests in the parish office but found only the receptionist, a dwarf. We presented our credentials again and again at the *cuartel*, trying to see the colonel who could give us permission to go up the few kilometers to where the fighting was, but the colonel was out, the colonel would be back, the colonel was delayed. The young officer in charge during the colonel's absence could not give us permission, but he had graduated from the Escuela Militar in one of the classes trained in the spring of 1982 at Fort Benning ("Mar-vel-*ous!*" was his impression of Fort Benning) and seemed at least amenable to us as Americans. Possibly there would be a patrol going up. Possibly we could join it.

In the end no patrol went up and the colonel never

came back (the reason the colonel never came back is that he was killed that afternoon, in a helicopter crash near the Honduran border, but we did not learn this in Gotera) and nothing came of the day but overheard rumors, indefinite observations, fragments of information that might or might not fit into a pattern we did not perceive. One of the six A-37B Dragonfly attack jets that the United States had delivered just that week to Ilopango screamed low overhead, then disappeared. A company of soldiers burst through the *cuartel* gates and double-timed to the river, but when we caught up they were only bathing, shedding their uniforms and splashing in the shallow water. On the bluff above the river work was being completed on a helipad that was said to cover two mass graves of dead soldiers, but the graves were no longer apparent. The taxi driver heard, from the soldiers with whom he talked while he waited (talked and played cards and ate tortillas and sardines and listened to rock-and-roll on the taxi radio), that two whole companies were missing in action, lost or dead somewhere in the hills, but this was received information, and equivocal.

In some ways the least equivocal fact of the day was the single body we had seen that morning on the road between the Río Seco and Gotera, near San Carlos, the naked corpse of a man about thirty with a clean bullet-hole drilled neatly between his eyes. He could have been stripped by whoever killed him or, since this was a country in which clothes were too valuable to leave on the dead, by someone who happened past: there was no way of telling. In any case his genitals had been covered with a leafy branch, presumably by the *campesinos* who were even then digging a grave. A *subversivo*, the driver thought, because there was no family in evidence (to be related to someone killed in El Salvador is a prima facie death warrant, and families tend to vanish), but all anyone in Gotera seemed to know was that there had been another body at precisely that place the morning before, and five others before that. One of the priests in Gotera had happened to see the body the morning before, but when he drove past San Carlos later in the day the body had been buried. It was agreed that someone was trying to make a point. The point was unclear.

We spent an hour or so that day with the priests, or with two of them, both Irish, and two of the nuns, one Irish and one American, all of whom lived together in the parish house facing the *cuartel* in a situation that remains in my mind as the one actual instance I have witnessed of grace not simply under pressure but under siege. Except for the American, Sister Phyllis, who had arrived only a few months before, they had all been in Gotera a long time, twelve years, nine years, long enough to have established among themselves a grave companionableness, a courtesy and good humor that made the courtyard porch where we sat with them seem civilization's last stand in Morazán, which in certain ways it was.

The light on the porch was cool and aqueous, filtered through ferns and hibiscus, and there were old wicker rockers and a map of Parroquia San Francisco Gotera and a wooden table with a typewriter, a can of Planter's Mixed Nuts, copies of *Lives of the Saints: Illustrated* and *The Rules of the Secular Franciscan Order*. In the shadows beyond the table was a battered refrigerator from which, after a while, one of the priests got bottles of Pilsener beer, and we sat in the sedative half-light and drank the cold beer and talked in a desultory way about nothing in particular, about the situation, but no solutions.

These were not people much given to solutions, to abstracts: their lives were grounded in the specific. There had been the funeral that morning of a parishioner who had died in the night of cerebral hemorrhage. There had been the two children who died that week, of diarrhea, dehydration, in the squatter camps outside town where some 12,000 refugees were then gathered, many of them ill. There was no medicine in the camps. There was no water anywhere, and had been none since around the time of the election, when the tank that supplied Gotera with water had been dynamited. Five or six weeks after the tank was blown the rains had begun, which was bad in one way, because the rain washed out the latrines at the camps, but good in another, because at the parish house they were no longer dependent entirely on water from the river, soupy with bacteria and amoebae and worms. "We have the roof water now," Sister Jean, the Irish nun, said. "Much cleaner. It's greenish yellow, the river water, we only use it for the toilets."

There had been, they agreed, fewer dead around

since the election, fewer bodies, they thought, than in the capital, but as they began reminding one another of this body or that there still seemed to have been quite a few. They spoke of these bodies in the matter-of-fact way that they might have spoken, in another kind of parish, of confirmation candidates, or cases of croup. There had been the few up the road, the two at Yoloaiquin. Of course there had been the forty-eight near Barrios, but Barrios was in April. "A *guardia* was killed last Wednesday," one of them recalled.

"Thursday."

"Was it Thursday then, Jerry?"

"A sniper."

"That's what I thought. A sniper."

We left the parish house that day only because rain seemed about to fall, and it was clear that the Río Seco had to be crossed now or perhaps not for days. The priests kept a guest book, and I thought as I signed it that I would definitely come back to this porch, come back with antibiotics and Scotch and time to spend, but I did not get back, and some weeks after I left El Salvador I heard in a third-hand way that the parish house had been at least temporarily abandoned, that the priests, who had been under threats and pressure from the garrison, had somehow been forced to leave Gotera. I recalled that on the day before I left El Salvador Deane Hinton had asked me, when I mentioned Gotera, if I had seen the priests, and had expressed concern for their situation. He was particularly concerned about the American, Sister Phyllis (an American nun in a parish under siege in a part of the country even then under attack from American A-37Bs was nothing the

American embassy needed in those last delicate weeks before certification), and had at some point expressed this concern to the *comandante* at the garrison. The *comandante*, he said, had been surprised to learn the nationalities of the nuns and priests; he had thought them French, because the word used to describe them was always "Franciscan." This was one of those occasional windows that open onto the heart of El Salvador and then close, a glimpse of the impenetrable interior.

At the time I was in El Salvador the hostilities at hand were referred to by those reporters still in the country as "the number-four war," after Beirut, Iran-Iraq, and the aftermath of the Falklands. So many reporters had in fact abandoned the Hotel Camino Real in San Salvador (gone home for a while, or gone to the Intercontinental in Managua, or gone to whatever hotels they frequented in Guatemala and Panama and Tegucigalpa) that the dining room had discontinued its breakfast buffet, a fact often remarked upon: no breakfast buffet meant no action, little bang-bang, a period of editorial indifference in which stories were filed and held, and film rarely made the network news. "Get an NBC crew up from the Falklands, we might get the buffet back," they would say, and, "It hots up a little, we could have the midnight movies." It seemed that when the networks arrived in force they brought movies down, and showed them at midnight on their video recorders, *Apocalypse Now*, and Woody Allen's *Bananas*.

Meanwhile only the regulars were there. "Are you going out today?" they would say to one another at breakfast, and, "This might not be a bad day to look around." The Avis counter in the bar supplied signs reading "PRENSA INTERNACIONAL" with every car and van, and modified its insurance agreements with a typed clause excluding damage incurred by terrorists. The American embassy delivered translated transcripts of Radio Venceremos, prepared by the CIA in Panama. The COPREFA office at the Ministry of Defense sent over "urgent" notices, taped to the front desk, announcing events specifically devised, in those weeks before certification, for the American press: the ceremonial transfer of land titles, and the ritual display of "defectors," terrified-looking men who were reported in *La Prensa Gráfica* to have "abandoned the ranks of subversion, weary of so many lies and false promises."

A handful of reporters continued to cover these events, particularly if they were staged in provincial garrisons and offered the possibility of action en route, but action was less than certain, and the situation less accessible than it had seemed in the days of the breakfast buffet. The American advisers would talk to no one, although occasionally a reporter could find a few drinking at the Sheraton on Saturday night and initiate a little general conversation. (That the American advisers were still billeted at the Sheraton struck me as somewhat perverse, particularly because I knew that the embassy had moved its visiting AID people to a guarded house in San Benito. "Frankly, I'd rather stay at the Sheraton," an AID man had told me. "But since the two union guys got killed at the Sheraton, they want us here.") The era in which the guerrillas could be found just by going out on the highway had largely ended; the only certain way to spend time with them now was to cross into their territory from Honduras, through contact with the leadership in Mexico. This was a process that tended to discourage day-tripping, and in any case it was no longer a war in which the dateline "SOMEWHERE BEHIND GUERRILLA LINES, EL SALVADOR" was presumed automatically to illuminate much at all.

Everyone had already spent time, too, with the available government players, most of whom had grown so practiced in the process that their interviews were now performances, less apt to be reported than reviewed, and analyzed for subtle changes in delivery. Roberto D'Aubuisson had even taken part, wittingly or unwittingly, in an actual performance: a scene shot by a Danish film crew on location in Haiti and El Salvador for a movie about a foreign correspondent, in which the actor playing the correspondent "interviewed" D'Aubuisson, on camera, in his office. This Danish crew treated the Camino Real not only as a normal location hotel (the star, for example, was the only person I ever saw swim in the Camino Real pool) but also as a story element, on one occasion shooting a scene in the bar, which lent daily life during their stay a peculiar extra color. They left San Salvador without making it entirely clear whether or not they had ever told D'Aubuisson it was just a movie.

AT twenty-two minutes past midnight on Saturday June 19, 1982, there was a major earthquake in El Salvador, one that collapsed shacks and set off landslides and injured several hundred people but killed only about a dozen (I say "about" a dozen because figures on this, as on everything else in Salvador, varied), surprisingly few for an earthquake of this one's apparent intensity (Cal Tech registered it at 7.0 on the Richter scale, Berkeley at 7.4) and length, thirty-seven seconds. For the several hours that preceded the earthquake I had been seized by the kind of amorphous bad mood that my grandmother believed an adjunct of what is called in California "earthquake weather," a sultriness, a stillness, an unnatural light; the jitters. In fact there was no particular prescience about my bad mood, since it is always earthquake weather in San Salvador, and the jitters are endemic.

I recall having come back to the Camino Real about ten-thirty that Friday night, after dinner in a Mexican restaurant on the Paseo Escalón with a Salvadoran painter named Victor Barriere, who had said, when we met at a party a few days before, that he was interested in talking to Americans because they so often came and went with no understanding of the country and its history. Victor Barriere could offer, he explained, a special perspective on the country and its history, because he was a grandson of the late General Maximiliano Hernández Martínez, the dictator of El Salvador between 1931 and 1944 and the author of what Salvadorans still call *la matanza*, the massacre, or "killing," those weeks in 1932 when the government killed uncountable thousands of citizens, a lesson. ("Uncountable" because estimates of those killed vary from six or seven thousand to thirty thousand. Even higher figures are heard in Salvador, but, as Thomas P. Anderson pointed out in *Matanza: El Salvador's Communist Revolt of 1932*, "Salvadorans, like medieval people, tend to use numbers like fifty thousand simply to indicate a great number—statistics are not their strong point.")

As it happened I had been interested for some years in General Martínez, the spirit of whose regime would seem to have informed Gabriel García Márquez's *The Autumn of the Patriarch*. This original patriarch, who was murdered in exile in Honduras in 1966, was a rather sinister visionary who entrenched the military in Salvadoran life, was said to have held séances in the Casa Presidencial, and conducted both the country's and his own affairs along lines dictated by eccentric insights, which he sometimes shared by radio with the remaining citizens:

> "It is good that children go barefoot. That way they can better receive the beneficial effluvia of the planet, the vibrations of the earth. Plants and animals don't use shoes."

"Biologists have discovered only five senses. But in reality there are ten. Hunger, thirst, procreation, urination, and bowel movements are the senses not included in the lists of biologists."

I had first come across this side of General Martínez in the United States Government Printing Office's *Area Handbook for El Salvador*, a generally straightforward volume ("designed to be useful to military and other personnel who need a convenient compilation of basic facts") in which, somewhere between the basic facts about General Martínez's program for building schools and the basic facts about General Martínez's program for increasing exports, there appears this sentence: "He kept bottles of colored water that he dispensed as cures for almost any disease, including cancer and heart trouble, and relied on complex magical formulas for the solution of national problems." This sentence springs from the *Area Handbook for El Salvador* as if printed in neon, and is followed by one even more arresting: "During an epidemic of smallpox in the capital, he attempted to halt its spread by stringing the city with a web of colored lights."

Not a night passed in San Salvador when I did not imagine it strung with those colored lights, and I asked Victor Barriere what it had been like to grow up as the grandson of General Martínez. Victor Barriere had studied for a while in the United States, at the San Diego campus of the University of California, and he spoke perfect unaccented English, with the slightly formal constructions of the foreign speaker, in a fluted, melodic voice that seemed always to suggest a higher reasonableness. The general had been, he said, sometimes misunderstood. Very strong men often were. Certain excesses had been inevitable. Someone had to take charge. "It was sometimes strange going to school with boys whose fathers my grandfather had ordered shot," he allowed, but he remembered his grandfather mainly as a "forceful" man, a man "capable of inspiring great loyalty," a theosophist from whom it had been possible to learn an appreciation of "the classics," "a sense of history," "the Germans." The Germans especially had influenced Victor Barriere's sense of history. "When you've read Schopenhauer, Nietzsche, what's happened here, what's happening here, well . . ."

Victor Barriere had shrugged, and the subject changed, although only fractionally, since El Salvador is one of those places in the world where there is just one subject, the situation, the *problema*, its various facets presented over and over again, as on a stereopticon. One turn, and the facet was former ambassador Robert White: "A real jerk." Another, the murder in March of 1980 of Archbishop Oscar Arnulfo Romero: "A real bigot." At first I thought he meant whoever stood outside an open door of the chapel in which the Archbishop was saying mass and drilled him through the heart with a .22-caliber dumdum bullet, but he did not: "Listening to that man on the radio every Sunday," he said, "was like listening to Adolf Hitler or Benito Mussolini." In any case: "We don't really know who killed him, do we? It could have been the right . . ." He drew the words out, *cantabile*. "Or . . .

it could have been the left. We have to ask ourselves, who gained? Think about it, Joan."

I said nothing. I wanted only for dinner to end. Victor Barriere had brought a friend along, a young man from Chalatenango whom he was teaching to paint, and the friend brightened visibly when we stood up. He was eighteen years old and spoke no English and had sat through the dinner in polite misery. "He can't even speak Spanish properly," Victor Barriere said, in front of him. "However. If he were cutting cane in Chalatenango, he'd be taken by the Army and killed. If he were out on the street here he'd be killed. So. He comes every day to my studio, he learns to be a primitive painter, and I keep him from getting killed. It's better for him, don't you agree?"

I said that I agreed. The two of them were going back to the house Victor Barriere shared with his mother, a diminutive woman he addressed as "Mommy," the daughter of General Martínez, and after I dropped them there it occurred to me that this was the first time in my life that I had been in the presence of obvious "material" and felt no professional exhilaration at all, only personal dread. One of the most active death squads now operating in El Salvador calls itself the Maximiliano Hernández Martínez Brigade, but I had not asked the grandson about that.

In spite of or perhaps because of the fact that San Salvador had been for more than two years under an almost constant state of siege, a city in which arbitrary

detention had been legalized (Revolutionary Governing Junta Decree 507), curfew violations had been
known to end in death, and many people did not leave
their houses after dark, a certain limited frivolity still
obtained. When I got back to the Camino Real after
dinner with Victor Barriere that Friday night there
was for example a private party at the pool, with live
music, dancing, an actual conga line.

There were also a number of people in the bar, many
of them watching, on television monitors, "Señorita El
Salvador 1982," the selection of El Salvador's entry in
"Señorita Universo 1982," scheduled for July 1982 in
Lima. Something about "Señorita Universo" struck a
familiar note, and then I recalled that the Miss Universe
contest itself had been held in San Salvador in 1975, and
had ended in what might have been considered a predictable way, with student protests about the money
the government was spending on the contest, and the
government's predictable response, which was to shoot
some of the students on the street and disappear others.
(*Desaparecer*, or "disappear," is in Spanish both an
intransitive and a transitive verb, and this flexibility has
been adopted by those speaking English in El Salvador,
as in *John Sullivan was disappeared from the Sheraton;
the government disappeared the students*, there being
no equivalent situation, and so no equivalent word, in
English-speaking cultures.)

No mention of "Señorita Universo 1975" dampened
"Señorita El Salvador 1982," which, by the time I got
upstairs, had reached the point when each of the finalists was asked to pick a question from a basket and

answer it. The questions had to do with the hopes and dreams of the contestants, and the answers ran to "*Dios*," "*Paz*," "El Salvador." A local entertainer wearing a white dinner jacket and a claret-colored bow tie sang "The Impossible Dream," in Spanish. The judges began their deliberations, and the moment of decision arrived: Señorita El Salvador 1982 would be Señorita San Vicente, Miss Jeannette Marroquín, who was several inches taller than the other finalists, and more *gringa*-looking. The four runners-up reacted, on the whole, with rather less grace than is the custom on these occasions, and it occurred to me that this was a contest in which winning meant more than a scholarship or a screen test or a new wardrobe; winning here could mean the difference between life and casual death, a provisional safe-conduct not only for the winner but for her entire family.

"God damn it, he cut inaugural ribbons, he showed himself large as life in public taking on the risks of power as he had never done in more peaceful times, what the hell, he played endless games of dominoes with my lifetime friend General Rodrigo de Aguilar and my old friend the minister of health who were the only ones who . . . dared ask him to receive in a special audience the beauty queen of the poor, an incredible creature from that miserable wallow we call the dogfight district. . . . I'll not only receive her in a special audience but I'll dance the first waltz with her, by God, have them write it up in the newspapers, he ordered, this kind of crap makes a big hit with the poor. Yet, the night after the audience, he commented with a certain bitterness to General Rodrigo de Aguilar that the queen of the poor wasn't even worth dancing with, that she was as common as so many other slum Manuela Sánchezes with her nymph's dress of muslin petticoats and the gilt crown with artificial jewels and a rose in her hand under the watchful eye of a mother who looked after her as if she were made of gold, so he gave her everything she wanted which was only electricity and running water for the dogfight district. . . ."

That is Gabriel García Márquez, *The Autumn of the Patriarch*. On this evening that began with the grandson of General Maximiliano Hernández Martínez and progressed to "Señorita El Salvador 1982" and ended, at 12:22 A.M., with the earthquake, I began to see Gabriel García Márquez in a new light, as a social realist.

There were a number of metaphors to be found in this earthquake, not the least of them being that the one major building to suffer extensive damage happened also to be the major building most specifically and elaborately designed to withstand earthquakes, the American embassy. When this embassy was built, in 1965, the idea was that it would remain fluid under stress, its deep pilings shifting and sliding on Teflon pads, but over the past few years, as shelling the embassy came to be a favorite way of expressing dissatisfaction on all sides, the structure became so fortified—the steel exterior walls, the wet sandbags around the gun emplacements on the roof, the bomb shelter dug out underneath—as to render it rigid. The ceiling fell in Deane Hinton's office that night. Pipes burst on the third floor, flooding everything below. The elevator was disabled, the commissary a sea of shattered glass.

The Hotel Camino Real, on the other hand, which would appear to have been thrown together in the insouciant tradition of most tropical construction, did a considerable amount of rolling (I recall crouching under a door frame in my room on the seventh floor and watching, through the window, the San Salvador volcano appear to rock from left to right), but when the wrenching stopped and candles were found and everyone got downstairs nothing was broken, not even the glasses behind the bar. There was no electricity, but there was often no electricity. There were sporadic bursts of machine-gun fire on the street (this had made getting downstairs more problematic than it might have been, since the emergency stairway was exposed to the street), but sporadic bursts of machine-gun fire on the street were not entirely unusual in San Salvador. ("Sometimes it happens when it rains," someone from the embassy had told me about this phenomenon. "They get excited.") On the whole it was business as usual at the Camino Real, particularly in the discothèque off the lobby, where, by the time I got downstairs, an emergency generator seemed already to have been activated, waiters in black cowboy hats darted about the dance floor carrying drinks, and dancing continued, to Jerry Lee Lewis's "Great Balls of Fire."

Actual information was hard to come by in El Salvador, perhaps because this is not a culture in which a high value is placed on the definite. The only hard facts on the earthquake, for example, arrived at the Camino Real that night from New York, on the AP wire, which reported the Cal Tech reading of 7.0 Richter on an earthquake centered in the Pacific some sixty miles south of San Salvador. Over the next few days, as damage reports appeared in the local papers, the figure varied. One day the earthquake had been a 7.0 Richter, another day a 6.8. By Tuesday it was again a 7 in *La Prensa Gráfica*, but on a different scale altogether, not the Richter but the Modified Mercalli.

All numbers in El Salvador tended to materialize and vanish and rematerialize in a different form, as if numbers denoted only the "use" of numbers, an intention, a wish, a recognition that someone, somewhere, for whatever reason, needed to hear the ineffable expressed as a number. At any given time in El Salvador a great deal of what goes on is considered ineffable, and the use of numbers in this context tends to frustrate people who try to understand them literally, rather than as propositions to be floated, "heard," "mentioned." There was the case of the March 28 1982 election, about which there continued into that summer the rather scholastic argument first posed by *Central American Studies*, the publication of the Jesuit university in San Salvador: Had it taken an average of 2.5 minutes to cast a vote, or less? Could each ballot box hold 500 ballots, or more? The numbers were eerily Salvadoran. There were said to be 1.3 million people eligible to vote on March 28, but 1.5 million people were said to have voted. These 1.5 million people were said, in turn, to represent not 115 percent of the 1.3 million eligible voters but 80 percent (or, on another float, "62–68 percent") of the eligible voters, who accordingly no longer numbered 1.3 million, but a larger number. In any case no one really knew how many eligible voters there were in El Salvador, or even how many people. In any case it had seemed necessary to provide a number. In any case the election was over, a success, *la solución pacífica*.

Similarly, there was the question of how much money had left the country for Miami since 1979: Deane Hinton, in March of 1982, estimated $740 million. The Salvadoran minister of planning estimated, the same month, twice that. I recall asking President Magaña, when he happened to say that he had gone to lunch every Tuesday for the past ten years with the officers of the Central Reserve Bank of El Salvador, which reviews the very export and import transactions through which money traditionally leaves troubled countries, how much he thought was gone. "You hear figures mentioned," he said. I asked what figures he heard mentioned at these Tuesday lunches. "The figure they mentioned is six hundred million," he said. He watched as I wrote that down, *600,000,000, central bank El Salvador.* "The figure the Federal Reserve in New York mentioned," he added, "is one thousand million." He watched as I wrote that down too, *1,000,000,000, Fed NY.* "Those people don't want to stay for life in Miami," he said then, but this did not entirely address the question, nor was it meant to.

Not only numbers but names are understood locally to have only a situational meaning, and the change of a name is meant to be accepted as a change in the nature of the thing named. ORDEN, for example, the paramilitary organization formally founded in 1968 to function, along classic patronage lines, as the government's eyes and ears in the countryside, no longer exists as ORDEN, or the Organización Democrática Nacionalista, but as the Frente Democrática Nacionalista, a transubstantiation noted only cryptically in the State Department's official "justification" for the January 28 1982 certification: "The Salvadoran government, since the overthrow of General Romero, has taken explicit actions to end human rights abuses. The paramilitary organization 'ORDEN' has been outlawed, *although some of its former members may still be active.*" (Italics added.)

This tactic of solving a problem by changing its name is by no means limited to the government. The small office on the archdiocese grounds where the scrapbooks of the dead are kept is still called, by virtually everyone in San Salvador, "the Human Rights Commission" (Comisión de los Derechos Humanos), but in fact both the Human Rights Commission and

Socorro Jurídico, the archdiocesan legal aid office, were ordered in the spring of 1982 to vacate the church property, and, in the local way, did so: everything pretty much stayed in place, but the scrapbooks of the dead were thereafter kept, officially, in the "Oficina de Tutela Legal" of the "Comisión Arquidiocesana de Justicia y Paz." (This "Human Rights Commission," in any case, is not to be confused with the Salvadoran government's "Commission on Human Rights," the formation of which was announced the day before a scheduled meeting between President Magaña and Ronald Reagan. This official *comisión* is a seven-member panel notable for its inclusion of Colonel Carlos Reynaldo López Nuila, the director of the National Police.) This renaming was referred to as a "reorganization," which is one of many words in El Salvador that tend to signal the presence of the ineffable.

Other such words are "improvement," "perfection" (reforms are never abandoned or ignored, only "perfected" or "improved"), and that favorite from other fronts, "pacification." Language has always been used a little differently in this part of the world (an apparent statement of fact often expresses something only wished for, or something that might be true, a story, as in García Márquez's *many years later, as he faced the firing squad, Colonel Aureliano Buendía was to remember that distant afternoon when his father took him to discover ice*), but "improvement" and "perfection" and "pacification" derive from another tradition. Language as it is now used in El Salvador is the language of advertising, of persuasion, the product being one or another of the *soluciones* crafted in Washington or Panama or Mexico, which is part of the place's pervasive obscenity.

This language is shared by Salvadorans and Americans, as if a linguistic deal had been cut. "Perhaps the most striking measure of progress [in El Salvador]," Assistant Secretary of State Thomas Enders was able to say in August of 1982 in a speech at the Commonwealth Club in San Francisco, "is the transformation of the military from an institution dedicated to the status quo to one that spearheads land reform and supports constitutional democracy." Thomas Enders was able to say this precisely because the Salvadoran minister of defense, General José Guillermo García, had so superior a dedication to his own status quo that he played the American card as Roberto D'Aubuisson did not, played the game, played ball, understood the importance to Americans of symbolic action: the importance of letting the Americans have their land reform program, the importance of letting the Americans pretend that while "democracy in El Salvador" may remain "a slender reed" (that was Elliott Abrams in *The New York Times*), the situation is one in which "progress" is measurable ("the minister of defense has ordered that all violations of citizens' rights be stopped immediately," the State Department noted on the occasion of the July 1982 certification, a happy ending); the importance of giving the Americans an acceptable president, Alvaro Magaña, and of pretending that this acceptable president was in fact commander-in-chief of the armed forces, *el generalísimo* as *la solución*.

La solución changed with the market. Pacification, although those places pacified turned out to be in need of repeated pacification, was *la solución*. The use of the word "negotiations," however abstract that use may have been, was *la solución*. The election, although it ended with the ascension of a man, Roberto D'Aubuisson, essentially hostile to American policy, was *la solución* for Americans. The land reform program, grounded as it was in political rather than economic reality, was *la solución* as symbol. "It has not been a total economic success," Peter Askin, the AID director working with the government on the program, told *The New York Times* in August 1981, "but up to this point it has been a political success. I'm firm on that. There does seem to be a direct correlation between the agrarian reforms and the peasants not having become more radicalized." The land reform program, in other words, was based on the principle of buying off, buying time, giving a little to gain a lot, *minifundismo* in support of *latifundismo*, which, in a country where the left had no interest in keeping the peasants less "radicalized" and the right remained unconvinced that these peasants could not simply be eliminated, rendered it a program about which only Americans could be truly enthusiastic, less a "reform" than an exercise in public relations.

Even *la verdad*, the truth, was a degenerated phrase

in El Salvador: on my first evening in the country I was asked by a Salvadoran woman at an embassy party what I hoped to find out in El Salvador. I said that ideally I hoped to find out *la verdad*, and she beamed approvingly. Other journalists, she said, did not want *la verdad*. She called over two friends, who also approved: no one told *la verdad*. If I wrote *la verdad* it would be good for El Salvador. I realized that I had stumbled into a code, that these women used *la verdad* as it was used on the bumper stickers favored that spring and summer by ARENA people. "JOURNALISTS, TELL THE TRUTH!" the bumper stickers warned in Spanish, and they meant the truth according to Roberto D'Aubuisson.

In the absence of information (and the presence, often, of disinformation) even the most apparently straightforward event takes on, in El Salvador, elusive shadows, like a fragment of retrieved legend. On the afternoon that I was in San Francisco Gotera trying to see the commander of the garrison there, this *comandante*, Colonel Salvador Beltrán Luna, was killed, or was generally believed to have been killed, in the crash of a Hughes 500-D helicopter. The crash of a helicopter in a war zone would seem to lend itself to only a limited number of interpretations (the helicopter was shot down, or the helicopter suffered mechanical failure, are the two that come to mind), but the crash of this particular helicopter became, like everything else in Salvador, an occasion of rumor, doubt, suspicion, conflicting reports, and finally a kind of listless uneasiness.

The crash occurred either near the Honduran border in Morazán or, the speculation went, actually in Honduras. There were or were not four people aboard the helicopter: the pilot, a bodyguard, Colonel Beltrán Luna, and the assistant secretary of defense, Colonel Francisco Adolfo Castillo. At first all four were dead. A day later only three were dead: Radio Venceremos broadcast news of Colonel Castillo (followed a few days later by a voice resembling that of Colonel Castillo), not dead but a prisoner, or said to be a prisoner, or perhaps only claiming to be a prisoner. A day or so later another of the dead materialized, or appeared to: the pilot was, it seemed, neither dead nor a prisoner but hospitalized, incommunicado.

Questions about what actually happened to (or on, or after the crash of, or after the clandestine landing of) this helicopter provided table talk for days (one morning the newspapers emphasized that the Hughes 500-D had been *comprado en Guatemala*, bought in Guatemala, a detail so solid in this otherwise vaporous story that it suggested rumors yet unheard, intrigues yet unimagined), and remained unresolved at the time I left. At one point I asked President Magaña, who had talked to the pilot, what had happened. "They don't say," he said. Was Colonel Castillo a prisoner? "I read that in the paper, yes." Was Colonel Beltrán Luna dead? "I have that impression." Was the bodyguard dead? "Well, the pilot said he saw someone lying on the ground, either dead or unconscious, he doesn't know, but he believes it may have been Castillo's security man, yes." Where exactly had the helicopter crashed? "I didn't ask him." I looked at President Magaña, and he shrugged. "This is very delicate," he said. "I have a problem there. I'm supposed to be the commander-in-chief, so if I ask him, he should tell me. But he might say he's not going to tell me, then I would have to arrest him. So I don't ask." This is in many ways the standard development of a story in El Salvador, and is also illustrative of the position of the provisional president of El Salvador.

News of the outside world drifted in only fitfully, and in peculiar details. *La Prensa Gráfica* carried a regular column of news from San Francisco, California, and I recall reading in this column one morning that a man identified as a former president of the Bohemian Club had died, at age seventy-two, at his home in Tiburon. Most days *The Miami Herald* came in at some point, and sporadically *The New York Times* or *The Washington Post*, but there would be days when nothing came in at all, and I would find myself rifling back sports sections of *The Miami Herald* for installments of *Chrissie: My Own Story*, by Chris Evert Lloyd with Neil Amdur, or haunting the paperback stand at the hotel, where the collection ran mainly to romances and specialty items, like *The World's Best Dirty Jokes*, a volume in which all the jokes seemed to begin: "A midget went into a whorehouse . . ."

In fact the only news I wanted from outside increasingly turned out to be that which had originated in El Salvador: all other information seemed beside the point, the point being here, now, the situation, the *problema*, what did they mean the Hughes 500-D was *comprado en Guatemala*, was the Río Seco passable, were there or were there not American advisers on patrol in Usulután, who was going out, where were the roadblocks, were they burning cars today. In this context the rest of the world tended to recede, and word from the United States seemed profoundly remote, even inexplicable. I recall one morning picking up this message, from my secretary in Los Angeles: "JDD: Alessandra Stanley from *Time*, 213/273-1530. They heard you were in El Salvador and wanted some input from you for the cover story they're preparing on the women's movement. Ms. Stanley wanted their correspondent in Central America to contact you—I said that you could not be reached but would be calling me. She wanted you to call: Jay Cocks 212/841-2633." I studied this message for a long time, and tried to imagine the scenario in which a *Time* stringer in El Salvador received, by Telex from Jay Cocks in New York, a request to do an interview on the women's movement with someone who happened to be at the Camino Real Hotel. This was not a scenario that played, and I realized then that El Salvador was as inconceivable to Jay Cocks in the high keep of the Time-Life Building in New York as this message was to me in El Salvador.

I was told in the summer of 1982 by both Alvaro Magaña and Guillermo Ungo that although each of course knew the other they were of "different generations." Magaña was fifty-six. Ungo was fifty-one. Five years is a generation in El Salvador, it being a place in which not only the rest of the world but time itself tends to contract to the here and now. History is *la matanza*, and then current events, which recede even as they happen: General José Guillermo García was in the summer of 1982 widely perceived as a fixture of long standing, an immovable object through several governments and shifts in the national temperament, a survivor. In context he was a survivor, but the context was just three years, since the Majano coup. All events earlier than the Majano coup had by then vanished into uncertain memory, and the coup itself, which took place on October 15 1979, was seen as so distant that there was common talk of the next *juventud militar*, of the cyclical readiness for rebellion of what was always referred to as "the new generation" of young officers. "We think in five-year horizons," the economic officer at the American embassy told me one day. "Anything beyond that is evolution." He was talking about not having what he called "the luxury of the long view," but there is a real sense in which the five-year horizons of the American embassy constitute the longest view taken in El Salvador, either forward or back.

One reason no one looks back is that the view could only dispirit: this is a national history peculiarly resistant to heroic interpretation. There is no *libertador* to particularly remember. Public statues in San Salvador tend toward representations of abstracts, the Winged Liberty downtown, the *Salvador del Mundo* at the junction of Avenida Roosevelt and Paseo Escalón and the Santa Tecla highway; the expressionist spirit straining upward, outsized hands thrust toward the sky, at the Monument of the Revolution up by the Hotel Presidente. If the country's history as a republic seems devoid of shared purpose or unifying event, a record of insensate ambitions and their accidental consequences, its three centuries as a colony seem blanker still: Spanish colonial life was centered in Colombia and Panama to the south and Guatemala to the north, and Salvador lay between, a neglected frontier of the Captaincy General of Guatemala from 1525 until 1821, the year Guatemala declared its independence from Spain. So attenuated was El Salvador's sense of itself in its moment of independence that it petitioned the United States for admission to the union as a state. The United States declined.

In fact El Salvador had always been a frontier, even before the Spaniards arrived. The great Mesoamerican cultures penetrated this far south only shallowly. The great South American cultures thrust this far north

72

only sporadically. There is a sense in which the place remains marked by the meanness and discontinuity of all frontier history, by a certain frontier proximity to the cultural zero. Some aspects of the local culture were imposed. Others were borrowed. An instructive moment: at an exhibition of native crafts in Nahuizalco, near Sonsonate, it was explained to me that a traditional native craft was the making of wicker furniture, but that little of this furniture was now seen because it was hard to obtain wicker in the traditional way. I asked what the traditional way of obtaining wicker had been. The traditional way of obtaining wicker, it turned out, had been to import it from Guatemala.

In fact there were a number of instructive elements about this day I spent in Nahuizalco, a hot Sunday in June. The event for which I had driven down from San Salvador was not merely a craft exhibit but the opening of a festival that would last several days, the sixth annual Feria Artesanal de Nahuizalco, sponsored by the Casa de la Cultura program of the Ministry of Education as part of its effort to encourage indigenous culture. Since public policy in El Salvador has veered unerringly toward the elimination of the indigenous population, this official celebration of its culture seemed an undertaking of some ambiguity, particularly in Nahuizalco: the uprising that led to the 1932 *matanza* began and ended among the Indian workers on the coffee *fincas* in this part of the country, and Nahuizalco and the other Indian villages around Sonsonate lost an entire generation to the *matanza*. By the early sixties estimates of the remaining Indian population in all of El Salvador ranged only between four and sixteen percent; the rest of the population was classified as *ladino*, a cultural rather than an ethnic designation, denoting only Hispanization, including both acculturated Indians and *mestizos*, and rejected by those upper-class members of the population who preferred to emphasize their Spanish ancestry.

Nineteen thirty-two was a year around Nahuizalco when Indians were tied by their thumbs and shot against church walls, shot on the road and left for the dogs, shot and bayoneted into the mass graves they themselves had dug. Indian dress was abandoned by the survivors. Nahuatl, the Indian language, was no longer spoken in public. In many ways race remains the ineffable element at the heart of this particular darkness: even as he conducted the *matanza*, General Maximiliano Hernández Martínez was dismissed, by many of the very oligarchs whose interests he was protecting by killing Indians, as "the little Indian." On this hot Sunday fifty years later the celebrants of Nahuizalco's indigenous culture would arrange themselves, by noon, into two distinct camps, the *ladinos* sitting in the shade of the schoolyard, the Indians squatting in the brutal sun outside. In the schoolyard there were trees, and tables, where the Queen of the Fair, who had a wicker crown and European features, sat with the local *guardia*, each of whom had an automatic weapon, a sidearm, and a bayonet. The *guardia* drank beer and played with their weapons. The Queen of the Fair studied her oxblood-red fingernails. It took twenty centavos to enter the schoolyard, and a certain cultural confidence.

There had been Indian dances that morning. There had been music. There had been the "blessing of the market": the statue of San Juan Bautista carried, on a platform trimmed with wilted gladioli, from the church to the market, the school, the homes of the bedridden. To the extent that Catholic mythology has been over four centuries successfully incorporated into local Indian life, this blessing of the market was at least part of the "actual" indigenous culture, but the dances and the music derived from other traditions. There was a Suprema Beer sound truck parked in front of the Casa de la Cultura office on the plaza, and the music that blared all day from its loudspeakers was "Roll Out the Barrel," "La Cucaracha," "Everybody Salsa."

The provenance of the dances was more complicated. They were Indian, but they were less remembered than recreated, and as such derived not from local culture but from a learned idea of local culture, an official imposition made particularly ugly by the cultural impotence of the participants. The women, awkward and uncomfortable in an approximation of native costume, moved with difficulty into the dusty street and performed a listless and unpracticed dance with baskets. Whatever men could be found (mainly little boys and old men, since those young men still alive in places like Nahuizalco try not to be noticed) had been dressed in "warrior" costume: headdresses of crinkled foil, swords of cardboard and wood. Their hair was lank, their walk furtive. Some of them wore sunglasses. The others averted their eyes. Their role in the fair involved stamping and lunging and brandishing their cardboard weapons, a display of warrior *machismo*, and the extent to which each of them had been unmanned—unmanned not only by history but by a factor less abstract, unmanned by the real weapons in the schoolyard, by the G-3 assault rifles with which the *guardia* played while they drank beer with the Queen of the Fair—rendered this display deeply obscene.

I had begun before long to despise the day, the dirt, the blazing sun, the pervasive smell of rotting meat, the absence of even the most rudimentary skill in the handicrafts on exhibit (there were sewn items, for example, but they were sewn by machine of sleazy fabric, and the simplest seams were crooked), the brutalizing music from the sound truck, the tedium; had begun most of all to despise the fair itself, which seemed contrived, pernicious, a kind of official opiate, an attempt to recreate or perpetuate a way of life neither economically nor socially viable. There was no pleasure in this day. There was a great deal of joyless milling. There was some shade in the plaza, from trees plastered with ARENA posters, but nowhere to sit. There was a fountain painted bright blue inside, but the dirty water was surrounded by barbed wire, and the sign read: "Se Prohibe Sentarse Aqui," no sitting allowed.

I stood for a while and watched the fountain. I bought a John Deere cap for seven *colones* and stood in the sun and watched the little ferris wheel, and the merry-go-round, but there seemed to be no children with the money or will to ride them, and after a while I crossed the plaza and went into the church, avoiding the bits of masonry which still fell from the bell tower damaged that week in the earthquake and its aftershocks. In the church a mass baptism was taking place: thirty or forty infants and older babies, and probably a few hundred mothers and grandmothers and aunts and godmothers. The altar was decorated with asters in condensed milk cans. The babies fretted, and several of the mothers produced bags of Fritos to quiet them. A piece of falling masonry bounced off a scaffold in the back of the church, but no one looked back. In this church full of women and babies there were only four men present. The reason for this may have been cultural, or may have had to do with the time and the place, and the G-3s in the schoolyard.

During the week before I flew down to El Salvador a Salvadoran woman who works for my husband and me in Los Angeles gave me repeated instructions about what we must and must not do. We must not go out at night. We must stay off the street whenever possible. We must never ride in buses or taxis, never leave the capital, never imagine that our passports would protect us. We must not even consider the hotel a safe place: people were killed in hotels. She spoke with considerable vehemence, because two of her brothers had been killed in Salvador in August of 1981, in their beds. The throats of both brothers had been slashed. Her father had been cut but stayed alive. Her mother had been beaten. Twelve of her other relatives, aunts and uncles and cousins, had been taken from their houses one night the same August, and their bodies had been found some time later, in a ditch. I assured her that we would remember, we would be careful, we would in fact be so careful that we would probably (trying for a light touch) spend all our time in church.

She became still more agitated, and I realized that I had spoken as a *norteamericana:* churches had not been to this woman the neutral ground they had been to me. I must remember: Archbishop Romero killed saying mass in the chapel of the Divine Providence Hospital in San Salvador. I must remember: more than thirty people killed at Archbishop Romero's funeral in the Metropolitan Cathedral in San Salvador. I must remember: more than twenty people killed before that on the steps of the Metropolitan Cathedral. CBS had filmed it. It had been on television, the bodies jerking, those still alive crawling over the dead as they tried to get out of range. I must understand: the Church was dangerous.

I told her that I understood, that I knew all that, and I did, abstractly, but the specific meaning of the Church she knew eluded me until I was actually there, at the Metropolitan Cathedral in San Salvador, one afternoon when rain sluiced down its corrugated plastic windows and puddled around the supports of the Sony and Phillips billboards near the steps. The effect of the Metropolitan Cathedral is immediate, and entirely literary. This is the cathedral that the late Archbishop Oscar Arnulfo Romero refused to finish, on the premise that the work of the Church took precedence over its display, and the high walls of raw concrete bristle with structural rods, rusting now, staining the concrete, sticking out at wrenched and violent angles. The wiring is exposed. Fluorescent tubes hang askew. The great high altar is backed by warped plyboard. The cross on the altar is of bare incandescent bulbs, but the bulbs, that afternoon, were unlit: there was in fact no light at all on the main altar, no light on the cross, no light on the globe of the world that showed the northern American continent in gray and the southern in white; no light on the dove above the globe, *Salvador del Mundo*. In this vast brutalist space that was the cathedral, the unlit altar seemed to offer a single ineluctable message: at this time and in this place the light of the world could be construed as out, off, extinguished.

In many ways the Metropolitan Cathedral is an authentic piece of political art, a statement for El Salvador as *Guernica* was for Spain. It is quite devoid of sentimental relief. There are no decorative or architectural references to familiar parables, in fact no stories at all, not even the Stations of the Cross. On the afternoon I was there the flowers laid on the altar were dead. There were no traces of normal parish activity. The doors were open to the barricaded main steps, and down the steps there was a spill of red paint, lest anyone forget the blood shed there. Here and there on the cheap linoleum inside the cathedral there was what seemed to be actual blood, dried in spots, the kind of spots dropped by a slow hemorrhage, or by a woman who does not know or does not care that she is menstruating.

There were several women in the cathedral during the hour or so I spent there, a young woman with a baby, an older woman in house slippers, a few others, all in black. One of the women walked the aisles as if by compulsion, up and down, across and back, crooning loudly as she walked. Another knelt without moving at the tomb of Archbishop Romero in the right transept. "LOOR A MONSENOR ROMERO," the crude needlepoint tapestry by the tomb read, "Praise to Monsignor Romero from the Mothers of the Imprisoned, the Disappeared, and the Murdered," the *Comité de Madres y Familiares de Presos, Desaparecidos, y Asesinados Politicos de El Salvador.*

The tomb itself was covered with offerings and petitions, notes decorated with motifs cut from greeting cards and cartoons. I recall one with figures cut from a Bugs Bunny strip, and another with a pencil drawing of a baby in a crib. The baby in this drawing seemed to be receiving medication or fluid or blood intravenously, through the IV line shown on its wrist. I studied the notes for a while and then went back and looked again at the unlit altar, and at the red paint on the main steps, from which it was possible to see the guardsmen on the balcony of the National Palace hunching back to avoid the rain. Many Salvadorans are offended by the Metropolitan Cathedral, which is as it should be, because the place remains perhaps the only unambiguous political statement in El Salvador, a metaphorical bomb in the ultimate power station.

". . . I had nothing more to do in San Salvador. I had given a lecture on the topic that had occurred to me on the train to Tapachula: Little-known Books by Famous American Authors—*Pudd'nhead Wilson*, *The Devil's Dictionary*, *The Wild Palms*. I had looked at the university; and no one could explain why there was a mural of Marx, Engels, and Lenin in the university of this right-wing dictatorship."

—Paul Theroux, *The Old Patagonian Express*.

The university Paul Theroux visited in San Salvador was the National University of El Salvador. This visit (and, given the context, this extraordinary lecture) took place in the late seventies, a period when the National University was actually open. In 1972 the Molina government had closed it, forcibly, with tanks and artillery and planes, and had kept it closed until 1974. In 1980 the Duarte government again moved troops onto the campus, which then had an enrollment of about 30,000, leaving fifty dead and offices and laboratories systematically smashed. By the time I visited El Salvador a few classes were being held in storefronts around San Salvador, but no one other than an occasional reporter had been allowed to enter the campus since the day the troops came in. Those reporters allowed to look had described walls still splashed with the spray-painted slogans left by the students, floors littered with tangled computer tape and with copies of what the National Guardsmen in charge characterized as *subversivo* pamphlets, for example a reprint of an article on inherited enzyme deficiency from *The New England Journal of Medicine.*

In some ways the closing of the National University seemed another of those Salvadoran situations in which no one came out well, and everyone was made to bleed a little, not excluding the National Guardsmen left behind to have their ignorance exposed by *gringo* reporters. The Jesuit university, UCA, or La Universidad Centroamericana José Simeón Cañas, had emerged as the most important intellectual force in the country, but the Jesuits had been so widely identified with the left that some local scholars would not attend lectures or seminars held on the UCA campus. (Those Jesuits still in El Salvador had in fact been under a categorical threat of death from the White Warriors Union since 1977. The Carter administration forced President Romero to protect the Jesuits, and on the day the killing was to have begun, July 22, 1977, the National Police are said to have sat outside the Jesuit residence in San Salvador on their motorcycles, with UZIs.) In any case UCA could manage an enrollment of only about 5,000. The scientific disciplines, which never had a particularly tenacious hold locally, had largely vanished from local life.

Meanwhile many people spoke of the National University in the present tense, as if it still existed, or as if its closing were a routine event on some long-term academic calendar. I recall talking one day to a former member of the faculty at the National University, a woman who had not seen her office since the morning she noticed the troops massing outside and left it. She lost her books and her research and the uncompleted manuscript of the book she was then writing, but she described this serenely, and seemed to find no immediate contradiction in losing her work to the Ministry of Defense and the work she did later with the Ministry of Education. The campus of the National University is said to be growing over, which is one way contradictions get erased in the tropics.

I was invited one morning to a gathering of Salvadoran writers, a kind of informal coffee hour arranged by the American embassy. For some days there had been a question about where to hold this *café literario*, since there seemed to be no single location that was not considered off-limits by at least one of the guests, and at one point the ambassador's residence was put forth as the most neutral setting. On the day before the event it was finally decided that UCA was the more appropriate place ("and just never mind," as one of the embassy people put it, that some people would not go to UCA), and at ten the next morning we gathered there in a large conference room and drank coffee and talked, at first in platitudes, and then more urgently.

These are some of the sentences spoken to me that morning: *It's not possible to speak of intellectual life in El Salvador. Every day we lose more. We are regressing constantly. Intellectual life is drying up. You are looking at the intellectual life of El Salvador. Here. In this room. We are the only survivors. Some of the others are out of the country, others are not writing because they are engaged in political activity. Some have been disappeared, many of the teachers have been dis-*

appeared. Teaching is very dangerous, if a student mis-interprets what a teacher says, then the teacher may be arrested. Some are in exile, the rest are dead. Los muertos, you know? We are the only ones left. There is no one after us, no young ones. It is all over, you know? At noon there was an exchange of books and *curricula vitae.* The cultural attaché from the embassy said that she, for one, would like to see this *café literario* close on a hopeful note, and someone provided one: it was a hopeful note that *norteamericanos* and *centroamericanos* could have such a meeting. This is what passed for a hopeful note in San Salvador in the summer of 1982.

THE Ambassador of the United States of America in El Salvador, Deane Hinton, received on his desk every morning in the summer of 1982 a list of the American military personnel in-country that day. The number on this list, I was told, was never to exceed 55. Some days there were as few as 35. If the number got up to 55, and it was thought essential to bring in someone else, then a trade was made: the incoming American was juggled against an outgoing American, one normally stationed in Salvador but shunted down to Panama for as long as necessary to maintain the magic number.

Everything to do with the United States Military Group, or MILGP, was treated by the embassy as a kind of magic, a totemic presence circumscribed by potent taboos. The American A-37Bs presented to El Salvador in June of that year were actually flown up from Panama not by Americans but by Salvadorans trained at the United States Southern Air Command in Panama for this express purpose. American advisers could participate in patrols for training purposes but could not participate in patrols in combat situations. When both CBS and *The New York Times*, one day that June, reported having seen two or three American advisers in what the reporters construed as a combat situation in Usulután province, Colonel John D. Waghelstein, the MILGP commander, was called back from playing tennis in Panama (his wife had met him in Panama, there being no dependents allowed in El Salvador) in order, as he put it, "to deal with the press."

I happened to arrive for lunch at the ambassador's residence just as Colonel Waghelstein reported in from Panama that day, and the two of them, along with the embassy public affairs officer, walked to the far end of the swimming pool to discuss the day's problem out of my hearing. Colonel Waghelstein is massively built, crew-cut, tight-lipped, and very tanned, almost a cartoon of the American military presence, and the notion that he had come up from Panama to deal with the press was novel and interesting, in that he had made, during his tour in El Salvador, a pretty terse point of not dealing with the press. Some months later in Los Angeles I saw an NBC documentary in which I noticed the special effort Colonel Waghelstein had made in this case. American advisers had actually been made available to NBC, which in turn adopted a chiding tone toward CBS for the June "advisers in action" story. The total effect was mixed, however, since even as the advisers complained on camera about how "very few people" asked them what they did and about how some reporters "spend all their time with the other side," the camera angles seemed such that no adviser's face was distinctly seen. There were other points in this NBC documentary when I thought I recognized a certain official hand, for example the mention of the "sometimes cruel customs" of the Pipil Indians in El Salvador. The custom in question was that of flaying one another alive, a piece of pre-Columbian lore often tendered by embassy people as evidence that from a human-rights point of view, the trend locally is up, or at any rate holding.

Colonel Waghelstein stayed at the ambassador's that day only long enough for a drink (a Bloody Mary, which he nursed morosely), and, after he left, the ambassador and the public affairs officer and my husband and I sat down to lunch on the covered terrace. We watched a lime-throated bird in the garden. We watched the ambassador's English sheep dog bound across the lawn at the sound of shots, rifle practice at the Escuela Militar beyond the wall and down the hill. "Only time we had any quiet up here," the ambassador said in his high Montana twang, "was when we sent the whole school up to Benning." The shots rang out again. The sheep dog barked. *"Quieto,"* the houseman crooned.

I have thought since about this lunch a great deal. The wine was chilled and poured into crystal glasses. The fish was served on porcelain plates that bore the American eagle. The sheep dog and the crystal and the American eagle together had on me a certain anesthetic effect, temporarily deadening that receptivity to the sinister that afflicts everyone in Salvador, and I experienced for a moment the official American delusion, the illusion of plausibility, the sense that the American undertaking in El Salvador might turn out to be, from the right angle, in the right light, just another difficult but possible mission in another troubled but possible country.

Deane Hinton is an interesting man. Before he replaced Robert White in San Salvador he had served in Europe, South America, and Africa. He had been married twice, once to an American, who bore him five children before their divorce, and once to a Chilean, who had died not long before, leaving him the stepfather of her five children by an earlier marriage. At the time I met him he had just announced his engagement to a Salvadoran named Patricia de Lopez. Someone who is about to marry a third time, who thinks of himself as the father of ten, and who has spent much of his career in chancey posts—Mombasa, Kinshasa, Santiago, San Salvador—is apt to be someone who believes in the possible.

His predecessor, Robert White, was relieved of the San Salvador embassy in February 1981, in what White later characterized as a purge, by the new Reagan people, of the State Department's entire Latin American section. This circumstance made Deane Hinton seem, to many in the United States, the bearer of the administration's big stick in El Salvador, but what Deane Hinton actually said about El Salvador differed from what Robert White said about El Salvador more in style than in substance. Deane Hinton believed, as Robert White believed, that the situation in El Salvador was bad, terrible, squalid beyond anyone's power to understand it without experiencing it. Deane Hinton also believed, as Robert White believed to a point, that the situation would be, in the absence of one or another American effort, still worse.

Deane Hinton believes in doing what he can. He had gotten arrests on the deaths of the four American churchwomen. He had even ("by yelling some more," he said) gotten the government to announce these arrests, no small accomplishment, since El Salvador was a country in which the "announcement" of an arrest did not necessarily follow the arrest itself. In the case of the murders of Michael Hammer and Mark Pearlman and José Rodolfo Viera at the Sheraton, for example, it was not the government but the American embassy which announced at least two of the various successive arrests, those of the former guardsmen Abel Campos and Rodolfo Orellana Osorio. This embassy "announcement" was reported by the American press on September 15 1982, and was followed immediately by another announcement: on September 16 1982, "a police spokesman" in San Salvador announced not the arrest but the "release" of the same suspects, after what was described as a month in custody.

To persist in so distinctly fluid a situation required a personality of considerable resistance. Deane Hinton was even then working on getting new arrests in the Sheraton murders. He was even then working on getting trials in the murders of the four American women, a trial being another step that did not, in El Salvador, necessarily follow an arrest. There had been progress. There had been the election, a potent symbol for many Americans and perhaps even for some Salvadorans, although the symbolic content of the event showed up rather better in translation than on the scene. "There was some shooting in the morning," I recall being told by a parish priest about election day in his district, "but it quieted down around nine A.M. The army had a truck going around to go out and vote—*Tu Voto Es La Solución*, you know—so they went out and voted. They wanted that stamp on their identity cards to show they voted. The stamp was the proof of their good will. Whether or not they actually wanted to vote is hard to say. I guess you'd have to say they were more scared of the army than of the guerrillas, so they voted."

Four months after the fact, in *The New York Times Magazine*, former ambassador Robert White wrote about the election: "Nothing is more symbolic of our current predicament in El Salvador than the Administration's bizarre attempt to recast D'Aubuisson in a more favorable light." Even the fact that the election had resulted in what White called "political disaster" could be presented, with a turn of the mirror, positively: one man's political disaster could be another's democratic turbulence, the birth pangs of what Assistant Secretary of State Thomas Enders persisted in calling "nascent democratic institutions." "The new Salvadoran democracy," Enders was saying five months after the election, not long after Justice of the Peace Gonzalo Alonso García, the twentieth prominent Christian Democrat to be kidnapped or killed since the election, had been dragged from his house in San Cayetano Itepeque by fifteen armed men, "is doing what it is supposed to do—bringing a broad spectrum of forces and factions into a functioning democratic system."

In other words even the determination to eradicate the opposition could be interpreted as evidence that the model worked. There was still, moreover, a certain obeisance to the land reform program, the lustrous intricacies of which were understood by so few that almost any interpretation could be construed as possible. "About 207, 207 always applied only to 1979, that is what no one understands," I had been told by President Magaña when I tried at one point to get straight the actual status of Decree 207, the legislation meant to implement the "Land-to-the-Tiller" program by providing that title to all land farmed by tenants be transferred immediately to those tenants. "There is no one more conservative than a small farmer," Peter Shiras, a former consultant to the Inter-American Development Bank, had quoted an AID official as saying about 207. "We're going to be breeding capitalists like rabbits."

Decree 207 had been the source of considerable confusion and infighting during the weeks preceding my arrival in El Salvador, suspended but not suspended, on and off and on again, but I had not before heard anyone describe it, as President Magaña seemed to be describing it, as a proposition wound up to self-destruct. Did he mean, I asked carefully, that Decree 207, implementing Land-to-the-Tiller, applied only to 1979 because no landowner, in practice, would work against his own interests by allowing tenants on his land after 207 took effect? "Right!" President Magaña had said, as if to a slow student. "Exactly! This is what no one understands. There were no new rental contracts in 1980 or 1981. No one would rent out land under 207, they would have to be crazy to do that."

What he said was obvious, but out of line with the rhetoric, and this conversation with President Magaña about Land-to-the-Tiller, which I had heard described through the spring as a centerpiece of United States policy in El Salvador, had been one of many occasions when the American effort in El Salvador seemed based on auto-suggestion, a dreamwork devised to obscure any intelligence that might trouble the dreamer. This impression persisted, and I was struck, a few months later, by the suggestion in the report on El Salvador released by the Permanent Select Committee on Intelligence of the House of Representatives (*U.S. Intelligence Performance in Central America: Achievements and Selected Instances of Concern*) that the intelligence was itself a dreamwork, tending to support policy, the report read, "rather than inform it," providing "reinforcement more than illumination," " 'ammunition' rather than analysis."

A certain tendency to this kind of dreamwork, to improving upon rather than illuminating the situation, may have been inevitable, since the unimproved situation in El Salvador was such that to consider it was to consider moral extinction. "This time they won't get away with it," Robert White was reported to have said as he watched the bodies of the four American women dragged from their common grave, but they did, and White was brought home. This is a country that cracks

Americans, and Deane Hinton gave the sense of a man determined not to crack. There on the terrace of the official residence on Avenida La Capilla in the San Benito district it was all logical. One step followed another, progress was slow. We were Americans, we would not be demoralized. It was not until late in the lunch, at a point between the salad and the profiteroles, that it occurred to me that we were talking exclusively about the appearances of things, about how the situation might be made to look better, about trying to get the Salvadoran government to "appear" to do what the American government needed done in order to make it "appear" that the American aid was justified.

It was sometimes necessary to stop Roberto D'Aubuisson "on the one-yard line" (Deane Hinton's phrase about the ARENA attempt to commandeer the presidency) because Roberto D'Aubuisson made a negative appearance in the United States, made things, as Jeremiah O'Leary, the assistant to national security adviser William Clark, had imagined Hinton advising D'Aubuisson after the election, "hard for everybody." What made a positive appearance in the United States, and things easier for everybody, were elections, and the announcement of arrests in cases involving murdered Americans, and ceremonies in which tractable *campesinos* were awarded land titles by army officers, and the Treasury Police sat on the platform, and the president came, by helicopter. "Our land reform program," Leonel Gómez, who had worked with the murdered José Rodolfo Viera in the Salvadoran Institute of Agrarian Transformation, noted in *Food Monitor*, "gave them an opportunity to build up points for the next U.S. AID grant." By "them" Leonel Gómez meant not his compatriots but Americans, meant the American Institute for Free Labor Development, meant Roy Prosterman, the architect of the Land-to-the-Tiller programs in both El Salvador and Vietnam.

In this light the American effort had a distinctly circular aspect (the aid was the card with which we got the Salvadorans to do it our way, and appearing to do it our way was the card with which the Salvadorans got the aid), and the question of why the effort was being made went unanswered. It was possible to talk about Cuba and Nicaragua, and by extension the Soviet Union, and national security, but this seemed only to justify a momentum already underway: no one could doubt that Cuba and Nicaragua had at various points supported the armed opposition to the Salvadoran government, but neither could anyone be surprised by this, or, given what could be known about the players, be unequivocally convinced that American interests lay on one side or another of what even Deane Hinton referred to as a civil war.

It was certainly possible to describe some members of the opposition, as Deane Hinton had, as "out-and-out Marxists," but it was equally possible to describe other members of the opposition, as the embassy had at the inception of the FDR in April of 1980, as "a broad-based coalition of moderate and center-left groups." The right in El Salvador never made this distinction: to the right, anyone in the opposition was a communist, along with most of the American press, the Catholic Church, and, as time went by, all Salvadoran citizens not of the right. In other words there remained a certain ambiguity about political terms as they were understood in the United States and in El Salvador, where "left" may mean, in the beginning, only a resistance to seeing one's family killed or disappeared. That it comes eventually to mean something else may be, to the extent that the United States has supported the increasing polarization in El Salvador, the Procrustean bed we made ourselves.

It was a situation in which American interests would seem to have been best served by attempting to isolate the "out-and-out Marxists" while supporting the "broad-based coalition of moderate and center-left groups," discouraging the one by encouraging the other, co-opting the opposition; but American policy, by accepting the invention of "communism," as defined by the right in El Salvador, as a daemonic element to be opposed at even the most draconic cost, had in fact achieved the reverse. "We believe in gringos," Hugh Barrera, an ARENA contender for the presidency, told Laurie Becklund of *The Los Angeles Times* when she asked in April of 1982 if ARENA did not fear losing American aid by trying to shut the Christian Democrats out of the government. "Congress would not risk losing a whole country over one party. That would be turning against a U.S. ally and encouraging Soviet intervention here. It would not be intelligent." In other words "anti-communism" was seen, correctly, as the bait the United States would always take.

* That we had been drawn, both by a misapprehension of the local rhetoric and by the manipulation of our own rhetorical weaknesses, into a game we did not understand, a play of power in a political tropic alien to us, seemed apparent, and yet there we remained. In this light all arguments tended to trail off. Pros and cons seemed equally off the point. At the heart of the American effort there was something of the familiar ineffable, as if it were taking place not in El Salvador but in a mirage of El Salvador, the mirage of a society not unlike our own but "sick," a temporarily fevered republic in which the antibodies of democracy needed only to be encouraged, in which words had stable meanings north and south ("election," say, and "Marxist") and in which there existed, waiting to be tapped by our support, some latent good will. A few days before I arrived in El Salvador there appeared in *Diario de Hoy* a full-page advertisement placed by leaders of the Women's Crusade for Peace and Work. This advertisement accused the United States, in the person of its ambassador, Deane Hinton, of "blackmailing us with your miserable aid, which only keeps us subjugated in underdevelopment so that powerful countries like yours can continue exploiting our few riches and having us under your boot." The Women's Crusade for Peace and Work is an organization of the right, with links to ARENA, which may suggest how latent that good will remains.

This "blackmail" motif, and its arresting assumption that trying to keep Salvadorans from killing one another constituted a new and particularly crushing imperialism, began turning up more and more frequently. By October of 1982 advertisements were appearing in the San Salvador papers alleging that the blackmail was resulting in a "betrayal" of El Salvador by the military, who were seen as "lackeys" of the United States. At a San Salvador Chamber of Commerce meeting in late October, Deane Hinton said that "in the first two weeks of this month at least sixty-eight human beings were murdered in El Salvador under circumstances which are familiar to everyone here," stressed that American aid was dependent upon "progress" in this area, and fielded some fifty written questions, largely hostile, one of which read, "Are you trying to blackmail us?"

I was read this speech over the telephone by an embassy officer, who described it as "the ambassador's strongest statement yet." I was puzzled by this, since the ambassador had made most of the same points, at a somewhat lower pitch, in a speech on February 11, 1982; it was hard to discern a substantive advance between, in February, "If there is one issue which could force our Congress to withdraw or seriously reduce its support for El Salvador, it is the issue of human rights," and, in October: "If not, the United States—in spite of our other interests, in spite of our commitment to the struggle against communism, could be forced to deny assistance to El Salvador." In fact the speeches seemed almost cyclical, seasonal events keyed to the particular rhythm of the six-month certification process; midway in the certification cycle things appear "bad," and are then made, at least rhetorically, to appear "better," "improvement" being the key to certification.

I mentioned the February speech on the telephone, but the embassy officer to whom I was speaking did not see the similarity; this was, he said, a "stronger" statement, and would be "front-page" in both *The Washington Post* and *The Los Angeles Times*. In fact the story did appear on the front pages of both *The Washington Post* and *The Los Angeles Times*, suggesting that every six months the news is born anew in El Salvador.

Whenever I hear someone speak now of one or another *solución* for El Salvador I think of particular Americans who have spent time there, each in his or her own way inexorably altered by the fact of having been in a certain place at a certain time. Some of these Americans have since moved on and others remain in Salvador, but, like survivors of a common natural disaster, they are equally marked by the place.

"There are a lot of options that aren't playable. We could come in militarily and shape the place up. That's an option, but it's not playable, because of public opinion. If it weren't for public opinion, however, El Salvador would be the ideal laboratory for a full-scale military operation. It's small. It's self-contained. There are hemispheric cultural similarities."

—*A United States embassy officer in San Salvador.*

"June 15th was not only a great day for El Salvador, receiving $5 million in additional U.S. aid for the private sector and a fleet of fighter planes and their corresponding observation units, but also a great day for me. Ray Bonner [of *The New York Times*] actually spoke to me at Ilopango airport and took my hand and shook it when I offered it to him. . . . Also, another correspondent pulled me aside and said that if I was such a punctilious journalist why the hell had I written something about him that wasn't true. Here I made no attempt to defend myself but only quoted my source. Later we talked and ironed out some wrinkles. It is a great day when journalists with opposing points of view can get together and learn something from each other, after all, we are all on the same side. I even wrote a note to Robert E. White (which he ignored) not long ago after he protested that I had not published his Letter to the Editor (which I had) suggesting that we be friendly enemies. The only enemy is totalitarianism, in any guise: communistic, socialistic, capitalistic or militaristic. Man is unique because he has free will and the capacity to choose. When this is suppressed he is no longer a man but an animal. That is why I say that despite differing points of view, we are none of us enemies."

—*Mario Rosenthal, editor of the* El Salvador News Gazette, *in his June 14–20 1982 column, "A Great Day."*

"You would have had the last interview with an obscure Salvadoran."

—*An American reporter to whom I had mentioned that I had been trying to see Colonel Salvador Beltrán Luna on the day he died in a helicopter crash.*

"It's not as bad as it could be. I was talking to the political risk people at one of the New York banks and in 1980 they gave El Salvador only a ten percent chance of as much stability in 1982 as we have now. So you see."

—*The same embassy officer.*

"Normally I wouldn't have a guard at my level, but there were death threats against my predecessor, he was on a list. I'm living in his old house. In fact something kind of peculiar happened today. Someone telephoned and wanted to know, very urgent, how to reach the Salvadoran woman with whom my predecessor lived. This person on the phone claimed that the woman's family needed to reach her, a death, or illness, and she had left no address. This might have been true and it might not have been true. Naturally I gave no information."

—Another embassy officer.

"AMBASSADOR WHITE: My embassy also sent in several months earlier these captured documents. There is no doubt about the provenance of these documents as they were handed to me directly by Colonel Adolfo Majano, then a member of the junta. They were taken when they captured ex-Major D'Aubuisson and a number of other officers who were conspiring against the Government of El Salvador.

SENATOR ZORINSKY: . . . Please continue, Mr. Ambassador.

AMBASSADOR WHITE: I would be glad to give you copies of these documents for your record. In these documents there are over a hundred names of people who are participating, both within the Salvadoran military as active conspirers against the Government, and also the names of people living in the United States and in Guatemala City who are actively funding the death squads. I gave this document, in Spanish, to three of the most skilled political analysts I know in El Salvador without orienting them in any way. I just asked them to read this and tell me what conclusions they came up with. All three of them came up with the conclusion that there is, within this document, evidence that is compelling, if not 100 percent conclusive, that D'Aubuisson and his group are re-

sponsible for the murder of Archbishop Romero.
SENATOR CRANSTON: What did you say? Responsible for whose murder?
AMBASSADOR WHITE: Archbishop Romero . . ."

> —*From the record of hearings before the Committee on Foreign Relations, U.S. Senate, April 9, 1981, two months after Robert White left San Salvador.*

Of all these Americans I suppose I think especially of Robert White, for his is the authentic American voice afflicted by El Salvador: *You will find one of the pages with Monday underlined and with quotation marks,* he said that April day in 1981 about his documents, which were duly admitted into the record and, as the report of the House Permanent Select Committee on Intelligence later concluded, ignored by the CIA; he talked about Operation Pineapple, and blood sugar, and 257 Roberts guns, about addresses in Miami, about Starlight scopes; about *documents handed to him directly by Colonel Majano,* about *compelling if not conclusive evidence* of activities that continued to fall upon the ears of his auditors as signals from space, unthinkable, inconceivable, dim impulses from a black hole. In the serene light of Washington that spring day in 1981, two months out of San Salvador, Robert White's distance from the place was already lengthening: in San Salvador he might have wondered, the final turn of the mirror, *what Colonel Majano had to gain by handing him the documents.*

That the texture of life in such a situation is essentially untranslatable became clear to me only recently, when I tried to describe to a friend in Los Angeles an incident that occurred some days before I left El Salvador. I had gone with my husband and another American to the San Salvador morgue, which, unlike most morgues in the United States, is easily accessible, through an open door on the ground floor around the back of the court building. We had been too late that morning to see the day's bodies (there is not much emphasis on embalming in El Salvador, or for that matter on identification, and bodies are dispatched fast for disposal), but the man in charge had opened his log to show us the morning's entries, seven bodies, all male, none identified, none believed older than twenty-five. Six had been certified dead by *arma de fuego*, firearms, and the seventh, who had also been shot, of shock. The slab on which the bodies had been received had already been washed down, and water stood on the floor. There were many flies, and an electric fan.

The other American with whom my husband and I had gone to the morgue that morning was a newspaper reporter, and since only seven unidentified bodies bearing evidence of *arma de fuego* did not in San Salvador in the summer of 1982 constitute a newspaper story worth pursuing, we left. Outside in the parking lot there were a number of wrecked or impounded cars, many of them shot up, upholstery chewed by bullets, windshield shattered, thick pastes of congealed blood on pearlized hoods, but this was also unremarkable, and it was not until we walked back around the building to the reporter's rented car that each of us began to sense the potentially remarkable.

Surrounding the car were three men in uniform, two on the sidewalk and the third, who was very young, sitting on his motorcycle in such a way as to block our leaving. A second motorcycle had been pulled up directly behind the car, and the space in front was occupied. The three had been joking among themselves, but the laughter stopped as we got into the car. The reporter turned the ignition on, and waited. No one moved. The two men on the sidewalk did not meet our eyes. The boy on the motorcycle stared directly, and caressed the G-3 propped between his thighs. The reporter asked in Spanish if one of the motorcycles could be moved so that we could get out. The men on the sidewalk said nothing, but smiled enigmatically. The boy only continued staring, and began twirling the flash suppressor on the barrel of his G-3.

This was a kind of impasse. It seemed clear that if we tried to leave and scraped either motorcycle the situation would deteriorate. It also seemed clear that if we did not try to leave the situation would deteriorate. I studied my hands. The reporter gunned the motor, forced the car up onto the curb far enough to provide a minimum space in which to maneuver, and managed to back out clean. Nothing more happened, and what did happen had been a common enough kind of incident in El Salvador, a pointless confrontation with aimless authority, but I have heard of no *solución* that precisely addresses this local vocation for terror.

Any situation can turn to terror. The most ordinary errand can go bad. Among Americans in El Salvador there is an endemic apprehension of danger in the apparently benign. I recall being told by a network anchor man that one night in his hotel room (it was at the time of the election, and because the Camino Real was full he had been put up at the Sheraton) he took the mattress off the bed and shoved it against the window. He happened to have with him several bullet-proof vests that he had brought from New York for the camera crew, and before going to the Sheraton lobby he put one on. Managers of American companies in El Salvador (Texas Instruments is still there, and Cargill, and some others) are replaced every several months, and their presence is kept secret. Some companies bury their managers in a number-two or number-three post. American embassy officers are driven in armored and unmarked vans (no eagle, no seal, no CD plates) by Salvadoran drivers and Salvadoran guards, because, I was told, "if someone gets blown away, obviously the State Department would prefer it done by a local security man, then you don't get headlines saying 'American Shoots Salvadoran Citizen.'" These local security men carry automatic weapons on their laps.

In such a climate the fact of being in El Salvador comes to seem a sentence of indeterminate length, and the prospect of leaving doubtful. On the night before I was due to leave I did not sleep, lay awake and listened to the music drifting up from a party at the Camino Real pool, heard the band play "Malaguena" at three and at four and again at five A.M., when the party seemed to end and light broke and I could get up. I was picked up to go to the airport that morning by one of the embassy vans, and a few blocks from the hotel I was seized by the conviction that this was not the most direct way to the airport, that this was not an embassy guard sitting in front with the Remington on his lap; that this was someone else. That the van turned out in fact to be the embassy van, detouring into San Benito to pick up an AID official, failed to relax me: once at the airport I sat without moving and averted my eyes from the soldiers patrolling the empty departure lounges.

When the nine A.M. TACA flight to Miami was announced I boarded without looking back, and sat rigid until the plane left the ground. I did not fasten my seat belt. I did not lean back. The plane stopped that morning at Belize, setting down on the runway lined with abandoned pillboxes and rusting camouflaged tanks to pick up what seemed to be every floater on two continents, wildcatters, collectors of information, the fantasts of the hemisphere. Even a team of student missionaries got on at Belize, sallow children from the piney woods of Georgia and Alabama who had been teaching the people of Belize, as the team member who settled down next to me explained, to know Jesus as their personal savior.

He was perhaps twenty, with three hundred years of American hill stock in his features, and as soon as the plane left Belize he began filling out a questionnaire on his experience there, laboriously printing out the phrases, *in obedience to God, opportunity to renew commitment, most rewarding part of my experience, most disheartening part.* Somewhere over the Keys I asked him what the most disheartening part of his experience had been. The most disheartening part of his experience, he said, had been seeing people leave the Crusade as empty as they came. The most rewarding part of his experience had been renewing his commitment to bring the Good News of Jesus as personal savior to all these different places. The different places to which he was committed to bring the Good News were New Zealand, Iceland, Finland, Colorado, and El Salvador. This was *la solución* not from Washington or Panama or Mexico but from Belize, and the piney woods of Georgia. This flight from San Salvador to Belize to Miami took place at the end of June 1982. In the week that I am completing this report, at the end of October 1982, the offices in the Hotel Camino Real in San Salvador of the Associated Press, United Press International, United Press International Television News, NBC News, CBS News, and ABC News were raided and searched by members of the El Salvador National Police carrying submachine guns; fifteen leaders of legally recognized political and labor groups opposing the government of El Salvador were disappeared in San Salvador; Deane Hinton said that he was "reasonably certain" that these disappearances had not been conducted under Salvadoran government orders; the Salvadoran Ministry of Defense announced that eight of the fifteen disappeared citizens were in fact in government custody; and the State Department

[handwritten margin note: immediate contradiction]

announced that the Reagan administration believed that it had "turned the corner" in its campaign for political stability in Central America.

ALSO BY JOAN DIDION

"A novelist with important things to say
about the dislocations of our time. . . .
Joan Didion is stellar."
—*Newsday*

AFTER HENRY

In this foray into the American cultural scene, Joan Didion
covers ground from Washington to Los Angeles, from a TV
producer's gargantuan "manor" to the racial battlefields of New
York's criminal courts.

Current Affairs/Essays/0-679-74539-4

A BOOK OF COMMON PRAYER

The intertwining story of two American women in the derelict
Central American nation of Boca Grande; one controls much of
the country's wealth and knows all of its secrets, while the other
vainly hopes to be reunited with her fugitive father.

Fiction/Literature/0-679-75486-5

RUN RIVER

Joan Didion's electrifying first novel is a haunting portrait of a
marriage whose wrong turns and betrayals are at once absolutely idiosyncratic and a razor-sharp commentary on the history of
California.

Fiction/Literature/0-679-75250-1

ALSO AVAILABLE:

Democracy, 0-679-75485-7
Salvador, 0-679-75183-1

VINTAGE INTERNATIONAL
Available at your local bookstore, or call toll-free to order
1-800-793-2665 (credit cards only).